Socialism in History

SOCIALISM IN HISTORY
Political Essays of
Henry Pachter

Edited and with an Introduction by
Stephen Eric Bronner

Columbia University Press
New York   1984

Library of Congress Cataloging in Publication Data

Pachter, Henry Maximilian, 1907-1980
Socialism in history.

Includes bibliographical references and index.
1. Socialism—History—Addresses, essays, lectures.
2. Communism—History—Addresses, essays, lectures.
3. Socialism—Addresses, essays, lectures.   4. Communism
—Addresses, essays, lectures.   5. Social history—
Addresses, essays, lectures.   6. Political science—
History—Addresses, essays, lectures.   7. Political
science—Addresses, essays, lectures.   I. Title.
HX21.P33 1984   335'.009   83-18904
ISBN 0-231-05660-5

Columbia University Press
New York   Guildford, Surrey

Copyright © 1984 Columbia University Press

Clothbound editions of Columbia University Press books are
Smyth-sewn and printed on permanent and durable acid-free paper.

Contents

List of Illustrations   *vii*

Acknowledgments   *ix*

Introduction, by Stephen Eric Bronner   *xi*

I.   Marxian Themes   *1*

1. The Right To Be Lazy   *3*
2. Three Economic Models: Capitalism, the Welfare State, and Socialism   *16*
3. Freedom, Authority, Participation   *36*
4. The Idea of Progress in Marxism   *65*

II.   The Thirties   *87*

5. Communism and Class   *89*
6. Fascist Propaganda and the Conquest of Power   *110*
7. Reflections on the Spanish Civil War   *147*

III.   Nationalism and Internationalism   *159*

8. The Problem of Imperialism   *161*
9. Notes on the Soviet Union   *200*
10. Who Are the Palestinians?   *203*

IV.   Teachers of Marxism   *217*

11. Marx and the Jews   *219*
12. The Ambiguous Legacy of Eduard Bernstein   *256*
13. Gramsci—Stalinist Without Dogma   *284*

14. Orthodox Heretic, Romantic Stalinist: On the Ninetieth
Birthday of Georg Lukács   *295*

Epilogue   *315*
Confessions of an Old-Timer: Aphorisms on Socialism   *317*
Notes   *333*

Illustrations

1. Paul Lafargue   *10*
2. Workers Loafing in *À Nous la Liberté*   *13*
3. The Iron-Rolling Mill   *52*
4. "This is how the Englishman colonizes"   *72*
5. Ernst Thälmann   *90*
6. Spanish Civil War: Popular Front Women   *152*
7. Spanish Civil War: FAI Tank   *153*
8. Vladimir I. Lenin   *163*
9. Beirut Bombed, 1982   *204*
10. Moses Hess   *236*
11. The New York Stock Exchange   *237*
12. Spranger Barry as Timon of Athens   *238*
13. Karl Marx as a Student   *241*
14. Otis Skinner as Shylock   *245*
15. Eduard Bernstein   *257*
16. Karl Liebknecht   *263*
17. Antonio Gramsci   *285*
18. Georg Lukács   *296*
19. Charlie Chaplin in *Modern Times*   *327*

Acknowledgments

All changes from Henry Pachter's previously published articles were made either from unpublished notes or for purely grammatical reasons. These changes were made in consultation with Hedwig Pachter, the author's widow, who also did the translations and to whom I owe an enormous debt of gratitude for her help with all aspects of this book. By the same token, I would like to express my thanks to Benjamin Barber, Rosalyn Baxandall, Joan McQuary, Joel Rogers, Charles Webel, and David Diefendorf for their suggestions and encouragement.

Stephen Eric Bronner
Rutgers University

Où marches–tu, gai compagnon?
Je m'en vais conquérir la terre.
J'ai remplacé Napoléon,
Je suis le prolétaire.

Pierre Dupont
1846

Introduction

When Henry Pachter died in 1980, a luminous intellect was lost. There were few who could boast of his enormous scholarly range, probably fewer still who could make equal claim to his intellectual rigor or his disdain for passing academic fads. The posthumous publication of his beautiful *Weimer Etudes* brought him a measure of renown which he never really experienced in his lifetime. Before then, some knew him only as the author of *Paracelsus: Magic into Science*, others as the contemporary European historian who had written *The Fall and Rise of Europe* and *Modern Germany*, still others as a publicist or a teacher.

In America, he was primarily regarded as an essayist. This pleased him too, for there was no form he loved as much as the essay — the *political* essay. The essay form allowed him to act as the gadfly and confront the specific thinker, issue, theme, or idea with which he, always a restless intellect, was concerned at the moment. Often his essays appear cantankerous, often they commit themselves to positions that stand in sharp contradistinction to the values of many on the contemporary American left. But each essay manifests the desire to explode a myth, expand an outlook, and provoke the reader into a confrontation with the values which he takes for granted. There is a purpose and an essential theme to each of these essays. Originally they were written as separate pieces; nevertheless, they rest upon an interconnected set of values and a certain tradition of inquiry. In this sense, they form a coherent world view that can only extend the socialist vision to which Henry Pachter dedicated his life.

The author of these essays was born in 1907 to a bourgeois Jewish family in Berlin. He grew up in a rigid, stuffy, and thoroughly Victorian atmosphere. It was surely in response that, as an adolescent, Pachter joined *Der schwarze Haufen*, one of the many groups which composed the German youth movement. This movement, commonly known as the *Wandervogel*, lacked a direct political purpose. There, however, Henry Pachter received his first taste of community, rebellion, and the possibilities of individual expression. The songs, the hikes, and the élan of a countercultural lifestyle had a pronounced effect. But the adult world could not be avoided forever, and it ultimately became impossible to ignore the movement's ideological reliance on neoromanticism, elitism, and irrationalism.

When the Youth Movement split in 1926, at the urging of his friend Karl August Wittfogel, who would later write the classic *Oriental Despotism*, Pachter joined the youth league of the German Communist Party (KPD). Later, in Freiburg, he took courses with Husserl and met his lifelong friend Hannah Arendt. There he also studied with a conservative professor of history named Georg von Below, who made Pachter's ideological transition to Marxism easier by emphasizing the romantic roots and the speculative character of that theory, which the old Junker despised. It was also von Below who advised Pachter, in the friendliest terms, to shift his scholarly focus from medieval history and concentrate on another area — medieval history was tacitly closed to Jews.

By the end of 1926, Pachter had returned to Berlin. There he met Karl Korsch — author of the influential *Marxism and Philosophy*, Minister of Justice in the short-lived revolutionary government of Thuringia, Reichstag representative for the KPD, and editor of the party journal *Die Internationale* — who would become the major intellectual influence on his life. Along with Georg Lukács and Antonio Gramsci, Korsch would emerge as one of the major contributors to the development of what would be called "critical" or "Western" Marxism. Included in this volume are essays on Lukács' intellectual development, analyzed in terms of the changes in the Communist movement to which the great theorist was committed, and on Gramsci, who is critically viewed with an eye toward his political activities.

Although Pachter never completed the essay on Korsch that he always wanted to write, it was from him that the student learned firsthand what was common to all three of these thinkers. From the perspective of Korsch, Lukács, and Gramsci, Marxism is neither a fixed "system" nor an objective "science" based on a causal notion of economic determinism. Instead, Marxism becomes a method of sociohistorical inquiry that can question even its own specific political or ideological usage from a critical standpoint. The working class and its aims therefore cannot be identified with any party that simply claims to incarnate its "true interests." For Korsch, and then for Pachter, there could be no evasions and no pseudo-"dialectical" sophistry. Socialism and the extension of democracy were inextricably bound; the goal of Marxism could only rest upon working-class *control* — and not mere *ownership*—of the means of production.

There was no way for Pachter to hide these heretical views from his Communist comrades. Trouble had been brewing for some time when he found himself expelled from the Communist Youth in 1928 over the question of "socialism in one country." In the meantime, however, he witnessed the complete degeneration of the KPD. This experience informs Pachter's essay on Gramsci; it is the reason for his critical detachment, his emphasis on Gramsci's political role and mistakes, beyond any admiration for this Italian thinker's theoretical contributions. Henry Pachter could never forget the "bolshevization" of the German party under Zinoviev's henchmen, Ruth Fischer and Arkadij Maslow, who later would themselves be dismissed and vilified in favor of the dull-witted Ernst Thälmann once Stalin's star had risen in the homeland of the revolution.

A dynamic of intraparty repression had allowed the ruthless persecution and expulsion of the KPD's finest members, including Korsch himself. Indeed, the mid-1920's also witnessed the transformation of Marxism into the codified dogma of "Marxism-Leninism"; the rise of the *apparatchik* mentality; the reliance on outright lies that were—sometimes cynically, sometimes naively—accepted as truth; and the concerted efforts of Stalinists and Nazis alike to bring the Weimar Republic to its knees.

After his expulsion, Pachter briefly frequented the bohemian cafes in Berlin. There he came into contact with the expressionist avant-garde and the cultural intelligentsia. He also got in touch with such splinter groups as the Communist Workers' Party (KAPD) and the

Socialist Workers' Party (SAP), a group for which he always felt great sympathy and through which he first became friendly with Paul Frölich, the pupil and later the biographer of Rosa Luxemburg.

This was also a time of great intellectual activity. Under the supervision of two renowned liberal historians, Hermann Oncken and Friedrich Meinecke, Pachter wrote his dissertation, *Das Proletariat des Vormärz*, which proved to be a superb treatment of the sociopolitical constitution of the German working class before 1848; that knowledge would also be put to good use later in the marvelous essay "Marx and the Jews," which is a small masterpiece in the sociology of knowledge. But Pachter didn't confine himself to scholarly pursuits; he also began to teach economic history in one of the workers' schools that flourished in the "red" districts of Berlin.

It didn't last long. Following Hitler's rise to power, Pachter led a shadowy existence. In concert with his wife, Hedwig, and Richard Löwenthal, whom he had first met in the Communist Youth, Pachter put out what was probably the first resistance journal, a little paper entitled *Proletarische Aktion*. That didn't last long either. By the end of 1933, Pachter had been forced to flee to Paris. There he took odd jobs, taught at the *Université Populaire,* agitated for creating a "popular front" of all antifascist forces, and ultimately served as a publicist for the POUM, a mixed group of Trotskyists and socialists that served the loyalist cause during the Spanish Civil War.

The collapse of Spain left a void. By the late 1930's the grand vision which the Russian Revolution initially projected had become a nightmare, while the Fascist barbarians had conquered much of Europe and sought to rule the rest. Gérard Sandoz (Gustave Stern), now a well-respected French writer and formerly a companion of Pachter's during their Paris exile, inscribed his *La Gauche Allemande* to his friend in 1970 with the words: "En souvenir de nos espoirs et désillusions." Henry Pachter found the inscription "fitting."

Throughout this time, Pachter still considered himself a revolutionary Marxist. That becomes clear from his first substantive work, *Wirtschaft unterm Rutenbündel.* The pamphlet, which emphasizes the economic sophistry of the Fascists and their reliance on cartels, is valuable insofar as it retains the flavor of those agitational writings that flooded the left in that period. It is a work of transition. The old ultra-left sentiments are there along with a somewhat mechanistic quality, reflecting a bit of the KPD style. Yet the brochure closes with the following: "No political miracle can save the proletariat; no god, no dictator, no tribune. Only the workers themselves can achieve their liberation through the social revolution."

Despite the emphasis on proletarian self-organization, however, there is a clear opening to the Social Democratic Party of Germany (SPD), which served as the bulwark for the Weimar Republic. After all, Pachter's call for a "social revolution" was unmistakable in the context. That concept was formulated by Karl Kautsky in his influential *The Social Revolution*, which appeared in 1902 and which argued that the attempt to build the socioeconomic power of the working class could not be divorced from a support for democratic political forms.

Henry Pachter's brochure was printed in 1932, after he formally joined the SPD. When he entered the party, few illusions remained about its revolutionary potential. The SPD had supported the kaiser in the First World War, opposed the revolutionary upsurges in Russia and Europe during the years that followed, and become a stalwart of the status quo in the new parliamentary regime. But it retained a working-class base, forced the passing of numerous pieces of very progressive welfare legislation, and emerged as a clear-cut opponent to the Nazis. Besides, the old aura of the past still had an effect.

In *Weimar Etudes*, Pachter describes some of his experiences in this socialist party that had grown bureaucratically petrified with its own success. But the flavor of the movement before its "great betrayal" in 1914, its contradictory commitment to orthodox Marxist theory and reformist practice, its belief in democracy, and its relation to contemporary developments are all explored in "The Ambiguous Legacy of Eduard Bernstein."

In a way, it makes sense that this should have been Pachter's last published essay. "The movement is everything, the goal is nothing" was the phrase that came to be associated with Bernstein, and Pachter liked its anti-metaphysical implications as well as its emphasis on concrete politics. Also, aside from Pachter's own long-standing commitment to pluralism, parliamentarism, and reform, the figure of Eduard Bernstein provided him with an example of intellectual courage, decency, and an honest willingness to exert the critical faculty, even if it meant clashing with the dominant dogma.

Nevertheless, the young ex-communist's political decision to join the SPD necessarily involved a philosophical confrontation with his recent past. Despite the forced, and sometimes over-complicated style, the first step was perhaps his finest article of the period, "Communism and Class." This essay appeared in the prestigious *Die Gesellschaft*, a journal edited by Pachter's SPD patron, Rudolf Hilferding, author of the classic *Finanzkapital* and twice Minister of Finance in the Weimar Republic.

The essay was first published in 1932, after Stalin's "left turn" of 1929. This change of line instituted what came to be known as the Social-Fascist thesis, which equated the Social Democrats with the Nazis. Insofar as both groups were hostile to the Communists, and so "twin brothers," any support for a KPD alliance with the SPD against Hitler could be seen as a "right-wing deviation" — even though this division of the working class would ultimately help the Nazis gain power.

In Pachter's view, a fundamentally different *Weltanschauung* provoked the break between these two competing organizations of the working class at a critical historical juncture. As far as the KPD was concerned, its revolutionary ideology had become split from what was essentially an opportunist practice. Whatever Lenin's merits, this situation derived from his "substitution" (Trotsky) of the Party — which, by definition, incarnates the "true" revolutionary consciousness of the proletariat — for the actual working class as the agent of revolution. But, following the theoretical lead of his friend and teacher Arthur Rosenberg, Pachter saw that such a substitution does not lead to a revolutionary identification between the party and the interests of this specific class. Quite the opposite: replacing class with party creates a vacuum that can be filled by any mass base.

As Pachter argues, lacking any check from below through its adherence to "democratic centralism," the party can choose any means to pursue that revolutionary goal which legitimizes it in the first place. Any tactic can simply be decreed a "revolutionary" necessity even as the immediate needs of the organization will take precedence over that final goal. As a consequence, where any mass can fill the vacuum of the base from the standpoint of the revolutionary vanguard, any party can assume primacy from the standpoint of the radical masses as long as it maintains a fundamental discipline that is *ideologically* directed toward the fulfillment of some chiliastic goal.

In this respect, Pachter provides one of the most interesting analyses of the ideological degeneration of the Communist movement as well as the crossover in membership between Nazis and Communists that was so striking toward the end of the Weimar Republic. Actually, however, Pachter probably overemphasized the implications of this overriding ideological moment for the KPD position on the "United Front." If means really take the place of ends, and if any tactic can be viewed as a revolutionary necessity, then there is no reason why the Communists should have ideologically excluded a "United Front" policy per se; such a policy could have been propagandistically justified as easily as the separatist course — and it would be proclaimed only a few years later in the "Popular Front" period.

What Pachter underplays in this essay is the ideological subordination of the KPD to the Soviet Union, and so the actual concerns that determined the party line. In fact, Moscow's "left turn" was anything but "left" insofar as it assumed that capitalism had "stabilized" and that all Comintern efforts should be directed toward supporting the industrialization campaign which would construct "socialism in one country."

As a consequence, the Soviet Union moved away from Lenin's emphasis on exploiting international class contradictions to exacerbating the conflicts between bourgeois states. From this new standpoint, Hitler's success could appear useful to the Soviet Union in disrupting the West, and Stalin's suicidal German policy would at least retain a certain deranged logic. But then, it would also follow that the "revolutionary" line which accompanied the "left turn" was pure fluff; the Communist claim that the Nazi state would only last five years at the most — under the slogan "After Hitler, Us!"— would therefore be nothing more than the fruit of a propaganda that veiled a defeatist policy.

Basically neither the orthodox Communists, despite the polemical efforts of Togliatti and Dimitroff, nor the Social Democrats were able to develop a coherent understanding of fascism. In his broad and insightful essay "Fascist Propaganda and the Conquest of Power," which was written for the UNESCO-sponsored volume entitled *The Third Reich,* Pachter attempted to make his contribution. Through his analysis of the Nazi propaganda effort, it becomes clear that the Nazi purpose was neither to persuade nor simply to deceive. Both persuasion and deception occur within a discourse that, at least potentially, allows for an opponent's response. The Nazi vision was much more radical: the very possibility of rational discourse had to be destroyed, arbitrary power had to prove decisive, and the audience had to be directly subjugated to the speaker's will.

Following the work of Franz Neumann and Hannah Arendt, Pachter argues that terror, symbols, and organizational details are all manipulated to prepare the psychological condition in which individuals become atomized into an amorphous mass to insure an immediate identification with the "leader." Real communication is therefore subordinated to the creation of a spectacle in which the entire society will participate. Through mass meetings, torchlight parades, and ideological bombardment, "an artfully contrived mass regression into the age of tribal magic" will occur that will also portray the human condition as one of perpetual combat readiness.

But combat against whom? The enemy mattered as little as the conflicting promises which Hitler offered to conflicting classes. Although Pachter does not ground Hitler's mass support in a sociopolitical analysis of the precapitalist groupings within German society, the image of the "little man" is useful. It was this "little man" —the peasant, the clerk, the small businessman, the petty aristocrat, the disillusioned army veteran, the civil servant — who felt his traditions, position, and possibilities being extinguished by the modern industrial classes of society, their political parties, and their institutions no less than by the values they affirmed. Indeed, Pachter beautifully shows how the cultural climate of the time militated against Enlightenment traditions in favor of irrationalist, vitalist, and neoromantic ideologies.

In Pachter's view, the Nazi rise was based on that movement's ability to harness the resentment, the moral indignation, and the frustration of these "little men" through the call for harmony, through the fanatical insistence on an abstract apocalypse, and through the demand for revenge on the representatives of modernity: the "bosses," the "Communists," the "democrats," liberals, intellectuals, and Jews. In this orgy of resentment, sadism took the place of a revolutionary impulse and became socially ennobled. Callousness, hatred, fanaticism, violence took on positive connotations. Intuition replaced reason as the criterion of truth; empty abstractions such as "destiny" gave primacy to myth as a form of social cohesion and dynamism. Intensity became its own end. Thus fanaticism, rather than any specific goals, will come to define Fascist propaganda.

Such fanaticism, however, will have to be perpetually fueled. The world will therefore be propagandistically portrayed as being on the brink of war, and the prophecy must become self-fulfilling. Only in this way is it possible to insure a perpetual dynamism—a dynamism without purpose or rational justification — which becomes the vitalistic, existential compensation for what Erich Fromm called "the escape from freedom."

But there were those in the 1930s who were not willing to hand over their freedom quite so easily. In France, the newly formed "Popular Front" sought to defend democracy against the fascist tide in the name of a progressive attempt to "reform the structure," while 1936 also saw the great experiment with revolutionary democracy and antifascist resistance in the Spanish Civil War. In that year, the military, the church, the aristocracy, and other reactionary classes unified behind Franco's leadership in a revolt against the Spanish Republic. Liberals, socialists, Communists, Trotskyists, and anarchists rose to defend it. While Hitler and Mussolini sent massive military aid and personnel to Franco, the Western democracies — despite the underground shipment of some arms and the enthusiasm of volunteer regiments — remained rigidly neutral. The only real defender of the Republic appeared to be the Soviet Union, whose "Popular Front" line was transported into Spain. Basically an antirevolutionary position, this policy came into open conflict with the revolutionary desires of the anarchist movement. That contradiction on the left would be tragically resolved in 1937 when Communist forces, with socialist support, slaughtered the revolutionary front of anarchists, syndicalists, Trotskyists, and their partisans in the battle of Barcelona.

During the intervening year and a half, Pachter wrote *The Spanish Crucible* — which would remain his favorite work. A testament to the anti-Communist revolutionary left and the struggles of the antifascist cause, it was republished in 1965; Pachter wished to include a new introduction, which is part of this volume. The revisions are startling and the criticisms are balanced.

Shrugging aside the later liberal historians who in retrospect argued for compromise on the left, Pachter notes that "the Civil War was inevitable precisely because the revolution was inevitable." Nor should the tragedy of Spain be simply seen as a prefiguration of World War II or a situation in which the international proletariat stood ready to defend the Republic. Casting aside the vestiges of nostalgia, Pachter is not even afraid to question whether the war should actually have been prolonged after late 1937 when it was known to have been lost; ruefully he points out how the zealous antifascists of the time "owed it to the militants to sacrifice them to the cause."

That cause itself was the splendid mixture of liberty and socialism which has become the transcendent symbol of the Spanish ordeal. To this cause, Pachter would remain committed. Indeed, there was enough blame to go around and, for him, the lessons of the Spanish Civil War are neither tactical nor organizational. The real lesson lies in the need to confront an unfinished dialectic of freedom and necessity, spontaneity and organization, along with those values that an emancipatory resolution projects: democracy, socialism, and individual dignity.

By 1941, Henry Pachter's second exile had begun in America. Through the influence of Otto Kirchheimer and Franz Neumann, the great theorists of law and the state, he became a consultant for the Institute of World Affairs and the Office of War Information. He also became a research associate for the Office of European Economic Research, which was a branch of the OSS, and it was for this organization that he wrote his little book on Nazi rhetoric, entitled *Nazi-Deutsch*. Afterwards, Pachter taught at the New School for Social Research, the City College of New York, and Rutgers University.

When the cold war began, Pachter maintained his commitment to social democracy. At the same time, however, any past traces of solidarity with the Soviet Union from the common front against

Hitler had vanished. In this regard, Pachter was no different from many of his friends — such as Franz Borkenau, Richard Löwenthal, Otto Kirchheimer, Fritz Sternberg, and Arthur Rosenberg — who had also experienced what Brecht called "the Stalin trauma."

Whatever criticisms may be leveled at their work, its intellectual quality is remarkably high and, when taken as a whole, a corpus appears that is a major contribution to socialist thought. All of these thinkers, including Pachter, contributed to the development of what might be considered a political realist approach to Soviet foreign policy. Many took part in the debate over the concept of "totalitarianism" and, in seeking to come to terms with their own past, this group consistently sought to analyze the roots of Stalinism and the degeneration of the international Communist movement. Indeed, it was these thinkers who perhaps most effectively attempted to develop a vision of socialism that would reject the "dictatorship of the proletariat" and bind the movement to pluralist parliamentarism and the reformist path.

As the years wore on, Pachter became known as one of many cold warriors, an impression that grew through his criticisms of the American revisionist historians and certain articles in *Dissent,* of which he was a co-founder and editor. Still, Henry Pachter was neither a mandarin, a McCarthyite demagogue, nor a reactionary moralist like Solzhenitsyn. There were some, like Merleau-Ponty, who tried to distance themselves from both superpowers in the name of what may be called "a-communism." But, though Pachter felt a certain intellectual affinity for this position, he fundamentally believed that such a stance was an evasion of the concrete political choice which had to be made.

Given this choice, Pachter and the political realists came down squarely on the side of the West. Although Pachter would criticize imperialist ventures like the Vietnam War, neither he nor his friends had any sympathy for or understanding of the New Left. Overly sensitive to the bluster of marginal elements of the New Left, Pachter's basic criterion of judgment was clear: he would always "prefer the most inefficient democracy over the most efficient dictatorship." Thus, he often found himself trapped in the position of stubbornly defending the status quo against a left that bore no real relation to Soviet authoritarianism. From his realist standpoint, he was perhaps also afraid that such domestic unrest would objectively weaken the United States in its dealings with the Soviet Union. In this vein, his overriding desire to defend American pluralism — especially given the lack of a coherent left alternative — was consistent with Pachter's original stance, which emphasized the political character of the socialist enterprise.

Besides, the revolutionary halo had long since been stripped from the Soviet Union, a point which is hammered home in his masterful historical study, *Weltmacht Russland,* whose introduction has been included in this volume. Thinking back to his teacher Friedrich Meinecke, Pachter suggests that Soviet foreign policy cannot simply be considered a set of discrete strategies which reflect the shifts in that country's leadership and ideology. Rather, Soviet foreign policy is viewed as a function of the Soviet Union's development as a state system whose basic principle is the old bourgeois notion of *raison d'état.*

The Soviet Union will therefore be seen as one nation among others — without any "revolutionary privilege" in its relation with other states. Consequently, it must be treated, not as the bastion of world revolution, but as a state with its own national interests. Although some will retain a residual loyalty for the "fatherland of the revolution," and others will view it as the devil incarnate, Pachter argues that dealings with this state must be stripped of any ideological biases. Where the Communist ideology is still used to justify any measures the Soviet Union will take, Pachter proposes that the degeneration of this ideology is tied to the fact that the Soviet Union can actually better pursue its interests without the fetters of Marxist-Leninist dogma. The Soviet Union is therefore neither inherently expansionist nor inherently peaceful. As a super-power, the Soviet state will respond to given circumstances as it evaluates its particular interests and their strategic importance.

Precisely for this reason, an opportunity presents itself to the Soviet Union's adversaries, since "only ideas know no compromise; interests know no principle." Coexistence, after all, is a meaningless concept for allies; it is necessary only between enemies, and imperative when the possibility of nuclear war threatens. In this respect, even Pachter's *Collision Course: The Cuban Missile Crisis and Coexistence*—which is certainly not the most even-handed study—involves a plea for coexistence as the only realistic response to the tensions that underlie the cold war.

Opposition to the Soviet Union must therefore be seen in tactical terms, and the tactics should not be confused with the strategic purpose: peace. Indeed, Pachter believed that the question of nuclear arms should be severed from any other foreign policy issues and, just a few months before his death, he even drafted an essay on unilateral disarmament entitled "A Suggestion for Surrender."

Nevertheless, the position that Pachter elaborated on the Soviet Union necessarily demanded a theoretical encounter with other issues and, in particular, Soviet imperialism. If the Soviet Union is a state with its own *raison d'état* and imperialist potential, then the traditional Marxist view of that phenomenon must be revised — whether that view intrinsically ties imperialism to the structure of capitalist accumulation, in the manner of Rosa Luxemburg, or whether it sees imperialism as a function of capitalist development at a particular stage, in the manner of Hilferding or Lenin.

Because "socialist imperialism" cannot be explained from traditional Marxist viewpoints, a new theoretical point of departure must be derived. In his essay "Problems of Imperialism," Pachter is unable to theoretically specify the relation between economic interests, the state, and imperialist policies. But he is able to develop a coherent position. Given his conclusion that imperialist policies are neither intrinsic to capitalist development nor even necessarily economically profitable for the capitalist class as a whole, Pachter will extend Meinecke's theory and view imperialism as a *political* phenomenon that, in the modern period, is tied to the nation–state.

This is the reason for Pachter's emphasis on internationalism in a period where nationalism is the dominant force. It is a theme that runs through his major work of the postwar era, *The Fall and Rise of Europe,* as well as many of his essays. Whatever its inadequacies, in Pachter's view, the United Nations, along with its many international agencies, as well as regional organizations such as the European Economic Community, needs to be strengthened. This position is also what set Pachter at odds with leftists who uncritically supported Third World dictatorships and the movements of "national liberation."

Despite his relentless criticism of Third World authoritarianism and his neglect of the many attempts to extend democracy, Pachter does not dismiss the profoundly legitimate grievances of oppressed communities and the tragedy of their plight. The point becomes particularly clear in his essay "Who Are the Palestinians?"

As an editor of *Dissent,* Pachter noted with alarm the increasing Israeli bias of the magazine and many of its contributors, such as Bernard Avishai, Gordon Levin, Irving Howe, and others. Indeed, it must be remembered that this article appeared long before the barbarous slaughter of Lebanese civilians in 1982, which jolted many on the left into reconsidering their positions on the Mideast. In fact, tensions rose on the editorial board and a minor clash ensued. Still, Pachter does not fall into the common mistake of those who, in criticizing the role of the oppressor, cast a romantic aura over the representatives of the oppressed.

Henry Pachter thought little of Arafat and the Palestine Liberation Organization. But the essential point remains. Terrorism becomes the policy of those who have no other way to voice their grievances — a policy which Zionists also followed — and if that plague is to cease, those grievances must be confronted by an Israeli government whose stubbornness, narrow-mindedness, greed, and arrogance have prevented an adjudication of the existing repressive state of affairs.

The essay's historical sweep exposes the illusory nature of the question "who settled the land first?" along with the diplomatic intricacies and deceits that have helped make any settlement so difficult. But while criticizing Israel for not allowing Arabs to return to their homes or offering economic compensations similar to those West Germany made to its refugees from Eastern Europe, Pachter also emphasizes how neighboring Arab states have used the Palestinians as a political pawn rather than allow the inmates of the refugee camps to settle on their territories. In line with Pachter's general theory of foreign affairs, ideology and questions of sentiment or prejudice must be cast aside in the Middle East. From this perspective, he suggests that the only rational position for Israel in the long run is the acceptance of a Palestinian state. Nevertheless, there is a measure of cynicism and the fear that authoritarianism will arise in the future state. From bitter experience, Pachter understood that identifying the Third World masses with the states that claim to speak in their name is as illusory as equating the interests of the international working class with those of the Soviet Union.

All these issues are tactical. And this follows from the political realist approach which, insofar as the existing international system and the structure of the parliamentary welfare state are accepted, tends to reduce strategy to tactics. An instrumentalist impulse dominates this type of political realism so that questions concerning the *content* of socialism — as an emancipatory alternative to the existing capitalist order — seem to vanish from the discourse. Henry Pachter always believed, however, that the content of the socialist goal could not be taken for granted, and, in this regard, he attempts to move beyond some of those other thinkers with whom he shared such strong intellectual and political affinities. For Pachter, the epistemological question of "What is socialism?" cannot be avoided if there is to be any relation between tactics and strategy or means and ends. Particularly in the popular imagination, "socialism" has too often been identified with the economic reforms of the welfare state on the one hand and Communist authoritarianism on the other.

"Three Economic Models" is one of Pachter's best-known essays. It seeks to explain the epistemological assumptions that underpin the economic workings of "pure" capitalism, the welfare state, and socialism. When one considers these systems as "ideal types" (Weber), it becomes clear that both laissez-faire capitalism and the welfare state presuppose the existence of private property as well as a mathematically based notion of efficiency that will judge the value of production solely in terms of its profitability. An iron rule therefore applies: new production methods must produce savings in excess of the capital which they make obsolete. Both forms will tie ownership of capital to decisions over investment, identify labor as a commodity, and seek to maintain a consistent flow of profits for the capitalist class.

Although the "pure" model of capitalism never existed since, as Pachter shows, some degree of state intervention was necessary from the beginning, under this system each individual will try to maximize profits in an ostensibly free market. On the other hand, the welfare state seeks to mitigate the inequities that result as well as the growth of monopolies and "imperfect competition" through various regulatory institutions. In a sense, then, the differences between pure capitalism and its welfare variant are matters of degree rather than kind. As Pachter puts the matter in "Three Economic Models":

> The basic relationships of buyer and seller, employer and employee, owner and nonowner, are no different from those prevailing under pure capitalism; but they are supplemented by state interference in two important areas: where classical capitalism is indifferent to the distribution of incomes, the welfare state at least tries to make income differentials less steep; where under pure capitalism the development of resources is an accidental by-product of the profit incentive, the welfare state sets itself definite goals of developing public and private facilities, consumer satisfactions, even tastes and standards.

But the iron rule remains, along with the market and the insecurity caused by private control over investment decisions, no less than the lack of control by the ultimate consumers. Although Pachter shifts his focus from the traditional socialist emphasis on producers and establishes no relation between these direct producers and the indirect consumers, for him the crucial issue of socialism is neither wages nor the simple "expropriation of the expropriators" (Marx) by some authoritarian party that demands national *ownership* of the means of production and full control over civic life. Rather, socialism focuses on the question of how the means of production, along with the public managers, can be democratically *controlled*. In this sense, abolition of what the young Lukács termed "reification" and the "commodity form" is necessary in order to direct investment toward projects which might not bring an immediately calculable profit, but which will make life easier and better.

Socialism and various forms of capitalism will therefore "provide different answers to the same questions." Consequently, socialism should not be identified with a new era of unrivaled productivity in terms of those criteria usually associated with the capitalist labor process. And if that is the case, the entire notion of what constitutes "progress" under capitalism must be reformulated.

Despite what would become Henry Pachter's practical identification with mainstream social democracy, he was always attracted to speculative thought. At the time of his death, he was still collecting notes for a philosophico-historical work on a problem which had passionately intrigued him for many years: the concept of time. This work was never completed, but he did finish what would have constituted a chapter: "The Idea of Progress in Marxism." There, Pachter criticizes those who would slip the values of the bourgeoisie into the Marxian construct. These are the theorists who equate Marx's conception either with the thought of Comte and the positivists or with Hegel's view which presupposes an immanent teleology within history that exists a priori.

The first position, common to both orthodox Social Democrats like Kautsky and Communists like Bukharin, leads to technological or economic determinism. From such a standpoint, the economic-technological realm, rather than the social relations in which these phenomena are embedded, provides the impetus for capitalist development. The forces of production are then seen as constrained by capitalist production relations and, as a result, a further development of production per se will demand a new system. The production process, along with capitalist criteria, will essentially remain intact while socialist ownership of the means of production will be substituted for the old production relations.

The second position, which does not necessarily exclude the first, wittingly or unwittingly equates the Communist Party with the Hegelian World Spirit insofar as the former contains that "true" revolutionary consciousness of a working class whose victory is "inevitable." Every tactic or ally of the party, at any given moment, can then be identified with "progress," since — by decree — a step has been made toward that victory. The bourgeois influence makes itself felt because, from either of these two positions, the liberation of the working class through its own conscious practice will vanish as a criterion of progress while any critical, normative standard will tend to be obliterated as well.

"Progress" is a value peculiar to the capitalist stage of development, and it was used by the bourgeoisie in its ideological struggle against the feudal order. But the very practice of this class, as Marx, Weber, and others have shown in various ways, will necessarily undermine the humanistic and emancipatory ideals with which the bourgeoisie was politically associated when it was still revolutionary and on the rise. In this sense, Pachter retains the traditional social democratic notion that the new socialist society will fundamentally involve the realization of those unactualized emancipatory ideals of the French Revolution. But then, given Marx's great advance in exposing the socioeconomic mechanism by which capitalism functions, the fulfillment of these aims will require a new consciousness by the working class of its own revolutionary possibilities, needs, and capacities for self-activity (*Selbsttätigkeit*). This is the goal that becomes the Marxian standard for "progress." Socialism must therefore be understood as the *transition* to a new society with new values that will bring the alienated socioeconomic and historical practice of individuals under conscious and democratic control with a view to the extension of humanistic, universal, participatory ends.

The manner in which this can be achieved becomes a part of "Freedom, Authority, and Participation." Aside from the many economic suggestions made in this essay, there are political ones as well that actually synthesize the traditional wisdom. Thus, while socialists are a minority, they can only press for reforms. Only when real inroads or majorities have been achieved can demands be made for fundamental changes, while a substantial majority is necessary for any structural transformation that assumes "the symbolism of revolution."

Unfortunately, this wisdom is both mechanical and static. Although the description of actual possibilities at any particular stage might well prove accurate, Pachter essentially ignores the dynamic as well as the problems of moving from one position to the next. If a socialist movement, in the first situation, can only propose immediate reforms, such demands can easily be absorbed by bourgeois parties so that the independent identity of the incipient socialist movement might well never emerge: this is precisely one of the crucial problems with the tactics of democratic socialism in the

United States. By the same token, the achievement of inroads through *exclusive* emphasis on a parliamentary path will necessitate programmatic compromises with other classes that would obviously water down the original vision to be fulfilled, build a bureaucracy with the dangers Robert Michels recognized, and potentially damage the class character of the movement. In fact, the very obeisance to what has been called "capitalist democracy" will create a situation in which long-term political goals will be transformed into short-term economic ones to the point where the very desire for a structural transformation will become dissipated within the socialist movement and anathema to its apparatus.

The moment of "revolution" is lacking in Pachter's later works; the Leninist conception is rejected, and the development of a new notion is ignored. Instead, he returns to the traditional social democratic view. Thus, Pachter is correct when, following Kautsky, he suggests a difference between the long-term gradual "social revolution" and the moment of political transformation that is tactical in character. But he forgets what Rosa Luxemburg and Karl Korsch both realized. Unless the development of radical political awareness is linked to socioeconomic activity at each point in the struggle — through working with mass organizations while retaining the integrity of the socialist identity and goal *in such practice* — the development of that class consciousness which Pachter identified with "progress" will not occur.

Yet in that same essay as well as in his humorous and prophetic "The Right To Be Lazy," Pachter reinvigorates the notion of what socialism can be. Thus, he breaks the immediate identification of socialism and progress with technological production per se. Indeed, he envisages socialism as stepping back from the single-minded emphasis on production and capitalist notions of efficiency that have dominated the mass organizations of the left. Nowhere is Pachter as emphatic as when he decries those views of socialism which identify it with some technocratic scheme to run the capitalist economy more "efficiently" or with an economy that has merely rid itself of "capitalist parasites." New criteria must become manifest in the newly planned and democratically controlled economy no less than in a shift from industries that may be profitable in the short term to the construction of hospitals, parks, and other projects, which would provide benefits for the community as a whole over a longer period of time.

Given that level of abundance, which Pachter views along with democracy as the fundamental prerequisite for socialism, whether the new society is as "productive" as capitalism is not the point. From his standpoint, the value of socialism lies in the priorities it will set; the manner in which people will be freed from the drudgery of labor; the way in which their capacities for participation, leisure, and creativity will be fostered.

Under capitalism, workers should greet the introduction of technology with joy since it might relieve them of labor, but unfortunately they must also fear that technology, since it might cost them their jobs. As Pachter puts the matter, under capitalism the worker will have to fight on two fronts simultaneously: "on the one hand for his 'right to work,' on the other for his 'right to leisure.'" This is the contradiction that demands resolution. In this vein, the assumptions and priorities that underlie both mainstream social democracy in the West and "actually existing socialism" (Bahro) in the East must be reformulated.

If the extension of democratic participation and the erasure of material misery are the twin criteria of socialist development, then socialism cannot be identified with any set of institutions at all, let alone those which would abolish the individual in the name of some authoritarian collectivity. Henry Pachter therefore reinstates the purpose of the socialist project and resurrects its identification with a freedom that is still to be achieved. That very identification becomes the standard for criticizing the deformations which have been carried on in the name of socialism. The question "What is socialism?" therefore receives an answer. It is a sociopolitical and intellectual process that remains unfinished as long as even the traces of oppression continue to exist. For someone like Henry Pachter, socialism really could be nothing other than "the highest stage of individualism — its fruition for all."

January 1983   *Stephen Eric Bronner*
                                                      Rutgers University

ONE

Marxian Themes

1

The Right To Be Lazy

What the Lord did on the eighth day the Bible does not state. It is permitted to speculate that He continued to rest and, for all that the last million years' record shows, never returned to the hectic working spree of the first six days. And when, after another million years, He will still be sitting in glory on His throne, with angels leisurely winging around Him, He will behold His arrangements with satisfaction and say, All is as it should be.

By definition, anyone who can offer Himself such a long vacation must be God; by the same token, the lesser breeds are earning their bread by the sweat of their brows. He will muse upon the sorry fate of the Devil, busily running the world, rushing hither and thither to aggrandize his little kingdom and really leading one hell of an existence. And He will take pity on the damned — Sisyphus rolling his rock uphill, Tantalus hopping for his apples, the Danaidae forever fetching water to pour into the leaking barrel.

For it's labor that is Hell and leisure that is Paradise. Mankind knew that even when it was very young. We never got over that first and most effective of all curses which was the punishment for the first sin. The curse has worked well indeed; we still think it's a sin to revive that blissful state which existed before the Fall. But the wisdom of the people has never forgotten: they imagine Heaven as the absence of pain and effort; they exalt royalty ("The king was in the counting house...") as representatives of the gods on earth —

Dissent, Winter 1956.

clearly because leisure is the measure of distinction, and pleasure is divine.

Anyway, the people were always wiser than the textbooks; they never believed that wealth makes no man happy. Neither do they believe that riches are usually come by the hard way. Experience shows that the harder the work, the less the pay. The dirtiest jobs are not paid in proportion to the marginal "disutility" or distaste of their execution, but in accordance with the disrepute in which a person stooping to them is held by his equals and betters. Society may teach children that work never dishonors anyone, but when they grow up they would rather work less and receive higher honors.

This, Aristotle would say had he lived to see it, is as Nature would have it; for it is debatable whether those who do the menial work have a soul, whereas those who have leisure to enjoy the pleasures of life must of necessity have richer experience and a larger scope of soul. The more leisure, the higher the rank on the social scale.

On the other hand, the most effective slogan of revolutionary class hatred has been: He who shall not work, neither shall he eat. That terrible revolution did happen, though the exact time of its happening is not quite clear. Sociologists generally credit the Reformation with bringing about a complete change in people's attitudes toward work. Martin Luther, it will be remembered, rejected "good works," apparently because they interfered with works *tout court,* good or bad; thus the rich and mighty would go to heaven despite their bad works and the poor to hell for their good works; he also admonished the princes to keep the peasants in their place and, failing that, to quarter, break on the wheel, blind, whip, and hang them. An even gloomier chap was John Calvin. When he governed Geneva, he declared it a sin against God and a burden on the city's treasury for any man to be idle; he sent the spiritual and temporal police into every household to make sure every man was working. He was one of the first churchmen to condone a modest amount of usury by calling it interest; stinginess he called thrift; and hoarding, diligence. His defense of the usurer was echoed by the staunch churchman Mellon, who never foreclosed properties unless the tenants were "weakened by bad habits and extravagant living" — which unfortunately he found to be the case fairly regularly. Calvin never married, and he forbade his followers all plea-

sures, luxuries and, above all, idleness, which gives a man ideas. Before
Freud he discovered that frustration can be converted into furious
work. His friend Ulrich Zwingli thought that "labor is a thing so
godlike. . . in things of life, the laborer is most like to God."

Their later followers, however, found it difficult to persuade sensible
men that this could be true, if only because the Catholics were having
a good time and still expecting God's forgiveness. Therefore they
invented the "Calling." It is difficult to explain the Calling if you can't
say it's another word for work. "Calling" means work as a crusade; it
means that a man has been identified with his work so intimately that
his life no longer consists of hours of work and hours of play or rest: it
is all work. If he does rest, it is to restore his energy for work; his
recreation, too, must be usefully employed; his play must exercise his
mental or physical powers. *Kraft durch Freude* was not invented by the
Nazis; this mentality had been there all along waiting to be topped off
with the usual German instinct for turning the all-too-serious into the
all-too-ridiculous. The Americans are only slightly behind the Germans; however, as is fitting, our example comes not from government
propaganda but from commercial advertising. A maker of foam rubber tells us to "rest efficiently" on his mattresses. Now I like foam
rubber, and using it for rest should be a pleasure, but that adman has
spoiled it for me. If I feel that even in my sleep I am being efficient, I
don't enjoy it any more.

Yet even Calvin's universe had its rewards. In the first place, work
was pleasing to God; then, to follow one's Calling brought recognition
among men. Some people's Calling did not call them to great deeds,
nor to great riches either, but just to fill their places as ordained from
on high. Doing one's job well was satisfaction in itself. Finally, a man
could look with pride at his work. Whatever he did was completely his
own; even if it was done in cooperation with others, he still had insight
into the whole process. Our language has retained a reminiscence of
this bliss: we still say "work" for both the act of creating and the
product. By contrast, we say "labor" for the expenditure of human
energy and for the supply of same. In the English language — and in
none other, as far as I know — the word "job" can be set aside to name
the social and economic relationship between the worker and his
working place.

Since language is prefabricated thought, a worker referring to his "job" is revealing a truth about modern society; he is "class-conscious." But if he naively says "my work," forgetting that he neither owns his product nor controls the process of its production, he is atavistically using conceptions from the craftsman's age. His parlance beclouds the fact that under the conditions of industrial capitalism the worker is separated from his product, first by a huge apparatus of machinery that does not belong to him, second by his contract that deprives him of the fruit of his labor, third by the market. All he knows is that for the time being he "has a job" requiring him to supply a specified amount of labor and to cooperate in the production of some merchandise his boss thinks he can sell. Usually he specializes in some phase of production and has very little insight into the whole process. He cannot possibly feel the satisfaction of an artisan looking at his work; he is not asked to be "creative" and has very little chance even to show ingenuity. All his pride is concentrated on the work process, which he can speed up and even improve, but which never leads to any fulfillment or end.

The more efficient the worker is, qua worker, the greater is his estrangement from the product. So much of it passes over his work-bench; he boasts of his inventiveness in cutting corners, getting out more production in a given time, making more money to take home. The myth of Productivity has driven out the friendly gods of old. In their place we have enthroned the religion of Efficiency. We love efficiency, paradoxically, for two reasons: it saves "labor," but on the other hand it makes working more productive. If efficiency were used only to speed up our working hours and extend our leisure time, it would be all to the good. But this is not the case at all, or very rarely so. My hero in technology always was that attendant boy who was too lazy to turn by hand all the valves on Thomas Newcomen's first primitive steam engine; he connected the various faucets with rods which later were attached to the flywheel, and thus invented the feed-back. This invention really was meant to save "work"; but when his employers later used it, they did so to save "labor."

Now here is the paradox: as a human being, the worker should be glad that machinery is being invented to relieve him of (at least some of) the drudgery; as an employee he has to fight hard not to be relieved entirely by the machine. Under capitalistic conditions he has to fight on two fronts — on the one hand for his "right to work," on the other hand for his "right to leisure." Fortunately, both birds can be killed with the same stone. The long history of class strife in the nineteenth century is a story of the gradual shortening of the working day. With this device, workers have assured themselves a place among human beings; they have won recognition for their desire to rest and play beyond the call of duty, and at the same time they have stretched the need for labor.

The price of better working conditions was the division of labor: the worker had to accept, and acquiesce in, the conditions of factory work; he was integrated into a huge organization of well-laid-out production processes and subjected to the requirements of machine production. In this organization, the worker no longer has control over his product; at best, he may have control over his machine, but in most cases the machine will have control over him. Only the top management has control over production, and the sales manager has control over the product. The worker often does not even see his product. When the first news of the atomic bomb was published, the most shocking revelation, to me, was not its enormous power of destruction but the report that thousands of people had been employed in its production without knowing what they were doing. Here all the traditional notions of "workmanship," "pride in one's work," "calling" had become devoid of any meaning. Professional prowess no longer lies in "creativeness" nor in anything that refers to the product; the satisfaction is not in creating the product; it is in productivity. The worker is completely estranged from his product, and opinion research probing a little beneath the surface will reveal that workers love their machines but are indifferent to what they produce. (Foundations please take note; this is a really worthwhile project that also might be interesting to management.)

Orthodox Marxist critics of capitalism first considered "alienation" a purely economic estrangement of the worker from his product. No amount of worker participation will overcome this condition—for the simple reason that even under the most favorable conditions the employers don't have control over the verdict of the market either. The condition, however, is also inherent in modern mass production as such; even an entirely state-controlled or cooperative enterprise cannot escape it. The remedy is trade union action, which gets for the worker as much out of the proceeds as the market will bear—a tonic that does not remedy the situation but makes it less obnoxious. The enterprise can give the worker a very decent or even a very high (monopolistic) wage and make working conditions for him really pleasant with Muzak, air-conditioning, coffee break, and other devices of "human engineering"—all justified as conducive to higher efficiency, of course.

Still, we are even more deeply entangled in the basic contradiction —that work and leisure are two very different things. The devices of personnel management only help to underline the basic fact that labor is measured by its disutility to the worker, that he strives to exert himself less, to spend less time inside the factory, has no pride in his work, and gets little satisfaction out of a job well done, except perhaps through a promotion that enables him to spend more time outside the factory and enjoy it better. This condition transcends capitalism; it is characteristic of all industrial societies, including a socialist economy based on industrial production. Isn't it significant that travelers to Utopia usually find themselves in garden cities suggesting a preindustrial society?

All the devices of human engineering and personnel relations are just so many acknowledgments of the fact that work generally is unpleasant, that office hours are a nuisance, and that work discipline is degrading. This unpleasantness is overcome by morale-building ideologies, such as "work ennobles the worker," "the joys of duty," "common interest goes before self-interest," "duty before pleasure," "there is a war on." Sportsmanlike nations can be persuaded to stage productivity competitions; warlike nations can be asked to outproduce the enemy. Totalitarian governments particularly have developed techniques of combining competition with war images; they constantly organize battles of the grain, battles of production, battles of the cradle, etc. Failure to increase production unfailingly results in a charge of sabotage, but the most potent device of totalitarian imposition is the myth of Productivity, which persuades the worker that his job is his duty and that Duty, or one's job, stands higher in the hierarchy of values than one's personal needs.

At best, such verbalizations are the results of utter confusion. When the philosophers speak of *homo faber*, they mean the inventor, the creator, the playful explorer, the craftsman perhaps, but never the industrial worker. Man is free and creative only when he plays; he transcends himself only when his work serves no purpose; he fulfills himself only when he has no "job" to do. He develops his personality only when he throws off the thralldom of labor. He creates "works" only when he is not in the position of a "worker." The nihilistic, fascist ideologist Ernst Jünger went so far as to "suggest the question whether workers are not of a third sex"; a robot need not be human.

That workers are people was most forcefully asserted by Marx's son-in-law, Paul Lafargue, in his slogan "The Right To Be Lazy." His pamphlet under this title tells the story of a hundred years' fight for shorter hours; but there is more to it. Lafargue, a West Indian mulatto, had not been brought up in the Calvinist virtues and did not believe in the pseudosocialist philosophy that work alone redeems man from this vale of miseries. He felt that man needed very much to be redeemed from the obligation to work and saw that industrial machinery might help him to get rid of the drudgery. Much as he welcomed this opportunity, he also saw the danger of man's enslavement by the machines. The bold speculations of his eminent father-in-law on the all-pervasiveness of labor made him uneasy; he did not deny that socialists should fight for "the right to work," but he was not so sure that they also should fight for the duty to work. To him, it was just as important to fight for the right not to work. He was a brave man who truly believed in freedom, and when he felt that his life had been played out, he allowed no duty to retain him; he quit, even in his last action asserting a man's right to take his life into his own hands.

Lafargue was thirty years younger than Marx, and in the meantime two more generations have passed. To disagree with Marx amounts to saying that today it is possible to see where Marx was a child of his age. His enemies were the leisure classes that were monopolizing consumption. The streak of the Jewish prophet and chiliast in Marx blinded him to the virtues of luxury and pleasure; his own life was that of a zealot; he poked fun at Lassalle's suggestion that the workers ought to increase their desiderata. So deeply was he steeped in the idea of

1.   Paul Lafargue
(Photo: International Institute of Social History, Amsterdam)

productivity that he even proposed labor service, and his idea of progressive education was to merge the factory with the schoolroom. Besides being an apostle of justice, Marx was a Victorian gentleman and a Prussian scholar; in neither capacity did he understand the workers. He had created for himself such a high image of the ideal proletarian (with arms growing thinner and fists raised higher) that the specimens he met in real life usually annoyed him. Philosophical materialist that he was, he liked them best when they were least concerned with the good life, and he honestly expected them to sacrifice their consumer interests to the beauties of the socialist society of pure producers.

Under the conditions of capitalism, the worker tries to welsh on his contract and deliver less labor than he is expected to; the employer, on the other hand, holds the unions responsible for the delivery of an honest day's work. Under state socialism or state capitalism, the worker's interest in his "job" is supposed to wax to enthusiastic proportions; it's "his" state he is working for and the benefit is supposed to accrue to all. As a consumer and taxpayer, the worker certainly should tell himself, as his own employee, to work harder; but unless he develops a split personality it does not happen that way. His participation in management is only vicarious. He may be his own boss in the abstract; but this abstract personality confronts him in the alienated shape of a supervisor, and the conflict can be resolved only by institutionalizing the split of personality: free trade unions must bargain as his representatives qua worker with management as his representative qua consumer. Management will still insist on labor-saving devices to cut costs, while the union will ask for work-saving devices even if they are costly. This applies notably to jobs that are dirty and demand great exertion but give little or no psychological satisfaction.

I simply do not believe that "socialist conscience" will drive anybody to volunteer for the job of groundhog, digging a tunnel under the Hudson River. Lowly jobs can be filled only by one of four devices: higher wages; special honors and/or some sense of adventure that may be connected with them; labor service or some other form of forced labor; or finally, the presence of a lower class or race whose members are prevented from rising to better positions. I reject the last two and consider the second too rare to be generalized. Groundhogs must be paid higher wages or given longer vacations after the first enthusiasm of exerting themselves for their own government has worn off.

The same, though less drastically demonstrable, is true of all government efforts to increase productivity. A socialist government wishing to stay clear of compulsion must recognize the freedom of trade unions and cooperatives. I cannot imagine a socialist society in which all is eternal harmony; least of all can I accept the ideal of a docile labor force, bent on furiously fulfilling its duty toward the socialist fatherland and enthusiastically improving its productivity. If capitalism were to be criticized only because it is wasteful and inefficient, I would have little quarrel with it; but it is wasteful with human happiness and economical only with material goods. I expect socialism to be rather wasteful with material resources but thrifty with unpleasantness imposed on human beings.

The most efficient, i.e., cost-saving, economical way of producing merchandise may not always be the best from the standpoint of the worker's comfort. Our technology has advanced efficiency to provide for everybody; we can well afford to be inefficient wherever it suits us better. Automation is precipitating a new industrial revolution before society has made the necessary adjustments to use the new efficiency for the benefit of all mankind. We have become slaves of Progress; we have not dared to stop the development of atomic power as long as the nations cannot agree on disarmament. Marx was correct in opposing the Luddites: industrialism and capitalism could not be arrested but had to be digested. Automation, however, is correct in opposing Marx, and we have not digested the implications yet. The age of the robot is here; mankind can sit back and relax; the need for efficiency no longer worries us; productivity no longer is the measure of human contribution to the process of production; our needs can be filled by pushbutton operations.

Our problem is rather to increase our ability to enjoy our leisure time. We need to develop the creative range of play; we need to learn what it means to be free from the drudgery of work. Up to now our play has been modeled after the image of our work; even in consuming we maintain producer attitudes, or even worse — the dull and dutiful attitudes of factory work. We have to forget, to unlearn the producer

2.   Workers Loafing (from René Clair's À Nous la Liberté)
(Photo: Billy Rose Theatre Collection. New York Public Library at Lincoln Center.
Astor, Lenox, and Tilden Foundations)

attitudes; we have to renounce efficiency and productivity as human attributes. We have to insist on our right to be lazy and just human.

Indeed, why efficiency? It is generally agreed that socialism will be a very cumbersome way of providing administration and planning. If we admit, with Lenin, that a woman, on one day, ought to have a go at running her kitchen and the next day at running the state, I am afraid we shall not only eat less well but also have more serious reasons to gripe—which, by the way, I think is absolutely necessary and healthy. If we rotate labor from town to country, from manual to clerical, from executor to executive, out go expertise and efficiency. Not that I believe in these silly devices; I refer to them for two purposes only — first, to show that even the fathers of socialist thought, who suggested them, must have been aware that socialism is not a way to organize society more efficiently; second, to show how distinctly they were aware of the problem of human values that I am discussing here. But in those days they could think only of making work more "humane"; they had to organize their ideas of socialism around man the producer. It was only natural that they should have come to contradictory conclusions. Now we can make the Copernican turn: not by thinking of better devices to organize *homo faber* shall we liberate him from the realm of necessity, but by resolutely acknowledging his human ability to enjoy life and to act creatively in purposeless play.

Once labor has been recognized as something to move beyond and leisure has been recognized as the legitimate and significant sphere of human endeavor, we might even expect those psychological changes that are just utopian dreams in the classical theory of socialism. The founding fathers all imagined that socialist production habits would create community spirit and other virtues that would prevent the recurrence of acquisitiveness and war. There was neither proof in theory for such possibilities, nor did experiment bear these hopes out, except where communities were founded on a strictly religious basis. If we succeed, however, in substituting a religion of laziness for the worship of industriousness, the acquisitive instincts, while they still cannot be killed, might find no cultural and social nourishment and no economic sphere in which they could become active. Indeed, Fourier's paranoiac conjecture of a new animal might for the first time be rationally discussed. Those who might find some of his suggestions strange are asked to consider that he believed in play, too.

Retouches to "The Right To Be Lazy"

When *Dissent* reprinted this and other articles to celebrate its twentieth anniversary, I was struck by the discovery that many of the little truths we had published in the 1950s were proclaimed as great revolutionary innovations by the New Left ten years later. At the time I wrote "The Right To Be Lazy," I was not aware of doing more than any socialist could have done: pitting human values against capitalist values, affirming cultural freedom against the cult of efficiency.

Perhaps what I said then could be misunderstood. I said we should not make Efficiency our god, but I did not say we should make a god of Inefficiency. I said that productivity should not be an end in itself, but I did not say we should discard it as a means. A philosophy of free human choices is possible only on the basis of a technology that has taken the drudgery out of work.

Precisely for an ecology-conscious generation, the problem of rationality has not ceased to be troublesome. We can now, thanks to technology, be relatively unconcerned about the productivity of human labor. But we must husband the earth's resources and we must once again be cost-conscious in terms of the materials we use, the landscapes we despoil, the damage we do to our environment. The paradox is that these are engineering problems and that to solve them we call on the same technicians who have caused the trouble in the first place.

It would be dishonest to deny that socialism is likely to increase overall consumption. We want all the people to have enough living space, to own a TV set if they want it, to use all the health services they need, etc. The right to be lazy includes the right to use the conveniences of modern life; it does not imply the obligation to forgo them.

Since a socialist commonwealth can be built only on technology, and since a commonwealth means interaction of people and mutual aid, society will demand of every citizen a minimum of work for the services it offers. Unacceptable is, on the one hand, the technocrat's claim that priorities are to be determined by technical criteria and, on the other hand, the citizen's claim that he has no obligation to his society at all.

2

Three Economic Models:
Capitalism, the Welfare State,
and Socialism

In the capitalist economy, business decisions are made by the owners of resources. Capital may take the form of money, real estate, or machinery and equipment. It may also take the form of claims and rights to use, or to dispose of, these resources, or of powerful positions in organizations. Since labor is also a resource and a commodity, the power to supply or to withhold it may fall under this definition of property as well.

In the welfare state these powers of free disposal have been curbed. They are regulated and controlled by political organs, and in large areas of economic activity government has substituted its purposes for those of independent agents. These purposes are determined politically; i.e., they may range from establishing a strong defense posture to a concern for the well-being of the greatest number of people.

In both systems income is related to the use of *property*. Under capitalism such property itself constitutes a claim on income, to be realized in the market; the welfare state, however, supplements the market by other institutions that create or distribute income. Moreover, it creates a demand for goods and services that results not from consumer preferences and producer expectations but from its own political purpose.

Dissent, Spring 1964 (expanded).

Socialism I shall call an economic system that has divorced income from property, and even from the exertion of labor. In contrast to state capitalism, which still recognizes the property of the state as a claim to income, socialism also divorces capital from production decisions.

Obviously, I am dealing here with pure types, disregarding intermediate systems such as monopoly capitalism, syndicalism, corporativism, and market socialism, which have in common this basic feature: the means of production are not owned by individuals but by collective bodies which, however, deal with their property claims as though they were individuals. An especially interesting case is the cartel général or state capitalism, where this feature has been carried to the extreme: all facilities are owned by one big corporation but the production relations are still governed by the market mechanism.

My purpose is to show what other assumptions must be made to realize each of these models as a working economic system and how each affects the allocation of resources, the general efficiency of production, and, above all, the welfare of its citizens.

However, I deliberately refrain from speculating on possible differences of cultural attitudes or changes of human nature in the three systems. I only assume that humans have a natural aversion to involuntary toil and a natural ambition to excel in self-assigned tasks, but that the degree of their acquisitiveness and cooperativeness is related to the environmental conditions that encourage or stifle their development.

I

Capitalist theory claims that all resources find their most useful employment when each owner tries to maximize his profit in a free market, where labor also finds its price.[1] Fortunately, such a pure capitalism has never existed, or else no one would have organized the police, provided courts of justice, built bridges, laid sewers, embellished the public parks, founded hospitals, or established public universities. It has always seemed to me that the fire brigade refutes the pure theory of free enterprise. What more essential service could one imagine? It ought to command a price and attract the venture capital of an enterprising speculator who wished to make a profit and would therefore allocate resources for this purpose. Yet nothing of the kind happened; instead of waiting for the free play of the market to prove the usefulness and determine the price of a fire brigade, a committee of the ruling classes on the municipal level went ahead and organized one.[2]

Likewise, the business community felt that private coining privileges led to public losses, and it gave central banks the power to regulate the flow of money, the rate of interest, the value of currency, and thereby also the direction of foreign trade, income distribution among various countries, and, to some extent at least, the business cycle. Even the most classically free capitalism is not an entirely "free" economy. To function properly, it polices itself. In the public debate, however, the question of controls usually is confused with the question of who should do the controlling. Business prefers the so-called indirect (orthodox or classical) controls: regulation of the rate of interest, reserve requirements, the marketing of Treasury bills — not because they are indirect or because they are not controls but because the controllers of these controls are businessmen.

On the other hand, business expects the state to protect it against foreign competition. Far from leaving the optimum allocation of material resources to the competitive spirit of rapacious speculators, it asks the government to enforce conservation practices, to protect patents, and to finance research. Even the most ardent theorists of economic liberalism — Professors Mises, Hayek, Röpke — point out that it can function only if a "strong state" enforces the laws of the free market and provides the services that free enterprise does not find profitable. In short, it simply is not true that the free market, left to itself, results in the optimum allocation of resources. Adam Smith himself advocated government intervention for specific purposes and opened the way for a general theory of "Expenses of the Sovereign and the Commonwealth."

Apart from such empirical observations, which undercut the ideal model of pure capitalism (and we have not spoken yet of the tendency toward concentration and monopoly, of the creation of artificial markets through advertising, or of manipulation through government orders or policy), at least two theoretical factors militate against the contention of the market theorists. Both are inherent in the model, and both have been freely admitted by the better representatives of liberal economics. One is the inequality of incomes and the other is the time limit within which investment is expected to pay a return but which may — and increasingly does in large projects of national interest — exceed a man's lifetime. It is generally conceded that both features are incompatible with the optimum use of resources. I shall explain the idea in greater detail.

Apologists for capitalism often say that a free market permits the consumers to "vote" for the goods they desire, and that the price mechanism tells producers which goods might give greatest satisfaction to the greatest number. Hence free enterprise equals democracy, QED. This analogy limps. The consumers must first *buy* their "ballots"; unless they are equipped with purchasing power, their desires will not become manifest to the producers. In other words, this "democracy" is based on unequal suffrage. Are those who have no votes incapable of satisfactions? If all votes were equal, the sum total of satisfactions would be substantially greater and the allocation of resources would be much closer to the optimum. Even from the angle of developing resources, therefore, pure capitalism does not produce the best distribution of effort. Apart from the haphazard method by which the market discovers what is in demand, it does not determine the common good but — at best — the maximum profit for all enterprises.

Paradoxically, this also is the aim of certain "socialist" economies, e.g., the syndicalism practiced in Yugoslavia and preached by Oskar Lange and his German disciples.[3] In the way these systems function they scarcely differ from capitalism, expect that the dividend is shared between workers and government instead of being paid out to the shareholders to be taxed later. The Yugoslavs claim two virtues for market socialism: it establishes that "consumer democracy" which capitalism cannot realize, and the producers' associations tend to acquire the power of true soviets, the best form of political democracy. One day, both claims might be validated, provided the Communist Party dictatorship disappears; today Tito's works councils are far from being soviets, and the consumers can express their preferences only months or years after the central planning board has expressed its views through investment priorities. In fact, if the Yugoslavian "socialist" economy is to work better than it does, more decisions on investment will have to be made by central boards. Syndicalism in an underdeveloped country tends toward state socialism.

In a capitalist economy, investment decisions are guided by the profit expectations of investors. But Mises correctly states that profit can be obtained only by meeting "a *comparatively urgent* demand" (italics mine). If there is no such demand equipped with purchasing power, it may be created artificially, through advertising or by inducing the government to finance it; that way, resources are misappropriated to suit a pressure group. Or a need may exist, but demand may not become effective and supply may not come forth because the projects are too big or too speculative: only big corporations, or monopolies, have the means or the foresight to allocate resources for long-term research and development on a large scale. It takes guts, plus a reasonable assurance that no competitor has the same plan,[4] to construct a bridge, a railway, or a power dam at a time when demand is not yet "urgent" — though money might be saved by anticipating it well in advance.

If not government initiative, then at least a government guarantee of capital and interest is required to bring forth investments in the infrastructure — roads, canals, harbors, rivers, and draining of marshes —which will rarely yield profits in the foreseeable future. A paper mill may establish a hundred-year cycle of timber exploitation; but this exception proves the rule, for in any event the mill expects to make a profit on the real estate. Similarly, one "octopus" after another used railroad construction as a pretext to acquire land and to exploit farm communities in the West. Even this incidental profit did not prevent carrier companies from going broke, and the United States would not have its marvelous rail network had not some speculators miscalculated! One too often forgets that our industrial empire arose over the bodies of expropriated capitalists and failed investors, or that incidental monopoly profits made up for losses sustained in the production phase of the enterprise.[5]

Because of this time factor, classical capitalism does not achieve optimum use of resources. Normally, wherever expectations of profit must be deferred beyond the planners' lifetime, the investment will be undertaken only for a reason of public policy — whether conservation, development, autarky, or strategy. The history of foreign aid shows that private capital will not take the risk of developing the infrastructure of the laggard countries in a time interval consistent with the rapid population increase and rising expectations. If rapid development is desired, colonialist monopolies or state capitalism seem to be the only alternatives.

II

After a glorious career of continued primitive accumulation, during which capitalism began to develop modern industrial production all over the world, it has now reached limitations that can be overcome only by more effective methods of organization — the giant trust, the monopoly, the government enterprise, state capitalism. The enterprise has become too large, the time span for the return of profits too long, and, on the other hand, the need for political investments too pressing for the free market to remain competitive. In distributing resources, competition no longer responds to consumer needs — if it ever did — and does not most effectively use all factors at the right time. It still is serviceable on the smaller scale of consumer industries; it may still pioneer in some areas of invention. But major research and large industry are now in the era of imperfect competition, and the claims that continue to be made on behalf of "pure" capitalism are based on a theory which no longer fits the facts. Even Mises admits that under monopoly rule "private profit and social productivity are at a variance"; hence, "however great an evil socialism might be, it would be less harmful than private monopoly."[6]

To make my point clear, what has been said so far does not amount to Hobson's and Lenin's charge that monopolies suppress technological progress. The few instances in which a significant invention was temporarily withheld from exploitation are far outnumbered by the inventions that originated in a monopolistic enterprise and could be exploited only by monopolistic practices. On the other hand, a socialist or state-capitalist system might actually find it necessary to delay exploitation of an invention that would make obsolete a recent huge investment. Imagine a new gimmick that would force each of us to buy a new television set: private industry would ruthlessly force the expense down our throats, while government-operated stations might mercifully continue to use the old system.

At a certain level of development the equations of exchange grow more rigid. More individual transactions become dependent upon one another, yet at the same time the number of independent variables increases while the number of indeterminate variables decreases. For instance, the population explosion and government-sponsored research cannot be captured in any system of equilibristic calculations. Finally, neither the external nor the internal reserves adjust themselves to the requirement of the equilibrium. There are no precapitalistic spaces left for capitalism to feed on, and the labor force does not obligingly contract while automation makes it obsolete.[7] On the other hand, even the unemployable now refuse to abandon a standard of living that has become synonymous with existence in the most advanced countries. As Marx pointed out, the human factor does not fit into the equations. Hence we must turn the problem around. State capitalism and socialism provide different answers to the question of how to fit such equations to the human situation. We therefore have to say a brief word on the importance of the equations, or what Arthur C. Pigou and Abba Lerner call The Rule.[8]

We said that technological progress is now speeding ahead much faster than old equipment can be written off, while production units are increasing in size and, in the more developed countries, demand is becoming more inelastic. Is greater efficiency the answer? In introducing new production methods, capitalism needs to consider only their cost to the enterprise. It does not consider the social cost of firing people — neither the "disutility" of their enforced leisure nor the money it costs to maintain them in social insecurity, the social losses in crime, disease, and illiteracy. The welfare state makes a conscious effort to assume these social costs, or it may even waste more money to fight those undesirable by-products of capitalistic cost-accounting; but it will not effectively force the company to take them into account — it cannot even control air and water pollution, protect us from the din of commercials and jet noises, or preserve scenic views and wildlife.

A state capitalistic system has the means to deal with the problem of social cost. It may maintain a railway stop that no longer pays in order to save the gasoline the commuters might have to use otherwise. Yet more often it will leave people to fend for themselves. Wherever state capitalism is operating today, it tends to suppress the problem rather than to solve it. Only a socialist system, operating under conditions of abundance, can make its investment decisions in full view of all economic, social, and human factors that might be affected. It may even make uneconomical investments which might not save labor hours and minimize cost but would save exertion and misery.

Any economic system that wishes to balance cost and revenue must earn its investments before it introduces new inventions, or the new production methods must produce savings in excess of the capital they make obsolete. That is the iron rule for all systems that aim to produce economically, i.e., that fulfill the exchange equations. A free market economy does so by trial and error, through wasteful competition, and at the cost of misallocated resources. It achieves a dynamic equilibrium at the cost of periodic depressions and, even at its best, through violent fluctuations that can be contained only through monopolistic practices — which destroy the free market.

III

State capitalism[9] fulfills the equations by systematizing monopolistic practices. It avoids the waste of the free market, and it does not permit investments to be misplaced in the development stage or to become obsolete in the stage of saturation. It can direct investments toward ventures that create new demands — Keynes' "pyramids," Tugan-Baranovsky's tower of equipment, a huge defense establishment, or a "New Frontier" — and it may even balance inefficient production units against overproductive units. Not for long, though: in the end, state capitalism too must balance its budget as well as its other accounts; it must instruct its managers to produce a profit and not to forget that they must earn interest and amortization charges on the equipment that has been placed at the disposal of each. For state capitalism, like classical capitalism, is governed by The Rule, and its current production must be burdened by past investments, some of which may no longer have physical counterparts. (The built-in debt charges in most government budgets are constantly increasing, and the French are still paying for conquests they have long since surrendered.)

In contrast to classical capitalism, state capitalism must be more prudent in using the resources that have been developed, and can be more daring in developing still unexploited resources. Since both, however, are laboring under the regime of scarcity,[10] commodities and services have prices that constitute costs for the producer. The relations between buyer and seller, employer and employee, debtor and creditor are the same under both systems. Whatever their system of equations, it must be capable of simultaneous resolution: service must be paid; capital must be amortized and bear interest; even though production may be nationalized, property relations still govern all economic calculations. It may seem that some national enterprises do not show a profit because the government is their only customer and it subsidizes them. Taxes and subsidies are hidden in the price system, which the government seems to fix arbitrarily for reasons of national policy.

In the Soviet Union, for example, military "hardware" is sold to the defense establishment at prices below cost. That makes the budget look smaller but has resulted in such confusion of bookkeeping that managers are now pressing for an honest price system. Today, Gosplan must keep two different sets of books — one of which shows the real cost of the subsidized articles. These subsidies, however, must be covered by taxes taken from the prosperous enterprises or from the consumers, and if the budget does not balance, inflation threatens to upset all equations. State capitalism, therefore, is striving to increase efficiency and to raise the productivity of labor even more diligently than free capitalism. The whip of hunger has been replaced by the guillotine of control figures: all accounts must resolve themselves, all equations must be fulfilled. While no shareholders expect a dividend, it is as though the managers were merely executing the abstract striving of capital to become remunerative.

Many people confuse socialism with state capitalism and nationalization with socialization. Oskar Lange was clearly thinking of state capitalism rather than socialism when he wrote: "The equations which have to be solved in a socialist economy are exactly the same equations, and they are solved by the same persons, as in a capitalist economy."[11] He claimed three advantages for his system of socialism:

> ——a greater equality in incomes, conducive to a greater welfare effect of production and to greater overall efficiency in the allocation of resources;
> ——substitution of social gain for private profit;
> ——planning: projecting needs, avoiding waste, and setting public goals.

These three improvements are of the greatest importance, but they will not liberate the economy from the dominance of value equations. Moreover, they are ambiguous: the "social gain" that is being substituted for private profit does not become available to the consumers or even to the producers. Some profit may be used to build public parks and art galleries; but its bulk must be invested in improvements of national resources. Lange knew that the workers would not get "the full proceeds of their labor," as some primitive socialists have demanded. His "socialism" must follow the market equations, i.e., his society must invest its surplus in the same enterprises that would look inviting to capitalists under the profit incentive. These investments are the "social gain" in Poland today [1964].

Recreation facilities and places of learning, however, do not emerge from the equations; their cost must be taken out of "surplus value." Strangely enough, instead of improving the standard of living, the Polish government has used a large part of its profits to rebuild destroyed cities in the quaint auld style of yore. The point is that under state capitalism, which Lange called socialism, the apportionment of surplus value among welfare and other national purposes is a matter of arbitrary decision. The government may allot its profits to industrial developments, to the creation of a national image, to military power, to welfare institutions and consumer satisfactions, or to a trip to the moon.

The equations neither prescribe nor prevent any particular use, and state capitalism therefore is neutral with respect to socialism. It is not incompatible with a distributive economy, but it is also compatible with systems of remuneration according to deserts or social rank. Under conditions of great scarcity, or of extreme stress for the sake of rapid development, state capitalism (national socialism) will reproduce the very worst features of early capitalism (or worse, as it did under Stalin); but under conditions of abundance it may develop features of the welfare state or even of socialism.[12]

Which path it follows, however, will depend upon the development of democratic institutions, and in this respect state capitalism is not so indifferent. It tends to favor bureaucratic dictatorships; or, more correctly, state capitalism and dictatorship enhance each other. Particularly if the dictator communicates to the nation a sense of urgency concerning plans for accelerated development, he may destroy the germs of pressure groups and of pluralistic bargaining. State capitalism always creates economic conditions that tempt the policy-makers toward national greatness. It is the ideal basis for a military or defense economy. Statism is not socialism.

The arbitrariness of statist production goals has inspired violent protests from partisans of a free economy, and not without reason have they denounced state capitalism as "the road to serfdom." Unfortunately, though, they gave it the name socialism, and this has created theoretical confusion. The socialists were actually the first to dissociate themselves from all theories of bureaucratic rule. At all times they have insisted that the state apparatus should be an instrument, not a taskmaster. In its decadent phase, bourgeois theory no longer has the ability to distinguish between the conceptions of "state" and "politics." Socialists do not say that the state should organize production and command consumption. They say that demand itself has come to be politicized.

IV

To explain this distinction, I must return to my introductory remarks. Ultimately the owners of resources make not one decision but two. They seek profit with only those means that previously they have decided to allot to gainful employment; but at the same time they have decided what part of their resources and time they wish to retain for themselves. As an owner of real estate I might decide to set some of it aside for hunting; as an owner of money I might decide to buy jewels or paintings rather than machinery; as an owner of labor power I might decide to become a monk, thus withdrawing myself from the market and raising the price of labor. According to the strict theory as taught by Mises and Hayek, all resources should compete in the marketplace for the highest profit, thereby ensuring the optimum allotment for the greatest satisfaction of the whole while granting workers the "marginal" wage that will induce them to serve.

In practice this has never been the case. Each owner is a monopolist who may decide to leave his resources idle, to consume them unproductively, or to use them for gain. Thus workers may decide that idleness gives greater satisfaction than work at low wages or for long hours, and by withdrawing labor power from the market they raise its price. They conspire to do that, just as landowners conspire to control the use of land and bankers conspire to maintain the value of the currency. These are different kinds of conspiracy, recognized as legal at different stages in the development of modern industrialism; together with the first kind of intervention we mentioned — governmental care for health, welfare, security, and communication – they become countervailing powers that mitigate the arbitrariness, brutality, uncertainty, and insecurity of the capitalistic market.

The welfare state implies a capitalistic economy that largely depends on the free market. At the same time, countervailing techniques have been politicized and are consciously employed to balance the economy, to develop the national resources, or to pursue fixed goals of social policy. Foremost among these goals are economic security, higher living standards for the poor, and conservation and development of resources. The fully developed welfare state has at its disposal a wide range of economic instruments, classical as well as Keynesian and statist. They include the government's power to regulate, to control, to intervene, to tax and redistribute the product, to plan and use its position as a buyer of 10 to 20 percent of the national product.

The welfare state may achieve techniques of maintaining full employment and minimum incomes; it may use industrywide planning, price-fixing, and overall control of development. But, although it will nationalize the coal industry in France and England, erect a TVA in the United States, and build a government steel mill for India, it stops short of expropriation.[13] On the contrary, its proclaimed aim is to preserve the structure of property and to protect the formation of a free market. Whatever expropriating is to be done must come through the free play of the market, as is happening in our farm economy despite price supports. The basic relationships of buyer and seller, employer and employee, owner and nonowner, are no different from those prevailing under pure capitalism, but they are supplemented by state interference in two important areas: where classical capitalism is indifferent to the distribution of incomes, the welfare state at least tries to make income differentials less steep; where under pure capitalism the development of resources is an accidental by-product of the profit incentive, the welfare state sets itself definite goals of developing public and private facilities, consumer satisfactions, even tastes and standards.

In contrast to pure, classical capitalism, which is totally producer-oriented, the welfare state may plan the deliberate increase of consumer satisfactions, whether in the form of more equal distribution of income, increased productivity, or enlarged public services. It does not always go that far. Such planning for satisfaction may stop at "full employment," which may be brought about through defense expenditure or pyramid-building without any noticeable increase in the general standard of living and without making people more equal. However, the welfare state must give its citizens more security than pure capitalism, and its planning usually results in higher wage rates, shorter hours, greater opportunities, or, at the very least, in the maintenance of satisfactions that might otherwise be lost.

By virtue of both its means and its ends, the welfare state therefore is often dubbed socialism on the installment plan or creeping socialism.[14] But we should not be misled by its efforts to plan, regulate, and control production, to distribute income, and to curb the uninhibited use of private property. At the hub of its mechanics, it is different from socialism. Although some prices and wages are determined politically, on the whole they are determined by the market, and that is true even of the public enterprises. The regime of property prevails throughout, with the dead weight of past investments burdening the calculation of profit and decisions on future investments, with at least a theoretical obligation to balance all budgets, and with remuneration still tightly ruled by a man's contribution to the value of the product. Public projects still must be justified in terms of national policy rather than human needs, and expenditure for defense and similar purposes still exceeds the welfare expenditure.

V

An economy totally controlled by the interests of the ultimate consumers is properly called socialism or distributive economy. We usually distinguish two stages. The ultimate, communism, permits every citizen to draw on the public resources according to his needs. This presupposes a degree of productivity and wealth that probably is not available in any country now, in addition to a development of public morality that may not be achieved in the near future. I therefore confine myself to the penultimate stage, socialism, where distributions may still be proportionate to deserts. Even at this stage, however, a *national dividend* may be distributed among all citizens in two forms: increased public services or the conversion of many essential services (such as higher education, health, transportation, housing, recreation, theater) from private to public operation;[15] secondly, the distribution of a minimum allowance sufficient to cover the expense of feeding, housing, and clothing a family.[16] The minimum allowance would not be generous enough to cover luxury expenses; there would thus remain an incentive to earn additional wages to keep up with the Joneses. Wage levels may be governed by demand and supply, collective bargaining will continue, and there will be wage differentials according to skill. But there will be a floor, thanks to the national dividend. A free market will provide goods and services, allowing demand and supply to regulate those prices that are not manipulated for purposes of public policy. Both public enterprise and entrepreneurs or cooperatives may compete for the consumers' favor.

Some prices may be administered to implement public policy. It is easy to imagine, for example, that each citizen is allotted a room of ten by ten feet; but if a man's need exceeds the standard house in his community, he may have to pay progressively increasing rent per additional square foot, window, or door. For all these transactions, money will be used as a means of circulation and for purposes of accounting. I can see no reason why a socialist economy should deprive itself of this useful invention — provided the money is not used to form capital and to acquire control of production facilities.

Capital formation may be prevented by a number of devices, such as steep income and inheritance taxes. This may be important for the period of transition if expropriated owners are to be indemnified. One may also think of "funny money," or a tax on all means of circulation and credit accounts such that money would lose a certain percentage of its value every month. That percentage might even be regulated for purposes of public policy in the same way that we now raise and lower reserve requirements or the rate of interest. The device is not primarily intended to reduce big bankbooks, and it does not even serve that purpose very effectively; its main purpose is to help in divorcing present from past production, a necessity I shall discuss presently. Here I only wish to insert a remark on private property.

It seems to me that socialists have overestimated the importance of expropriating the expropriators; the symbolic value of this measure far exceeds its economic significance. What matters is not ownership but control, and all systems by now are moving in the direction of more public control. A man like Mattei had a stranglehold not only on the whole Italian economy but on Italian foreign policy, too, though he did not own a single drop of the oil on which he had built his power. Or, closer to home: if one must have a dictator, one might think of better men than Robert Moses, but he has so much power that if any man were to claim as much merely on the ground that he owns a lot of the state's real estate, he would be harassed by D.A.s in every borough and hounded by tax inspectors in every district. The real question is how a democratic society can control the controllers and the managers of public enterprises.[17] Owners may be parasites, but economically speaking they are mere *faux frais,* or overhead. Their unearned income is not a personal tithe which they exact from the community but a payment for the use of their capital. In the capitalist lore, it is indeed the tribute to capital, not to its owner.[18]

VI

A socialist economy does not earn "wages of capital"; in fact, it severs the umbilical cord between capital formation and production or, in Marxian language, between past labor and current employment. This may sound utopian, and some readers who so far may have gone along, figuring that the national dividend also is nothing but an extension of welfare state services, may accuse me of economic dilettantism. Indeed, every major economist who has given the matter some thought has emphasized the need for a socialist economy to heed the equations, to follow The Rule, to amortize capital, and, if it wishes to invite expansion, to pay itself interest and even ground rent. Schumpeter said that any other notion was "irrational," Abba Lerner worked out schemata showing how the ultimate costs must equal prices, and Mises thought he had refuted the viability of socialism by showing that under that system "calculation would be impossible." Only Kautsky had an inkling of the importance of "freeing prices from values," but he failed to follow up his idea. It was an outsider, Peter F. Drucker, who put his finger on the crucial point: "The wage rate is the traditional symbol for the real conflict rather than the issue itself. The basic problem is a conflict between the enterpriser's view of wage as cost, and the employee's view of wage as income. The real issue is not an economic one but one over the nature and function of wage."[19]

Since we already have severed income from cost in Section V, we now have a similar conflict between the state enterprise's view of capital as cost and the consumer's view of capital as expenditure. The issue is not how much interest capital might earn to remain fair in a socialist society, but what its function can be in such an economy.

The difference between a socialist and any other economy is in the divorce of production from capital or property claims. *In the socialist economy, capital goods, once created, enter into the consumption funds of the society, to be drawn upon as the need occurs.* There is no need to amortize them in any given time or to realize a profit on them. Even today we are using facilities, such as roads, which our fathers built, and we are building facilities, such as airports, which our children may use. Strangely enough, such facilities are being paid for out of the current municipal, state, and federal budgets but are not carried on the books of these bodies as "assets"; just the same, bonds representing the value of these assets are being held and serviced for generations.

Other examples of divorce between real capital value and use challenge the sense of outrage. Daniel M. Friedenberg has shown how tax advantages make it profitable for owners to tear down houses that still might be of service for years,[20] while at the same time rat-infested slums are maintained because they still yield a profit. All I suggest is that a socialist society might use this same divorce of past investment from present enjoyment, but for a better purpose. We already have seen that state capitalism is capable of taking losses in one industry while earning profits in another. All that was required to satisfy The Rule was that the profit-and-loss accounts cancel each other out. We know that in practice the balance is never achieved in any particular year. But why must the year be the unit? Why not the decade? Why not the century? In practice we draw on present resources to unbalance the budget, otherwise we could have no development. Then, however, having established those new facilities, we forbid ourselves their enjoyment and say, in effect: "Now we must tighten our belts and pay for these goodies." Though we may have created the new investment in order to work less, we now must work more to pay for it. If this is not irrational, words have no meaning.

It is, indeed, a fetishistic way of looking at "value" that makes us demand that capital goods must produce value in all types of economies. Capital assets do not affect the prices of goods unless someone claims that they "belong" to him and he must be rewarded for letting us use them.[21] It is the same fetishistic view of man creating "values" that makes us demand that all equations be resolved simultaneously. They don't have to be; in a distributive economy we don't have to wait until we find a buyer to turn over the merchandise. Such an economy may destroy unserviceable assets or abandon created values — don't we do that to our military hardware anyway? — and yet it need not suffer the kind of loss which spells failure for the capitalist to whom it happens, for the loss really has occurred when the goods were first erroneously produced.

I shall admit that this kind of economy encounters certain difficulties. It is rather wasteful; it cannot account for all its transactions in one set of books; its measurements of efficiency are uncertain, and a number of indeterminate variables enter into its cost calculations, not to mention the numerous political factors that determine its prices.[22] All this is small discomfort, however. A distributive economy is possible only at a fairly advanced stage of development. One cannot distribute poverty; only wealth. Once we have conquered scarcity and are systematically opening further possibilities to augment our resources, we can tailor production not only to needs: we can consider capital a free resource that may enable society freely to decide at every moment whether to use certain developments without fears about meeting the dividends. Indeed, *what Mises counts as a refutation of socialism, its indifference to proper cost accounting, I would claim as its virtue.*

Nevertheless, no society has unlimited funds, and even the most liberal economist must economize somewhere. Plans must be developed with an eye to citizens who might be stingy with their time. Certain materials may indeed be scarce, and someone must calculate which of two possible substitutes might be more easily developed. In that case, "easily" means fewer hours of labor, less waste of other materials, cheaper transportation. In other words, a socialist economy may keep a second set of books where all transactions are calculated, either in hours of labor or in prices (provided the price system has not become too distorted). This set of books will have to allow for a kind of waste unheard of in our present economy: time wasted in experimentation, machines bought not to increase efficiency but to make work easier, committee meetings and grievance procedures, and special privileges granted to attract workers. On the other hand, the surplus value also will be enormous, as workers demand parks, playgrounds, nurseries, and other special distributions. In short, the bookkeepers will be aware that capitalistic enterprise could be much more efficient, and that is the reason why socialist economy must not be managed by the bookkeepers. Indeed, it can survive only as long as it is controlled by organs of democracy on all levels, from the planning board down to the workers' council.[23]

A socialist economy also can afford to experiment with different sorts of enterprise — communal, cooperative, municipal, union-owned — and to cater to other preferences. It can even allow a free market and marginal forms of private property (as it certainly will in farming). Enterprise cannot be "free," but the enterpriser as promoter and manager may be welcome (he cannot encounter more difficulty in pursuading a state office to place resources at his disposal than he has today in persuading a bank that he can make a profit). Thus socialism can be more "liberal" than state capitalism; it is not a regime of technocrats but a form of economic management that leaves ample room for pluralism and democratic processes of decision-making.[24] In fact, the danger may rather be that, under socialism, the economy could become too politicized and that logrolling would supplant calculating. Anyway, it is obvious that state capitalism is more conducive to dictatorship, while socialism is compatible with many forms of government.

3

Freedom, Authority, Participation

Learn to read and to write so that you may be relieved of labor and become an official with honor. The scribe is a master. His writing pad distinguishes him from the humble oarsman.

An Egyptian father to his son, about 1400 B.C.

Socialism: The Highest Stage of Individualism

Socialism strives to abolish exploitation and inequality. It seeks a society where merit and character are the only marks of distinction; where economic resources are controlled by public agencies, themselves under public scrutiny; where production is geared to the human needs of all and the product is distributed equitably; a society, finally, where man is no longer utilized as a means for purposes alien to him.

In practice, however, socialism has usually come to be identified with collectivism, and two of its best-known features are public ownership of the means of production and a comprehensive "plan" of production and distribution. Both are indeed characteristic of states that now call themselves socialist. But a moment's reflection will show that they are inadequate to define socialism. Nationalization is not socialization, and a plan must have a purpose: it may be

Dissent, Summer 1978.

designed to enhance the development of man's potentialities or it may be the instrument of national ambitions.

In the Inca state and the Egypt of the pharaohs we have both public ownership and a plan, but paired with servitude and exploitation. Spartan communism subjected all citizens to equal political oppression. Bismarck nationalized the railroads and the health service; Hitler's war machine was powered by a planned war economy. Some modern states have adopted a rapid-industrialization plan that — though praiseworthy in its intention — ruthlessly subordinates the citizens' desires to the needs of the state. Others have abolished the market for political reasons without, however, freeing the production units from the tyranny of profit calculations that continue to keep the workers under the yoke of exploitation.

To call all this socialism is to misuse a good word. Socialism is not a technocratic scheme designed to run the capitalist economy more efficiently; nor is it an economy that has merely been rid of capitalistic parasites. Socialists hope to liberate people from subservience to goals that have been imposed on them either by arbitrary masters or by abstract laws of economic development. They aim to make people responsible for their own destiny and to give everyone a chance to fulfill his aspirations as a person. This dream has been expressed in the socialist literature of all times: "In place of the old bourgeois society, with its classes and antagonisms, we shall have an association in which the free development of each is the condition for the free development of all." In most anthologies this sentence is the conclusion of the *Communist Manifesto,* for it is indeed the end of its theoretical exposition. It must be assumed that Marx and Engels worded this ending with special care, and it is therefore noteworthy that they said "association" instead of "state," and that they did not consider the development of the whole a condition for the development of each but, on the contrary, *the development of each the condition for the development of all.*

Marx and Engels were not oracles, but it is significant that these alleged collectivists placed the individual ahead of the collective. True, they proposed to abolish private property, but not to put state property in its place. Their "association" was supposed to abolish the relationship of property between capital and worker, between dead and living labor; it was to substitute a direct, human relationship of cooperation for the mediated, material relationship of property and profitability.

Socialism has inherited this emancipatory dream from a long tradition of democratic revolutionary thinkers; as is well known, their revolutions were sidetracked and ended in capitalism—with individualism frozen in the property relationship and opportunity confined to the owners' class. Socialism continues the movement of liberation that was started in the eighteenth century, and it means to spread individualism to all, removing the fetters that capitalism has clasped on the fulfillment of many human aspirations. Freedom is not a luxury, to be enjoyed only by the members of a ruling elite, but a basic human aspiration that was brought to flower only in the unique development of western civilization, and it is still waiting for a full and generalized realization: civil rights and human rights are still expanding, and their wider scope is on the agenda of socialism. *Far from abolishing the individual, socialism is the highest stage of individualism—its fruition for all.*

As an association of people, the socialist society certainly must reflect the democratic structure and behavior of its origin—the socialist movement. In this passage from the *Manifesto*, Marx and Engels fell into the language of Rousseau, although on other occasions they were highly critical of theories that attributed the founding of the state to a "contract." When they wrote the *Manifesto*, they still saw the socialist revolution as the direct outgrowth of the democratic revolution. Imbued with the democratic spirit of that revolution, they saw "the association" as the means to mediate between the demands of society and the rights of the individual. Indeed, they could not conceive of a socialist society—much less a state—that would set itself goals other than those the citizens themselves had made their own.

Yet socialism begins with the insight that the whole is more than the sum of its parts. The association can envisage goals that unassociated individuals might not even be able to conceptualize. This is an opportunity as well as a danger. The following pages will discuss problems that have arisen for socialism out of the conflict between the will of the whole and the will of the parts: how much freedom may smaller associations (the shop, the region, the profession, the ethnic or religious fraternity) reserve vis-à-vis the big association (the nation, an international authority)? How much discipline or obedience can the larger community expect from the smaller and from the individual? When does the public ethos prevail over the private conscience?

The Distributive Economy: A Political Economy

The socialist economy is designed to meet human needs; its production is for use, not for the creation of value. But it cannot claim, realistically, that it will do away with drudgery, that it will not demand exertions and sacrifices, that it will be able to satisfy all demands. It can only promise that burdens and benefits will be shared as evenly as possible. It seeks equality in three areas:

——equality of opportunity for the self-fulfillment of all;
——equality of citizens' sacrifices and services;
——equality of basic rewards for each citizen (the national dividend).

This does not exclude differences of talent, achievement, and ambition. It is assumed, however, that some rewards of excellence will be sought in the shape of nonmaterial satisfactions, such as honors and responsible functions. Material rewards will be held to a token level or taxed so that private accumulation of wealth is confined to tolerable limits.

Private enterprises, such as small businesses and family farms, are not incompatible with an economy in which large-scale industries, utilities, and financial services are nationalized and cooperative enterprise is encouraged. What matters is that major investment decisions and overall industry targets are controlled by public boards. In the light of experience it can be said that the extent and speed of the early nationalizations in Soviet Russia and those in Eastern Europe after World War II were politically motivated and economically unwise, and that some reprivatization has paid off in Eastern Europe without endangering the regimes.

At a certain level of technological development, the minimum that is guaranteed to all citizens can be large enough to reduce inequality to marginal amounts. As a random proportion, the permissible maximum income could be twice as large as the median and four times as large as the minimum. Since basic needs are guaranteed to all, it would be the choice of each individual whether he or she wishes to work longer, acquire special skills, develop new lines of personal fulfillment. The border between work and play should become blurred. In a socialist society nobody should be called a parasite because he chooses to write poetry rather than advertising copy. Each citizen should have free choice of occupation after he has delivered the minimum service that all are required to supply.

Unfortunately, Marx called this requirement "labor service," and Hitler gave the same name to his premilitary training corps. It goes without saying that socialists, by contrast, have in mind those unpopular but necessary jobs that cannot be filled by special incentives in an economy of abundance — e.g., street cleaning, digging ditches, mining — and that could not be made a required stage in career training. This public service could be limited to, say, two years but it should be obligatory for all able-bodied citizens. There might be a choice of the age at which one fulfills this obligation, and also a choice between kinds of service. But it should be admitted that such jobs must be filled after the reservoir of generous, public-spirited volunteers has been exhausted.

Conscription of labor can be held to a minimum if a system of incentives is available to those who engage in a career. At some point the government may have to choose between increasing the incentives, lowering the minimum sustenance, and extending the years of required service. Obviously, abundance is always relative, and no utopia can elude unforeseen problems. Marx did not know about erosion and pollution, and he took the threatening exhaustion of natural resources all too lightly; the neo-Malthusian Club of Rome builds its utopia on the premise of scarcity or even impending famine. Against this kind of panic reaction, Marx's prediction was correct for a hundred years: population movement and the rate of inventions did adjust to the capabilities of a given economic system. From now on, however, it will be necessary to husband and plan the use of resources so that the threat of scarcity may no longer serve as an excuse for inequality. "Relative abundance" means that we have now the technical means to control the factors that used to produce relative scarcity: the growth of population can be controlled; the development of resources can be planned; investment in new technology can be directed to meet true requirements; the enormous waste of resources that occurs under capitalism can be reduced.

Contrary to widespread misconceptions, socialism may not open up a period of unrivaled development. It may broaden consumption but provide no incentives to produce bigger cars and more sophisticated household equipment. A planned economy may postpone the use of an invention that might be marginally useful but would require excessive resources and unwarranted social costs. By contrast, it might develop industries that are not profitable today but would provide intangible benefits to the community. Indeed, this is not utopian: states and municipalities have always built parks, sewers, harbors, waterways, and roads — certainly to help business but also to make the environment more livable; partial public planning has always been a necessary complement to "free" enterprise, which will not provide services deemed essential by the community.

Competitive and unnecessary expansion and a runaway rate of growth are illusionary benefits. A rapid rate of investment reduces the resources available to consumers and strengthens the scarcity argument that the rate of surplus value must be increased, that management should be given more authority, and that there is not enough wealth to allow equal rations for all. A socialist economy is not subject to the whiplash of competition to expand production for the sake of profit, and it does not have to make work for the unemployed. It will distribute as much as possible of the national dividend and will allow improvements and innovations only where they benefit the consumers or save labor and resources. It will take into account environmental and social costs. It may spend more on safety measures and health protection, or on machines that do not save labor but reduce drudgery and discomfort.

The development of these conditions requires a different notion of efficiency from that which exists today. The socialist plant manager need not strive for maximum profit, nor seek the most cost-effective means. He may measure his performance — in a certain way similar to the old guild craftsman or the artist — by aesthetic criteria, sanitary standards, satisfaction of the workers with their work, environmental impact of his operations, but not necessarily by the quantity of output and the efficiency of how he uses the equipment. He may not need to earn the amortization of invested capital; he may be able to reduce labor hours instead of dismissing workers or seeking additional outlets.

Obviously, a socialist economy will make mistakes; the question is, what would be the consequences of these errors? Misinvestments in a capitalist economy lead to depression. A socialist economy can write off the losses and shift production; it can localize mistakes and smooth out fluctuations. Technological shifts, population movements, even fashion changes can produce problems very similar to those that occur in capitalist economies; but a socialist government need not take these catastrophes as God-given laws of nature against which man is powerless. A new society will be equipped to deal with social change, and the structure of the socialist economy is so designed that it will absorb unforeseen irregularities.

To Control the Controllers

Some hints must be given on the structure of the socialist economy. Underdeveloped countries will rely largely on a central plan to develop their industries, but it should be kept in mind that, in so doing, they will also depend on the population's ability to produce needed articles within the family, or else to do without them. Even more advanced countries, such as the Soviet Union, have had crash programs rather than an integrated plan; what was called a "plan" involved merely the speedy development of certain key industries that failed to provide satisfaction to their consumers. In Eastern Europe, planning has usually meant the development of heavy industry, at great cost to workers' well-being, and utter chaos in regard to consumer satisfaction. *These models,* which have given a bad name to socialism, *are not the poorly managed samples of a basically sound structure, but monstrosities in their very conception.*

A socialist economy must be so designed that its functioning depends not on the vigilance of a government department but on self-adjusting mechanisms, steady feedback, and corrective action. Modern socialist theory has found that a certain freedom of the consumer markets and the price mechanism is an aid to flexible responses, while an authoritatively imposed plan may lead to gross disregard of consumer needs. In the Soviet Union, managers frequently have no incentive to follow demand, and hence merely fulfill the quantitative "plan target" — with the consequence that for a month people can buy gloves of only one size. Under "market socialism" consumers would have a choice of goods.

In a capitalist society, on the other hand, cartels may serve as tools to organize the market, or the government may act as buyer of last resort to set prices and production goals. A socialist government can use similar mechanisms for different purposes: not to maintain high prices but to regulate production in accordance with needs. The techniques of guiding the markets have been worked out by the corporate economy and the relevant government departments, regulatory agencies, and international authorities (European Coal and Steel Community, Common Market farm program, etc.). They need not be discussed here, because new techniques that a socialist government might add to them will not make a substantial difference. The purpose of these controls, however, should be different, and four possibilities present themselves:

> ——control can largely reside in the hands of corporate managers who are in close contact with the regulatory bureaucracy;
> ——control can be imposed by a bureaucracy that politically dominates the industrial managers, as in the case of a strong dictatorship;
> ——control can be exercised by democratic institutions through a bureaucracy (an unstable setup that may easily be transformed into either of the preceding types);

——control can be directly exercised through democratic movements at every level of production and distribution.

The problem is to institutionalize democratic types of control and organization in such a way that the new institutions cannot set themselves up as governing elites or merge with them. This problem is compounded by the need to adjudicate the conflicts that are likely to arise among industries, regions, control agencies, and between workers and management, planners and consumers, surplus producers and subsidized areas. The complex apparatus of a modern industrialized economy cannot be ruled by administrative fiat, and the courts are unable to resolve conflicts that arise out of social change.

Inevitably, therefore, economic questions will have to be thrashed out in the political arena, and from a socialist perspective this can only be done in a democratic way. A dictatorship may suppress conflicts for some time but will experience undesirable reactions (black markets forcing the state to become more tyrannical, economic deformities creating pressures in other areas). A better way would be to let conflicts come out into the open and to stress the associative features of the socialist-democratic processes — by developing cooperation and codetermination, letting the governed participate in decision-making, and allowing a proliferation of committees and representative bodies. Although such a multiplication of participatory bodies may have its negative and even unpleasant or dangerous aspects, at the moment it is merely necessary to emphasize that the only alternative is some form of corporate, bureaucratic, or state capitalism. Liberal capitalism was characterized by the total separation of the state from the economy; the twentieth-century economy, by whatever name, is characterized by its thorough politicization, and under democratic socialism economic decisions would be political, too.

Democracy: A Prerequisite of Socialism

Widest participation of the governed in the processes of decision-making is desirable not only on all levels of economic activity but also in schools, municipal affairs, and all organizations of public

interest. According to David Spitz, democracy has "two ingredi-
ents. . . the free play of opinions [and] the constitutional responsibility of the rulers to the ruled," while Robert MacIver calls it "a way
to determine who shall govern and, broadly, to what ends." These,
however, seem to be merely *formal* determinations that say nothing
about the economic system and which class is to rule. Yet, as
democracy increasingly becomes majority rule, it will tend to per-
vade more and more areas of public life; it will develop a policy on
education, family life, and health protection, on workers' rights,
and, above all, on overall economic policies. The purely "formal"
or procedural features of the democratic process are converted into
substantive measures, and democratic government comes to be
defined — and was already so defined by Aristotle, who hated it for
that very reason — as a government that serves the interest of the
majority.

It still is hated for the same reason: it will impose higher
wages and shorter hours, health protection and medical insurance, social security, the dole, inheritance taxes, regulations of business, environmental protection, codetermination and grievance
procedures, as well as civil rights and integration. None of these
measures is socialist in itself. Together they not only impose elements of a distributive economy on an acquisitive system; they are
also launching pads for further demands, and they support the
movement for a more comprehensive change of system. This is why
socialists of the last century embraced democracy so fervently. They
were confident that a majority of the people would act as a government for the people, breaking down the formal separation of the
state from the social life of the country. In contrast to the liberal-
republican state, the democratic state is not a limited state; it absorbs
influences from the community, and it is allied with socialism by
unbreakable ties.

This is certainly true as long as socialism has not been totally
victorious, and even during this period socialists will not rely exclusively on parliamentary institutions but will have to pursue their
goals through active, ever-renewed movements to counter the
capitalistic-oligarchic influences on the liberal-representative state. It
is a mistake to reject those institutions because they give access to

the levers of power all too impartially to the rich and to the poor; the answer is to find means of making the system work for the majority.

Quite a different problem arises when socialists obtain a majority and come into a position to impose their own system, i.e., create irreversible changes that might infringe on the rights of minorities. From Plato to Hegel and his latter-day disciples, political theorists have maintained that the state should represent not the interest of the majority but that of the whole, or "the general will." In defense of democracy, Rousseau put forward the sophistry that the elector does not vote his interest but what he thinks the majority will guess to be the general will. Khrushchev, when asked why there were no free elections in the Soviet Union, snapped back: "What if the people vote incorrectly?" The argument hinges on the assumption that someone—the philosopher, the dictator, the party—knows what is the interest of the whole. Most parties also claim that what they represent is not really a particular interest but "the best interest of all" or everybody's interest "if rightly understood." This presumably entitles them to disregard the minority, or even to prevent it from ever becoming a majority again. To state the argument in this form is almost tantamount to destroying it.

Ultraleft utopians have given it an even sharper, or perhaps more ludicrous, form. It seems to them that under socialism people will undergo a fundamental change of character; not being alienated, they will have neither different interests nor different opinions, but will gladly cooperate in any reasonable assignment that the government decides upon. The government, a fortiori, would be possessed of infinite good will and wisdom, and therefore the people would have no need for democratic organs of control.

No one has the right to make such assumptions. Under socialism, governments will continue to blunder and people will continue to want to control them and commit their own blunders. As Rosa Luxemburg was fond of saying, "The wisdom of the wisest Central Committee cannot be a substitute for the experience people gain by making their own mistakes." It is strange that some "socialist" philosophers should expect a total psychological change and then not trust the "new man" to take part in decision-making. If socialism is to develop a social dynamism, it will need all the collaboration and self-criticism, all the participation it can get in the selection of leaders and in drawing up programs. In the long run, the health of the socialist system will depend on the amount of "self-activity" or "self-movement" — words Karl Marx and Rosa Luxemburg repeated again and again. This means free discussion, free expression, free access to the means of criticism and to the media, the right to question yesterday's truth and correct yesterday's mistakes, the freedom to assemble, organize, and petition, the right to choose representatives and to form parties — even the right to refuse cooperation or to strike.

Fortunately, we don't have to choose between welfare and freedom, democracy and socialism. But if such a choice had to be made, it would surely be better to accept inequality under a democratic government than to accept a despotic government that offered equality. For under democracy it would be possible to fight for more equality, while despotism would inevitably bring back inequality. The leader who claims to represent the general will is the most dangerous of all: he carries aggression abroad and rules by oppression at home. For socialists it is better to claim that they represent nothing more than the will of the majority (if they do) and the democratic means to carry out that will.

This leaves the question that was slurred over a moment ago: what justification does the majority have when it passes over the will of the minority to impose structural changes? The problem has been put most succinctly by John Stuart Mill, in *On Liberty:* "The 'people' who exercise power are not the same people over whom it is exercised; the self-government spoken of is not the government of each by himself but of each by all the rest."

There are a number of conventions people accept because they are practical and their observance does not impinge upon either our individual rights or the system that has been acepted. But consider abortion: if the right to have an abortion implies the right to have it in a public clinic (as I believe it does) — by what right can I campaign for a law that would force Catholics to contribute, through their tax payments, to acts their religion forbids? As Friedrich von Hayek has noted, in recent times the concept of law has moved from rules of

conduct, mostly restrictive, to substantive commands, mostly coun-
terdiscriminatory. To create equal opportunity for all indeed means
to write laws that affect different groups differently. Advocates of
affirmative action have hammered this lesson home, and there is no
reason to believe that a socialist community may not discover problems requiring similarly discriminatory laws: either the majority
would become persuaded of a need for remedial action, or minorities would form logrolling coalitions. Whatever the mechanics of
forming a majority, there is no virtue in ignoring the fact that its
will overrides the will of the minority.

A gracious or guilt-ridden majority might grant certain dissenters
conscientious-objector status; or Catholics could be given a tax
remission for services, such as school and abortion, which they do
not require. Conflicts of this sort can be resolved by appropriate
accommodations within the prevailing system and, following Mao
Tse-tung, may be considered nonantagonistic or intrasystemic conflicts. The other type of conflict, obviously, is of a nature that cannot
be resolved within the "system" — which is an interconnected set of
institutions, each functioning to permit all others to function properly. To introduce a socialist economy means to create institutions
that would be difficult to repeal. It means to create a situation where
those advocating repeal cannot easily be accommodated. Imposing
majority will in order to introduce sweeping measures of socialization, therefore, places considerable responsibility on that majority.
To appreciate this it is necessary to examine more closely what is
meant by revolution.

Political and Social Revolutions

Revolution is usually seen as a single political act accomplished in
a relatively short time, sharply separating two different systems or
epochs. Thus, for most people capitalism in Russia ended in November 1917, and socialism began shortly thereafter. Even those
who would see a period of transition might be surprised to learn
that as late as 1921 Lenin wrote: "We have elements of a capitalist
economy, of state capitalism, of socialism, and of a cooperative

economy in our country." Likewise, 1789 is seen as a watershed, even though de Tocqueville showed how much of the ancien régime survived and how much of the new age it had anticipated.

The need to dramatize, to symbolize and periodicize is satisfied when a new epoch is proclaimed, and the proclamation helps people feel that indeed they owe allegiance to the new age. This stabilizes the revolutionary regime and relieves it of the need to justify itself again and again. Thus, the dismantling of the soviets after Kronstadt and the NEP, Stalin's crimes and the pact with Hitler, the imperialist policies since World War II — all this is seen, not as so many steps away from socialism but as means to fortify its power in the Soviet Union. *L'esprit de système* prevents the cool analysis of each action on its merits; one gives the system the benefit of every doubt and does not ask whether perhaps its behavior indicates a change in its nature.

Revolution is a powerful symbol. It reassures the revolutionary government that it can be dislodged only by counterrevolution; that it can fire unsympathetic teachers, officers, civil servants, judges who may have tenure; that it can swiftly create new offices and institutions to supersede the old; that it can take emergency measures to paralyze its enemies; that it may stay in power for more than one election period. Even if a socialist government did emerge nonviolently from ordinary election processes, it must fear a coup or foreign intervention. When the Kapp Putsch in Germany nearly overthrew the Republic, the Austrian socialists adopted a program envisaging a defensive dictatorship against reactionary plotters. Hostile powers have also been able to create conditions similar to civil war that eventually seem to justify intervention by the armed forces against a lawfully elected government (Spain 1936, Chile 1973). It therefore is necessary to make the following distinctions:

> ——As long as socialists are a minority or only a weak majority they can press for reforms, may join governments committed to reforms, but are not in a position to introduce fundamental changes in the social-economic system.
> ——Even where socialists and their allies may have won slight majorities, they must try to avoid the impression of revolutionary inroads

but should quietly strengthen their positions in all democratic institutions, increase the pressure of mass organizations, and then, having proved that they can govern, ask for a clear mandate for major structural changes.

———If socialists and their allies have reason to foresee a substantial majority for a program of large-scale structural reforms, their campaign may assume the symbolism of revolution. It is vital to tell the voters the truth: introducing socialism behind their backs would only entail a prolonged dictatorship. (I think it is now time for socialists to speak candidly about Allende's mistakes; although he remains a martyr, he need not be a model. Allende came to power without a clear mandate, either in numbers or by force of his program; he allowed supporters whom he could not contain to carry the revolution into the countryside before he could obtain its consent, thus uniting his enemies. While recognition of such mistakes will in no way excuse the counterrevolutionary, fascist repression that followed, it must be asked whether the bloody coup would have been possible if the Chilean socialists had refrained from "revolutionary" gestures. After all, this happened in a country that had enjoyed democratic government for forty years and had the experience of the antisocialist coup of 1932.)

———Where there is no tradition of democratic government and socialists come to power in the wake of civil war against a dictatorial or colonial regime, the chances for immediate transition to a left-wing dictatorship are greater, but a heavy price has to be paid.

If a revolution is to legitimize a socialist government, it must respond to a deeply felt desire of the population. No idea, be it ever so convincing and pure, can be a substitute for the democratic expression of consent that makes it unnecessary for the revolution to suppress dissenters. We come here to a fundamental distinction that used to be taken for granted in the older socialist literature but became blurred in the minds of our contemporaries because of the brilliant imagery of the political revolutions in Russia, China, and Cuba, all based more or less explicitly on the model of the French Revolution.

The alternative to this Jacobin–Bolshevist scenario was spelled out by Karl Kautsky in his 1902 pamphlet *The Social Revolution*. Kautsky distinguished the *social* from the *political* revolution, which in his time meant the establishment of majority rule. This, he explained, was only half the battle; after it there would follow a period of intensified class struggles, in the course of which the working class would expand its power in all areas: press, business, politics, the judiciary, the school, the theater, etc. Foreseeing fascism, he warned that reactionary gangs would try to turn the clock back by force. To meet them, the working class would need state power, but that would be only one episode in a long-drawn-out process.

Today we may amplify these insights by our better knowledge of the process of revolution. Even in the French Revolution, political events did not reflect the deep social upheaval that shook French society. But the classes that were most active in pushing the revolution to its consummation were not the ones that finally substituted themselves for the ancien régime. We call it the bourgeois revolution because of its outcome, but the third estate was much larger than the bourgeoisie, and even at the height of the terror the masses were not in power. Likewise, in the Russian Revolution the seizure of power by a Marxist party was not tantamount to a proletarian revolution. Lenin had foreseen only a bourgeois-democratic revolution under the "hegemony" of workers and peasants. But with the pressure of circumstances — the unique opportunity provided by the physical disappearance of the ruling class and the total collapse of the economy — the political revolution ran far ahead of the possibilities for a socialist revolution in Russia. The Bolsheviks had to retreat from War Communism when the radical impetus of 1917 was exhausted and was followed by a period of stabilization. Trotsky later wondered "whether we did not introduce Thermidor ourselves."

The Russian Revolution led to the nationalization of most enterprises, and this model has been followed throughout Eastern Europe. In the West nationalizations have been more selective, and some are still on the agenda. The Russian and East European revolutions have also made the society of these countries more egalitarian and have given the workers security and welfare from the cradle to the grave. But they did not abolish exploitation, did not promote self-administration, did not increase productivity beyond the rate that was to be expected through technological advances,

3.   Adolf von Menzel's <u>Das Eisenwalzwerk</u> (The Iron-Rolling Mill), 1875
(Photo: Ullstein Bilderdienst, Berlin)

and have left the working population woefully behind their Western colleagues with respect to both income and supply, not to speak of freedom and happiness.

If the social revolution was to improve the living conditions of working families, the slow, undramatic advances in the West have added up to more than the leap in the East. The price Western workers have paid for their greater freedom is the seesaw battle of class war, the pressure to succeed, the lack of security. The democratic process has resulted in permanent improvements and institutions, confirmed — and often expanded — even by right-wing governments that had originally opposed them. However, the system is enormously wasteful and frustrating; its redeeming feature is that the effects are clearly seen and openly discussed.

Comparing the two systems, one feels entitled to ask: Was it necessary to go through the painful process of revolution and to submit to bloody dictatorships only to end with a working class lagging behind those that had not made a proletarian revolution? Is it necessary to mobilize the symbolism of revolution in order to give the working classes of the West the assurance that the system works for them? To the first question Robert Heilbroner has answered: What about the suffering that is prevented by a revolution (the unborn children, or simply what Marx describes in the first volume of *Capital*)? It seems to me more fruitful to deal with historical questions as history: in some countries, we have seen, the social revolution was accelerated by a political revolution that also established a certain type of state, the dictatorship of the Bolshevik Party. Because of this accident of history, the socialist revolution has come to be identified with such a seizure of political power.

Marx coined the phrase "dictatorship of the proletariat," but he always meant it in a sociological sense, and he envisaged it for only a brief period. Moreover, it was to be the dictatorship not of a party but of the organs of socialist democracy opposed to the old state apparatus. Originally, Lenin and Trotsky also thought of the soviet dictatorship as an organ of popular democracy. Only later, when this was narrowed down to the dictatorship of the Politbureau, was the myth of the salvationist dictatorship created. Instead of seeing the need for dictatorship as a misfortune, Bolshevik propaganda had to insist that it was a virtue. This historical accident had great ideological consequences. The dictatorship was then passed off as the model for all other revolutions. The vision of the social revolution became confused with the myth of the seizure of power.

Dictatorship and Progress

Where underdeveloped countries have not produced an enterprising middle class, the task of modernization devolves on the new elites: army officers, urban intellectuals, civil servants, and classless students trained abroad. None of these classes has economic power of its own, but they all hope to use state power as the vehicle of their aspirations: to develop the country's resources and to prepare it for the race with other countries. For both purposes, they offer elite leadership; progress can no longer be left to the spontaneous processes of undirected growth.

Where no tradition of democracy exists, technocrats and bureaucrats are seen as pioneers of progress. The great prerevolutionary historian Vasili Klyuchevsky thought that in Russia the state had always been ahead of society in promoting development; in fact only the West has been modernized by spontaneous social forces rather than by the will of the princes.

State elites are more acutely aware of the dynamics of power than of the awakening nation's human desires. The more urgent the need for speedy development and the more compelling the thrust for national power, the less will the leaders feel inclined to develop democracy. Nationalism is their justification, with socialism added on as an ideology, and both are then identified with their own usurpation of power.

A modernizing nationalism in some countries goes by the name of socialism but in others, as in Taiwan now and in Japan before World War II, under the name of a corporate economy. Historical parallels are also relevant here: despotic governments helped the development of capitalism; kings gave commercial privileges to their courtiers, established royal manufactures, sent the poor to workhouses, and drove the peasants off their meager holdings — under pretext of making them more efficient in the name of national power and a higher economic rationality. This system was called mercantilism, and its greatest contemporary representative is the Shah of Iran.

Some friends of the Third World have argued that underdeveloped countries cannot hope to make adequate progress while remaining democratic. This was the ideology of Indira Gandhi — who was brought down by antimodernizing forces. But it would be sophistry to extol every dictatorship as progressive or to accept its claim of being socialist. So far most dictatorships have not raised the living standards in their countries. When the time comes that technological and financial infusions achieve an expansion of their national product, then it will also be time for vigorous democratic and labor organizations to fight for a share in decision-making and its results. In a milder form, the argument for dictatorship points to the huge and powerful bureaucracy that is needed to cope with all the tasks of a socialist economy. Usually one hears this argument from the enemies of socialism, and socialists tend to minimize its seriousness. Nevertheless, there are two sides to this problem.

Bureaucracy as a Tool of Socialism

Socialism has two uses for bureaucracy. In the age of welfare reforms, government agencies have been created to control the anarchy of the markets, shield the environment, protect people from exploitation, and curb the rapacity of business. No wonder bureaucracy has a bad press in capitalist countries. Only recently, the rejection by Congress of the proposed Consumer Agency was greeted as "a blow against overweening bureaucracy."

Second, bureaucracy may accomplish what private enterprise fails to provide, or may provide it better (how wonderful are European railroads!); it also is a necessary agent of public services.

In addition, bureaucracy may develop programs and points of view that grow out of its assigned routine but point toward new possibilities: projects that may lead beyond the welfare purposes, or even critical views of existing policies and institutions. It is well known that Marx used British government reports in writing *Capital,* and to this day practically all information on capitalistic malfunctions is based on official surveys, reports, investigations; it could not be otherwise. People in government agencies may have to look beyond the present system and project policies requiring a more rational economy. Any public official who has to think about the future of energy supply must get impatient with the influence of the oil companies.

Fear of *1984,* of the "bureaucratization of the world," of the "technocentric society" is based on the perception that these technocrats, who see the need for a centrally directed economy, may also want to use their strategic position — society's need of their skills in commanding functions — to seize power and make themselves the dominant class. The men with these ideas, however, usually are not the doers, and the so-called power elite is divided into at least three different strata:

———the experts: scientists, technologists, officers, professionals;
———the bureaucrats: administrators, corporate directors, civil servants;
———the politicians: the party or military junta, the parliamentary parties.

A complicating factor is that members of the elite groups may be employed by the government, the academy, or private industry, and that, as C. Wright Mills has claimed, these elites tend to merge into what Eisenhower called the military-industrial (and I would add academic) complex. For our purposes, however, it is preferable to divide the "new class" into two large groups:

———the political avant-garde, the innovators in government and business:
———the bureaucracy proper, the civil service and corporate managers.

While the first is flexible and dynamic, and derives its legitimation from the claim that it represents "the people," the second has the "civil service mentality" of honesty, obedience, predictability, and sluggishness. These are ideal types, and one must be careful not to compare the vices of one group with the virtues of the other. Usually, business claims the dynamism for itself and blames dullness on the bureaucrats; but there are as many bureaucrats working in business as in government, and for all the talk of oppressive, immovable bureaucracy, the loudest complaints are heard when a dynamic bureaucracy tries to move an inflexible business corporation.

An excess of bureaucratic virtues may be harmful, even oppressive, and if decision-making is left to the bureaucracy, the system may become self-serving and unresponsive to the needs of the community. But let us not forget that part of the clumsiness of bureaucratic procedures is due to the safeguards against abuse. The danger that the administrative and technical bureaucracy will set itself up as the new master is comparatively small: to do that, the bureaucrats would need the leadership of a political elite. (After Stalin's death, Beria found out that a modern country like Russia cannot be governed by the police, and Malenkov that it cannot be governed by the economic and administrative bureaucracy. It took a politician like Khrushchev to organize power, and when he turned against the party, he was ousted too.) The bureaucracy will usually serve the system in which it works, but it does not create a system. It does not produce a political will but is the organ of the will. The Great Wall of China was not built beause labor became available but because the tyrannical will of Shih Hwang-ti made it available. The computer does not produce solutions for problems that have not been fed into it.

This analysis disagrees with the theories of Saint-Simon, Bell, Djilas, Orwell, Burnham, Wittfogel, Brzezinski, and Birnbaum, who all assume that somehow a managerial bureaucracy, a "technocentric structure" or "new class," emerges from the pores of our society — as the capitalist class developed in the interstices of the ancien régime. The antisocialists among them will then push the analogy further: just as the popular revolution of 1789 ended by bringing that capitalist class to power, so the socialist revolution of our time will end, or has ended in some countries where it was tried, by bringing the technocrats and bureaucrats to power. But Stalin was not merely the "top bureaucrat," and the Communist bureaucrats are not an exploitative class in the same sense as were capitalists and feudal lords. In the nonrevolutionary advances of Western socialism, by contrast, each wave of social legislation leaves, like a sediment, a bureaucracy that implements and institutionalizes it.

These bureaucracies tend to stabilize and perpetuate the new social relations. Their very mulishness will prevent reactionary forces from reversing the trend, and socialists depend very much on the self-preserving instincts of bureaucracy to protect social progress from political attacks. Harold Laski was merely witty but not profound when he said that experts should be on tap, not on top; in practice the technocentric structure is as much an ally of the labor movement as an impediment to stronger dynamism. Also, as Horace Orlando Patterson remarks in his outstanding *Ethnic Chauvin-*

ism, "a big impersonal state may be a better guardian of libertarian values than a small unit with its cronyism."

Although the various strata of the ruling class interchange functions and recruitment, they also are rivals. Dutch sociologists have invented the term *verzuiling* (roughly, column-building) for the process of splitting society into professional camps: the corporate structure, the administrative stucture, the military structure, the medical structure, the academic structure, the judicial structure, the political structure, each with its top layer of a dominating elite. I find this model not only more persuasive than the myth of the technostructure; it is also more practical. Rather than call upon the whole of society against "big brother," democrats could suggest two remedies against his domination: encouraging mobility within each column, and encouraging rivalry between the columns. In each of the columns we find politicians who articulate the technical plans that come from their respective bureaucracies. The bureaucrats determine only feasibility, maybe desirability; it is for the political leaders to choose, to bargain among different interests, to hammer out a balance that can then be presented as the "general will."

Pluralism

Socialists attempt to expand the jurisdiction of public bodies and to institutionalize their material achievements. Eventually a point is reached where the haphazard historical gains must be consolidated and systematized — if only to prevent them from getting into one another's bailiwicks. Then a grave decision will have to be approached: a new economic constitution must be codified, and it will tend either toward state capitalism and eventually fascism, or toward democratic socialism. The latter presupposes strong independent mass organizations and established traditions of constitutional government. Strongly centralized, overarching organs of decision-making will favor state capitalism; fragmentation of power will serve the interests of democracy. This includes the customary division of power among executive, legislative, and judiciary, between federal and regional, but also between planning agencies and claimant groups, between economic and political authorities, and between employing agencies and producers.

The term totalitarian suggests the monolithic identity of the various elites and conceals the fact that oppression is first of all political. Stalin called upon "the people" to help purge the bureaucrats and especially those who had developed some appreciation of the limitations of their power or maybe even a certain affection for the people under their jurisdiction. So did Mussolini, so did Hitler: generals whose advice was professional had to go. As long as only bureaucrats rule, they will be "corrupt," i.e., responsive to the parameters of their jobs. What is dictatorial and tyrannical is the General Will. Bureaucracy is a check upon it, and all the more so the less it becomes a monolith in its own right. It must be fragmented to reflect the plurality of interests and functions in a modern society — differences of class, region, race, philosophy, profession. Anchored in its various "columns" it cannot become an autonomous machinery of oppression. The divergent groups and antagonisms can act upon the system.

This hope of rivalry has been translated into a political theory called pluralism. It does not mean direct participation of the governed in the process of government, but it gives the representatives of interest groups access to the levers of decision-making. It guarantees a certain diversity of impulses that are brought to bear upon the decision-making process and to that extent is a safeguard against arbitrary government. How well this device will work obviously depends on the vigor and number of independent, articulate forces in the society. Once again, it is clear how merely "formal" requirements can be translated into substantive measures.

Self-Government and Participation

Self-government means actual participation of the governed in the process of decision-making and in the design of measures to carry out those decisions. It can be realized only if the governed have access to all levels of government. For this purpose, a number of devices and designs rival for attention. Here only a brief rundown can be given.

———The councils or soviets: a revolutionary organization that became an executive organ in the Russian Revolution and then also the model of movements in Europe. It was prominent in the Hungarian revolution of 1956 and in the German revolution of 1918. It means direct participation on the lower echelons but indirect participation through delegates on the higher levels.

———The syndicalist system: shops are run cooperatively by the trade unions and are free to compete, though investment decisions may be made centrally. This system was used in the Spanish Civil War and in parts of Israel. A combination of the council and the syndicalist systems has been used in Yugoslavia.

———Codetermination: the system remains capitalist or state capitalist, but workers' representatives are elected to sit on the board of directors. The system, operative in West Germany and partly in France and other areas of the Common Market, involves shop stewards and trade unions in questions of management and gives them access to the books, a strong voice in personnel questions, and, where public officials also sit on the board, the chance to form majorities.

———Sweden's Meidner Plan, under which control of each company would gradually pass into the employee's hands.

———Capitalistic variations of the codetermination scheme, for instance the Volkswagen system, where workers own shares in small denominations, or the Sears Roebuck plan, where the employees' pension fund owns the shares.

———The public corporation model, preferred in England, where control is in the hands of an authority or public board.

Characteristic of all codetermination schemes and also the Yugoslav form of the council scheme is participation on the lowest, most direct level — the shop. It leaves the plan bureaucrats in control of the industry and fails to reflect other concerns of the masses — as consumers, as members of a church, etc.; it also gives them little access to policy-making on the national level. The large figures of "participation" that are often cited for Yugoslavia thus reflect only a rather truncated democracy. Moreover, these councils are split locally. A real workers' representation requires an independent national union. Real professional and industrial representation requires national chambers of the various professions, farm associations, and other organizations. In Yugoslavia these have neither political nor economic power. The Weimar Constitution foresaw a National Economic Chamber, which, however, never acquired real power.

Reluctantly one must conclude that the councils are more likely to become the instruments of a strong political leadership, transmission belts between the national government and the shop, rather than true organs of democratic control. They could be that only if they were to develop their own political organs that would feed information to independent parties and trade unions. There is no substitute, no gimmick, organization, or scheme of participation that can or should take the place of political parties.

One must also admit that the Yugoslav democratic system of economic self-administration has not diminished the dictatorship of the party; nor has it prevented the growth of a sprawling bureaucracy on county, regional, and national levels, whose infighting is a burden to the country. Moreover, the syndicalist and participatory schemes offer little protection against parochialism, industry egoism, and communal rivalry. (Nor should one be oblivious of recent examples in the United States, where even Paul Goodman, perhaps the most ardent American advocate of local self-government, called on the central New York school board to assert its authority.)

The most serious enemy of self-government, however, is apathy and indifference. It not only strikes all spontaneity and participation with paralysis but also makes participatory schemes the playground of sectarians and fanatics. The fatigue of drawn-out committee meetings, the disgust with factionalism, all too easily leave the field to determined groups that take over and make a mockery out of the best scheme. Nor should this problem be shrugged off with assertions that under socialism people will be different. Dedication and spontaneity come in bursts, or at best in waves, and there is no guarantee that only the capable and well-intentioned will constitute themselves as the permanent avant-garde.

Participatory experience on the local and factory level, therefore, is welcome as a recruiting school for trade union and party activities;

it is a contributing factor to decentralization; but it should not be used as a pretext for withholding essential political and ideological freedoms.

The Continued Relevance of Class War

My conception of democratic socialism is as far from revisionism as from utopian visions of a world without problems and conflict. I do not recommend any specific set of institutions, organization schemes, or election procedures. I am concerned with the involvement of the greatest number of people in the management of their destiny on all levels of economic, cultural, and political decision-making. Whether they do this in the form of a council movement, in the form of trade unions or cooperatives, or in parliamentary forms, success will always depend on the amount of interest and action they put into the organ of self-administration. No government or party can place self-administration on a platter and hand it to the people by decree; they must develop it by their own efforts and ingenuity. Not only that, they must continue to develop it even after it has been institutionalized. Any human institution can become obsolete, rigid, perverted, alienated from its original intentions.

The East European examples, which seem to contradict the possibility of democratic socialism, should not deter us; they are based on the experience of countries that never or rarely enjoyed democratic institutions and citizens' rights. In the Western nations there is a long tradition of independent judges, of an independent press, freedom of the universities, undiminished rights of assembly and of parliamentary representation. The continued presence of opposition parties, of alternatives, and of constitutional guarantees will ensure that under any social-economic system the further evolution toward greater freedom will not be permanently abridged.

Democracy is a movement of people, a constant struggle to enlarge their rights and to bring more of them into the circles of power. This can be achieved only by their own participation, by pressures, even by fighting. The aim of socialism, of course, is to make further frictions as tolerable as possible, to achieve a consensus that is not imposed from above but agreed to by the interested parties. Unless the society is stagnant, new claimant groups will appear or new problems of adjustment will be discovered. The mere fact that material worries have been removed may bring psychological and family troubles to the fore. Recent experience even indicates that such problems may lead to asocial, antagonistic behavior. Precisely because paradise cannot be expected, socialists must be prepared to allow conflict, movement, evolution, even revolution. Not all conflict may be susceptible to litigation. Political outlets must be available for those who, rightly or wrongly, do not feel that their aspirations can be fulfilled within the existing institutions.

In all the so-called socialist countries, revolutionary or quasirevolutionary action may be required to overthrow the oppressive political dictatorship. This revolution would be supported by a large part of the technical intelligentsia, which sees both the material possibilities and its own ambitions curbed by the dictatorship. In the underdeveloped countries, popular revolutions are less likely to succeed; they may topple one kind of dictatorship only to fall prey to another, or else they may have to pay for freedom by readmitting alien capitalism.

In most of the Western countries, a system has emerged that combines representative government and civic freedom with welfare-state institutions: partly nationalized industries, guidance and manipulation or direct controls, public services, some redistribution of income through taxation and services. But on the whole, there remain the criteria of profitability for economic activity. Trade unions and consumer organizations confront corporate power; civil-rights claimants, farmers, and church groups fight for influence. Reformist action by labor parties and governments has reached limits where further major progress can be made only by measures that seem to go beyond the welfare state; notably, overall planning of social welfare, distribution of a national dividend, and a preponderance of public enterprises whose rationale is not profitability. Further reforms would be "structural" — i.e., instead of alleviating the condition of individuals they would change the way the system operates.

What prevents the adoption of these measures is not political oppression but their inherent risk along with the absence of organizations that have a clear and popular plan and are ready to fight for it. New ventures are introduced piecemeal, and often without the clear awareness that their full benefits could become visible only in a totally different context.

Here we come once more to the problems of the "system": socialism today does not confront the capitalist model with a utopian model. It is not a predesigned plan that can only be accepted or rejected in toto. On the contrary, it is an open development of the economy based on an equally open movement for the betterment of living conditions. It is a movement, more and more, of all the people and not only the laboring classes. The new possibilities of the welfare state have brought to the fore problems that previously had been hidden by the need to fight first for material satisfactions. Socialism has become (again, as in Marx's own time) a cultural movement striving not only for the improvement of material conditions but for the liberation of the individual personality. It certainly is not a movement of technocrats for a more efficient organization of society. It is a movement of people, and its idea cannot be divorced from their eternal yearning for freedom.

4

The Idea of Progress in Marxism

The public and even many scholars see the appeal of Marxism in its grandiose view of history: free man and slave, overlord and serf, capitalist and wage earner, finally the free association of producers — this seems to be an escalator irresistibly carrying mankind upward. The *Communist Manifesto* portrays the inevitable triumph of industrial capitalism over feudal and Oriental backwardness and then goes on to assure the workers that to win socialism they need not strive after ideals (utopias) but can confidently rely on a great law of history that will carry them unfailingly toward the good society.[1] *Capital* proves the same scheme more scientifically: it begins with a preface enunciating "laws... working with iron necessity" apparently so universal and so stringent that "the country that is more developed industrially only shows, to the less developed, the image of its own future," pursues the theme of capitalist expansion through three volumes, and ends triumphantly with the "necessary transition to the reconversion of capital into the property of the producers, no longer as... private... but as social property."[2]

Concurrent with this progression of economic stages, there marches a parade of political and ideological revolutions: from despotism to feudal law to constitutional monarchy to republican and democratic regimes; from superstitious demonology to monotheism, metaphysics, and eventually to scientific humanism. Thus

Social Research, Spring 1974.

economic, political, and intellectual freedom will come, not because the grievances of the vast majority are just but because their victory is necessary.[3]

Man Makes His History

Not since Saint Augustine had the disinherited been given such a firm time schedule for their ultimate redemption. But while the bishop of Hippo had allowed his world ages to follow each other in rather haphazard fashion and also depended on God's grace for final redemption, Marx had inherited from Hegel a much more reliable scheme of development: its progression was propelled by an inner logic! For indeed, progress is not an arbitrary sequence in time but one whose links are connected by lawful relations so that the later stage is always in some way "higher" or more perfect, more complex, or more highly developed than the earlier stage, and at the same time derived from it.[4] The sequence 25, 19, 71, 57 obviously makes no sense; the series 1, 4, 9, 16, 25 does. In his *Science of Logic,* Hegel does not simply enumerate the categories but develops them, and his whole system reads like the unfolding of Reason itself. The same inevitable progression governs history: in the ancient Orient, one man was free; in Greece and Rome some were free; among the Christians, all are free. For "world history is progress of the consciousness of freedom," and the three aspects are always necessarily connected: development in time, development in logic, greater perfection. We do not call "development" or "progress" an increase in syphilis, crime, or pollution, nor improvement of deadly weapons, except in ironical quotation marks.[5] Marxism assumes that any new conditions, even those as yet developing in the old society's womb (both Marx and Engels loved this biological metaphor), are necessarily higher, and that certainly the result of the ensuing conflict leads to a higher form.

There is one apparent difficulty with such a system. How do we know what is "up"? Are we not simply confusing late with high, and last with best? To speak of progress we must assume a striving for some goal, an end of development that is somehow prescribed in its beginning — as a hyperbolic equation indicates the infinite approach to its asymptote. Indeed, Hegel's World Spirit knows where it is going as it unfolds itself through a series of various national spirits: from self-alienation to self-realization, from separation through unhappy consciousness to reconciliation with the universal mind. "Freedom alone is the purpose which realizes and fulfills itself.... This final aim is God's purpose.... Freedom... comprises within itself the infinite necessity of bringing itself to consciousness.... It is the ultimate purpose toward which all world history has continually aimed."[6]

But people have not at all times striven toward such freedom, and their actions were not always obedient to the logic of history. This does not bother an idealistic philosopher who, since he is in possession of Reason, is sure of the purpose History is pursuing. He explains that people are possessed by "false consciousness," unaware of the ultimate consequences of their actions, which Providence, however, has arranged behind their backs. This is the "cunning of history," which always achieves its end.[7]

One may find similarly confident formulations in the works of the later Marx, but they are extremely rare and, as we shall see, they always occur in a specific context. By 1844 Marx had decided that history is not propelled by philosophy, inner logic, higher purpose, or entelechy, but by social action. As a materialistic student of human affairs, he had to deal with efficient causes, not with final causes, and therefore was unable to trust any preordained course of history. From his new point of view, Hegel's "progress of the consciousness of freedom" was a mystification — all the more so as the end station of this progress was not freedom but the Prussian state.

Contrary to the allegations of many critics,[8] Marx rejects historicism and any notion of Providence. When Proudhon suggested that all history was pointing toward equality, Marx answered sarcastically: "Suppose... that social genius produced, or rather improvised, the feudal lords with the providential purpose of transforming *peasants* into *responsible* and *equal* workers."[9] History does not know where it is going, and if any pattern can be discovered in its course, it has been read into it by men with a purpose (Sorel would call it a myth); this is all there is to progress of the consciousness of freedom. Man not only makes his history, he also interprets it and thereby determines what is to be called "higher," more perfect.

No "objective" criterion tells us what direction Progress must take. The decision belongs to human praxis. This is the basic reason why the mechanical increase in technological advances is not enough to define progress — and, incidentally, why a dictatorship that legitimizes itself only by the claim that it modernizes and industrializes a country is not progressive in any Marxian sense: the bourgeoisie also brought political and religious liberation; Messrs. Amin and Qaddafi have done nothing of the kind.

On the same ground, Marx had to reject the world-historical scheme of Auguste Comte, his older contemporary. Comte's "law of three stages" smugly stated that man's knowledge develops from religious through metaphysical to scientific concepts, but it fails to tell us why and how these changes occur. It therefore discovers no mechanism that might bring forth further progress; on the contrary, while recognizing past revolutions, it precludes future ones and abandons mankind to the scientific care of positivist managers. This is exactly why Marx rejected the utopian system of Saint-Simon, for whom, as a person and thinker, he had much more respect than for Comte. Any "progress" that did not promote and expand the autonomous action or "self-activity" (*Selbsttätigkeit*) of the revolutionary class did not interest Marx.

The Laws of Social Development

If we cannot use either the Hegelian World Spirit or any providential escalator — or, for that matter, any utopian or positivist foreknowledge of the desirable end station of social development — what then makes Marx so bold as to predict the further course of mankind? What idea of progress lends itself as a tool of historical analysis and prophecy? Was Marx thoughtlessly repeating the commonplace notions of "progress" that were current among his contemporaries? After all, in the nineteenth century progress was taken so much for granted that even conservatives made a point of being for it, though not "with it." In his funeral oration for Marx, Engels candidly admitted that Marx had not discovered any law of progress: even as the notion of evolution had existed long before Darwin showed the specific means by which the species can emerge from chance variants, so the idea of social transformation had previously existed; but Marx showed the specific mechanisms by which one type of society may be superseded by another.[10]

Engels' reference to Darwin is corroborated by Marx in his letters: two to his friends, where, after reading *Origin of Species,* he announces with rare enthusiasm: "This is the foundation, in natural science, of our philosophy"; a third to Darwin, in which he asks the master to accept the dedication of *Capital* (the honor was declined).[11] These declarations are of methodological importance. Obviously, *Origin of Species* does not imply, but rather excludes, the notion that man had to emerge as the crown of creation. Like a family tree, the tree of evolution may end in any number of creatures each claiming some kind of perfection in its own way. Natural evolution is multilinear. All systems of social evolution, by contrast, claim a unilinear, necessary development. A philosophy of history, however, that implies foreknowledge of its outcome has to be either metaphysical and idealistic, or more mechanical and deterministic than a revolutionary party, or even a reformist one, can tolerate.

It is not necessary to dwell too long on the misunderstanding of "economic determinism." Marx himself repudiated it at all periods of his life and in each of his major works. In *The Poverty of Philosophy* he chides Proudhon for assuming "immutable laws, eternal principles, and ideal categories."[12] This, however, was the view the first generation of Marxists presented to the public and, more important, it was the view the masses embraced ardently when they flocked to the banner of socialist revolution. They did so under the illusion that Marx had placed History and Philosophy on their side. Had he not discovered those "iron laws" which inexorably prescribed the course of mankind from primitive to civilized, from slave-owning to free societies? Were not these developments solidly based on material conditions — the handmill determines a society of small producers, the steam mill industrial capitalism — and "science"?[13] As socialists learned in party schools, on its ladder of ascent history's irresistible plan provided for the expansion of large-scale industry to a point where the producers themselves could take over its management and thereby introduce a new civilization that would compare with all previous eras as known history compares with prehistory.

If Marxism is what such a view assumes it to be, then it cannot escape these contradictions: either the laws of social development are comparable to those in the natural sciences, and the results of history are then not necessarily "higher" in any moral sense than their causes; or Progress means a necessary and logical unilinear unfolding from the imperfect to the perfect, and then the specific scientific laws of development would be rather in the nature of foresight. To an activist like Eduard Bernstein, this was intolerable. Despairing of the "trip wires of dialectics," he renounced historical materialism and, although he was the executor of Marx's and Engels' literary estate, became the father of "revisionism." On the other hand, Karl Kautsky assumed the task of defending an orthodox system of deterministic Marxism but could do so only at the price of making it completely academic and depriving it of its activism. Only a few outsiders, such as Hermann Gorter and Rosa Luxemburg in the generation of the Second International, tried to develop Marxism as Marx might have done himself.

Interestingly enough, the new orthodoxy of the Communist International also rejected the more radical approaches and planted its own theory solidly in the soil of Kautsky's "materialism." Some dissenters, like Georg Lukács and Karl Korsch in the 1920s, tried to deal with progress as an ideology of the bourgeoisie (which will be developed later) but were quickly shouted down.[14]

The present generation of young Marxists now enjoys the benefit of newly published manuscripts that Marx and Engels had abandoned "to the gnawing criticism of mice" after their conversion to communism, and it has become fashionable to play off the "young Marx," a radical Hegelian humanist or disciple of Feuerbach and a Jacobin, against the all too mature Marx of Capital.[15]

For the problem of progress, the "young Marx" legend has a special significance. The views he held before 1845 often resemble those of the "German Socialists," or "True Socialists," whom the

Communist Manifesto was to trounce so badly. Some of them were his close collaborators and friends (the manuscript of *The German Ideology* has come to us in the hand of Moses Hess.) It can safely be said that in these manuscripts Marx was still under Hegel's influence and that his concern still was something very close to Hegel's salvation scheme: man's return to his essence, which Marx calls, in the manner of Feuerbach, "species being" (*Gattungsmensch*). Although his idea of this event and of this "new" man obviously was different from Hegel's, it nevertheless appears in a similar plan as the goal of history. And although the concept is also different from the noble savage, it nevertheless is sufficiently similar to that creature for Wilhelm Reich and Herbert Marcuse to have claimed a Marxian heritage when they proposed to liberate him.[16] The mature Marx, however, had no use for an "essential man," and the word *Gattungsmensch* does not recur in his works after 1845. Even so, Marcuse's error is based on a misreading of the German text: Marx never spoke of *Begattungsmensch;* his concern was man the creator, not the procreator.

The Dialectic of Progress

Confronted with so many interpretations of Marx's idea of progress, we must try to proceed philologically. But when we list, in Marx's and Engels' works, the passages containing the word *Fortschritt,* "progress," the result is both disappointing and confusing. Direct references are rather few, and those that occur are divided into two conflicting kinds: on the one hand, contemptuous remarks about soft-hearted liberals who believe in automatic and gradual steps toward enlightenment and justice; on the other hand, an almost savage admiration for the historical progress achieved by the triumphant expansion of capitalism, by British colonialists in India and Prussian militarists in Europe. Moreover, we do not find the word progress in places where we should expect it. For instance, when Marx speaks of the achievement of the ten-hour day, he refrains from using any such word but calls it "the victory of the economy of the laboring class over the economy of the bourgeoisie."

4.   "This is how the Englishman colonizes."
(From *Simplicissimus*, a collection of satirical drawings by Thomas Theodor Heine,
ed. by Stanley Appelbaum, New York: Dover, 1975)

By contrast, Bismarck's victory over Napoleon III promotes *Fort-schritt*.

Finally, Marx fails to use the word progressive in the sense much favored by present-day Communists — when they refer to their temporary allies or to movements they hope to exploit for their own purposes. Unlike unavowed Communists, Marx never used the word progressive as a synonym for his own party; nor did he condescend to hide behind other people's ideas or to gloss over ideological differences. While he certainly was not sectarian, he always insisted on honest separation in ideology and organization. He would hardly have awarded the title progressive to such assorted leaders of bourgeois nationalism as Nehru, Nasser, Chiang Kai-shek, or to petty-bourgeois sentimentalists like George McGovern, Henry Wallace, or even F.D.R., as the Comintern has done at one time or another. And he had good reason to keep at arm's length people who in his own day called themselves progressive.

The term *Fortschritt* had been preempted in German politics by a middle-class party advocating free trade, constitutional government, and a liberal approach to matters of culture, religion, and mores. Although this party claimed the heritage of the Gironde, it never caught up with the latter's historic audacity; on the contrary, it was known for its indecisiveness. Having missed its historic hour in 1848, it collapsed before the authoritarian initiative of its deadly enemy, Bismarck. But it spread the illusion that progress, justice, peace, and freedom could be achieved through gradual reform, and therefore it proved an irksome obstacle to revolution. In 1850, after that party's defeat, Marx called petty-bourgeois democrats "far more dangerous to the workers" than the liberals.[17] Later, their timidity and confusion provoked much derisive comment from Social Democrats like Karl Kautsky and Rosa Luxemburg. Only the non-Marxist, reformist wing considered the Progressives genuine vehicles of social transformation and honest allies of the workers. In southern Germany they had working alliances with the Liberals; in England they supported Liberal candidates and then formed a Labour Party that had no socialist commitment. It is deeply ironic, therefore, that Lenin and Stalin should have reintroduced progressivism on the grounds of Marxian orthodoxy.[18]

Progress with a capital P, as seen from the vantage point of revolutionary Marxism, is the ideology of the old middle class in its struggle against the traditionalist powers of the landed aristocracy, the church, the princes and bureaucrats, the monopolies and guilds. The *Communist Manifesto*, as we saw, contains the most enthusiastic paean to this historical role of the bourgeoisie ever written: how it carries modern industry to the remotest corners of the earth, drives out tribal customs, abolishes superstition, and not only liberates gigantic powers of production but also frees minds from oppressive backwardness. Indeed, in its ascending phase, the bourgeoisie is seen as the seedbed of enlightenment and as the agent of the greatest liberation of productive forces in all history. The word "progress" is reserved almost exclusively for the action of the *grande bourgeoisie* in developing the forces of production. To an extent most Marxists today might find embarrassing, Marx gave credit to the British colonialists in India. In his contributions to *The New York Tribune* on this question he certainly betrays a feeling of Western superiority over the "stagnant" society of an Oriental India.[19]

An interesting detail shows the ambivalence of Marx's position vis-à-vis the bourgeois revolution. In his draft for the *Communist Manifesto*, Engels wrote candidly that "since the Communists cannot look forward to the decisive showdown between themselves and the bourgeoisie before the latter is in power, it is in their interest to help the bourgeoisie seize power in order to overthrow it later."[20] This proto-Leninist conception is somewhat weakened in the *Communist Manifesto* to read:

> In Germany [the Communists] fight with the bourgeoisie whenever it acts in a revolutionary way, against the absolute monarchy, the feudal squirearchy, and the petty bourgeoisie.
>
> But they never cease, for a single instant, to instil into the working class the clearest possible recognition of the hostile antagonism between bourgeoisie and proletariat, in order that the German workers may straightway use, as so many weapons against the bourgeoisie, the social and political conditions that the bourgeoisie must necessarily introduce along with its supremacy.[21]

Taking its cue from Hegel's philosophy of history, the *Communist Manifesto* ascribes this revolutionary role not to the bourgeois themselves but to a cunning of reason that seems to force on them the part of an "unwilling carrier of progress." Earlier, in his *Outlines of a Critique of Political Economy* of 1844, Engels first accuses Adam Smith of hypocrisy but then stops himself to ask: "But was Smith's system... not an advance?" and answers:

> Of course it was, and a necessary advance at that. It was necessary to overthrow the mercantile system, with its monopolies and hindrances to trade, so that the true consequences of private property could come to light... so that the struggle of our time could become a universal human struggle.... It was necessary to carry the immorality contained in the old economics to its highest pitch.[22]

This sounds like pure Hegel: progress is necessary. However, it is not a constant climb toward a high goal, achieving greater and greater approximation and perfection. On the contrary, it is progress toward the apogee of evil — Engels specifically mentions the theory of Malthus, "the crudest, most barbarous theory that ever existed"[23] — if not toward the apocalypse. Progress is logical, but it is also dialectical, negative: first evil must reach its logical climax, then it can reverse itself (*umschlagen*) into its opposite. The apologists of free trade are worse monopolists than the mercantilists; liberal economists are less humane than defenders of absolutism. Just as liberal theology must either relapse into scripturalism or progress into atheism, so the liberal economist must either return to monopolism or transcend private property.

Marx reasons similarly in his essay on India, where British capitalism is praised for tearing the nation loose from its sleepy past, but simultaneously condemned for depriving the Indian population of its livelihood. Then he adds that India will have to go the way of Europe, and concludes in surprising ambiguity:

> When a great social revolution shall have mastered the results of the bourgeois epoch, the market of the world and the modern powers of production, and subjugated them to the common control of the most advanced peoples, then only will human progress cease to resemble that hideous pagan idol who would not drink the nectar but from the skulls of the slain.[24]

In the American Civil War, the International naturally favored the North and (true to the strategy of the *Communist Manifesto*) tried to push the bourgeois democrats into a conflict with the notion of property by demanding emancipation of the slaves. When Lincoln was reelected, Marx sent him a congratulatory address in which he said that slavery was "an obstacle to progress and to the development of power for the working class." Nowhere is progress celebrated as such but always in relation to the development of the proletariat, "the greatest of all forces of production."

The Reform of Consciousness

As Marx explains in numerous places, the working class does not come to power before the bourgeoisie has developed all the forces of production and has reached a point where (1) it cannot develop them any further without bursting its own framework of socioeconomic institutions (production relations), or (2) these forces themselves begin to rebel against that framework.[25]

Marxists have often charged that monopoly capitalists are holding back the exploitation of new inventions. What the founders of "scientific" socialism had in mind when they accused capitalism of turning into a hindrance to further progress, rather, was something more Hegelian. For them, progress could never be a mere accumulation of scientific and technological knowledge; it had also to be moral and historical. If the bourgeoisie could invent only railways and plumbing, that would not be much to crow about; it earned the epithet "revolutionary" when in the process it also raised the consciousness of people, spread enlightenment, and liberated them from oppression. It was not the mechanical progress of industry that was threatened by a prolonged regime of capitalism but the logical continuation of that process of liberation: from political equality to social equality, from mastery over nature to the conscious management of social production, from individualism to community. This process is described at the most significant place in Marx's entire *oeuvre:* not in some unpublished note by the young disciple of Feuerbach, but virtually at the end of the only volume of *Capital* that Marx himself was able to publish (disregarding a coda on colonialism which points to volume 2):

> Hand in hand with this centralisation, or this expropriation of many capitalists by few, develop... the co-operative form of the labour-process, the conscious technical application of science... the entanglement of all peoples in the net of the world-market... [the] grow[ing] revolt of the working class. Centralisation of the means of production and socialisation of labour at last reach a point where they become incompatible with their capitalist integument. This integument is burst asunder. The knell of capitalist private property sounds. The expropriators are expropriated.... It is the negation of negation.[26]

This is one of the few passages where the mature Marx returned to a Hegelian formula, and he was taken to task by Professor Eugen Dühring and many subsequent critics who charged that he was deriving future history from the abstract scheme of dialectics. Their interpretation, however, is erroneous and was rejected by both Marx and Engels. They explained that their method, on the contrary, was "materialistic" — that is, that the law had to be derived "from real life processes" and that in this particular instance the process had been spelled out in detail before the handy Hegelian formula was used to summarize it.[27]

Why then use it at all? In *The German Ideology* Marx had declared that the Hegelian categories "have no value in themselves but help to bring some order into the historical material." Some order! If, in his defense, Marx asserted that he "had turned Hegel from his head, where he had stood, onto his feet," then he was turning the materialists' philosophy inside out. Since *they* were in a passive mood, he used Hegel's method to make philosophy humanly active, as he had announced in his "Theses on Feuerbach." The "order" of things obviously does not derive from an "iron law" inherent in them but from human insight and will. To quote once again the famous letter to Ruge (see note 7, p. 336):

> We do not face the world in doctrinaire fashion with a new principle.... We develop new principles for the world out of the principles of the world.... The reform of consciousness exists *merely* in the fact that one makes the world aware of its consciousness.... Our entire purpose [is to bring] the religious and political problems into the self-conscious human form.[28]

The Hegelian element of consciousness here connects dumb history with clear-minded morality; in his social epistemology Marx assumes that the next step in the development of society is not seen before the class of the future has a conception of the desired solution. The interpretation is part of history. Obviously, the class of the future has a partial view of history, but one that becomes total the moment its consciousness envisages the solution. Granted, this is a distorted or selective view of history. But to impose unity on a large tract of history, one has to rule out that which does not fit.

Any view of history claims to put order into what otherwise may be confusion. It imposes unity on a disconnected series of events, converting them into a sequence; it tries to make sense out of sound and fury; it imbues with intelligence that tale told by an idiot. The bourgeoisie has been largely an unwitting agent of progress, or it has recognized this historical task only in the reified form of a hypostatized "Progress." The revolution of the proletariat, by contrast, has to be all consciousness.

Progress: Discontinuous, Decisionist

As a stagnant class, the bourgeoisie has no philosophy of history. Meanwhile it has fallen for prophets of doom like Spengler or skeptics like Toynbee. In Marx's own day the decline was visible almost from decade to decade. Hegel's grandiose vision of a march of the World Spirit through World History toward the Fulfillment of Reason was no longer believable. In his "Theses on Feuerbach," Marx begins with the complaint that in its most radical philosophy, materialism, the bourgeoisie assigns no active part to man. It sees human progress in no other light than evolution in nature: it happens, it is automatic and irresistible; it requires neither a special effort nor any "qualitative leap," as the young Hegel had taught and Marx—at least as a young socialist—had assumed.[29] The bourgeoisie, meanwhile, as we have seen, produced manipulative systems like that of Auguste Comte, which rested on previous progress but foresaw no basic change in the future. It believed in scientific, technological, and even social progress without feeling compelled to draw any moral and political conclusions. Eventually, in the philosophy of Herbert Spencer, the bourgeoisie abandoned itself to pure naturalism. Evolution now was defined as the progression from simple to more complex organizations. At the end of the century, T.H. Huxley explicitly denied that evolution led to any forms that were ethically "higher," and Ernst Haeckel, whom Engels still quoted as a scientific authority, denied that evolution applied to society at all.

In the meantime, the oppressive nature of capitalism had overshadowed its dynamic features. Accordingly, the bourgeoisie had abandoned the philosophical banner its fathers had fought under; it had turned pessimistic or agnostic and reactionary to the point of doubting progress and even abjuring the scientific world view. At that moment the fallen banner was picked up by the spokesmen of the ascending class, the proletariat, which thereby legitimized itself as carrier of the future interest of all mankind. For according to *The German Ideology,* the revolutionary class is distinguished precisely by this: that its own survival coincides with the further development of the productive forces which an ancien régime keeps fettered.

Progress, for Marx, is discontinuous. It is not automatic and unilinear but decisionist. Far from thinking that the laws he had discovered made capitalism a necessary development, he seriously studied other alternatives, in particular Oriental societies and the problems of bureaucratic despotism. He also said repeatedly that the transition from capitalism to socialism was not guaranteed by any providential law and that, instead of socialism, the outcome might be a *relapse into barbarism.*

Although Marx foresaw neither the world wars nor fascism and Stalinism, Karl August Wittfogel, Daniel Bell, and Shlomo Avineri have shown that these were serious alternatives for Marx. He did not see history as an escalator bound to carry mankind from one floor to the next in predetermined stages.[30] Moreover, closer examination of the *Communist Manifesto* reveals that Marx and Engels did not mean to picture a gigantic pageant of man's progress through the millennia but to discuss progress as the dynamism of capitalistic society only. They describe in purple prose its triumph over feudal and Oriental powers and its coming into conflict with the forces of progress it has called into being. They show how for capitalism progress is at the same time the condition of its survival and the threat of its obsolescence; how the progressive ideas that had been necessary for the victory of the bourgeoisie become embarrassments that can be turned against its domination as so many weapons.

Capital thus becomes its own grave-digger. In Marx's unpublished manuscripts and in Engels' publications from the early 1840s, we gather an even more gruesome picture: the progress that so powerfully modernizes the world is at the same time regression for millions of people who become uprooted from their livelihoods, their customs, their families, their culture. While capitalism places at man's disposal the most powerful and sophisticated machines and produces goods one would never have imagined even a hundred years earlier, it also deprives people of their property, of their relationship with their fellow men, of their control of the products they make, even of their self-respect. It dehumanizes man.

The young Marx, before he had shed his Hegelian plumage, drew from this dialectical development the direct dialectical conclusion:

when this dehumanized condition has grown unbearable, it will turn against itself; humankind will overcome its alienation to get reconciled with its true nature. The mature Marx simply stated that the paupers will see no way but to revolt, and since theirs will be the greater number, they will overthrow capitalism. In either case, progress is not the linear continuation of the status quo but its inversion; capitalism is marching to its triumph and its doom at the same time; the revolution does not blossom from rising expectation but explodes from despair. Like Dante, Marx takes us through Hell before he leads us to Paradise. This, it should by now be clear, is what the negation of the negation means: not progress but the cataclysm.

The Moral Criterion of Progress

In the last section of *Capital,* where Marx discusses "the so-called primitive accumulation," he destroys the notion that capitalism grew in small, easy steps. He shows how capital came into the world "dripping from head to foot, from every pore, with blood and dirt."[31] History, he had read in Hegel, is a slaughter bench of nations. But he could not, like Hegel, fall back on the comforting idea that all's well that ends well (he left that for Mussolini's and Stalin's court philosophers to derive from Hegel). He could recognize no abstract promise of future reconciliation through a World Spirit; what counted was the concrete human praxis of the class that, he believed, represented along with its own interests those of all society.

This liberation, however, could be achieved only by a class that did not wish to become the ruling class. And it could be achieved only by the autonomous action of that class, not by its vicars or representatives. A bureaucracy ruling over nationalized factories and mobilized hands can invoke the name of socialism only blasphemously. This name was reserved, in the minds of the first generation of socialists, for those who had not forgotten the humanist roots of their philosophy.

It is at this point that the Marxian concept of progress differs most sharply from the epigones' progressivism, from vulgar Marxism, bolshevism, and Third World romanticism. All the modern dictatorships, like the mercantilist and absolutist monarchies of the seventeenth century, can easily be justified by the claim that they help—or helped—to develop the forces of production. At the same time, of course, like capitalism, they develop the ugly features of ruthless exploitation, of utter alienation, of oppressive state organizations. While they destroy the old ruling classes as well as their local, national, and imperial overlords, tribal authorities, comprador bourgeoisie, and colonial rulers, they also establish a new ruling class: a bureaucratic or military dictatorship, a "state bourgeoisie," a party or technocratic elite. Some of these rule in the name of "socialism"—though it usually is hyphenated: national socialism, Arab socialism, African socialism, people's democratic socialism, etc.

Obviously, Marx could not have recognized any of these regimes as socialist or communist. The criterion for him was precisely whether material progress was converted (the Hegelian word *umschlagen* is in order here) into the release of new human resources: abolition of classes, self-administration of production units, transformation of private or state property into associative use of facilities, the withering away of the state. In his *Critique of Hegel's Philosophy of Right,* Marx denied that bureaucracy was "the universal state" and showed that, on the contrary, bureaucracy was a state within the state, a particular interest clothing itself in the mantle of general interest.[32] When in *The Eighteenth Brumaire of Louis Bonaparte* and *The Civil War in France* he returns to the subject of bureaucracy, he is speaking of a different kind of state: no longer a *separate* interest, a feudal state, but the *bourgeois* state, which is the executive organ of the ruling class. Any reversion to bureaucracy would not be progress but a relapse into precapitalist conditions.

Moreover, in his economic-historical studies Marx meanwhile had recognized bureaucracy as the characteristic of the "Asiatic society" that capitalism was working hard to overcome. No wonder he did not appreciate the "new middle class" as a progressive force when he encountered it in the third volume of *Capital.* Since only the proletariat had a role in the drama of salvation, that part of the business administration which was "progressive" and had a function in the scheme of production was styled into a part of the new proletariat. Bureaucracy as such was not progressive.

Marx recognized at least four different types of bureaucracy: (1) the ruling class of "Asiatic society;" (2) the absolute state preceding the bourgeois revolution and monopolizing the "universal interest" as the special interest of one class; (3) the business and political administration of bourgeois society, which is part of the ruling class but may, under conditions of equilibrium between the classes, make itself independent (Bonapartism, fascism, Nasserism); and (4) the functional administrators who may join the proletariat or already represent the model of future socialist functionaries. He considered the intellectuals strictly a service class, handmaidens to the historical producer classes, neither free-floating nor "vanguard" nor "guardians."[33]

It is misleading, therefore, to say that "bureaucracy... runs through Marx's writings after 1843... and is central to the understanding of the modern state."[34] Actually, after 1843 Marx saw bureaucracy in a new light and he never included it in his paean to the progressive forces of capitalism. While he hailed "concentration," he did not foresee, let alone desire, the formation of bureaucracy as a new stage of capitalism or of society. To him, it could not be progressive and therefore it could not be a new stage. As administrative functions are taken over by salaried employees, they grow ripe for socialization; therefore the state as a separate organization becomes obsolete. It merely serves the reactionary purpose of defending the bourgeois order, hence it must be abolished. Although it was Engels who coined the famous phrase, "the state withers away," Marx saw its abolition in the same vein: it loses its raison d'être and becomes increasingly superfluous. Its flowering certainly has no progressive features.

It should be especially noted in this connection that nationalized property is as much alienated as is private property in the means of production. Wage earners are in the same position with a private as a government employer. "The condition of the *laborer* is not overcome but extended to all men... The community is only a community of labor..."[35] We must conclude, therefore, that the strategy Marx had worked out for the bourgeois revolution would apply also to national and bureaucratic revolutions: to support them as long as they were subversive of a more repressive system, but to turn against them the weapons they had developed as soon as they were established and became repressive themselves.

Progress, we have seen, is a harsh reality which has its dark side. Its positive features must not be allowed to extenuate the negative ones; on the contrary, the conflict must be hastened to prevent the suppression of human progress by material progress. Revolution is on the agenda against all oppressive — even "progressive" — states.

Marx versus the Marxists

In the Soviet Union and in China, Marxism has become, or has been made into, an oppressive philosophy. Dialectics has been sterilized by canonization. All the proper formulas are being piously recited and — to the annoyance of students, for whom this is dry routine — are being taught in schools.

The emasculating operation, however, has not been very subtle: there once was a revolution, hence no further development needs to be revolutionary; contradictions once were antagonistic for all societies, and they still are antagonistic as between the nonsocialist and the socialist camps, but they cannot be antagonistic inside the socialist camp. Progress, therefore, will continue smoothly and orderly, according to a well-conceived plan. Where there is dissent, it cannot originate in inner contradictions of the socialist society; it is not an engine of progress and must be suppressed as an alien force. Paradise has no history.

Marx thought that the socialist revolution should "end the prehistory of mankind," and Trotsky expected the flowering of a new culture. Marx left the actual content of further progress open to the spontaneous creativity of socialist men; in his essay "Repressive Tolerance," Marcuse — substituting himself for the World Spirit — knows where mankind is supposed to go and what the "real" wants of socialist man are. So does the Soviet government: both are sure of their authority to suppress whatever stands in the way of their own notion of progress.

Meanwhile, Hegel's contradictions have been frozen into a system of dialectical materialism. Progress and progressivism have been elevated to the status of ontological essences — abstract and universal "laws" governing man and nature. Like any good divinity, these metaphysical entities are at the beck and call of their conjurers, and "progressive" equals whatever is useful to the Soviet government, its allies of the day, and its sycophants. Progress has become a tool of mass manipulation.

While this twofold deterioration — transfer of the dialectical mainspring from internal conflicts to the East-West confrontation and ideologization of the concept of progress — came naturally to the Russians, it needs explanation in the case of the Frankfurt School, some of whose original members had been raised in the Communist Party or in sufficient proximity to it. In exile, some members of the Institute came to prominence who had never been part of the traditions of Hegel and Marx. Their thinking stemmed from Nietzsche, Heidegger, or Kierkegaard; they were culture critics or, better still, cultural pessimists. Horkheimer and Adorno's *Dialectik der Aufklärung; Philosophische Fragmente* (Amsterdam: Querido, 1947) saw eighteenth-century philosophy no longer as the triumphant opening of the bourgeois era but as the beginning of Western decadence. They treat the development of Western thought as a steady progress of alienation and reification, with Marx himself not a mean contributor to that trend.

For these critics of Western culture, the gulf between man and society, which Marx had tried to bridge through philosophical praxis, has become unsurmountable. Only a complete return to a pre-Feuerbachian age, to the "root" *(radix),* would be satisfactory — and that is impossible. Thus Horkheimer ended in mysticism, and Marcuse's final utopia is no longer the outcome of dialectical progress. Although he continues to use Marxian language and method, Marcuse as a philosopher has left the Marxian framework and, as Stephen Bronner noted, has returned to Schiller. [36]

The career of Marxism began with the assertion of a "scientific" way to secure progress from capitalist to socialist society. In Karl Kautsky's hands, this scientism became sterile but still served as an ideology for the Second International. The Comintern replaced it by a more philosophical ideology that, however, was no less rigid and orthodox: As "dialectics," it almost restored the teleological metaphysics Marx had thought dead. Ironically, Marxian tools of scientific investigation are still used precisely by those sociologists and social critics who no longer believe in the prophecy that had once been connected with Marxism as a philosophy.

TWO

The Thirties

5

Communism and Class

A proletarian united front against fascism is possible whenever there is a specific goal that demands struggle: in most cases just a human life or a house to be defended — any action of simple solidarity whose initial political impact is only minimal. A proletarian united front becomes impossible as soon as it is conceived in political terms, as soon as it requires a concrete notion of joint actions, as soon as the workers' parties are to conclude even a mere truce (*Burgfriede*) regarding agitation and theory. This is not very surprising. If a united front were possible in political practice, we would not need diverse parties. Ernst Thälmann quite rightly said:

> Are we sincere when we say we want an antifascist united front? What a question! Every day the brown plague murders our comrades, strikes down our best fighters, undertakes provocative attacks on our party buildings.... And in the face of this fact, in the face of the ominous peril that Germany may be turning into a country of the gallows and the stake, how can we Communists fail to be sincere about an antifascist proletarian united front?
>
> However, the issue of sincerity is an issue of *fighting*, of mobilizing the masses. Hence, we are asking you: Is it just the reactionaries that disarm the working class? No: the ADGB and SPD[1] leaders are disarming it by banning strikes, newspapers and demonstrations, by splitting the movement, by coalitions and truces with the bourgeoisie, by their policy of making concessions!

5.   Ernst Thälmann, 1928
(Photo: International Institute of Social History, Amsterdam)

And later on:

> We are supposed to keep quiet about the fourteen years we have gone through! We are supposed to keep quiet about the ADGB's failure to mobilize the four million colleagues against the Papen government!... So, we are supposed to side with the SPD in defending the present system of bourgeois rule![2]

Thälmann is right on two counts: (1) if you consider the other party's policy that criminal, you cannot conclude even a truce with it; and (2) the failure of the united front is not due to lack of sincerity but to the total lack of all the essentials upon which a joint fight would have to be based.

To begin with the second point. If we in the SPD denounce the Communists for not being sincere when they offer us a united front, that clearly does not justify our declining the offer. But in substance, too, the denunciation is unfounded. The Communists are organizationally unable to exploit the windfall — unsystematic, unearned, and inexplicable even to themselves — which they harvested in the election of last July; they are not anchored in the factories and trade unions; they are more vulnerable to the government's and the Fascists' attacks than are the Social Democrats; their chances of influencing German politics are minimal; and any insurance they might supply to Russian foreign policy is becoming more and more dubious. After failing to hitch a ride with the successes of the Fascist movement, their only chance of survival will lie in tying their fate as tightly as possible to that of the Social Democrats.

The KPD is in a fix — in a conflict between reality and ideology, between the needs of practical, day-to-day politics and a thirteen-year history that we must not pass over in silence. At the present time, more than at any previous point in its history, the KPD is a prisoner of its own ideology; what most truly prevents any united front is the *Weltanschauung*, the split that has historically developed within the working class.

There are two ways to get around the difference of *Weltanschauung*. We can either politely reassure each other that basically we both want the same thing — in this case, socialism and the dictatorship of the proletariat — or else we can candidly face the clash of philosophies, regard today's ally as tomorrow's opponent, and attempt to demonstrate that the opponent's philosophy is irrelevant for today's relevant practice. Neither response is possible here. In the course of historical development and as a reaction to the failures of proletarian policies, both sides have affixed their philosophies to specific institutions. Hence, there can be no united front without a discussion of ideology; eclecticism would be opportunism. While it is easy to charge the Social Democrats with paying too little attention to their own ideology in coalitions with other parties, the KPD's actions often have served no other purpose than to buttress its dogma.

> The KPD's opponents often misunderstand its idealism: This party starts from the erroneous premise that noncommunist proletarians are really misled communists who could quite easily see how correct the communist demands are, were it not for those spiteful people who,... by means of material and spiritual corruption, prevent that insight.[3]

This ideology assumes a vacuum that can be filled by any movement: which way those freely and spontaneously erupting energies will go depends on the party agitators' skill. That is why, wherever the KPD has awakened a readiness to place all trust in the party's word, fascism reaps great success. Obviously this explanation rests on a number of assumptions. But the Communists themselves know that best of all. Dimitri Manuilsky, on the eleventh plenary session of the Executive Committee of the Communist International, complained: "The methods of our agitation are the worst conceivable. We approach the workers as if we had a communist audience... of people who have ideologically broken with social-democracy and merely need a certain push to join our ranks."[4] Well, here the Communists themselves acknowledge this phenomenon as a tactical flaw — thus refuting the suspicion that this is their basic attitude. Obviously such psychological explanations will not suffice. Arthur Rosenberg, in his recent book,[5] has offered a convincing political portrait. Since he is a Marxist, his books are distinguished by the way in which he bases his analyses on the objective economic facts. But since he is not a "vulgar Marxist" who believes in the metaphysics of economic facts, he refuses to identify reality with rationality or allow the Hegelian World Spirit to move people like chessmen. For him, the acting persons, organizations, classes actually make their own history. According to Rosenberg's method and reasoning, the basis of Communist idealism is the bourgeois concept of the revolutionary vanguard and the chiliasm of the radical-utopian masses; that is to say, Communist politics is not characterized by an excessive identification of the vanguard party with the proletarian class, but rather by the classlessness of its views. This is an attitude that derives from Hegel: "Hence representation cannot now be taken to mean simply the substitution of one man for another; the point is rather that the interest in itself is actually present in its representative."

This is in line with Hegel's view of the state:

> "In considering freedom, the starting point must be not individuality, the single self-consciousness, but only the essence of self-consciousness; for whether man knows it or not, this essence is externally realized as a self-subsistent power in which single individuals are only moments."[6]

This idea of party and state is obviously tailored to the bourgeois constitution and to the bourgeois revolution. But that concept is used by the Communists. It is the Jacobin concept in which the party represents not just the actual will of its followers, but also what really "ought" to be their will. The party will then incarnate the "true" interest of its followers.

But if that is the case, then the party is not identical with the class and it will not have to represent the empirical interests of the masses. Rather, it will embody the contradiction between "appearances," the day-to-day interests of the masses, and the "essence" that is their true revolutionary destination.

If "appearance" and "essence," the immediate interests and the future goal, are linked in practice, there is no problem. Unfortunately, however, the two become divorced in the the very practice of the party. Instead of emerging in the "appearance" of everyday practice, the revolutionary goal — or "essence" — assumes the status of an independent entity. The relation between the theoretical goal (the essence) and the exigencies of immediate practice (appearance) assumes the form of a contradiction that cannot be resolved. Consequently, that contradiction will attempt to be covered up. The revolutionary goal (the essence) will take on an ideological reality that will justify an immediate party tactic (appearance) even if there is no relation between reformist means and revolutionary ends. In short, the resolution of this contradiction will take place merely inside the head, through an act of identification with the party.

Marx, at least before 1848, employed similar philosophical concepts. But later on, he seemed to conclude that the party — as a propagandistic organization — was simply the most advanced part of the proletariat rather than the metaphysical incarnation of its true interests. Lenin, on the other hand, was a genuine Jacobin. In his programmatic pamphlet *What Is to Be Done?* (1902), he says:

> "We said that the workers *could not have* a social-democratic consciousness. It could be brought to them only from without. History teaches that the working class, by its own efforts, can merely accomplish a trade-union consciousness.... The socialist doctrine, however, has grown out of those... theories that were discussed by the educated persons of the propertied classes, by the intelligentsia.... The view that the workers' political class consciousness could be developed *from the inside,* from the economic struggle as it were... such a view is fundamentally mistaken.[7] (Lenin's emphasis.)

Holding this Leninist view, the party will never represent the real proletariat, but always its essence. It will represent that essence all the more single-mindedly the less the proletariat has become conscious of its own idea and the less use that proletariat has for such a "revolutionary" representation; in fact, the party will represent that essence most explicitly when there is no proletariat at all. The party embodies the historical category "proletariat, the liberator of mankind," the idea of the proletariat as a revolutionary force. Along these lines, the party does not absolutely need the proletariat to carry out its mission; the proletariat is merely its most appropriate helper. In well-known passages (*Critique of Hegel's Philosophy of Right, The Holy Family*), Marx calls upon the proletariat to come to the aid of philosophy but still describes the proletariat's role very ambiguously:

As philosophy finds its material weapon in the proletariat, so the proletariat finds its spiritual weapon in philosophy.... The head of this emancipation is philosophy, its heart is the proletariat.

When socialist writers ascribe this historic role to the proletariat, it is not...because they consider the proletarians as gods. Rather the contrary. Since the abstraction from all humanity... is practically complete in the full-grown proletariat... it cannot abolish the conditions of its own life without abolishing all the inhuman conditions of life.... The question is not what this or that proletarian, or even the whole of the proletariat, at the moment considers as its aim. The question is what the proletariat is, and what, consequent on that being, it will be compelled to do.[8]

This concept perfectly meets the needs of the bourgeois revolution. While the proletariat is the executive organ, "philosophy" is what gives the revolution its meaning. The proletariat is unaware of the movement's "idea," of its "essence"; it is enough that philosophy knows of it. This conception made good sense in 1848, on the eve of a bourgeois revolution in which the proletariat could play a part but not yet stage its own drama; "philosophy" — and in later parlance the party — had to perform wearing the proletariat's mask.

Now Lenin, on the eve of another bourgeois revolution, but with his eyes on the great, organized workers' community of the West as against his undeveloped Russian workers, was consistent: there is a second vacuum in his Jacobin conception; thus he can declare that the masses, too, are interchangeable. He strictly adheres to "philosophy," which is incarnated in the party, but the proletariat is no longer his exclusive helper. He does not even have much use for the proletarian revolution; he draws up an exact strategy of "revolutionary-democratic dictatorship of the proletariat and the peasantry."[9] The decisive point is that the "vanguard" is the one to take power; let the proletariat and the democratic strata put themselves into its hands, for it alone can guarantee the proletarian character of the revolution.

The party becomes the central concept; for the sake of its purity Lenin split the Russian Social Democratic Party, in 1902, in London. In the 1917 revolution, the epochal event is not the dissolution of the bourgeois parliament nor the achievement of council democracy but the party's seizure of power. In the course of the revolution, and to this day, the party has remained the representative and embodiment of the proletariat and its revolutionary mission; the councils — the soviets — never ruled for a moment; and had they ruled, the revolution would not only have lost it meaning, but its very existence would have been gravely imperiled.

In 1917, one month before the seizure of power, Lenin wrote: "Like any other political party, our party wants power *for itself.* Our goal is the dictatorship of the revolutionary proletariat. . . . We regard going back to the pre-July demand, All power to the soviets, as a mere compromise."[10] The dictatorship of the proletariat is thus not identified with the soviets but with party rule. The party, so to speak, represents the World Spirit, which makes the "essence" of history visible.

It is harder to understand, however, why this vanguard theory became credible in a country that *had* known highly developed class war. In Germany, some small group might have been able to cling for years to beliefs born in an era of immediate revolution — defending the revolutionary "essence," the proletariat, against the "appearance" of social democratic reformism. During nonrevolutionary periods, however, a mass party cannot retain such theoretical purity without falling into considerable contradictions with its own practice and with the actual proletariat as a whole; essence and appearance will fall apart; truth will no longer be concrete.

The Communist contradiction between theory and practice will of necessity find its expression in centrist, eclectic ways if the reformist day-to-day event is given a revolutionary halo. In that case, a unity of opposites can be manufactured only within the acting person or party, so that a party legitimized by its revolutionary goal need only pursue a policy of strict party egoism; whatever it does will then be a revolutionary deed. Only such a party can satisfy the chiliastic desires of the utopian-radical, unorganized masses, which neither want to recognize that the proletariat is on the defensive nor intend to forgo their cherished day-to-day reforms. They wish to hold on to the revolution emotionally without being able to hold on practically. Hence, the masses believe faithfully in a party that frees them from anxiety over this contradiction; and, in turn, they make such a party possible.

If, however, the masses — as seen by the party — fill a vacuum that any other mass could fill just as well, then the party leadership — as seen by the masses — is a vacuum that any other party could fill as long as it meets their quasireligious desires. A party that bases its propaganda on this principle, therefore, runs a clear risk of actually working for another party. That is why lately we have so often seen those moves back and forth between Communists and Nazis and why, for the KPD more than for any other party, ideology is the wellspring of action. Theoretically, its followers never permit it any pact with the powers that be, not even a make-believe pact; practically, it has to draw certain ideological lines of its own in order to affirm its basic revolutionary attitude.

Either way, a quasi-religious approach to political issues will result. Inevitably, the party will acquire the characteristics of a church; the shibboleth by which its followers can be distinguished will be their belief in socialism ruling the Soviet Union, and their trust in the Soviet Union's particular institutions. As a result, faith becomes attached to specific symbols and phantoms involving the party. But faith prevents political mobility.

Here is a characteristic example, presented by Thälmann at last year's plenary session of the Central Committee (note that he uses the Russian word soviets instead of the German *Räte*):

> What are the organs of the people's revolution? The soviets — and this issue cannot be watered down. Today we do not yet have a ripened revolutionary crisis that would supply the preconditions for the creation of soviets, or even parts of soviets, as organs of the People's Revolution. If in spite of that we were to create such organs, they would become discredited. Haven't we gone through this before? Absolutely! I'll just remind you of the shop stewards which in 1923 – 24 were supposed to replace the soviets, or the so-called Workers' and Soldiers' Councils in the first year of the revolution; all they did was discredit the real soviets."[11]

This is pure theology! On the one hand it is considered permissible to substitute the slogan of a "People's Revolution" for the proletarian revolution. On the other hand, one theologizes about a specific revolutionary organ and then passes it off for a new type, which, however, cannot be realized in practical terms. Of course the

real, practical, successful organs of revolution must not be used —
the icon of the party might be destroyed. The symbol that once
represented the practice of a bloody revolution has now, through
the creation of the Soviet Union, become binding and mythical; out
of the nether regions of the dirty, earthly struggle it is elevated into
the Soviet heaven. Clearly, religion gets into the KPD's way not just
where the party is asked to revise its politics, but in the very planning
of its politics.

This ecclesiastical bent of the KPD generates an increasing timidity about symbols. Like any newly emerging theology, the Communist type narrows its scope. Where the party gains an ever greater
liberty to carry on opportunistic maneuvers and adventures that
sacrifice principles to party egoism, the room available for such
maneuvers will shrink; the ideology will become dogma while the
party church will become the most important carrier of that dogma.

Only recently, there has been a grotesque instance of this development. The Holy Father of the church, Stalin, was told by some
educated people that Marxism denies the impartiality and objectivity of science. Logically, since there can be no truth outside the
church, the Holy Father decided that *all* thinking had to be strictly
partisan; it would have to be controlled by the Party and adapted to
Party needs. At this point his youngest deacon, Kurt Sauerland,
presented him with a canon entitled *Dialectical Materialism,* which
says a little more about the matter and draws the political consequences. Near the end of the Epistle, Sauerland writes:

Dialectical materialism is not simply the philosophy of the proletariat.
Rather, it is the philosophy of the most advanced parts of the revolutionary proletariat, of those who best, most clearly, and most consistently
express and defend the interests of the entire working class. It is the
theoretical basis of the vanguard of the proletarian class, i.e., the philosophy of the party that is the revolutionary proletariat's leader; and inasmuch
as this party is the vanguard and the highest form of the class organization
of the proletariat, party theory is the highest and most advanced form of
the proletarian class ideology. . . . It has to arrange these tasks and subor-
dinate them to the revolutionary war which, being waged on two fronts,
inexorably exposes and criticizes the theoretical roots and the opportunism of any deviation from revolutionary class and party theory and from

the line of the Communist International, leader of the revolutionary proletariat of the world.

On the very last page, the purpose of his reasoning is divulged — a solemn absolution from all opportunistic sins:

How all opponents screamed when the KPD issued its Program of National and Social Liberation! Compromises with National Socialism, deviation from Marxism, they said. Was that so surprising? I don't think so. If someone calls the Second International's dogmatism Marxism, how will he ever be able to understand all this?"[12]

Somewhat similarly, Stalin — who turns out to be not just an important politician but also a philosopher and historian — in a recent, much discussed letter decreed that Lenin had been a Leninist all his life and did not need to develop his views through fighting reaction. As we can see, the ludicrous external marks of ecclesiastization emerge as well. In fact, ecclesiastic jealousy has reached the point where the bourgeoisie is denied the privilege of having a church. Deacon Sauerland wrote in his Epistle of 1932 — the year when the bourgeoisie was clamoring for fascism: "The bourgeoisie has no use for any leading party; it cannot allow itself to be led, being itself the ruler."

Let us take note of this sentence, since it is politically important; meanwhile, listen to the one immediately following:

The proletariat, on the contrary, creates its leadership: the party, which, in order to represent the common interests of the entire class, must always march at the head of the working class, show it the way, and raise the backward proletarian masses to a higher level of class consciousness. [13]

In this theory of the party there are dangers for the entire proletariat. If idealistically the party is not considered a tool of the movement but its leader; if the party merely *takes cognizance* of its surroundings but otherwise, unimpressed by the masses, centers its policy on seizing power; if the party embodies the essence of the proletariat; if eventually it becomes the sole court of appeals for all issues affecting the proletariat; if in this totally unmaterialistic way the party becomes the savior, while nothing but its mere good intentions and its followers' mere good faith can guarantee any correlation between its form and the substance of its struggle—then this party may not necessarily be the one that will accomplish the redeemer's function. The connection between party and class will be dissolved, since neither the party elite nor the masses themselves are defined in real class terms. Class-determined institutions, which again and again would impel the return to a class-determined politics, are replaced by a symbolism, a religious catechism, meant merely to force an identification of the masses with the party; democratic control is replaced by the church synod.

Only one watchword will then allegedly be retained: belief in the final goal. But instead of having its existence proved hourly through a relevant policy, and instead of getting visibly developed from the policy, this legendary final goal will become a mere pretext for opportunistic policies. In an idealistic way, the unity of theory and practice will be established simply through a "personal union," through the "partiality" of thinking.

In fact, a peculiar reversal of the "spontaneity doctrine" will supplement this vanguard theory. The combat will be directed, and power will be seized, by the party elite rather than by the proletarian masses who will organize themselves in that combat; ironically, the elite action will be occasioned by the spontaneous action of the indifferent masses and will then be exploited by the party.

Clearly this theory has connections to fascism, or is bound to generate them. A proletariat that, because of the educational work of a Communist Party, has gotten used to this idealistic course of history will no longer be tied to its party by material institutions. The masses may then surrender to any party that offers the strongest symbolism. They may simply change the elite they are willing to trust. And trustingly, they may surrender their power to this elite without reserving for themselves the right of democratic control; the elite need merely display a credible idealism. *The party turns into the central category of politics.*

Once a proletariat has gotten used to this view, it has no theoretical arms against fascism. The Communist International never produced any theoretical writings against fascism — and that is no accident. It had to make do with pointing out practical shortcomings as they occurred; there is no difference in strategic principles.

A materialistic politics is bound to match, exactly and visibly, and at every single point of the political struggle, the means to the end. Thus, what distinguishes the parties from each other is not just the final "ends or means" question: in fact, the means of the political struggle alone determine the quality of the ends. He who makes the party into a central category and is therefore able to justify any opportunism by claiming party interest, takes his place in the general trend toward fascism. The means become the end rather than being an instrument to concretely realize the goal. When a party's organizational and tactical structure arbitrarily determines its character, its original theory will ominously split off from its practice.

The theory then, far removed from actual practice, will draw its own circles around a dogmatic center; dogmatic battles lead to splits, and the party will be cut off from all groups that mean to hold on to pure theory, pure practice, or a desire to harmonize the two. Being of a strictly ecclesiastical persuasion, the ones who split — like the KAPD — will merely attempt to found a new, better, and purer church, or else join a different church. One way or another, they are lost to the proletarian movement. Either they will become even more sectarian than the old party, or they will find another party with similar features and just a different symbolism. Consequently, since the means do not fit the ends in the KPD, the Communist voter can easily desert to fascism.

At this point let us recall the strange assertion Deacon Sauerland made: the bourgeoisie cannot have a class party. The statement is a political confirmation of our thesis that the Communist Party is classless, for it implies that the Communist Party can become the leader of all other classes as well. The party-dictatorship doctrine and the Communist Party itself, both made into absolutes, are joined together; the vanguard of the proletariat turns into the leader of the nation. In the colonial countries this development has already been accomplished: there the Communist Party strives to lead the bourgeois revolution, and it thus fulfills the functions of a fascist party. In Germany, it tried the same scheme last year with the People's Revolution slogan. The ideological link with fascism and with the fascist party ideal is all too clear. The party is totally severed from the class. Of course, I am not saying that the Communists deliberately support fascism; I am saying that the theoretical propaganda of the abstract term "dictatorship" is preparing a fascist turn of mind.

The KPD, being a mass party, is different from its sectarian spin-offs, like the KAPD, in that it does not foster pure, abstract theory but tries to affirm its ideology in its practice. But to cover up the antinomy between theory and practice, and for the sake of its ideology, the KPD will resort to practical actions that have little practical value, or none at all, but that simply serve to define the party in ideological terms. Just one example: last year's plebiscite, where, in tandem with the Nazis, the Communists tried to overthrow the democratic Prussian government. Here, theory — isolated from practice and made absolute — created its own "essence"-oriented practice.

It is clear that the Communists, while aware of the need for a united front, do not believe it is feasible except within the framework of the Communist Party or at least with the KPD in the lead. Hence the vacuous prattle of a "united front from below" and the thesis, "The united front is with us." Both are mere synonyms for ordinary party propaganda among the masses. To begin with, of course, a kind of united front must be established between the party and the masses affected by its propaganda, but it is only a new word that cloaks an old politics. The narrowed ideology prevents the establishment of a real united front and requires the fabrication of a caricature.

The history of the KPD shows how this contrived politics has always outweighed the trend toward a realistic approach. After all, the united-front spirit rose long before this year. The first attempt was made in 1921. When the Comintern abandoned hope for world revolution and Russia simultaneously introduced the New Economic Policy, the workers' fatherland needed to come to terms with the capitalist powers. As a result, the international Communist movement's relation to the reformist workers' parties changed drastically. Russian foreign policy called for amicable dealings with the Social Democrats, who had proved to be the stronger force within the labor movement. The interests of the European labor movement called for a change of Communist policy from outright revolutionary struggle to a revolutionary opportunism. The Communists therefore gave the daily struggle decisive priority in the hope that it would develop into a revolutionary struggle. As early as 1920 Lenin had written his programmatic polemical treatise against the ultraleft KAPD: *Left-Wing Communism — An Infantile Disorder.* This made the KPD into a centrist successor to the old prewar Social Democratic Party. The old centrism, too, had accepted reformism as the immediate watchword for action; its goal had been to gain the trust and allegiance of the working masses in this struggle and thereby lead them into the revolution.

The final-goal ideology, however, has always been a mere excuse for current powerlessness; gradually, and self-evidently, the decisive watchword became concrete, day-to-day action. One proof: at that same time another theory was advanced which held that the reformist leaders did not even carry out their own reformist jobs; accordingly, in the reformist struggle the KPD actually sought to substitute itself for the SPD. No doubt this theory was much more serious and much more practical; but for this very reason it actually implied, at that time, the ideological liquidation of the KPD. No longer was it necessary to have a revolutionary party; a reformist one was needed which, however, would use any means at all, even those that had never been used in German reformism (though they had been in other countries — remember, for instance, the nine-day general strike in England in 1926).

Most significantly, the KPD leaders with a USPD background did their utmost to prevent this from happening. They, indeed, intended to continue the revolution no matter what; they did not want the old organization but a new, revolutionary party; they therefore vehemently opposed Karl Radek's united-front slogan. They had little understanding of the famous vanguard theory, and therefore were able to see that liquidation would begin as soon as the revolutionary nature of the KPD was no longer to be guaranteed by material, militant action but instead by a Communist elite that idealistically and personally was identifying itself with the revolutionary goal. Actually, some Moscow factions at the same time seriously toyed with the idea of liquidating the Comintern (for details see Rosenberg's book). United front at that time definitely meant reunifying the divided branches of the labor movement.

At any rate, a partial liquidation of the Comintern had already been implied: the revolutionary slogan "dictatorship of the proletariat" was replaced by the "workers'-and-peasants'-government" slogan when in 1923 Communists and Social Democrats formed coalition governments in central Germany. Heinrich Brandler, at the time still a KPD leader, stated that under the Weimar Constitution a dictatorship of the proletariat could be established. Even then, the only valid reason for the existence of the KPD was the Social Democrats' lack of energy in matters of reform.

The "left wing" of the KPD, which called for unconditional autonomy of the Communists from the Social Democrats, consisted mainly of those strata which, feeling insecure, no longer trusted their ability to continue a revolutionary politics without theology. The defeat in 1923 of the "Red October" — which the KPD had undertaken only in order to emulate the "Russian October" — revealed the failure of the liquidationist policy and returned this pseudoleftist wing to power.

From 1925 to 1928 a united front was again attempted. This time, Russian foreign policy led the way much more actively. The Soviet Union sought to come into closer contact with the Labor and Socialist International and, through it, with governments influenced by Socialists. The British Communist Party adopted the slogan of "international trade union unity" and in 1925 sponsored the Anglo-Russian Trade Union Committee, which was to promote trade union cooperation. The KPD sent its followers into the Free Trade Unions. Prodded by Trotsky, Bukharin even admitted the existence of a plan to form a "political bloc."

Meanwhile, however, within the Comintern the theologization of ideology, the self-styled "bolshevization of the national parties," had advanced too far; a liquidation of the Comintern could no longer even be suggested. At no time was the party's ecclesiastical character more distinct than when it virtually abandoned its *political autonomy* by sponsoring, for instance, a plebiscite for the expropriation of the German princes, a Working Men's Congress, trade union unity — all lacking specific Communist concerns. As if to make amends for these mundane practices, the KPD simultaneously retreated into its own ordained reservation: its *philosophical and organizational autonomy*. At that time its left wing began to consider KPD and SPD simply two firms that were competing for the same political merchandise and whose eventual cartelization simply depended on accidental contingencies.

Characteristically, this view of a united front ran parallel to a process of bolshevization, i.e., of an ever-narrowing contraction of party ideology into a central line. It was ideology that later on, in conjunction with the Soviet Union's "left turn" in 1929, forced the KPD to abandon the united-front policy. By then, philosophy and organization had both strongly concentrated on specific objects; it had become impossible to find a common basis without recognizing the rule of socialism in the Soviet Union, the soviet system, and the role of the party. Philosophy and autonomous organization had developed too vigorous a life of their own and acquired too great a following among workers for anyone to push them aside out of hand. Thus, because of its inconsistency this policy failed.

Now the KPD entered upon the opposite course. As it withdrew from a trade-union united front, the classless and vanguard-oriented features of its agitation gained new strength. The so-called People's Revolution was invented — with the philosophical implications I have cited. It tried to climb on the coattails of the Fascist movement. By now, its philosophy was so closely connected with specific symbols, institutions, and persons that its believers had grown unable to perceive political differences, to reason about political strategies and their appropriateness; instead, the members had become oversensitive about issues of dogma. This is why the defeats of Social Democrats, and of democracy in general, evoked unconcealed jubilation, while responses to the Fascists' stunning successes in the July election were rather cool. After all, what distinguishes the Communist from the Social Democrat is his world view; with the fascists there is merely a difference of a plus or minus sign which the Communist can hope to reverse.

Now what is the great philosophical concern that, by contrast to the politically nonrevolutionary actions of the KPD, informs it with the sense of being revolutionary? I have hinted at the trinity: van-guard party, socialism in one country, and government by soviets. An opposite philosophy would imply participating in relevant German institutions and adopting the ideology of democracy. About this latter ideology the Communists are indeed extremely sensitive, and they do their utmost to maintain their opposition to it. In doing so, they erroneously associate the dictatorship of the proletariat with the soviet system, and democracy with a political system of representation constituted under the name of parliamentarianism; thus they consider democracy, as opposed to the soviet system, a system of government. "Democracy" is supposed to be an actual entity, an absolute essence, which is the same anyplace and at any time.

Just as the party had been reified — essence as against appearance — and just as this reification had contradicted the actuality of class, now governmental forms have become reified; they are seen as Platonic ideas rather than results of class relations and human actions. Again and again in Communist conceptions we come across metaphysics, i.e., the bourgeois form of theology. The Communist thinks that by studying class wars in an economy based on the commodity form, he has overcome fetishism; but as he studies the totality of social relations, the entire capitalistic metaphysics, fully developed, infiltrates his theories from a totally unexpected quarter.

As we have seen, the Communists themselves meant to base the dictatorship of the proletariat not on the soviet constitution but on the Party regime. True, there is a linkage with the soviet constitution; although it is purely ideological, it stems from the historical example of a workers' government created with the help of the soviets. We must, however, strictly differentiate between the history of how this power was created and the system into which it has been frozen. In 1917 the Russian soviets were organs of democratic control set up against a government that, contrary to the popular will, continued the war and delayed radical social change. These soviets became the organs of the revolution: more and more widely, the broad masses began to exert control over the country's political, social, and administrative problems. The soviets organized the proletariat, which had been poorly organized under czarism, and they defended the revolution against intervention as well as reaction.

But the soviets never actually ruled Russia. When they showed signs of interfering with Party rule, a governmental crisis arose; the Communist Party emerged victorious. From organs of the revolution, the soviets were promoted to a constitutional establishment; they became the administration. No longer organs to provide democratic control over the government, they became the government. There is not just a difference but a diametrical contradiction between their function in 1917 and their function today. Then, they were the organs that were to effect the state's withering away; now, they have a flourishing state life of their own, complete with a fully developed bureaucracy and parliament and even with a separation of legislative from executive power.

Conversely, in the German revolution the councils failed. Just the same, the dogmatic German Communist, predictably, makes a historically specific political form into an absolute. Fighting for a soviet constitution, he expects everyone's mind to work the same way. He can tell his friends and comrades-in-arms by this symbol, and his enemies by the way they use political rather than ideological criteria to judge a constitution. Denying class criteria, all the Communist needs is to associate, on theological grounds, a specific constitutional system with the proletarian dictatorship he seeks to achieve. The farther his concepts depart from practice, the more absolute his concept of dictatorship, to the point where it becomes totally severed from the working class. The Communist argues like Shylock: dictatorship — nothing else. Soon he considers political democracy his most intimate enemy.

The more forceful this process of creating absolutes, the easier the transition to fascism. Again it is *Weltanschauung* that prepares the transition and creates the ideological soil for fascism. In proletarian minds, capitalist fetishism indulges fetishist orgies. What obstructs the unification of the proletariat is not an accidental philosophical education but a typical result of capitalistic thinking: relationships between classes turn into "systems"; a partial aspect becomes the whole. Society is defined by legal rather than by economic categories; and then, in a bourgeois manner, these categories become "eternal" and universally valid. When one has a specific conception in mind, no alternatives are permitted.

Citizen Hegel, of all people, defined revolution as the attempt "to validate abstractions in reality." Calling for dictatorship at the very moment when the bourgeoisie is calling for dictatorship is bound to create credit — at the very least ideological credit — for fascism. At this point, if the only issue is "dictatorship of the bourgeoisie or of the proletariat?" a no-win strategy results. That is what happens when the Communists generalize the particular, when in their radical discourse they speak of "the" democracy, "the" dictatorship, "the" system, when they call every government the absolute government (a proposition that can easily become a self-fulfilling prophecy), when they forgo examining the development of class relations in a state through concrete sociohistorical analysis.

The developments of the past fourteen years have taught the Social Democrats to be on their guard against this fallacy. To be sure, before the war they had used terms for democracy similar to the ones that the Communists use for dictatorship today; in 1918 the SPD desired an absolute democracy so fervently that, after first trying to achieve it in revolutionary ways, it proceeded too fast to establish a formal "system." Instead of developing proletarian power by polemicizing against the apparatus of the ruling class, the SPD developed a belief, derived from its prewar ideology, in a final, ideal society; it thereby prevented itself from using democracy to suppress reaction.

Today, however, this ideological ideal of a nondenominational democracy, this historically developed mistaking of form for substance, appears to have yielded to a more sociological turn of mind. Today there is not one group among Social Democrats that, were the labor movement to rise anew, would reestablish the Weimar democracy unchanged. Nor is there anyone who fails to perceive that democracy has acquired a new function over the years: in the face of the growing trend that seeks to turn government institutions into absolutes, defending or retrieving democratic liberties has become an important revolutionary task for the proletariat. Incidentally, many Communist workers responded to this challenge when on July 20 they spontaneously demanded that both workers' parties defend democracy in Prussia.

So here we have arrived at the answer to our question: how is a proletarian united front possible? Its theoretical premise would be the renunciation of abstract ideologies and the return to a class-oriented sociological analysis. On its practical feasibility, let us listen to a strategic expert:

> If two or more states combine against a third, this constitutes, politically speaking, only *one* war. However, this political union also has its degrees.
>
> The question is whether each state in the coalition possesses an independent interest in, and an independent force with which to prosecute, the war, or whether there is one among them on whose interests and forces the others lean for support. The more the latter is the case, the easier it is to regard the different enemies as one alone, and the more readily we can simplify our principal enterprise to one great blow; and as long as this is in any way possible, it is the most thorough and complete means of success.
>
> We would, therefore, establish it as a principle that if we can defeat all our enemies by defeating one of them, the defeat of that one must be the aim of the war, because in that one our blow strikes the common center of gravity of the whole war. [14]

Just so. In the class war of our time, the forces of social reaction are in this same situation: they can strike all their proletarian enemies with one blow. Today, democracy is that enemy. Hence, we ask the Comintern to at least partially liquidate its ideology. This demand is less unfair than it seems to be. The issue of liquidating the Comintern is just as timely today as it was in the days when the idea of world revolution was abandoned. The autonomy of the KPD is threatened by the interests of Russian politics and by the German situation.

The ideological barriers, however, have grown higher in the meantime. If the KPD collapses, it will be the Social Democrats' job to offer the Communist workers an equivalent ideology and, even more important, militant activities filled with socialist spirit. The theologization of the Communist philosophy has not yet advanced to the point where it would permit an unprincipled bloc; but the threat to our very existence, which calls upon us all to fight back, is growing. So it appears that the united front cannot be "manufactured" but will, in practical terms, be formed wherever the class enemy tries to strike both his enemies with one blow.

6

Fascist Propaganda and the Conquest of Power

Propaganda and Violence

Totalitarian propaganda is a form of violence.[1] To the faithful it promises a share in the exercise of power. The bewildered, the wavering, and the hesitant it browbeats into joining in the pleasures of "conquest." The recalcitrant it warns not to obstruct the "wave of the future." Enemies it threatens with "annihilation." Its argument is imposition; its counterargument, intimidation.

> The masses do not understand unless they are made aware of the master. The cruder and more brutal your language, the larger the crowd that will be ready to listen to you. (Hitler)

Hitler's method was not persuasion; nor, incidentally, was it deception, as so many of his adversaries have charged. His aim was to subject the audience to his will — to do violence to their minds.

> It is wonderful to exert power over guns. But it is still more wonderful to exert power over the hearts and minds of men. (Goebbels)

What in this confession seems to be a figurative use of the word "power" has, if taken literally, a sinister meaning. The Nazi propaganda specialist understood that it was his business to wield power and to conquer. When he boasted that "propaganda made the Third Reich," he hardly thought of well-phrased arguments, but he remembered the beer-hall battles in which he "conquered Berlin." For example, he and his Storm Troopers would go to a meeting of the

From M. Baumont, J.H.E. Fried, and E. Vermeil, eds., *The Third Reich* (New York: Praeger, 1955). By permission of Unesco and the International Council for Philosophy and Humanistic Studies.

Red Veterans' League in "Red" Wedding, the most decidedly Communist borough, and break it up with clubs and a judicious use of panic. The following day, as Goebbels gleefully reports in his account of his stewardship, applications for membership began to swamp his office.

Communist militiamen frequently went over to the Nazis after their party decided to avoid armed encounters. Republican defense-squad leaders kept complaining that the republican and Social-Democratic press gave too little publicity to their heroic resistance. Hitler, on the other hand, openly sanctioned the terror his troops practiced in the streets, and in court he proudly declared that he "stood by the boys" who in cold blood had murdered a young Communist miner in the Silesian village of Potempa. The assassins of the German statesmen Rathenau and Erzberger were glorified as heroes by the Nazi movement.

"Individual terror," abhorred by Marxists, was sanctioned by the fascists — provided, of course, that no risk was involved.

"Punitive expeditions" must be successful to be good propaganda. The Fascist Party in Italy and its shock troops, the *Squadre d'Assalto* or *Arditi* ("the bold ones"), trembled when workers occupied factories in northern Italy; but as soon as that movement broke down — for reasons that will not be discussed here — the Fascists organized their rise to power through systematic terrorism. The famous "March on Rome" could hardly have taken place — much less succeeded — had the military been willing to oppose it; but it was excellent propaganda in the Fascist sense. And terror propaganda reached its apex when Mussolini assumed responsibility for the assassination of his widely respected antagonist, the member of parliament Giacomo Matteotti. Then the Aventinian coalition, the center and left parties boycotting Mussolini's parliament, collapsed.

Terror and Propaganda are not alternative methods of conquering power. For the Fascists, terror is propaganda at its highest pitch. The Nazi professor of political science, Eugen Hadamovsky, candidly disclosed the essence of psychological civil warfare in his book, *Propaganda und nationale Macht — Die Organisation der öffentlichen Meinung* (Oldenburg: Stalling, 1934):

> The ordinary person, and the masses still more, will almost infallibly succumb to the power of the spoken word, no matter whether it is true

or not. Propaganda, if it is applied with the correct tactics, will influence the human will. It is thus more secret, deeper, and therefore more powerful than the open force of suppression.

Propaganda and force are never absolutely opposed to each other. The use of force can be part of the propaganda. Between them lie different grades of effectively influencing people and masses: from the sudden excitement, the attention, the friendly persuasion of the individuals to incessant mass propaganda [a precious differentiation!]; from the loose organization of convinced people to the creation of semiofficial institutions; from individual terror to mass terror; from the authorized use of the force of the stronger one to the military enforcement of obedience and discipline through the death penalty.

The most effective form of mass demonstration is the visible exhibition of power, as, for instance, the number of participants, the size of the meeting, and all that which demonstrates power: armed people, people in uniforms, weapons of all kinds.[2]

The "Crowd"

Hadamovsky belonged to that circle of German army psychologists who, in the First World War, developed the concept and practice of *Menschenführung* — how to lead people. When they sent Hitler to preach against the Republic, they gave him their manual as a guide, and in *Mein Kampf* he expounded their theories, which originally applied to subjecting army recruits to discipline.

The Nazi mass meeting imitated the conditions of army discipline by placing people under the spell of its power display. Insignia and flags, brass bands marching in front of armed formations, men in uniform, the party anthem intoned in unison; everthing was designed to impress and overawe the onlooker, or rather to make him into a participant. Other movements that have used similar devices did so to provide the public with a spectacle; for the Nazis the pageant is the movement itself, with the theatrical devices integrated into the performance of a ritual that expresses its spirit.

In the Nazi meeting the speaker is a "drummer," not an advocate. He marches in front of the audience; he does not confront them. He does not plead and argue; rather, his speech is a mock performance of the fight into which he is going to lead them. The oration is not a discourse, open to debate; it is a ceremony of exorcising the enemy before giving battle — one is tempted to say a propitiatory rite. It culminates in another ritual, the mass chorus vowing obedience to the Leader: "Führer, command, we shall follow thee," or, "Duce, at your bidding we shall attack," with hands extended toward the leader in the Roman salute, symbolizing surrender to his will.

After that, a question period would of course be an anticlimax. Debate is definitely discouraged; even the occasional heckler, whom a democratic speaker would welcome as a counterfoil, is ruthlessly silenced by the Storm Troopers, the SA. The very idea that anybody can debate with the leader is sacrilegious. Hitler spoke sarcastically of the "philistine" speakers who enjoy criticism. Successful propagandists, he insisted, do not argue: they manipulate or command.[3] They deliberately cater to the submissive traits in human nature and may, on occasion, go out of their way to tell the crowd how deeply they despise it and how low they rate its intelligence.

In the mass meetings the speaker has authority over the crowd, and conditions for manipulation are ideal. The audience is inert, inarticulate, and shapeless, abandoned to the superior willpower of anyone who has the courage to mold it into his image. It is swayed by hope and fear, easy to lead and to deceive, ready to be whipped into frenzy and shape; moreover, it tends to forget the natural bonds of family, class, religion. Business interests and other social determinants, which under ordinary conditions keep the critical abilities on the alert, are relegated below the threshold of consciousness:

> The mass meeting is necessary, if only for the reason that in it the individual who, by adhering to a young movement, feels isolated and is easily seized with the fear of being alone, receives for the first time the picture of a greater community, something that has a strengthening and encouraging effect on most people... When he steps for the first time out of his small workshop or out of the big enterprise, in which he feels pretty small, into the mass meeting and is now surrounded by thousands and thousands of people with a like conviction... he himself succumbs to the magic influence of what we call mass suggestion.[4]

The "magic" Hitler praises is the technique of severing each individual from the covenant of civilization and of reducing the whole crowd collectively to the dehumanized status of the herd, ready to follow the primitive tribal instincts which, psychologists assert, emerge when the bars of personal integrity are lowered and the ties of social responsibility are loosened. The German army psychologists who were Hitler's tutors found this theory in the writings of Gustave Le Bon, a Frenchman who had undertaken to debunk the propaganda successes of labor and other democratic mass movements. Mussolini, too, was familiar with Le Bon's analysis of "crowd psychology," and he deliberately used the methods that, as his teacher claimed, the Social-Democrats were using by instinct.

Le Bon's bias is too obvious to deserve discussion here. He gave the name of inarticulate "crowd" to the socially articulate, democratically organized group or class which, at the end of the nineteenth century, was striving for recognition of its interests. He chose to misinterpret their show of strength, originally intended to impress the authorities with the group's power and to extort concessions from them, as if this had been a method of obfuscating the issues and confusing the demonstrators' minds. Hitler took this *quid pro quo* at its face value; he never used the mass meeting as an instrument of policy, but he found it propitious for creating a mental state of exaltation and of low critical resistance in which suggestion may result in submission. Contemptuously he called the crowd "feminine," and he lusted after subduing it.

If I approach the masses with reasoned arguments, they will not understand me. But if I awaken in them the appropriate emotions, then they will follow the simple slogans I give them. In the mass meeting, the reasoning power is switched off.... The larger the crowd, and the more there is a mingling of different kinds of people, such as peasants, workers, and public employees, the sooner will the typical character of the "crowd" become apparent. Never try to speak to meetings of the intelligentsia, or to trade associations. Whatever you may be able to teach them by reasoned enlightenment will be eradicated the next day by opposite information. But whatever you tell a crowd when it is in that receptive state of fanatical abandonment, that will remain like an order given under hypnosis; it is ineradicable and will withstand any reasoned argument.[5]

Hitler gave much thought to the means of creating this "crowd mentality." He went into such details as the advantage of calling a mass meeting in the late hours of the evening rather than in the daytime because resistance is lowered when people are tired after a day's work, or because the night is traditionally the time for spiritual experiences; Mussolini, for the same reasons, would often call meetings with high party functionaries at midnight, or even in the small hours of the morning. Hitler advised his propagandists to avoid close reasoning, which invites questions and sharpens the wit; instead, he preferred to talk in images and symbols. Of particular interest is his shrewd remark about special interests. His adversaries have often wondered how he managed to reconcile rural and urban crowds, employers and employees, the interests of producers, traders, and consumers. It was the essence of his propaganda that he did not even attempt to reconcile them; he endeavored not to mention group interests at all but to sever the individual from his social group. In the "amorphous crowd" of the mass meeting, the particular and concrete ties of family, business, and class are dissolved, and group consciousness is superseded by, and submerged, in tribal emotions, as Le Bon had taught.

After they seized power, of course, the fascist leaders were able to force every citizen to participate in the rituals that made him an unreasoning member of the crowd. The whole nation now joined in the rhythmical conjurations, such as the joyful *Eia Eia Alala,* the metrical idiocy of *Ce-du-Ce-du-Ce-du,* the thundering evocation of the Fatherland in *Deutschland, erwache!,* or the breathtaking exercise of *Heil! Heil! Heil!* The nation became an extension of the mass meeting. Even with complete domination of the radio, Hitler and Mussolini never rose to the reasoned intimacy of the "fireside chat." They had to address real crowds — for only in that situation can the magic ritual be performed; the whole nation, listening in, participates vicariously in the experience of those present.

In these mass meetings the communication is not one of thought or discourse; it is a "performance." The symbols of power dominate the audience; words of command are heard; the chorus greets the Leader; the names of the party's martyrs are called, and to each name the crowd shouts: "Present!" The leader consecrates a new flag by touching it with one hand, while with the other he "draws" the spirit of the old Party combatants from the famous "blood flag" that he had used in the abortive Munich putsch. His charisma creates the crowd.

Words here are spells rather than a message: they are not supposed to challenge but to bind. Judiciously employing the "archcraft of rhythm" (Ernst Krieck, a Nazi professor), the Leader drowns out each listener's private thoughts and makes his own words sound as the sole and true voice that rings in each heart — until all individual will has been transferred onto him and he truly speaks in the name of those who listen or, rather, participate.

To call this "mass suggestion" is misleading. It is an artfully contrived mass regression into the age of tribal magic, an extinction of personal identity such as today, among civilized nations, is achieved only under combat conditions. To the "lonely individual" whom — as Hitler, unknowingly quoting Durkheim, says — society has reduced to a "dust particle," Nazi propaganda offers an escape from anxiety, thus offering him a means of enjoying the amputation of his humanity. The experience, the *Erlebnis* of the mass meeting, of singing and marching in community, of identifying himself with the Leader (or even with the *corpus mysticum* of a movement, or with destiny) affords him the delusion of a harmony that is otherwise inaccessible to his dissonant mind. In fact, the SA, with an almost irresistible magnetism, attracted many unemployed and uprooted "philistines" because it gave them a sense of "belonging" and offered them a place in society — a place of sorts.

The Sham Revolution

The "little man," however, was interested not in social adjustment but in revenge. The Leader promised him not a job but a share in power, an opportunity to get even with the "bosses." Le Bon taught that crowds thrive on hostile feelings and destructiveness. Using this negative approach, the Nazis were able to pose as more revolutionary than any other critics of capitalism. When their speakers incited the masses to hatred and violence against individual "pluto-crats," Jews, and "bosses," and promised that not one of them would survive, they sounded more radical than any party that would re-form society. But they let the gluttons and racketeers live.

Moral indignation was substituted for politically relevant action. The hatred on which agitation thrives was buttressed, but had to remain impotent. This self-perpetuating cycle of frustration and rebellion gave the "little man" no chance to come to grips with his enemy or with his problem. Instead, the imagery of "the Night of the Long Knives" supplied him with the daydream of vicarious gratification. Any acting-out of the pent-up hate feelings was chan-neled to suit the Nazi design: sadism took the place of revolution.

"Heads will roll in the sand," Hitler prophesied, and Göring added sarcasm when he promised the leaders of the democratic Republic that the Nazis would be "polite all the way up to the top gallows step." On a different plane, the Italian Fascists exploited President Roosevelt's disability to the hilt; their constant reference to *il Paralitico* was in character — infirmity made him the proper target for their malice. By the same token, the Nazis had their fun with defenseless prisoners; castor oil humiliated the victim as much as it seemed to justify the humiliation. In cartoons the Jews were shown as "vermin" inviting extermination; salacious anecdotes characterized them as morally depraved, emasculated or to be emas-culated, and dangerous only as long as their tricks were not exposed. The verbal sadism was self-righteous; moreover, its decidedly sub-versive ring gratified secret desires. It afforded, or at least promised, revenge for all past resentment and frustration. In a nutshell, its theme was: "We may not be smart, but we are not cowards."

Hitler considered sadism a morale-builder: "You can win the soul of a people only... by annihilating the enemy... The masses do not understand handshakes.... They want to see... the destruction of the weaker or his unconditional subjection."[6]

Sadism thus became socially significant, even ennobled. It was particularly attractive to the decadent intelligentsia, who took so much pride in the "shattering of bourgeois values," who glorified vice, and craved to express the "wisdom of the blood."[7] Depraved students became notorious for thinking up refinements of cruelty; Heinrich Himmler, a schoolteacher, organized the most abhorrent system of mass torture and execution ever invented.

Yet it is not sufficient merely to denounce the Nazi appeal to sadism. We must also try to understand why at this particular juncture of history such an appeal could be successful. We cannot explain the effectiveness of Nazi propaganda unless we recognize the rebellious, insurgent elements within it.

The "animal protest" against "humanist culture" had been smouldering in European philosophy for a long time. Irrationalism, vitalism, and existentialism rebelled against the high court of Reason. Years before Fascism and National Socialism appeared on the political scene, futurism in Italy and the romantic youth movement in Germany gave expression to ideas about the new way of life that were brewing in a new generation of anti-Victorians and anti-Wilheminians. Some saw the soldier's allegedly carefree existence as salvation from philistine moralism; but mostly there was the rebellion of the "open collars" again the "stuffed shirts," striving to gain recognition for the senses, the instincts, and the emotions. These movements, which at first conceived their programs as attempts to expand the sphere of human experience, soon degenerated into a violent attack on all intellectual values. Nietzsche's "revaluation of all values" turned into devaluation. The sensuousness of Wagner and d'Annunzio was transformed into a negation of civilization. Thomas Mann clothed it all in the noble armor of "true culture's" fight against the *"literati."*

The Nazis were able to identify the rigors of social and intellectual rationality with "democracy," and the nihilism of young hoodlums with a manly " will to power." Plebeian resentment against highbrow culture was crossbred with the guilt feelings of the "little man" who failed to succeed in a world apparently planned to suit his "betters" with their higher abilities.

The common denominator of all these undercurrents of European civilization was the new feeling that "life" had been slighted. It expressed itself in a vitalistic philosophy, which the Nazis bowdlerized into a murderous racism, the Fascists into a swaggering nationalism. Transposed onto the political scene — where it did not belong — this pseudo-rebellion appeared as sadism, clothed in the glitter of heroism. The rebellion of the instincts condemned a world where "bleeding-heart altruism" could succeed. "Whenever I hear the word 'culture,' I uncock my gun," says the storm trooper in Hanns Johst's play. The spook will disappear if one bangs one's fist on the table; only weakness is evil.

Strange to say, the Nazis and Fascists were convinced that they were fighting for freedom. The authoritarian record of their regimes after they had come to power has overshadowed the rebellious and revolutionary sources of their strength, which distinguished them from ordinary reactionaries. In contrast to the latter, Nazis and Fascists did their utmost to give the impression that they, and only they, spoke the down-to-earth language of the plain people and knew their grievances. They systematically depicted Italy as a "pro-letarian nation," Germany as a "have-not"; many a storm trooper honestly believed that he was fighting for a social revolution — and consequently he had to be eliminated after the conquest of power. The Nazis not only dwelt on all the social evils that the Republic had failed to confront; they also articulated the antiphilistine, anti-bourgeois, or anticapitalist resentments of the frustrated masses and moreover supplied a complete imagery of rebellion: abolishing the parliamentary Constitution, "slamming the door" at the League of Nations, "tearing up" written treaties, "bursting the shackles of the thralldom of interest," "hanging traitors," "liquidating Jews." No wonder, then, that an analysis of their propaganda theme is a cata-logue of what they were against. They were antirepublican and antimonarchist, anticapitalist and antilabor, antibourgeois and anti-libertine, anti-Semitic, and anticlerical — in short, anti-everything at the same time. They could even pose as antimilitarists.

The Great Deception

Since the Nazis and Fascists were so effectively "against" every-thing, it mattered little what they were for. Their critics have vainly attacked their conflicting promises: to the peasants higher prices and

to the consumers a lower cost of living; higher profits to the capitalists and "socialism" to the workers; to the big corporations free
enterprise, and "guilds" or "the corporate state" to small business.
They were for the strong state, of course, but also for the freedom
of the individual. Looking back, some may be amazed to find Hitler
polemicizing against "omnipotent government" in *Mein Kampf;*
Mussolini, like his predecessor Louis Bonaparte who gloried in the
honorary title of "liberal emperor," asserted in 1920: "I start out
from the individual and I strike out at the state." Just as the manipulator tries at the same time to arouse the subversive and the submissive inclinations of the audience, so he promises them freedom and
dictatorship at the same time. Those critics missed their target
because ambiguity was an asset, not a fault.

Observing the rise of Bonapartism in the 1840's, Heinrich Heine
said that it attracted malcontented people "who do not know exactly
what they can do or what they want [the republic or the monarchy]":

> The Napoleonic Empire itself was nothing else but neutral soil for people
> of the most heterogeneous views. It was a useful bridge for those who
> had saved themselves from the raging stream of the revolution and who
> for twenty years ran back and forth on the bridge, trying to decide
> between the right and the left bank of the mainstream of contemporary
> opinion.[8]

Likewise, Fascists and Nazis were consistently sitting on the fence
on the issue of capitalism and its abolition; always in advance of and
at the same time lagging behind progress, they successfully avoided
taking sides on the burning issues of the day. While exploiting to the
hilt the social malaise, they refused to relate its causes to the shortcomings of society; while fanning discontent into blazing hatred,
they eschewed the responsibility of relevant action toward social
change. In their verbal orgies of hate and violence, they shifted the
focus of aggression from the scene of the present society, where
specific reforms were needed, to the abstractions of heroic-sadistic
daydreams, to the vices of the outgroup and the depravity of the
enemies across the border. Incidentally, in its vagueness as well as in

its false "determinacy," the Nazi language was an adaptable tool of this duplicity.

Nazi and Fascist propagandists expressed general indignation at the state of the world, but maintained a ready duplicity and light-hearted unconcern whenever they were asked what they intended to do about it. They never expected their followers to discover the ambiguities or to mind any of their glaring inconsistencies. And their judgment was correct: democratic counterpropagandists, endeavoring to exploit these contradictions, only reaped laughter. Pounding at the irresponsibility of Nazi propaganda, they failed to understand that it was successful exactly because it was irresponsible; trying to expose the Nazi lies, they overlooked the fact that the Nazis never told a lie their followers did not want to hear. Debunking such lies was like taking a dangerous toy away from a child; it only made the debunker more odious — the more so as Nazi minds are usually devoid of any sense of humor.

With the emotional core of their challenge to the powers-that-be well anchored in their followers' minds, the Nazis could afford to be eclectic in their methods and ideas. They might take part in a strike, but that did not alienate their middle-class faithful; they might use the legal mechanisms of the courts or the parliamentary procedures of elections, but the followers understood that they did so only to pervert the institutions of democracy or to make a mockery of them. "We shall be within the law until the nooses are around their necks," Göring jeered.

Two random examples will show that the followers never expected responsible action from the Nazis. Alleged Polish atrocities had always been a showpiece of Nazi propaganda, which accused the government of "selling out to the Polacks." Chancellor Brüning, hoping to put the Nazis on the spot, asked them to rally behind him in a protest action. Hitler, of course, refused. To the applause of his adherents, he denied the Republic the right to come to the rescue of Germans oppressed by Poles. Anti-Nazi propaganda was unable to draw any benefit from such an "outrageous betrayal of German nationalism." Nor did the unemployed storm troopers blame Hitler when, during his "struggle for power," he refused to divulge his mythical plan to create jobs. They understood better than the democratic counterpropagandists that Hitler was not supposed to raise anybody's well-being and that he could not be expected to fight for the realization of ideas, or to formulate any.

In both cases Hitler irresponsibly refused to make any constructive contribution toward the solution of burning questions. Instead, he told his followers to wait for the "total change" to overturn "the whole cursed system" which was rotten beyond remedy and reform. Dealing in discontent and thriving on frustration, he deliberately widened the gap between the ugly "now" and the blissful "then." In the use of this device, he was apt to go to ridiculous lengths. Once he told a delegation of women that in the Third Reich each of them would have a husband — thus dodging the issue of women's rights. The Nazis never said *what* should be done; for them, *who* should do it was the all-important question of the day.

Their propagandists made ample use of the devices Whitehead has called "the fallacy of misplaced concreteness" and "the fallacy of misplaced abstraction." They would point to a particular "boss" or "Jew" and comment: "There you have the whole system"; vice versa, when they had to deal with a concrete situation requiring action, they shrugged their shoulders: "Nothing can be done while 'they' are in power." This pseudorevolutionary radicalism is typical of the "little man" who despairs of his ability either to fit into the world or to change it. Projecting his sadomasochistic daydreams into the image of Destiny, he expects the general cataclysm any minute. Although he is unable to relate the now to the then, he trusts that the party and the Führer will somehow steal away from the general doom and that he himself will then join the "we." For what was needed in this extremity the Nazis used the word fanaticism. Hitler praised this as a virtue in a significant context:

> The conviction that it is right to employ the most brutal weapons is always associated with the fanatical belief in the necessity of a new and revolutionary transformation of the world. A movement that does not strive for such aims will never be capable of using such extreme methods.[9]

Propaganda for War and by War

Even without deep psychological insight, no one can doubt that the extreme means really are the aim, and that the ideals are a mere adornment. Fanaticism is the prerequisite for the Night of the Long Knives. It is the fanaticism of the means (turned ends), and not any specific content, that makes this propaganda "fascist." No transition negotiates between total doom and total salvation.

The Wagnerian setting was an essential prerequisite of Nazi propaganda. No other movement has capitalized on its martyrs as zealously as the Nazis — though they actually had fewer than their enemies. Only the Nazis could conceive of the idea that all Germany should perish with its leaders. Goebbels basked in the pageant of funeral rites after the destruction of a German army at Stalingrad, and he instituted what has come to be known as the "propaganda strategy of gloom."[10] Unlike Churchill's now famous phrase of "blood, toil, tears and sweat," it implied more than a supreme appeal to sacrifice in the face of supreme danger: it climaxed two decades of Nazi complaints that Nazi Germany was always slighted and frustrated, that traitors and archenemies were constantly scheming to bring the Führer's grand designs to naught, and that the world at large was full of horror and damnation. Even a few months before Hitler seized power, he was full of ill bodings for himself and his movement:

> I am fighting against this system today, as I fought thirteen years ago, just as I shall fight the fight today and ten years hence. I have chosen to fight, and I shall remain faithful to the fight until the earth covers me. They may kill my friends, they may kill me, but we shall never desist.
>
> When I shall be dead, this our flag shall cover me, and my epitaph shall read: Here lies a man who has fought all his life, who was hated by many who failed to understand him.[11]

Destructiveness, self-destruction, and the desire to be destroyed met in the term tragic realism, coined by Ernst Jünger, one of the fathers of Nazi philosophy.

In this gloomy philosophy, which was sometimes passed off as "heroic," the alternatives are not a poorly organized and an improved world, but "they" and "us," underdogs and top dogs. The Fascist propagandist assumes that the masses will join his gang because its more ruthless methods promise greater assurance of victory. And in adversity he expects them to stick with him because, like criminal conspirators, they will fear that they might all perish together. When Germany was on the verge of defeat, Goebbels conjured up before his fellow Germans' eyes the picture of a vengeful mankind (symbolized as "international Jewry"), holding them collectively responsible for the crime against humanity which, he said, united them in a community of guilt: "No German can escape by saying, 'I have always been a democrat, only the Nazis prevented me from showing my true feelings.' In the eyes of international Jewry, every German will be guilty. The Jews will never forgive us for it."[12]

The same phrase, "The Jews will never forgive us," had appeared in a broadcast at the height of victory in Russia, in the winter of 1941. In fact, the habit of reminding the listeners of the "Covenant of the Gangsters" tying them to their leaders (as Ernst Kris appropriately called the device)[13] was more than a mere propaganda device. It appeared in the earliest Nazi documents as a central concept of the Fascist war myth. Its reek pervaded the novelistic interpretations of the First World War, from which the young shock-troop leaders came home with the appalling notion: what we have done there is irremediable; we cannot readjust to civilian life; war has become the eternal state of things.

Jünger developed his concept of "total mobilization"; his fellow writer Schramm criticized the conduct of the First World War on the grounds that it had not been a war "for the sake of the profound idea of warriordom." Mussolini rejoiced that "war alone can carry human energies to the maximum of tension" and asserted that "war is for man what motherhood is for woman." D'Annunzio and the futurist Marinetti raved about the beauty and virtuousness of war; young officers jeered at the "desk generals," whom they scorned as "philistines." Hitler despised the humdrum nationalism which never could elevate its spirit above such ancient patriotic instructions as "dulce et decorum est pro patria mori." The totalitarians thought more highly and deeply of war; it was not to be degraded into serving some purpose. Conversely, all civilian activities had to be imbued with warlike purposes and attitudes.

So the SA began "marching in closed ranks," as Mussolini was "one who marches." The movement's organization, its symbols and rituals, its language — all became propaganda of war, for war, and by war. The propaganda kept referring to "struggle," "fight," and "death." Later it had its "battle of employment," battle of the grain, battle against mice, "battle of the cradle" (*Geburtenschlacht* – literally battle of births!). There was exaltation in the "blood sacrifice" – until the final self-annihilation. Folk wisdom was right when it dubbed Hitler's peace offers a "peace offensive." A Fascist is always at war, "living dangerously." Reversing Clausewitz's famous dictum, he considers diplomacy "war conducted by other means."

Fascist war propaganda is, therefore, more than glorification of a patriotic sacrifice: it denies civilization. It does not preach war but assumes war as the natural condition of man. The effectiveness of propaganda resides in the manipulator's ability to shape all forms of everyday life in the image of war.

Sham Dynamism and "Destiny"

A warlike philosophy, warlike attitudes in civilian and political matters, a warlike organization and warlike phraseology gave the Nazi and Fascist "movements" their revolutionary flavor. Any political move had to be executed *schlagartig* (as a crash program, with lightning speed); war itself became "lightning war," the blitzkrieg; and even Hitler's greatest diplomatic victory, the 1938 Munich Pact, was spoiled for him because he was not allowed to overrun Czechoslovakia. His interpreter Paul Schmidt reports how bitterly Hitler fought, during the decisive conference with British and French leaders, to save at least the propagandist appearance of a military action. Thinking it undignified to declare war formally, he meant the world to learn that formal peace was an abnormal state of affairs and war was normalcy.

"The heroic mind," says Jünger, "does not look upon war as an act of man. Total mobilization is not made; it happens. Modern integration can neither be chosen nor declined. It is unavoidable. Freedom and obedience are identical. Domination and subservience are all the same."

This passage makes it clear what the war myth does for Nazi propaganda. While appearing to be extraordinarily "dynamic," actually the soldier-propagandist accepts the powers-that-be and teaches his audiences not to bow to them, as a mere reactionary would do, but to recognize them as their own "Fate." The freedom that Fate promises is that of the runaway railroad engine, or of the tank on the battlefield. In fact, Hitler once asked his finance minister, Count Lutz Schwerin von Krosigk, who was plagued by doubts and qualms about the direction of Nazi policy: "Did you ever try to get off an express train in motion?"[14]

In the Nazi universe, people are lined up behind the leader in a prearranged order, and things are laid out so no one can escape his "Destiny" — a word which had never before been used so often and in so many contexts as during the Nazi regime. It was the destiny of the German race to dominate others, just as later it was its destiny to go down in a spectacular cataclysm. Where human beings might have rebelled against that fate, the "wave of the future" took over; man became a mere cog in that "dynamic machine racing toward its destiny."

> War has a beauty of its own because it brings forth the mechanical man who is perfected by the gas mask, the terrorizing loudspeaker, and the flamethrower, or is enshrined in the armored car which stabilizes man's mastery over the machine. War has a beauty of its own because it starts the dreamed-of metalization of the human body.[15]

What matters here is not the insane content of the message but the pseudorevolutionary dynamism of its tenor — that particular blend of motion where no one moves, with freedom where everyone is obedient. Reactionaries tell the people that they must submit to unalterable facts or expect to be pushed around by them; revolutionaries either debunk the claim of unavoidability, or rebel against it; Fascist propaganda — in its most effective specimens, at least — achieves the mystical identification of man and material. It denies change and development, but it substitutes the pseudorevolutionary dynamism of abstract "movements," races, nations, or whatever is suitable at the moment, for concrete actions of people. Geopolitics, which in proper hands may be a subject of military instruction, becomes an effective doctrine for propaganda where power lines, triangles, and pressure centers are conquering each other all on their own account, with the humans "sucked into the stream" or "seized by the spirit of the *matériel*" (Ernst Jünger).

The relations between man, society, and nature are perverted. Even the grammar and language of the fascist propagandist reflect his confused state of mind. In terms like *Geburtenschlacht, Opfer an der Idee* (sacrifice unto the idea), *battaglia del grano,* and similar high-pressure slogans, and in many sentences written in "Nazi German," subject and complement are interchangeable.[16] Frequently, statements are completely vague. For instance, in a passage by Hitler to which we will refer again later, he speaks of "the annihilation of an idea and its dissemination," leaving the reader guessing whether or not he wants to annihilate the dissemination of the idea. Again, it is typical of this language that nouns take the place of verbs, as if human action were contained in a bureaucratic ukase. (This emasculation of the language, however, is not a deliberate device; it happens along with the worldwide trend toward dehumanizing man. Thus, in a country not under discussion here, a wartime appeal to students to breed rabbits was telescoped into the "rabbitization of youth." Such perversions of speech tend to establish a totalitarian outlook on life in the speakers' minds.)[17]

Worse still is the stylistic confusion in literature. Who is acting, and what is being acted upon, never becomes clear. Redundant, high-sounding verbs hardly conceal the absence of action. A torrent of big talk simulates candor, where the first relevant word would give away the absurdity. It is amazing to find how little ever happens in Nazi novels; even when they are full of "action," the characters never develop, and in each case the implicit lesson is to deny history.

The race doctrine states this philosophy in explicit terms and carries it to ultimate extremes. The author of *Das Dritte Reich,* Arthur Moeller van den Bruck, who did not believe in racism, nevertheless said: "There is no evolution, only creation."

The world is structured rigidly. "Germany" is always strong and beautiful, though at times she may be asleep and needs to be "awakened." The enemy is consistently depraved and weak. Although he may assume different shapes at different times, he is always the same, identical enemy; appearances to the contrary are the work of traitors and treacherous magicians working through underhand juggling — a very strong propaganda device. Particularly "the Jew" — consistently used in the singular, as if there were no room for individualization — is always evil; a specimen of the Jewish race that seems to be fair-haired or fair-minded is only that much more proof of Jewish deceptiveness. No Jew can deny his base origin, just as no German can renounce his share of the German blood, be he ever so alienated from the homeland. An irrevocable fate binds the German-Americans to Germany's Germans; nor can citizenship in a foreign country release the Japanese from their obligations to their emperor.

The uncanny dynamism of "the movement," of the war machine, or of the geopolitical symbols has its counterpart in the immobility of the individual. Not only evolution is denied; the propaganda arrangements are so laid out that the individual no longer sees any choice. Where everybody is "marching," those who are out of step will be trampled by the collective foot. It was not by accident that a philosophy which stressed freedom of choice gained great popularity in the underground movements of the resistance.

Devaluation of Ideas

The mystique of the movement, the cult of dynamism for its own sake, had still another function. "Vitality" relieved the propagandist of the embarrassing obligation to make specific contributions to the solution of current problems. Instead of ideas and programs, he had flags and marching columns. Instead of social content, his imagery offered "fronts." The names of totalitarian parties betray nothing. "Fasci," "Falange," "Arrows," "Frontism," or (in England, where imagery is least successful) simply "New Party," in Mexico "Silver Shirts" — all these names suggest dynamism without any specific direction. Mussolini's reluctance to give his party any idea is well known; he even made a point of it: "A doctrine must be a vital act and not a verbal display. Hence the pragmatic strain in Fascism, its will to power, its will to live, its attitude toward violence, and its value." Or, bowdlerizing a famous saying of Mazzini's: "Like all sound political conceptions, Fascism is action and it is thought; action in which doctrine is immanent, and doctrine arising from a given system of historical forces in which it is inserted and working on them from within."[18]

Hitler's approach to programmatic ideas is even more startling. His "Twenty-Five Points" are incoherent and of various relevance; but once they were announced, he declared them to be the "unalterable foundation of the movement":

> The task of today's and tomorrow's members of our movement must not be a critical revision of these theses but, on the contrary, a pledge to them. Otherwise, the next generation might think itself entitled to waste its energy on yet another spell of such purely formalistic work within the party instead of winning new members and, thereby, new strength for the movement. The majority of our followers will see the essence of our movement less in the letter of our theses than in the meaning which we shall be able to give them.[19]

> "And what about agrarian reform, the abolition of 'thralldom of interest,' and the nationalization of the banks?" I [Rauschning] objected.
> "Now you, too, bring up the platform," Hitler replied impatiently. "Do I have to tell you, of all people, what the platform means? Simpletons may interpret it literally.... I shall not alter the platform, and it is meant for the masses.... It is like the dogma of the church. Is the significance of the church contained only in its dogma, or does it not rather lie in its activities and its rites? The masses need something for their imagination and also firm doctrines that cannot be altered. The initiated know that nothing is unalterable."[20]

Hitler claimed that he had learned this principle from the Roman Catholic Church, which also will not sacrifice one iota of its dogma although it may be dated: "Its [the church's] power of resistance is not due to its. . . adjustment to the day's scientific findings. . . but to its rigid adherence to the once-established dogma."[21]

Unlike practically all other political parties and mass organizations in history (including the churches), Fascist parties do not claim that their ideas are better; they appeal to people who distrust ideas in general and intellectuals in particular. Mussolini called intellectuals "babblers"; Hitler poured vicious irony on them because they thought that people could be moved by arguments. "To be a leader means to know how to set the masses in motion. The talent for shaping ideas has nothing whatsoever to do with ability of leadership."[22]

The Nazi revolt against the foundations of Western civilization started when it first rejected reasoned argument in propaganda. Declining to meet their enemies on their own grounds, the Nazis undermined their values. They refused to match ideas against ideas and facts against facts, proposing to exterminate both with clubs:

> The use of violence alone, without the impulse from a basic mental concept as its prerequisite, can never lead to the annihilation of an idea and its dissemination, except in the form of an absolute extirpation of the very last supporter and the destruction of the last tradition.[23]

This is the characteristic jumble of noun-bloated grammar which usually betrays Hitler's efforts to impute his own mentality to his enemies. He seems to be charging that they fight ideas with clubs rather than ideas; but actually he is the one. All he ever tried to do was to suppress ideas, to eliminate ideological contests. The symbol of civilized debate was the place where argument had been institutionalized: parliament. The Nazis referred to the Reichstag as a *Quasselbude*, a prattle shop; they did their best to make it unworkable and then accused it of inefficiency. They fanned hatred against this institution to blazing heat until, finally, the building itself went up in flames. The device was effective; it attracted all those who did not believe in compromise and reasoning — just as the propaganda against the League of Nations attracted the isolationist rabble that did not believe in diplomacy.

After their conquest of power neither Nazis nor Fascists, with all the powerful propaganda apparatus of the state at their disposal, ever took any chances with freedom of debate. They established a tight monopoly on publicity and information, which they constantly perfected and never relaxed. Not that Goebbels or Mussolini lacked confidence in their technique and devices (at which their adversaries marveled, erroneously attributing to them the Fascist successes); but there would have been much less to marvel at had the Fascists not refused to meet argument with argument.

All democratic propaganda is essentially discussion. Even the most ruthless demagogue, who shuns no calumny and appeals to all prejudices, at least pretends to respect the reasoning power of his audience. Even the professional liar thinks that he must deceive people by twisting his arguments. Obviously the Nazis did lie and deceive; but their lies were neither more skillful nor more effective than any propaganda of their opponents, whether truthful or false. On the contrary, the Nazis were most effectual when they bluntly told the truth and said that they did not think people were capable of judgment and understanding. They wanted them to believe in the Führer, and their arguments were words of command. Their appeal was directed neither to interest nor to insight but to duty and faith. For this reason, they also appeared to cut across all the other parties, each of which represented a group interest.

Again, democratic propaganda implicitly assumes that the audience knows its own interests or those of the country. Its arguments rest on the belief that people want to help themselves, and listeners are supposed to believe that man — eventually at least — can be perfected. Fascist propaganda, on the contrary, tells its audience that the leader knows best, that he will fight for them, and that people generally are not smart enough to learn from experience. It is based on the proposition, however, that man can be manipulated.

Manipulation can of course be best achieved through a monopoly of information. While he still has to compete with others for the voters' attention and allegiance, this propagandist must disrupt and negate the mechanism by which public opinion is forming in free discussion. His second-best chance of success, next to the "absolute extirpation" of his competitors, therefore, is to deny that he is debating with an enemy. He does not appeal to the audience as to a jury that hears his case as well as the opponent's; he addresses the entire nation as though it were already lined up behind him, ready to follow his call to "action," though often benumbed by enemy deception or mentally imprisoned by vicious conspiracy. The nation as a whole, not each individual, is supposed to hear the master's voice of command — *"a noi"* or "awake," "march," and "close the ranks."

The Captive Audience

Fascist propaganda, therefore, has only one problem and uses only one basic device: to place the unconquered minds under the spell of its symbols of power as if their resolve were already a foregone conclusion, putting the entire nation into the position of a captive audience.

An audience is captive when it cannot avoid seeing or hearing the full content of an advertisement — e.g., the public in a motion-picture theater or, better still for our metaphor, the passengers on a bus. While the mad armored tank is taking the Nazis to their destiny, they are fed the Nazi slogans. The problem for Goebbels was not what to tell people but how to get them on the bandwagon. The Nazi propagandist's first job was to make himself conspicuous, then to arouse constant and ever-increasing curiosity, and finally to be omnipresent in the minds of the public at large. Goebbels achieved these ends by presenting the Nazi movement as the great threat, and he succeeded in keeping this threat constantly in the public eye. When finally all nations expected their daily Nazi surprise, he had won.

As was necessary for this policy of keeping the world's nerves on tenterhooks, the Nazis tried to be seen and heard as often as possible, through demonstrations, through mass meetings, by plastering the towns with their posters, by inducing newsdealers to display their papers prominently, but above all by the eccentricities of their policies. "What will they do next?" everyone had to ask himself every day, first in Germany, then all over the world.

Here again the basic propaganda device is terror. The Nazi antics, however inconsistent they might have seemed to outsiders, were always converging on this double aim: to disrupt the social-political pattern of the republican regime, and to sever the Nazi followers from its mechanism. Opposition to the government and its policy was to be wrought into absolute negation; there was to be no salvation outside the Nazi movement. For good reason, therefore, organization and propaganda are dealt with together in the same chapter of *Mein Kampf*:

> The first task of propaganda is the winning of people for the coming organization; the first task of the organization is the winning of people for the carrying-on of propaganda. The second task of propaganda is the disintegration of the present state of affairs and the permeation of this state of affairs with the new doctrine, whereas the second task of the organization must be the fight for power in order to secure through it the final success of the doctrine.[24]

Here the specious meaning of the term "doctrine" in Fascist propaganda is clearly stated. The doctrine consists in propaganda for "the disintegration of the present state of affairs," and the immediate object and principal device of this propaganda is "organization." To be sure, all political movements use propaganda to strengthen their own ranks. This is so obvious that we must suspect a more specific thought in the passage just quoted. Indeed, the relation between "propaganda" and "organization" is much closer in Fascist parties than anywhere else. Loyalty is not built up on behalf of an idea but for the leader and his hierarchy. Hatred is preached not so much against doctrines and institutions as against certain "types" of people and their organizations. The conflict of programs is reduced to the level of a conflict between persons: on the positive side the leader, who is always right; on the other side the vermin, who are always incapable, immoral, and degenerate. Generally, even the fascistoids concentrate their propaganda on this pseudomoral aspect of politics.

The "system" is always characterized by its abuses; its standard-bearers are all profiteers or knaves; their corruption is matched only by their infernal designs. The Nazis managed to conduct a year's campaign on the basis of a fur coat which the wife of Berlin's mayor allegedly could not account for; the pornographic defamations spread in Streicher's weekly acquired worldwide notoriety.

Of course scandals have always made good copy for any opposition party, but content analysis shows that fascist propagandists rely on them to a far greater extent, using more exaggeration and vituperation than do their opponents, and that references to scandal not only abound in quantity but also occupy a central place in their imagery. They are not mere examples of the mismanagement of the attacked regime but somehow define its very essence. A closer view shows that this technique exposes the enemy as morally and physically depraved, disintegrating, and doomed. The device knocks down several pillars of the enemy's castle at one stroke, without committing the agitator to any positive policy or program.

At the other end of the value scale, the propagandist consistently exalts the moral and physical strength of his own organization and, in particular, of the leader. No Fascist movement has ever been successful without a leader cult. A huge mass audience is far from equivalent to an organization built on obeying its leader's command. The closely forged machines of totalitarian hierarchies and the iron discipline of the followers argue the strength and virtue of the leader, while the leader myth of omnipotence, infallibility, and incorruptibility is the supreme argument of any totalitarian party. Faith in the movement's future might be halfhearted at times, but faith in the leader and his mission can never fail. "Loyalty is my honor," says the motto of the SS. [25]

The leader cult also made it possible for propaganda to operate on very different levels with very different approaches and promises at the same time. The intelligentsia, always sensitive to points of doctrine, could be silenced by an appeal to its ability to believe; the man in the street, who might like to "see results," could be prevailed upon to prove his loyalty to the leader. "Give me four years!" Hitler asked his followers when he took power, and they gladly consented to wait that long for the kingdom to come. From the Führer's deputy down to the last SA man, and further on to the simple block warden and private soldier, everyone finally accepted his place within the regime. "Command from above, obedience from below," said Göring. But this was not a mere result of Nazi education; it was the essence of the movement from its inception. In *Mein Kampf* Hitler had already asserted that the movement must anticipate the new society in its structure and intent.

"Organization," then, is hardly differentiated from propaganda. It expresses the movement's spirit better than words. It is the living denial of debate and of intellectual values. The strength of the machine, its hierarchy, a man's rank in the movement, his loyalty to the leader, all these are the values that determine the personal success of the agitator and the success of propaganda. The scale of values does not run from right to wrong, or from correct to incorrect, or from right side to left side; it only knows weak and strong, soft and ruthless, dissecting and integrating. Its criterion is not reason but faith: the leader can do no wrong. Pacifism, for instance, might be either good or bad; but those who cherished pacifist ideals certainly were displaying softness, if not moral depravity. The Nazis therefore did not bother to disprove antimilitaristic ideas; they simply denounced them as despicable, or treasonable. When, however, the Führer made one of his ominous peace maneuvers, he did so "from strength" or wisdom.

Finally, organization was entwined with propaganda not only in this intimate quasimetaphysical way. It also had a direct technical aspect. The Nazi organizers had a very shrewd judgment of strategic procedure in propaganda. They did not wait for their mass appeals to reach a scattering of people and then for these converts to form cells; they pinpointed their propaganda in locations where they could hope to achieve the greatest immediate results in building up machines and forming nuclei for the further spreading of organization and propaganda. In advancing from village to village, they tried to win first the doctor, pharmacist, and teacher, if possible the pastor — not through methods of mass persuasion but through personal approach, involving the victim in their oganization even before they found it necessary to discuss their doctrine with him. In the cities they selected strategically situated pubs or poolrooms where they installed their headquarters and organized a certain to-do and coming and going, with guards visible from the street and occasional sallies into "enemy" territory conducted under propitious auspices. Thus they were able to conquer street by street.

The Big Lie and the Big Truth

Propaganda must constantly work on three levels: to indoctrinate and strengthen the followers; to paralyze, divide, or mislead the enemy; and to win ascendancy over the undecided. In democratic countries and democratic parties the job of propaganda is also to arouse people to action. Fascist leaders are less interested in that aspect; instead they use fake "calls to action" as a means to win ascendancy. The annual Winter Help campaign for charitable donations — which had to be given anyway as compulsory contributions — was actually designed to rally the population behind the Nazi chariot rather than to bring aid to those who had been crushed under its wheels. "I fanaticized the masses in order to make them into a tool of my policy," Hitler confessed.[26]

These words really summarize all there is to fascist propaganda. Neither Hitler nor Goebbels nor Mussolini had at their disposal any special powers of persuasion which their opponents could not have used had they been equally unscrupulous. A careful examination of the top Nazi and Fascist pronouncements on the subject, and of their techniques, does not reveal any new invention, nor any of the "startling insights into human weaknesses" with which some pundits of the left have credited them. The myth of the irresistible spellbinders suited the losers well enough; it implied that they had been defeated by blows below the belt, and it somehow seemed to cover up their own failure to offer, at decisive moments, a positive program for reconstruction, a way out of the political and social crisis. Actually, it came to pass that they tried some pitiful imitations of Nazi methods and slogans — a game in which they were bound to lose — instead of putting forth new and forceful ideas. They were beaten, not because they lacked the strength or the personal courage to fight the ever-bolder Nazis, but because they lacked what it takes to fight bewilderment and despair — and the Nazis quite openly played on just that.

There was never any secret doctrine or magic formula for fascist propaganda. Hitler, for example, candidly proclaimed his techniques in the wordy and clumsy tirades of *Mein Kampf* as early as 1925. Moreover, they are simple enough. He insisted, first, that propaganda must appeal to the emotions rather than to reason. Its intellectual level must be adapted to the understanding of the morons: "Its effect must always be directed more toward the emotions and only under very special conditions toward the so-called intelligence... and its intellectual level must be adapted to the capacities of the stupidest."[27]

Also, according to *Mein Kampf,* propaganda must pick out a few striking points and hammer a few slogans into unforgettable images: "[It is necessary to limit propaganda] to a very few points and to use these, in sloganized form, until even the last person will be sure to associate what we want with the word."[28]

Again, propaganda must not be subtle by ridiculing the adversary. Making fun of somebody still leaves a certain tie of friendliness with him. On the contrary, the adversary must be presented as brutal and inhuman. Fascist propaganda must not be "fair" to the opponent and must never concede that there may be two sides to a question.

> Would anyone advertise his soap by admitting that other soaps might be good, too?... The task of propaganda is not to weigh which side is right in this or that respect, but the exclusive emphasis on the one side. It is not to search objectively for the truth insofar as it favors the other side and then put it before the masses with doctrinaire sincerity, but it must uninterruptedly serve its own side.[29]

Hitler goes on to berate "knee-jerk objectivity" *(Objektivitätsfimmel),* which deprives the German people of its ability to stand on its rights, and he condemns all "half-measures" *(Halbheit).* Even an outright lie will be believed if told over and over again with brazen impudence; and the bigger the lie, the better:

> The bigness of the lie is always a certain factor for its being believed, because the people at large... in the primitive simplicity of their minds are more easily made victim by a big lie then by a small one, since while they themselves sometimes use petty lies they would be too much ashamed of lies that are too big. An untruth of that magnitude will not even occur to them, and they will be incapable of believing in the possibility of such an enormous impudence of the most infamous distortion on the part of others; even after confutation, they will continue doubting and wavering and assuming that at least there was some true ground behind it. That is why even of the most impudent lie something always will remain and stick.[30]

Yet, notorious and utterly unscrupulous as especially the Nazis were in the use of the technique of the "big lie," it must be added that they scored many a propaganda success by using the technique of the "big truth" — and in particular by combining the big lie with the big truth.

By the technique of the big truth I mean two things: exposing bluntly and mercilessly the weaknesses of the system and of the political parties that were to be eradicated; and being deliberately crude and frank whenever their own ultimate ends were announced. Before the Nazis and Fascists came into power, their agitators never tired of telling the people how badly off they were, and that the others had no policy and offered no leadership. On the other hand, Nazis and Fascists never made a secret of their own nostrum against all evils: foreign conquests. Were not Italy and Germany "late-comers" in the distribution of the world's territories and riches, while others had done the grabbing? Italy and Germany, too, would gain in might and prestige by acquiring more of the world's natural resources. The middle classes, whom Marxist propaganda clumsily threatened with "proletarianization," would receive commissions in the armed forces or in the administration of dependencies. "One cannot deprive a nation of its wealth without giving it glory and honor instead," said Mussolini.

Much of that had a ring of truth and seemed obvious, especially since the moderate and left parties rarely offered alternatives to such suggestions. In fact, they often believed that the best defense against fascist chauvinism and militarism lay in attempts to outdo them in nationalism. Even in 1919, the behavior of the Italian delegation at the Paris Peace Conference intensified the impression, ceaselessly propagandized by the Fascists, that Italy was being nationally humiliated by its fellow victors. Another example: surrendering to the ideology of the Nazis, the German Communists joined them in a referendum against the Young Reparations Plan.

A district-by-district analysis of subsequent election returns showed that Nazi progress was fastest in the districts where this Communist stratagem had succeeded. Nor had the traditionally nationalistic and militaristic parties any defense against fascist demands. Mussolini and Hitler had merely to state that they stood for the same goals, only more so, and that they were ready to use more ruthless methods. Again, everyone, from the moderate left to the extreme right, was of course against "Bolshevism"; but the Fascists and Nazis could show blood on their hands as proof that their hatred was more genuine.

Once middle-of-the-roaders were no longer prepared to stand up for a Communist's civil rights, even non-fascists came to conclude that fascist methods were the most effective in dealing with the Communist danger. This weakness of the moderate parties when confronted with a revolutionary bogeyman has been exploited by virtually every counterrevolutionary dictator-to-be for the past four hundred years. It was Hitler's and Mussolini's pet device, too.

Whether lie or truth, fascist agitation made it a rule that propagandists must always stick to their guns, avoid any change, repeat the great outlines *(die grosse Linie)* over and over, and, if forced to digress, in the end return to the original slogans:

> You will be amazed what gigantic, almost incomprehensible success is the reward of such perseverance. Any publicity, whether in the field of business or of politics, carries success in the permanence and unchanging uniformity of its application.[31]

Having grasped how effective repetition could be, Hitler concentrated his fire on one outstanding adversary at a time. This not only afforded him the chance of channeling all pent-up aggression into one direction and to combine all real and alleged evils into one personification; it also made repetition more versatile. For instance,

President Roosevelt would be used as a symbol of bolshevism as well as of plutocracy; "Jewry" for suppression as well as for subversion. This leads to the question of why eventually all totalitarian propaganda will find its proper vehicle in anti-Semitism. Even Mussolini, who personally did not hate Jews, ended by denouncing the "Jewish World Conspiracy."

Polarization

In propaganda analysis the device of building up an archenemy is called polarization; it has long been a standby of political and, particularly, of sectarian agitation. The Nazis perfected it by making their counterimages as "total" as they were themselves. The archenemy was universal, he was everywhere, he was the intangible and worldwide evil, ever-present in a thousand disguises.

Once the picture of an archenemy has been firmly established in the mind, it can be used like a clothesrack, to be endowed with any hostile symbols and emotions. The imagery that populates the agitator's universe is very stable. As in a serialized cartoon, the "types" never change; they are stereotypes. This is true of all propaganda, but it is extreme in the symbolic thinking of these publicists, and it can be explained by the very nature of fascist propaganda aims. While other publicists, however demagogically they may deal with their audiences, must eventually invite discussion, give explanations, exhibit principles, and above all must propose specific remedies for specific ills, their Fascist counterparts must avoid all this and deal in images of positive and negative characters — the "we" and the "they." "We" and "they" must, of necessity, be immutable. For example, such matters as the various phases of the economic cycle, or problems of taxation, or wage calculations with which "they" deal in their discussions and speeches, are rather complicated matters; the solutions "they" offer are often difficult to grasp and equivocal. "The Jew," on the other hand, is always equally hateable in the pseudopalpability of his abstract "essence." Likewise, the image of the "plutocrat" may or may not fit any number of individual millionaires, but everybody knows the "type," and all bankers, bosses, racketeers, and schemers are instinctively rolled into one composite mastermind which commands an international network conspiring to make the people poorer and the rich richer. Again, the sinister and mysterious conspiracy may be the work of "the Freemasons," or "the Jesuits," or "communism," or "international finance capital." At the height of the battle of Stalingrad, when the tide of military successes changed and the numbed population felt the beginning of the end, Goebbels produced the pyramidical "Jewish bolsho-pluto-democratic International."

For Nazi propaganda, however, the real archenemy was "the Jew." The other archenemies were either allied or identical with him. In this connection a word must be said on political anti-Semitism as distinguished from mere Jew-hating or Jew-baiting: it is a technique of mass domination designed to divert hatred from the ruling class and to shift it onto a mythical symbol of "otherness," of the Devil. Such a dark power is handily provided by the image of a "Jewish World Power" that allegedly — according to the notorious forgery, "Protocols of the Elders of Zion" — directs the destinies of all nations, organizing revolutions as well as counterrevolutions, pulling the strings of the stock exchange just as it commands the labor movement, surreptitiously dictating the course of history for some unavowedly sinister purpose, conspiring to frustrate the hopes of all decent people but using them for deceptive shadow play. At all times, this myth has fed the imagination of the lunatic fringe of the disinherited. But the Nazis made it a cornerstone of their propaganda. It was simple and striking; at once, it satisfied the need to "explain" the common man's frustrations and the desire to attribute them to some irrational cause. It was the perfect mystery, demystified just imperfectly enough to leave it mysterious. Hitler's great mystifier, Alfred Rosenberg, went so far as to detect the symbols of the secret Jewish world government in the design of German coins.

The concept had two outstanding advantages. In the first place, it "explained everything." Anything that appears to show the absurdity of the idea is, on the contrary, proof of a clever Jewish deception, contrived to conceal the great conspiracy and to mislead the "Aryan simpleton, who is much too good-natured." The poor Jew whose ragged clothes aroused the sympathy of a decent German,

Goebbels wrathfully warned, had been placed in that position by his wealthy cousin on Wall Street for no other purpose than to divert attention from the Jewish World Conspiracy — against which an "anti-Jewish uprising" was justified and timely: a world revolution would make it possible for the Nazi strategists to pose as friends of all peoples while subverting all nations. Hence their "internationalism."

Second, the notion of the Jewish World Government provided a rationalization for the Nazi conquest of world power. The conclusion was obvious: if the world had to be run by a conclave, then why not by one that was virtuous and of purer blood? The conspiracy could be overcome only by a counterconspiracy. The battle, then, was joined on very simple terms: the Jews or us?

"My Jews are a precious pawn, left in my keeping by the democracies. In all countries a propagandizing anti-Semitism is the all-but-indispensable means of disseminating our political fight. You will see in how short a time we will overthrow the whole world's concepts and standards, simply and solely by our fight against Jewry. For that matter, the Jews themselves are our best helpers in this struggle. Despite their dangerous situation, they always mix with the foes of order and with subversives' ranks insofar as they are poor, and they are far and wide conspicuous as owners of huge riches which everybody envies them. Hence, it is easy everywhere to furnish down-to-earth evidence for our claims by pointing out popular and concrete instances occurring right next door. As soon as, by specific exposure of the Jews, the race principle has made its entry, everything else will take care of itself promptly. People will be forced, then, to dismantle, step by step, their political and economic order and to absorb the new ideas of biological politics."

[Hitler] said that anti-Semitism was doubtless the most significant part of his propaganda arsenal and almost everywhere was dead certain to succeed. That was why he had given Streicher *carte blanche* in his job. Moreover, Streicher had an amusing and very clever way of doing his job, and it made him wonder where in the world Streicher got that new material all the time. He looked forward eagerly to each new issue of *Der Stürmer*, and it was the only paper he liked to read and did read from the first to the last line....

I asked him if he meant to say that the Jew should be annihilated altogether. "No," Hitler replied. "We would have to invent him. You need a visible foe, not merely an invisible one." The Roman Catholic Church, he said, found the Devil insufficient; it needed visible foes in order not to slacken in its fight. "The Jew always sits inside us. But it is easier to fight him in a living shape than as an invisible demon."[32]

Any word of comment would be anticlimactic. The point here is not to show Hitler's cynicism but his insight into his cynicism. He knew how explosive was the scheme he unleashed and how it could best be exploited. By depicting the poor Jew as the enemy of law and order he would subvert the domestic and international order. By inveighing against the wealth of Jews he would undermine other nations, the better to capture their own wealth. The last part of the quotation shows his awareness of the psychological mechanism that made polarization so powerful a propaganda weapon. The evil had to be shown to the people as being "outside" of them in order to paralyze the spirit of compromise "inside" them; liberation from all evil "inside" was promised to those who would recognize the need for an unconditional victory of the movement over the evil "outside."

Sooner or later all totalitarian movements avail themselves of the tremendous propaganda opportunities residing in anti-Semitism or equivalent polarization devices. The visible existence of total evil, the archenemy, can best justify the movement's claim to achieving a "total" purge. If national tradition fails to provide such an archfoe, propaganda must create one or build up an existing enmity into total rejection. It is for this reason that totalitarian policy against the archenemy cannot stop at administrative measures, however harsh — just as Nazi anti-Semitism could not stop at administrative measures to "curb Jewish influence" — but has to aim at "total annihilation."

Victims of Their Own Cunning

After the conquest of power, the same psychological mechanism continues to operate and calls for continuously growing radicalism in propaganda. Since the "evil," the "archenemy," exists not only in its original form, the Movement-State must fight it in its other forms too. The dynamism of its own demagoguery thus drives the Fascist state to find new enemies at home and to destroy the last vestiges of possible resistance. Not that the fascist regime, with all its police power and its monopoly on propaganda, need fear these remnants of opposition. On the contrary, it could not exist without constantly proving that opposition still exists. How necessary, therefore, is its cruelty against the "traitors," and how mistaken is the simple-minded follower who thinks that the sinister "conspiracy" has long since been stamped out! Hence, if the police destroys the opposition, propaganda must reinvent it.[33]

In order to export their ideas abroad, the Nazis did not even have to invent the Jewish danger. Their own persecutions at home produced a "Jewish question" in countries into which the destitute and homeless endeavored to emigrate — often, in fact, being driven to violating some of those countries' immigration laws. Gleefully, the organ of the SS, *Das Schwarze Korps*, pointed to "the scum of the earth, the wanderers without citizenship, without means of livelihood, without passports, and therefore without rights, who wherever they went became the living proof that their persecutors had been right after all." With satisfaction the Foreign Ministry noted in a circular letter "to all senior Reich authorities and the NSDAP Bureau for Foreign Affairs," shortly after the government-directed pogroms of November 1938:

> The emigration movement of only about 100,000 Jews has already sufficed to awaken in many countries the interest if not the understanding of the Jewish danger.... Germany is very interested in maintaining the dispersal of Jewry. The assumption that as a consequence boycott groups and anti-German centers would be formed all over the world disregards the following fact, which is already apparent: the influx of Jews in all parts of the world invokes the opposition of the native population and thereby forms the best propaganda for the German Jewish policy.... The poorer and therefore the more burdensome the immigrant Jew is to the country absorbing him, the more strongly the country will react and the more desirable is this effect in the interests of German propaganda.[34]

Once a movement of this type is in power, it can cause things to happen according to its own predictions. It is able to create propaganda facts at home and even abroad. Since it is ever ready to attack the status quo anywhere in the world, it can freely select the field where it wishes to go of its own choosing at a time of its own convenience. Since it is not bothered by considerations of principle, its fifth-column organizations can execute peace maneuvers or war threats; they can cooperate with friendly governments or try to disrupt hostile ones as the need arises. In doing this, propaganda often not only precedes the event on which it is built, but actually determines the course of events. It was for reasons of propaganda, or morale-building, that Hitler wanted Italy to join the war, although his military advisers cautioned him that it would be a liability rather than an asset. Mussolini, in turn, somewhat put to shame in the eyes of his more fervent and reliable followers by his belated rush to join the winner, then had to start a war all of his own: against the advice of his generals, he attacked Greece. Likewise, Hitler's war against the Soviet Union might have brought him less disaster had he conducted it with less regard for the requirements of propaganda — trying to take Moscow, to advance to the Caucasus and to the Volga, to hold on to untenable lines.[35]

Propaganda thus becomes responsible for the truly weird aspect of reality in the fascist world. Facts can no longer be evaluated in their own terms. Decisions are made according to the way in which events fit into the pattern of ideological propaganda, rather than in relation to actual events. Reality becomes a front, a shadow play, an affirmation of power. Not only the propagandist, but even the allegedly all-powerful leader and policy-maker, loses his grip on the real world and ends by chasing his own fantasies.

The Fascist propagandist, who started out by falsifying and distorting reality, is finally caught at his own game. He has to precipitate the *Götterdämmerung* he had predicted.

Long before the final holocaust, however, the spell of propaganda has lost its magic. With its symbols worn thin, its slogans emptied of meaning, and its language grown trite, its devices become self-defeating, its rituals are mockingly performed in the face of belying reality, its images are evoked in ironical quotation marks: "Of course, we all follow the Führer — into death," quoth the Berlin worker. The winking of the eye now accompanies every communication as the mirage of a sham reality vanishes.

What is true of the totalitarian party in power also applies to the totalitarian movement on its rise to power. Unless the leader can provide the daily miracle or delusion, his charisma wears off. Unlike other parties, founded upon more permanent interests, totalitarian movements rarely survive defeat. Unless they proceed to quick conquest, they falter; their membership is fickle, their vote-gathering appeal subject to wide fluctuations. Experience has shown that they thrive on being appeased, especially if their enemies make ideological concessions giving nourishment to their dreams; it has also shown that, confronted with determined opposition and firmly forced to face real problems, the leader will lose his power and his magic will dissolve.

7

Reflections on
the Spanish Civil War

Introductory note:

In 1938 my book *Espagne Creuset Politique* (Spain: A Political Crucible) was published in Paris. It dealt with the Spanish Civil War up to the battle fought in Barcelona during May of 1937. In that battle the anarchists, supported by syndicalists, Trotskyists of many shades, and homeless socialists, engaged the Communist forces supported by Russian army officers and advisers and by the central government. The anarchists lost, and that was the end of the revolution within the civil war. One last, short chapter of the book, entitled "La Guerre dévore la Révolution" surveyed the events of the following few months; its last line read: "Mais le peuple espagnol n'aura pas dit son dernier mot"(But the Spanish people has not yet spoken its last word).

Almost thirty years later, a publisher in Buenos Aires decided to republish the book in Spanish. He was unable to find me, and for good reason: *Espagne Creuset Politique* had been published under a pen name — though a transparent one to my friends: *Paechter* is the German word for dirt farmer, and *Rabasseire* the Catalan word. Only after the book had been translated and set in print did the editor happen to locate me in New York; by then it was too late for major changes. He allowed me to add, after that final line, a section on the international repercussions of the war and, in particular, on the hideous story of "nonintervention."

Here is the introduction I wrote in 1965 for *España Crisol Político*:

Sweet is the remembrance even of bitterness. As long as one does not forget the tragedy one has watched, one clings to the hope that it has not been in vain. This book, written under the direct impression of the events, is therefore a gift which the past has given to the future. It carries the thoughts and the illusions we cherished during the Popular Front years; it carries our judgments and mistakes, our hatreds and hopes. It is lived history. The emotions and the opinions it reflects may be rejected as untrue by historians; at the time I wrote them down they were true and sincere.

As I look through my book, I find myself in a strange position. To be sure, the information we have now is much more solid; it can either confirm or refute the prevailing hypotheses of 1938. Still, I do not dare rewrite *Espagne Creuset Politique* in the light of recent research or straighten out judgments that would no longer stand up to rigorous examination. I have a feeling that this book is a human document which belongs to the companions of yesteryear, and that any changes would do violence to it. That is why I warmly assented when I was invited to republish the book as a simple document without depriving it of its original freshness and its contemporary flavor. Oh yes, I would have liked to dig in archives, to read again all those memoirs, all those pamphlets; but that would have taken years, and it would have been a completely new book. Anyway, the bibliographic note at the end of *España Crisol Político* shows that by now there are enough books that sum up the new information.

I therefore contented myself with adding three short chapters to round out the book, with correcting a few outright errors in the text, and with completing the bibliographical notes, the references, and other useful information. The revisions I did make are of a rather technical nature, and I marked them as later additions.

I did not change any of the opinions expressed — not because I am doctrinaire but, on the contrary, because then I would have had to change too much. The perspective of 1965 superimposes important corrections on the historical panorama of 1936. In the first place, we can tell now that the Spanish revolution was not the beginning of a new era but the end of a chain of occurrences that started with the English revolution of 1642, went through the French Revolution, the 1848-49 revolutions, the Paris Commune, and the Russian revolutions of 1905 and 1917 — to mention only the most classic events. The debates reflected in this book have much in common with those between Cromwell and the Levelers, the discussions in the Paris Commune, and Lenin's arguments with the syndicalist opposition. In the Chinese revolution and those of Algeria and Ghana we do not find parallels; there, and even in Cuba, the totalitarian party imposed its nationalist ideology and its anticolonialist concept — elements that never played a part in the great social transformations before the war.

The Second World War was, I believe, a historic turning point. The political evolution after it was radically different from preceding developments; so we cannot hope that the lessons of the Paris Commune or of the Spanish Civil War can be directly transferred to future battles. The problems will take an entirely different shape. Not that the place we accord the Civil War in our view of history, or in our hearts, would be diminished in any way. But those who come later will emphasize the fundamental human attitudes rather than the political lessons to be drawn from it. The paltry quarrels will recede into the historical netherworld where they deserve to be buried; the great examples, the principles, the ideas will assume highest importance.

In 1938 I still saw Spanish events in the context of the strife between the Popular Front and the Axis powers. Behind Franco, enemy of the Republic, stood Hitler, enemy of all mankind. Antifascism was the ideology of the Second World War, as it was the ideology of the Spanish Civil War. Moreover, the epic Russian defense against the Nazi invasion recalled the Spanish people's resistance to the intervention. This resemblance, however, is superficial; it ignores the reversal of coalitions in 1939. The Second World War, unleashed by the aggressive alliance between Hitler and Stalin, was waged for national aims, while the Spanish Civil War began as a class war and its international repercussions — which we exaggerated at the time — proved to be negligible. Actually, the defense of the Republic had nothing in common with the wars of conquest that shook the world from 1939 to 1945, and ever since.

It has been said that the Spanish Civil War was "the dress rehearsal for the Second World War." That indeed is what it looked like to us, in 1938. We assumed that the great democracies and the Soviet Union would be forced, sooner or later, to unite against the fascist aggressors; we could not believe that France would permit the establishment, right across the Pyrenees, of a military government that would be Hitler's and Mussolini's natural ally. Nor was it a secret that Indalecio Prieto and Juan Negrín — both socialists, both high officials in the republican government — had no hope for the Republic except in a world war between the fascist and the antifascist powers.

In fact, none of this came to pass. Stalin was Hitler's ally until Hitler pushed him into the arms of Churchill and Roosevelt — and as it happened, all four of them were enemies of the Spanish Republic. The Germans and the Italians pulled out of Spain, and Franco surprised everybody by proving very independent from his soul-mates. The British, having bet on him, enjoyed his benevolent neutrality after France had fallen. In short, I fail to see what so many view as the continuity between the Spanish Civil War and the world war. At the most, we can say that the international intrigue had grafted itself on the civil war which, just the same, had peculiarly Spanish roots.

This leads me to ideas which in 1938 would have seemed entirely heretical and even suspect to me. We saw the Spanish Republic, and the International Brigades defending it, as the vanguard of world antifascism. Hence, it was essential that they should hold out as long as humanly possible — until the final day of reckoning with the Axis powers. No matter what one may say of Negrín and the Communists, of their desperate stubbornness, their inordinate resistance, even their terrible and cruel mistakes, which, in the battles of Teruel and on the Ebro, cost so many lives — all that seemed to fall into a superior strategic plan which in its turn justified all that blood and all those tears.

Looking back, I wonder if one had the right to prolong the suffering beyond the point where Franco was in a position to demand unconditional surrender. If the coup of Colonel Segismundo Casado, trying to secure an honorable surrender to Franco, had happened before the battle of Teruel, at a time when the republican army was still a formidable force and France could still threaten to open its borders to arms deliveries, perhaps one could have obtained more favorable peace terms. But our antifascist sensibility and our republican uprightness did not allow such thoughts at that time. They were permissible only to those who, even at that time, recognized that the Civil War was a Spanish matter. Who would have said that? We were convinced that the Civil War had universal significance. To realize the difference between that worldwide repercussion of a national event on the one hand and the particular interaction between that event and the international situation on the other — to realize *that* difference one had either to be a monster of professorial logic or lack all moral sense. One *owed* it to the militants to sacrifice them to the cause.

In recognizing the Spanish character of the Civil War, we are led to wonder: was it also necessary, beyond the material sacrifices, to sacrifice so many spiritual concerns to the conduct of the war? In my 1938 introduction I had said:

> War is the supreme judge who divides people, ideas, and social organisms, who imposes his laws even on those who want to exempt themselves. War requires everyone to take sides and take responsibility. The bullet hits not only the enemy; it shakes up the ranks of the undecided and, by ricochet, acts on the ranks of the friendly. War establishes the liaison between disparate events; civil war expands onto the international plane, and vice-versa.... War requires everyone to select his alliances. Groups that thought themselves enemies discovered they were marching together. The ballot was replaced by other means of expression: rifles, and feet. The great organizations found themselves reduced to the most primitive state, to the purest ambiance they had ever known, where the love of the brother-in-arms and the hatred of the enemy replaced every other idea, every mystic final aim. The end is nothing, the movement is all; violence constitutes law.

Today I am more inclined to see this deadly concatenation as the great tragedy of revolutionary Spain. Spain permitted the war to make the law, and Spain died of it. Even while the war was in progress, there were those who, rather than assuming responsibility for conducting the war, rather than bowing to its necessities, would have preferred to maintain the purity of libertarian ideas. I did not

6.   Spanish Civil War: Popular Front Women, 1936

(Photo: Ullstein Bilderdienst, Berlin)

share their way of thinking, and I am still proud of the antifascist unity which, until May 1937, manifested itself so gloriously in the cooperation of all the labor organizations; but I now give greater credit to Diego Abad de Santilla and Professor Camillo Berneri, who at an early hour criticized this attitude: they warned us that one cannot put an ideology or a revolutionary organization on ice and hope to find it fresh when the war is over.

This debate, which has its echo in my book, is the old problem of ends and means. When the libertarians submitted to the discipline of war, they did not think they were disarming their cause. As for the Communists, they have always boasted of being Machiavellians; they never hesitated to make use of all the means necessary to attain

7.   Spanish Civil War: Departure of Federación Anarquista Ibérica (FAI) Tank from
Madrid to the Northern Front, 1936

(Photo: International Institute of Social History, Amsterdam)

an end — in this case to establish a war machine. I believe that the
Spanish Civil War can teach us an important lesson on the relationship between ends and means. The anarchists proved themselves
men of responsibility and discipline when they felt it was necessary
to submit to the laws of war. In doing so, they did not abandon their
essential position; on the contrary, they recast the terms under which

Spanish society could be transformed. But instead of taking this transformation into their own hands, they allowed others to organize it. These others, the Communists, proved themselves irresponsible and terror-minded when they imposed the transformations needed for the war.

Today I believe that the difference between anarchists and Communists was primarily a rivalry not between social-revolutionary and individualist-counterrevolutionary ideologies but between two different ways of fighting, between two different types of people representing two different attitudes to life and to politics. I know that many of my old comrades will not agree; but it seems to me that we have become immobilized, to no good purpose, in a purely ideological position. Certain comrades have argued that the workers of the world would have risen to defend a Spanish revolution had it not been suppressed by the Communists. Well, we had better admit that this was an illusion. The French workers — to mention only them — were neither ready to overthrow the counterrevolutionary Chautemps and Daladier governments nor prepared to risk war with Hitler. This is the simple truth even if it is sickening.

It is equally hard to admit that certain positive measures taken by the Negrín government grew out of the situation. That does not mean we should endorse this cabinet's negative and counterrevolutionary measures. Indeed, to ask "war or revolution?" is to frame the question falsely, as if there always were just that one choice. As if one could not defend the Republic in its war without repressing the revolution. As if the success of the revolution would have been impossible without abandoning the Republic—the way Negrín and his admirers, the historians Hugh Thomas and Gabriel Jackson, understand it. To a faulty question there can be only faulty answers. We must reject the choice. The challenge was exactly to defend the Republic without abandoning the power which the libertarians, defending it, had gained.

I want to say a word about the Republic and the republicans too. As I reread my book, I feel that I may have treated them too condescendingly, or that I may have given an impression that nothing good could have come out of their parliamentary system. At that time we were very impatient. But the more recent experience of so many revolutionary governments has shown us the difficulties which a revolution in an underdeveloped country faces. We must count Spain among the nations that were, both politically and economically, poorly prepared for democracy. Every single time it set out to solve one of its central problems — the latifundia, the power of the church, education, the army, the monopolies — it risked civil war.

I would say therefore that the civil war was inevitable precisely because the revolution was inevitable. Certain writers have pondered the possibility of a more conciliatory politics, or they have tried to pinpoint the group or the leader that was the culprit. Presumably they were swayed by notions of a worldwide Popular Front or of an international conspiracy that incited innocent Spaniards to kill each other off; or else they charged "foreign influences" — a notion that lives on in the indestructible legend that Largo Caballero had himself called "the Spanish Lenin." We must realize that Spain is unique and original and that the ideas as well as the fury of its war are altogether Spanish.

I admit that next to Don Quixote there is always Sancho Panza. But it is the Quixotic trait that has given the Civil War universal significance and has made this experience into a deeply human epic. The Spanish libertarians accepted the battle because they abominated voluntary submission more than they feared defeat. Whenever they had to choose between submission and resistance, the Spanish people chose rebellion.

The rebellion against injustice defines justice; insurgence against servitude defines freedom; revolt against evil defines good. Every thought starts out as a negation of something imperfect. To ensure the future we must find fault with the present. To affirm that man is good we must admit that people are foolish. Here is the simple explanation of the mystery that libertarian thought is at the same time naive and subtle, affirmative and censorious. Man becomes human by outgrowing the animal; society becomes human by outgrowing foolishness.

We hope that the boy, as he learns to master his capacities, will grow into a man. The same way, we hope that society will civilize itself. But unlike the child, who has mentors to teach him, humanity has to teach itself, and it can grow only by rebelling against itself. The adolescent is the enemy of the child, man is the enemy of the youth.

As long as man is deprived of the right to develop, he will be a rebel. The humanist ideal drives him to rise against those who would deny him, and often his need to aspire after the common weal is stronger than his instinct to survive. Man is able to conceive this ideal and to sacrifice himself for it. Rebellion thus is a natural force that one cannot deny without mutilating the very idea of man.

This is an attitude rather than a politics, and if I want to be of service to my friends, I have to risk being rude. We cannot achieve a humane society by neglecting the problem of power. The Spanish experience has shown that power cannot be left to those who love power. The defeat of the libertarian movement in Spain was not an accident. The movement abounded with magnanimous ideas and ardent hopes. But it lacked precise theories. Its social aims were as vague as its organizational principles. It was utopian in the sense of counting upon a profound and spontaneous transformation of human attitudes responding to a rapid transformation of the social climate. Well, a paradox occurred. Anarchism, a warrior's system par excellence, was undone by the war. The humane rebellion against the inhuman system did not automatically produce a humane system. Here is a movement that has to renew itself after each victory. It can never be content with a battle won; it must always pit the humanitarian ideal, remote and unrealized, against reality, contemporary and limited. The ideal is infinite; life unrolls finitely. Politics, by definition, is the application of practical and feasible means to obtain gradual progress. The integral revolution, by contrast, the one that anarchist theory had forecast until 1936, was an apocalypse—the famous "leap into the realm of Freedom" of which Engels had spoken.

One would like to go on dreaming that this leap is possible — or rather, one would like to think of liberation as a cause always to be pursued, a cause one can approach but never reach. A romantic and revolutionary thought, worthy of the greatest libertarian thinkers. But Augustin Souchy, in his beautiful book *El Socialismo Libertario,* is right in calling the idea of a permanent revolution absurd: Far from liberating the individual, it would put him in a state of progressive militarization. This is exactly the criticism which libertarians raise against the pseudorevolutionary systems of Nkrumah, Sukarno, and Mao Tse-tung: the warriors of the totalitarian and permanent revolution cannot maintain their dynamism without unearthing "enemies" (especially abroad), "spies," and "traitors," and without pushing their *aficionados* further on the totalitarian and military road.

Here is the profound difference between the Spanish resistance to totalitarian attack and the postwar totalitarian revolutions. We live in a new age where people voluntarily submit to domination by political, economic, and mechanical machines. We must start anew to pass judgment on the great bureaucracies, on the apparatuses of state and party, on managers and opinion-makers.

The libertarian fight, culminating in the supreme effort of the Spanish workers in 1936, has to constitute itself in new forms in the postwar societies. Certain demands for the improvement of daily life have been fulfilled; in certain countries the poor enjoy television as they remain disinherited; certain countries, formerly under the colonial yoke, are now "free" even though the people are still deprived of any participation in conducting their affairs. The conditions have changed; the task is still the same; the problems, too, that stand in the way of the noble libertarian cause are still the same.

THREE

Nationalism
and Internationalism

8

The Problem of Imperialism

The Question Asked: There are superpowers that maintain bases and troops on foreign soil, wage war in faraway countries, provide others with arms worth billions of dollars a year, and influence the foreign as well as domestic policies of other countries. These superpowers define their own foreign policy in terms of a historic world struggle with one or two other expansionist powers, and it is on the ambitions of these mighty nations that smaller countries rely for their own protection. Clearly, any such power must be called imperialist by any definition of that term.

Yet, to say this is not to say much. Any structure as powerful as the United States, the Soviet Union, the People's Republic of China or, for that matter, the Lever Brothers Company, the United Fruit Company, Metro-Goldwyn-Mayer, the Ford Foundation, or the Roman Catholic Church, is bound to engage others of its kind in a power struggle that affects the interests, and often the fate, of the bystanders. Size itself provides opportunities and engenders a dynamism of its own; expansion feeds on further expansion, and hegemony makes enemies. To be rescued by Big Brother may seem almost as painful as to be swallowed by the Big Bad Bully.

The limited concerns of small nations are distorted when they are projected on the screen of world politics, which is of much more vital interest to the larger nations. Such big-power supremacy is resented, even if exercised without malice and intent — as Gulliver found out in Liliput.

Dissent, September–October 1970.

Still, a definition that explains imperialism as a mere byproduct of size is unsatisfactory. Imperialism is a deliberate, well-profiled policy, executed with powerful means and accompanied by an ideology that justifies the striving for empire and domination. Size with direction, expansion with deliberate intent, display of power, the wielding of influence abroad — these are the characteristics of imperialism. The question is: Whose interests does this effort serve? What motives or instigations stand behind it?

The question cannot be begged through including these driving forces in the definition. If one were to follow Lenin in viewing imperialism as "the last stage of capitalism,"[1] that would be an answer. But then another word would have to be found for the policies of Japan in 1894, in 1905, in 1931, and in 1941; obviously, when Japan first took Korea and Formosa it was not capitalistic, and when it attacked the United States it was not in the last stage of capitalism. If one were to follow Ronald Segal, whose book has been widely acclaimed in Europe,[2] imperialism would be seen largely as a matter of white domination over colored races — which, again, puts the analyst at a loss to explain the U.S. interventions in the Caribbean area and Europe, or the Soviet invasions of Hungary and Czechoslovakia. The only correct way to approach the question is by first isolating the phenomena of imperialism and colonialism and then asking whether they are perhaps connected and how they are related to the social structure of the country afflicted by these practices.

The answer is pregnant with political consequences. Should we conclude that America is inherently racist, colonialist, and expansionist, that our interventions in Cuba, Santo Domingo, and Vietnam were prompted by corporate influences in the White House, that the wars this country has fought were the *inevitable* consequences of our not-so-free enterprise system? Then our political outlook would have to be gloomy. On the other hand, we might start with the more benevolent assumption that blunders have been committed by individuals who were perhaps ignorant or had miscalculated the effects of their decisions; that we had stumbled into quagmires from which we did not know how to extricate ourselves and had gotten involved without knowing how.

8.   Lenin on Red Square, Moscow, May Day 1919
(Photo: Keystone Press Agency, New York)

In the first case, imperialism is the manifestation of a rotten system that will produce My Lais over and over again; any attempts to reform the monster then are futile, naive delusions, and unless a revolution comes to rescue us, we can only watch and wait for humanity to be blown to pieces.

If, however, imperialism is not institutional or "systemic," if it is not inherent in the structure of American politics and business, if imperialism is but a policy one can adopt or reject, perhaps a series of blunders, perhaps even the willful extravaganza of idealistic dreamers or the brutal pursuit of special interests by the military, certain corporations, or demagogues who thrive on chauvinism — then wise reforms or political action can curb such arrogance of power, and the outlook will be more hopeful.[3]

The latter view is held by the followers of Senators Eugene McCarthy and James William Fulbright, by the large majority of those engaged in the Moratorium movement, by the democratic left and all those whom Lenin contemptuously called petty-bourgeois pacifists; their protest is in the populist tradition of Bryan and La Follette. But the same view is also held by neoisolationist writers who are not necessarily committed to social reform, such as Professors Morgenthau and Kennan, and even by many people who must be counted among the right: followers of the old isolationist school, the Republican opponents of American intervention in the two world wars and the Korean war, the late Senators Taft and Langer, and the *Wall Street Journal*, which is as critical of the Vietnam War as it was of the Korean.

The pessimistic view is held by the New Left, by the more militant leaders of the Black Liberation movement, by the orthodox Marxist-Leninists who reject America as the country of monopoly capitalism. Despite Khrushchev's doctrine of coexistence, most Communists abroad, too, hold to Lenin's vision that imperialism is the apogee of capitalism and its apocalypse. None of this is surprising. What comes as a shock is that a large non-Marxist segment of public opinion in the Western countries and in the underdeveloped world also views U.S. policies as determined basically by the structure of its economy.

This kind of economic determinism is no longer tenable. *Specific* class and professional interests and certain industries or corporations do stand to profit from imperialistic policies and armament. But to name these, to analyze, denounce and fight their influence, is not tantamount to the proposition that "American capitalism" — an abstraction—brings forth another abstraction, imperialism. Nor is there an "intermediate position" or third choice: it is necessary to decide whether American capitalism is inevitably, inextricably, and fatally bound up with imperialism, or whether the two must be dealt with in separate, different ways. Before going into details, however, here is a preliminary definition: imperialism is a complex of political, diplomatic, military, financial, and economic strategies to secure the hegemony of one nation over others. Overlapping with, but distinct from, imperialism, the term colonialism shall mean — for the length of this essay — the subjection of one nation by another for purposes of economic exploitation. Our aim is precisely to determine the relationship of these two terms in the conduct of U.S. foreign affairs.

Economic Interpretations

The indictment of U.S. imperialism as inspired by business needs is neither new nor convincing. "Confident access to raw materials is a necessary precondition for industrial expansion into new or existing fields of technology.... America's ability to procure at will such materials.... is one of the keystones of its economic power.... The stakes are vast...."[4] This view was very popular before the First World War; Karl Kautsky, one-time grand oracle of Marxism, defined imperialism as the policy of an advanced power to secure sources of raw materials, and he observed that the United States needed no overseas colonies, for it treated its South as a colony.[5]

Strangely, the same argument has also been used in reverse. Apologists of imperialism claimed *Lebensraum* for their respective fatherlands and proposed to make them self-sufficient (autarkic) in case of war. To such ideologies Sir Charles Dilke and other British opponents of imperialism replied that you don't have to own a country to buy from it. Provided you pay a fair price, the colonies will be only too glad to sell; in fact, they may complain—as do our Latin neighbors today — that the metropolis does not buy enough from them.

Here three different processes must be distinguished: the conquest of a colony in order to fence it off for plunder; the use of political and economic advantages to exploit a country commercially by selling dearly and buying cheaply in its market; the "opening" of a country, pulling its economy out of the precapitalist and into the capitalist orbit. Often the three will appear in intimate symbiosis. In India, for instance, the British first reaped enormous extra profits, which they used partly to build up their own industries.[6] Then they excluded others and also prevented the Indians from founding native industries. Eventually, however, they were bound to recognize that in order to sell you have to buy. There is a limit to robbing a country of its treasures, and the primitive methods of enriching one country at the expense of another, which certainly had played a great role in the beginnings of capitalism, lost much of their significance — proportionally — as the forces of capitalism grew. Not that the hunt for gold and diamonds ever stopped, but the method of exploitation had to take a capitalist form. As Marx wrote in the Communist Manifesto: "The need for a constantly expanding market chases the bourgeoisie over the whole surface of the globe. It must settle everywhere, establish connections everywhere. It has given a cosmopolitan character to production and consumption in every country."

This is the third and final mode of expansion: the transformation of precapitalist, self-sufficient producers into capitalist suppliers and customers of the market.

Rosa Luxemburg tried to show that the motor of capitalist accumulation itself creates the need for expansion into noncapitalist areas; as capitalism engulfs all underdeveloped countries and plants become more sophisticated, the struggle for markets grows fiercer; militarism, colonialism, and imperialism are summoned to forestall the crisis.[7] She drew attention to contradictions in classical and Marxian economics, and to real conflicts in capitalist development.

Modern economists have not sustained her theory. Empirically, it fits early capitalism better than the most highly developed countries, which are each other's best customers. It fits America poorly because when the geographical frontier was reached and closed in 1898, new industrial frontiers were opened in depth; capital found outlets for expansion at home and became protectionist. By contrast, if the American farmer wished to retain his liberal orientation, he had to support a foreign policy that was antiimperialist in ideology, though in practice that does not mean antiinterventionist. The farmer, almost everywhere, was chauvinistic. He also was anticapitalist; for he was the victim of the market mechanism. Professor Williams shows that populists, agrarians, free-silverites, and other farm spokesmen tried to impose a "market mentality" on other nations.[8] "Make the Chinese eat American food!" exclaimed one farm editor; cotton exporters felt threatened by the Special Treaty Rights obtained in China by England, Russia, Japan, and Germany. No doubt those who upheld these interests were glad when 2,500 American Marines joined the expeditionary corps to subdue the Boxer Rebellion in 1900; and therefore Williams has called the U.S. "Open Door" policy the fountainhead of imperialism.[9] But President McKinley made it clear that the marines would be withdrawn — and they were — as soon as other nations withdrew their forces. I find it difficult to call this American counterinvention "imperialist" or "colonialist." The interest and aim of American policy in China clearly was to safeguard the political, financial, and commercial independence of the old Middle Kingdom. The point is that the interests of the United States, a latecomer to the power game, happened to coincide with the interests of China, its victim. Today the Soviet Union is in a similar position: as a latecomer, it often can coordinate its interests with those of underling countries. In neither case, though, does the relationship of itself necessarily imply an intention to exploit or dominate.

Naive or demagogic muckrakers are always shocked when they hear the word "profit." Of course America's intervention in China was not motivated by philanthropic concerns. On the contrary, the presidents were defending ordinary business interests. But if words have any meaning, "imperialism" implies an uneven relationship; the safeguarding of trade interests is not the same thing as imperialism. What American business was doing in China and elsewhere reminds us of Karl Marx's paean to the revolutionary force of capitalism, which "has dislodged old wants... creates new wants instead of those satisfied locally... draws even the most barbarian nations into civilization, and batters down every Chinese Wall."

Allegedly, business interests encouraged the annexation of the Philippines as a stepping-stone to the "great China market." Business, however, was hostile to both the Spanish war and the Boxer expedition; U.S. consuls in China constantly complained about the "apathy of American business," and exports to China totaled $16 million in 1910. The "big China market" was, according to Paul A. Varg, "a myth."[10] Nor were our two great rivals in the China tangle, Russia and Japan, "capitalist" powers. The roots of empire lie deeper than trade! (See Political and Psychological Theories, below.)

Big-Business Imperialism

Attempts to reduce "imperialism" either to the desire for imports or to the need for markets in general have been unsuccessful. In 1902 John A. Hobson offered a theory that has remained most influential because it links big business, and in particular monopoly, with both imperialism and colonialism: monopoly prevents a fair distribution of purchasing power; therefore the economy of the metropolitan states becomes more vulnerable to depressions; investment becomes risky and the trust magnates find more money on their hands than they can employ profitably; hence they seek new investment opportunities abroad.[11]

"The adventurous enthusiasm of President Theodore Roosevelt must not deceive us," Hobson wrote. "It was Messrs. Rockefeller, Pierpont Morgan and their associates who needed Imperialism... because they desired to use the public resources of their country to find profitable employment for their capital which otherwise would be superfluous."[12]

Hobson felt that a more equal distribution of incomes, tougher antitrust laws, and vigorous trade union action could eliminate the calamity of surplus capital in the hands of Morgan. Hence, for him imperialism was not inevitable. It was a cancer, a parasitical, retrogressive, stultifying force, a bastard child of capitalism that honest business could and would have to repudiate. Although he denounced the "economic taproot of imperialism," he thought the interests that were riding the nationalist bandwagon were illegitimate; their unhealthy influence could be defeated.

Many Americans share a vulgarized version of this view. They think that directors of, say, United Fruit or Grace Line or ESSO routinely inform the State Department or the president about American interests in each particular country. Do not their agents abroad work hand-in-glove with the U.S. ambassadors? Do not their lobbies dominate a Congress that is as uninformed as its voters? By default, its decisions usually favor the special interests. Presidents have indeed performed small and large services for their corporate campaign contributors; ambassadors have naively assumed that what is good for American corporations is good not only for America but for the natives, too. They identify (or confuse) the presence of American corporations abroad with American prestige and influence.

This is not peculiar to the twentieth century. Goethe wrote that "the Trinity of trade, war, and piracy cannot be split"; Sir Thomas More complained that "everywhere do I perceive a certain conspiracy of rich men seeking their advantage under the name and pretext of the Commonwealth." The reek of corruption that Hobson smelled in imperialism had been there for a long time — even in antiquity, when as virtuous a senator as Marcus Junius Brutus used the army to collect a debt from a Greek city. Corruption, however, is not an explanation but an effect; scandal-mongering and moral indignation do not overthrow the capitalist system.

The Marxists Rudolf Hilferding and V.I. Lenin used Hobson's theory by turning it right-side up:[13] imperialism is not the bastard child of capitalism but its legitimate scion, "the last stage of capitalism" — "last" in three senses: the latest, the most highly developed, and the terminal stage; capitalism at the point of its supreme organization but already toppling over into ruin and waiting to be replaced by socialism. The brilliance of Lenin's work resides entirely in this Hegelian approach: imperialism is systemic, inevitable, and fatal. Its root is not corruption, but corruption is the inevitable consequence of monopoly capitalism as it has developed in this century, with its intertwining of finance and manufacturing capital, its cartels and trusts, its fierce struggle for hegemony in the world. This capitalism has become destructive and is digging its own grave; but it has not stopped revolutionizing the world. In its deterministic radicalism Lenin's theory is unsurpassed and still attractive to modern Marxists who feel that a revolutionary theory must give a comprehensive picture of a system of evil riding to its inevitable doom. Magdoff and Baran have offered American versions of Lenin's view.[14] I shall address myself to this theory later; first I wish to complete my survey with a brief glance at the noneconomic theories.

Political and Psychological Theories

Pizarro may have looked for gold; the Spanish king and nobles wanted domination, rule over others, power. When Kipling speaks of the white man's burden, he certainly does not mean profit; he is describing a way of life — that of the master race, the warrior caste. Even Hobson saw that the imperialist interests "appeal to the lust of domination surviving in a nation from early centuries of animal struggle for existence." He characterized imperialism as an atavism, "a remnant of the roving instinct."[15] And numerous are the literary documents exposing this instinct to rule over the nether breeds.

On this foundation Joseph Schumpeter built his denunciation of imperialism as an atavistic hangover from the feudal order and from barbarian conditions.[16] Speaking from the no-nonsense viewpoint of the enlightened capitalist, he held that war is bad business and empires cost too much. Pointing to the Assyrians, the Babylonians, the Egyptians, and the Romans, he denied that empire-building has any specific connection with capitalism, which is by nature rational; in contrast, he emphasized the irrational nature of imperialism, its restless, mindless drive for more and more expansion, its hunger for power and more power without any reasonable objective or definable limit. In fact, this compatriot of Freud called imperialism a disease, the madness of a ruling class going to seed, a sure sign of decadence, the fulfillment of a death instinct. Drawing on the experience of his native Austria, Schumpeter saw monopoly and imperialism as creatures of the feudal state; militarism and chauvinism he saw as means to maintain the hierarchical structure of society.

An obvious objection to this view is the question, Why, then, did the middle class so avidly follow imperialist ideals? Is it not reasonable to assume that the bourgeoisie was using the feudalist fantasies, the Holy Grail, the Quest for Glory, Superman, and National

Honor merely as a screen for its very material interests? In the framework of a capitalist society all ideologies must serve the profit motive. This answer underestimates the radicalism of Schumpeter's attack on the only imperialism he knew: in its servility the bourgeoisie had adopted the values of its feudal rulers. It had not outgrown its political swaddling clothes even while it enthusiastically supplied the "sinews of war"; it did so enthusiastically, no matter how badly its material interests were hurt, precisely because those atavistic notions were stronger than economic rationality. This was even more true of the peasants, though their interests were even less identical with those of imperialism.

Leaving psychology aside, most historians define imperialism simply in terms of power. It occurs when one national state encroaches on the power of other nation-states. It is nationalism writ large when it enters world politics. Carlton Hayes, authority on nineteenth-century history, doubted that "the flag has to follow trade or investments." Although he admitted that "once flag-raising became common and competitive, economic considerations undoubtedly spurred [the Powers] to greater efforts," he held that "basically the new imperialism was a nationalistic phenomenon; it followed hard on the wars that created Germany and Italy and that brought Russia within sight of Constantinople." He considered England's and France's conquest of Africa "a fearful reaction [to Bismarck's successes], an ardent desire to recover national prestige."

Other historians saw imperialism before the world wars as the struggle for "mastery in Europe."[17] Is it not a fact that the great ententes of 1902 and 1907 settled the colonial rivalries between France and England in Africa, between Japan, England, and Russia in the Far East, between England and Russia in the Near East and Central Asia? Is it not a fact that England offered the German kaiser advantageous arrangements in the Near East and Africa if only he would renounce the naval race? Is it not a fact that German diplomacy used its business interests in the Maghreb and in Anatolia merely as small change on the bargaining counter of "high policy," where the stakes were not profits but superiority and power? The First World War broke out, not because the Powers could not agree on how to distribute the colonies — they had agreed — but because none could back down in a game of chicken without losing its standing in the concert of Europe. This also applies to the cold war.

Whose interests were being served by these contests of prestige, which ultimately hurled Europe into two world wars? James Mill called imperialism "a vast system of outdoor relief for the upper classes." Hobson remarked that in jingo politics the sports-loving upper crust is joined by the sensation-hungry mob. Hannah Arendt has shown how the dregs of all classes—lumpen proletariat, lumpen bourgeoisie, lumpen aristocrats, and lumpen intellectuals — find expression of their resentments in racism and imperialism.[18] Healthy, progressive capitalists create fields for innovation at home; the misfits, the adventurers, the freebooters — an Evelyn Cromer, a Cecil Rhodes, a Carl Peters — go abroad, found empires, and fire the imagination of other rootless people. It is not surprising to find their jingoism in frequent alliance with anticapitalist, pseudosocialist, anti–Semitic ideas.[19] Likewise, the shaky businesses are the ones that lobby for protective tariffs, empire preference, and similar schemes to milk the nation instead of serving it. Agriculture — the one industry that in most European countries is least capable of survival and decidedly underdeveloped — also is the most protectionist and jingoist.

In England, Austria, and Germany the big estates were the cradle of the caste that provided the empires with army officers and satraps. For both Junkers and gentry, protectionism and imperialism were vital in their fight to stay in power. Their estates could not compete with American farmers; their privileged position in the hierarchical structure of European society was under attack.[20] Their pernicious alliance with big industry in the conservative parties made the First World War inevitable. Professor Fritz Fischer has shown the intertwining of business and state interests in the kaiser's "world political" saber rattling.[21] His research brings out two things: the middle class could hope to gain prestige only by throwing itself into the role of the military caste; and in prewar imperialism the retrogressive, parasitical interests were far more prominent than the modernizing interests. We may add a third conclusion, to be drawn from the literature of imperialism: the empire was a safeguard of the domestic class structure. It absorbed those who did not fit into the establishment and diverted those who might have attacked it. It overawed those who might have doubted the wisdom of the upper classes, and forced all to find their places on the ladder of domination.

Imperialism and Colonialism

It is easy to cite outrageous feats of financial piracy or enormous profits made by some freebooters and imperial freeloaders. Some of these operators may have had an illegitimate, surreptitious influence in some policy-makers' back rooms. But this proves the opposite of Lenin's thesis, for the colonialists were not typical capitalists. The great pre–World War I struggle between the powers was for supremacy in Europe — a supremacy that certainly included economic power but must be seen in the context of domination, hegemony, exercise of power, rivalry, and security.

This brings me to a further distinction. Normally, we can point out an empire on the map: the Egyptian, the Roman, the Inca empire, they all had boundaries. The Chinese emperor even built a wall; in England and Germany we still see the ruins of Hadrian's wall, which once enclosed the Roman Empire. In Berlin a wall was erected under our very eyes. In brief, an empire seems to be a well-defined area, a territory dominated by one nation. When speaking of the British and Dutch empires, however, a map is not sufficient; one needs a globe. There is no land connection between the various parts of the empire.

This is usually called colonialism, a term based on the "saltwater fallacy": if an army conquers a neighboring country by the sword, riding on horses, or rolling in tanks, that may be imperialism but it is forgiven sooner or later; who cares today about the independence of the Circassians or Texas? People get used to seeing a larger area on the map colored yellow or blue and forget that a subjugated nation lives there. If, on the other hand, a ship is boarded to cross salt water to conquer a foreign tribe, that is colonialism — very reprehensible and never forgotten or forgiven. The Decolonization

Committee of the United Nations cannot by its Charter debate "contiguous territories." It cannot deal with Biafra, Kashmir, the Kurds, or with the Baltic and Caucasian nations in the Soviet Union; neither with Tibet and Sinkiang nor with the blacks in the Sudan or the Berbers in Morocco. The Russian invasions of Hungary and Czechoslovakia also concerned contiguous territories: they were imperialistic but by the U.N.'s definition not colonialist — even though those countries are clearly exploited and subjugated. Nehru refused to be bothered by the invasion of Hungary because that was not colonialism; India holds sovereignty over the Nagas. It would be better to speak of colonialism only where the relationship is exploitative, where it benefits one side more than the other in terms of money. One should speak of imperialism when a relationship is primarily of a political and military nature. Although in many cases the two will go together, more often than not they are distinct and different.

Imperialism Without Empire

The U.S. empire cannot be found on any map or globe, yet it is worldwide. The United States has no colonies to speak of; the few it has retained serve strategic purposes. But it has been accused of financial colonialism or neocolonialism, and the loudest outcry against American domination comes, not from underdeveloped countries whose raw materials the United States buys but from the most highly industrialized nations, which have themselves practiced imperialism and colonialism in the recent past: France and Japan.[22] Through political pressure U.S. corporations have infiltrated the allied economies and exploit them in subtle, and often not so subtle, ways.[23] A "superimperialism" is said to overarch the old colonial and neocolonial countries. Thus we have the following types of domination:

> 1. Territorial imperialism: old-fashioned rule over conquered nations.

2. Naval colonialism: exploitation of less-developed nations by settlers and managers, usually with political rule.

3. Neocolonialism: domination of newly independent countries by investors or traders, usually without political rule.

4. Superimperialism: domination or hegemony of a superpower over developed economies and independent countries that themselves may exploit other countries, thus forming a pyramid of primary and secondary dependencies.

In this tableau the United States is in very distinguished company. Ancient Athens certainly was an imperial power, although it owned no territory beyond the barren rocks of Attica. Medieval Venice was built on even less land, but it ruled the waves and financed the crusades, which always ended up in places where the Venetians needed trading posts. Of course, all these major naval powers — Athens, Venice, the United States, Genoa, and even the Phoenicians — were commercial republics, and they were ruled by the rich. Socrates could afford to loaf in the marketplace because his wife managed a lucrative export business. The Athenians were democratic at home, but they spoke harshly to their allies and they dealt brutally with defectors. Here is how they lectured the unhappy citizens of Melos:

> Of the Gods we believe and of men we know that by a necessary law of nature they rule wherever they can. We did not invent this law, we are only following it.... If you are well advised, you will not think it dishonorable to submit to the greatest city in Hellas when it makes you the modest offer to become its ally without ceasing to enjoy the country that belongs to you.[24]

In Thucydides, this speech is only a few pages away from that other Athenian oration, the first and proudest manifesto of democracy — Pericles' famous celebration of the virtues of Athens and of its idea of government. Indeed, all these maritime republics share one remarkable trait: they fight ideological wars — against dictatorships, against the barbarians, against the infidels. Democracy, freedom, humanism are ideas that claim universality, precisely because they are not nationalistic. Indivisible freedom cannot tolerate areas of servitude. It was natural for Athens to fight for the freedom of cities in Asia, for Venice to fight against the closed society of the Moslem Turks. The United States fought for Freedom of the Seas and proclaimed the principle of the Open Door against those imperial powers that conceived of their empires as fenced-in territories.[25] Woodrow Wilson fought for Collective Security; Franklin D. Roosevelt first quarantined the dictators and then fought for the Four Freedoms and the Atlantic Charter. Truman had to clothe his power conflict with Stalin in the ideological drapes of Anticommunism, Free Enterprise, and Collective Security.

Does this sound suspicious? Are these democracies imperialist because they are commercial?[26] Open Door has meant that a new imperialism tried to pry open some doors that older imperialisms held closed. It has been said that the Monroe Doctrine was proclaimed to fence South America in as a preserved hunting ground for U.S. capital. The trouble with this theory is that in 1823 the United States had little to sell to the American republics and no capital to invest. All documents of that time show that the doctrine was a diplomatic move, designed to assert the independence of U.S. policies. The ideology on which the doctrine was based, however, certainly expressed both America's interests and its "way of life."

Dollar Diplomacy

The Monroe Doctrine was political and self-serving, but it also served the interest of other American nations. Although it asserted the United States' hegemony in this hemisphere, that alone did not mean financial exploitation. The reverse is true: the financial troubles of the Caribbean republics were exploited to ascertain the political ascendancy of the United States. The dollar was the means rather than the motive or the purpose of policy. In China, likewise, the Open Door policy was to stop the Russo-Japanese partition of Manchuria; the State Department asked the ill-famed railroad tycoon Edward Harriman — grandfather of the present champion of liberal imperialism — to save Manchuria by investing a few million dollars there. But Harriman and Morgan found the proposition unprofitable and asked for a government guarantee. When Woodrow Wilson came to power, he refused to endorse the scheme. Ultimately, only thirty miles of railway were built — not in Manchuria but far to the south in Fukien; not one dollar was invested in Manchuria. But the Chinese government could use these tokens of American interest to maintain its independence until the First World War. It is all too clear that U.S. imperialism could not be financial in essence.[27]

If neither trade nor finance drove the United States into expansion, what did? Oddly enough, Jefferson — hardly a representative of finance — talked of annexing Cuba.[28] As the Louisiana Purchase showed, Jefferson had a strong sense of geopolitical realities; he was pursuing power politics, and the presidents after him who coveted the Isthmus of Panama or moved to build a canal and deployed the Marines to protect it, too, were thinking in terms of strategy. Jefferson may be called an imperialist in the old sense, but not according to Lenin's definition.

Nor did the dollar always call in the big stick. President Taft wanted to replace the big stick with subtler means. He defined "the purpose of the present administration... to encourage the use of American capital in the development of China by the promotion of essential reforms." He promised to "remove countries in this hemisphere from the jeopardy involved by heavy foreign debt and from the danger of internal complications due to disorder at home."

His Secretary of State, Philander Knox, sounds almost modern when he says that he could imagine no better use for American dollars than to replace insecurity by stability in neighboring states. "The malady of revolutions and financial collapse is most acute precisely in the region where it is most dangerous to us. It is here that we seek to apply a remedy."[29] Taft and Knox called the technique they were using dollar diplomacy — meaning the deliberate, purposeful exploitation of commercial and financial interests in order to bind other countries to the United States, to further strategic projects, to counteract designs of other powers.

Alas, it is well known where Taft's lofty resolutions led: to outright intervention by Marines in Nicaragua, Honduras, Mexico, Santo Domingo — and this under Woodrow Wilson, of all presidents, who had begun his administration by repudiating dollar diplomacy in China! The United States was talking to its neighbors as Athens had talked to Melos. There is no doubt that its concern with the Caribbean area, its solicitude for the safety of the Panama Canal, its fear of foreign intervention on this continent generated naval and financial imperialism. Inevitably, the United States established five protectorates—states that remained nominally independent but that were governed by U.S. commissars—and interests of a commercial and financial nature were grafted upon this empire.

In the period before the first world war this must still be called hemispheric imperialism. America was not yet a world power. It played no role in the rivalries that led to the catastrophe of 1914; and as we have seen, its imperialism was not primarily motivated by financial interests. Its trade with the Latin American countries was minimal, its investments there negligible; above all, being poor in capital it had no need to export it. The compulsion to expand was not economic but strategic. Financial imperialism — the so-called dollar diplomacy — was a tool, one of the means available for an overall policy; but this tool was soon to dominate the scene. In trying to develop techniques of humane, peaceful intervention, Knox created precisely those financial interests which Hobson and Lenin denounced as the roots of imperialism; the seeds that were planted sprouted like dragons' teeth. It may be necessary to invent a special term for this relationship—pseudocolonialism.

Dilemmas of Power Politics

This leads to a second observation about means, ends, and intentions. In the long run, intentions don't really count. The attempt to stay out of the power game leads straight into it. The Open-Door policy required meddling in the affairs of China; the design to stave off foreign intervention called for intervention; the wish to substitute dollars for bullets ended in more bullets. Worse: ultimate motives and ends initially seem to permit a wide choice of means — some of them, in the beginning and in the intention, even quite humane; but the means then take over and tend to determine the ends.

When the United States established itself as the tutor and guardian of the smaller American republics, it set up exactly the kind of preserved hunting ground that it said it had to deny to the Russians and Japanese in Manchuria. When the United States created a safety zone in this hemisphere, it provided for American capital exactly those opportunities that then, in turn, had to be protected by the Marines. In opposing its competitors' imperialism, the United States had to develop the weapons used by the other imperialists: a two-ocean navy, a military establishment, the draft, a propaganda agency. It occupied bases abroad and tried to influence, nay to dominate, other governments.

Even granting that all this was not done from imperialistic motives, the means certainly were imperialistic, and the old motto of all absolute pacifists was proven once again: in resisting evil one ends by doing evil; in fighting the totalitarians, the United States came to imitate some of their methods. This is the tragedy of all politics, the tragedy of power: it becomes absolute, independent of its purposes. The question is not for a theologian alone; it confronts the honest politician every time he must make a decision that may hurt someone.

The choice of means is hardly a dilemma for dictatorships; they can mold their ideology to fit their policies. The problem plagues democracies whenever they engage in world politics: At some point their ideology will find itself at odds with policy.

The United States has found it expedient, for example, to do business with dictators who are repugnant to this country's democratic sensibilities — Trujillo, Batista, Somoza, Chiang Kai-shek, Diem, Franco. Some say that such alliances disclose the true, reactionary nature of U.S. imperialism. Is guilt revealed by association? The United States did not "support" Franco, but he extorted an exorbitant price for a piece of real estate the U.S. Navy thought it needed; that is a different story. For similar reasons of self-interest the United States "supported" Tito, Nasser, Sukarno, and other part-time heroes of the left. Through the CIA, it even supported Ho Chi Minh[30] and worked against Diem.[31] It caused the downfall of Trujillo and Batista by withdrawing support from them; it offered to support Castro's farm reform.[32]

There may be, in certain circles within and outside the U.S. government, a predilection for military dictators. They are considered reliable anticommunists; their insatiable appetite for military hardware is viewed as a guarantee of their continued dependence on U.S. subsidies; and their notorious inefficiency is supposed to keep them beholden to U.S. "advisers." Lately, however, rats have been found in this brew. Some dictators don't stay bought but find the Russians just as eager to provide them with hardware, or even more amenable than the United States; their appetite transgresses the boundaries that the U.S. deems safe — and the Russians provide them with ideologies and propaganda techniques; they discover expansionist goals of their own, which enhance their popularity. Some proceed to expropriate U.S. property. Still others, like Duvalier, Thieu, Papadopoulos, become so embarrassing that at least part of the U.S. establishment would rather get rid of them.

The U.S. government is not always of one mind. In the case of Greece, for instance, it is well known that the CIA supported the king rather than the generals; in South Vietnam, two factions of the CIA seem to have been pulling in different directions; and its former director, Richard Helms, is known to have been at odds with military intelligence for years. Thus, while the record is by no means edifying, we might conclude this section with the following observations:

U.S. interests have led U.S. policy-makers to support regimes of various descriptions, republican and dictatorial, progressive and reactionary. Among the dictators the United States has supported we must distinguish between those, like the Brazilian and Guatemalan, for which U.S. agents bear direct responsibility, and those, like the Greek and Argentinian, with whom fate has forced the United States into harness on a limited number of policy issues. The record is not consistent and clear at all, but it shows a frequent wavering between extremes. For a while the United States would not recognize any Latin American dictator; then it decided to give the *abrazo* to any leader who actually was in possession of a country.[33] Often American interests pulled in different directions, with the CIA, the army, the ambassador, business interests, and the State Department backing different contenders.

The Rationale of U.S. Interventions

It is often said that the United States supports dictators because they protect American business. Some do protect American business interests, but the conjunction "because" is erroneous. The national interest is not to protect individual American firms but to preserve a system of business, which the American public identifies with its way of life and which the American government considers the alternative to the rival system of communism. In this matter, the American government agrees with Stalin, who said that whoever conquers a territory introduces his own economic system into it. The American empire expresses its presence and exercises its influence through the capitalist mode of operation, for which it keeps as much of the world "open" as possible. It also generally prefers democratic governments that guarantee the free exchange of goods and ideas.

There was an elightened self-interest behind the Marshall Plan and the containment policy of the late 1940s — the twin weapons of the so-called cold war. No doubt it was in the interest of both the American and the European democracies to keep the Soviet armies at bay and to avert the danger of a Communist take-over. To do that, the European economies had to be rebuilt and the reconstruction site had to be shielded. These policies not only helped to restore a capitalist world market, the interest of all parties also demanded a restoration of democracy in those countries of Europe that had lost it; democracy, of necessity, became the watchword of the Western coalition. Hence, like Athens, America fights an ideological war.

In Europe the United States found congenial forces — democratic and capitalistic — to work with. It never was equally chummy with

European dictators. Contrary to the charge that it always uses dictators, it often collaborates with democratic forces and institutions where they are available. Unfortunately, there are not many of them, especially in the Third World — and some that the West mistook for democrats, like Diem, were a disappointment. Yet the United States has given $7 billion to Nehru despite his preference for socialism and his pronounced anti-Americanism; it could not save U Nu in Burma; it loyally supported the socialist Adoula in the Congo against Tshombe, an avowed puppet of the Société Générale. It tried to defend democracy in Argentina against the dictator — to no avail, but not for want of trying. In Peru the U.S. ambassador supported the Acción Popular with President Belaunde and even Haya de la Torre, the venerable leader of the APRA (American Popular Revolution Alliance); in Bolivia the United States supported Paz Estenssoro, in Costa Rica Figueres, in Venezuela the liberal President Betancourt and his successor Leone; in Chile it rooted for Frei. The French even accused the CIA of aiding the Algerian rebels. And Velasco, the Peruvian darling of certain New Leftists, now advertises for American capital!

Where U.S. Business Comes In

Clearly, American and other business interests find a more favorable climate under republican governments than under such populist-nationalist generals as Perón, Ovanda, Velasco, or Nasser. Such pseudorevolutionary leaders were analyzed 120 years ago by Karl Marx; his pamphlet on Louis Napoleon has not been improved upon, nor has the original model. Some of the dictators find it profitable to cast themselves in an antiimperialist role — even while soliciting American investments.[34] In all countries entering the industrial age, labor is being exploited, by native even more cruelly than by foreign capitalists. What is actually a *social* question is made to appear as a *racial or national* question.

In the distorted view of demagogic dictators, class war is being deflected into "wars of national liberation." Paul Baran and Herbert Marcuse have characterized the pseudoprogressive, national-revolutionary governments as "the last and most dangerous disguise of business rule" over developing nations. Indeed, Libya throws the Americans out only to call in the French, and Western firms can do business with dictators of the left as well as of the right. American firms were prepared to work for Castro until he forced a showdown, and only after he had opted for the Russian orbit did Eisenhower break with him. Ceylon and Indonesia were allowed to expropriate oil because, unlike Cuba, they did not at the same time fall into the Russian or Chinese orbit.

These pragmatic policies have paid dividends that could hardly have been expected by the policy-makers. The Marshall Plan was supposed to stop the Russians in Europe, but at the time of its conception American capitalists would not bet their own money on European recovery. They were mistaken.

The Divorce of the State from Business

In recent years something new has been added to the economic structure of the West: the international corporation. Books are already being written about these new corporations, which know no borders and no nationality. They may establish themselves in one country for production purposes, in another for tax purposes. They may be owned by nationals of one country and managed by nationals of another. They know no government and no homeland and are international freebooters, following their interests to any place that may suit them. They even plan across national frontiers. German firms built chemical plants in South Carolina and electric power plants in South America with World Bank financing. Mutual funds overseas also sell shares in U.S. corporations.

The importance of international corporations in world trade is staggering. The gross value of goods produced by U.S.-owned firms or affiliates abroad alone is twice our export of manufactured goods and the equivalent of total consumer expenditure in a good-sized country like Italy. In another context, A.A. Berle has compared the new corporations to nations. They account for a certain percentage of world trade. For all that, it is interesting to note that some of these ventures are not profitable but must be pursued, nevertheless, because businesses are in a growth competition and must be "present" — just as the U.S. government must show a "presence" abroad — wherever a rival has established affiliates. The directors of big business care little what dividends are paid to the stockholders; big business is in a power game just like a state. On the other hand, they think it good business to help build "socialism" in the Soviet Union: Fiat, Mannesmann, and Ford extend credit lines to the "Reds" and calmly listen to the speeches that condemn them as colonialists and imperialists.

The planning of such firms is now global, with loyalties determined by the political situation on each of the continents. Often the profits have to be reinvested locally, so the companies are Arab in the Middle East, Pan-European in the countries of the Common Market; in Latin America they enjoy solidarity with the Hochschilds, the Patiños, and the Aramayos. Far from serving any American interest in Peru, the American owners of the Cerro mines plead in this country the leftist Peruvian junta's case. What matters here is not where the profit goes but where the power resides; while financial control may remain in New York, the thinking of the corporation assumes a "colonial" coloration, and something similar to the managerial revolution might be in the making, eroding the prerogatives of ownership and substituting functional criteria for all other motives.

International corporations may contribute to the development of some countries. More often now they merely seem to transfer business, plant, and managerial staff from a high-tax, high-wage country to one that offers low wages and taxes; or, as in the case of recent investments in Europe, they wish to get in under a customs wire. Such runaway businesses reexport into the United States or to other countries, and the AFL-CIO has charged, not without reason, that they are taking thousands of jobs from American workers, especially from minority people and hard-core poverty areas. These workers are not, as Lenin charged, sharing the profits of colonialism. When State Department officials are confronted with Latin American demands for lower tariffs, they actually may be dealing with front men for international corporations. Nevertheless, it remains U.S. policy to encourage private investment abroad; for governmental and international development aid cannot provide an adequate substitute for the formation of new capital in the under-developed countries themselves.

Now I would submit that these new corporations constitute a phenomenon that is the opposite of imperialism.

Imperialism is definitely and unmistakably tied to the policies of one country or government. The term makes no sense if one cannot point to a government that supports the imperialist or economic interests. An international corporation knows no exports or imports; whether its policies are good or bad, progressive or reactionary, coinciding or colliding with any government interest, they cannot be identical with American imperialism. A corporation may be an octopus, but without a navy it cannot be imperialist; we must stay with our definitions, and we shall see later on that these definitions have social-political meaning.

On balance, of course, more U.S companies operate abroad than foreign companies do here; more U.S. citizens draw income from overseas sources than vice-versa. Nonetheless, the international solidarity of capital seems to be guaranteed institutionally much more firmly than in any previous decade: the new arrangements to protect currencies from speculators, the International Monetary Fund and the World Bank, international cartels and trade agreements constitute an international directorate of banking, industry, and commerce. When, sixty years ago, Walther Rathenau wrote that the world was "ruled by two hundred people who know each other,"[35] who communicate with each other and understand each other, he may have thought of Greek ship owners, Armenian cannon kings, Latin American copper barons, Dutch oil men, Jewish bankers who acquired British knighthood, and also American heiresses who guilded rusty escutcheons. But his hyperbole might come true now in half of the world at least, with interlocking directorates extending into many countries.

While the international corporations have lost their identification with the country of their origin, nations in turn do not any longer identify their interests with those of the corporations. Lord

Palmerston still could call upon the might of the British Empire on behalf of a Maltese Jew who happened to be its citizen; the United States no longer protects the passengers of its airlines from kidnapping. President Harding still considered U.S. corporations in Mexico at least partially extraterritorial; Presidents Eisenhower and Nixon recognized the right of any country to nationalize corporations in its territory. For their part, the corporations often act in flagrant contradiction to national policy or even become spokesmen for the country in which they operate. American oil companies, which once thought they had the sheiks in their pockets, now plead with President Nixon to change America's Near East policy in favor of the Arabs — fortunately in vain, but that will not change the popular prejudice that oil determines U.S. policies in the Near East.[36]

Incidentally, even on occasions when the U.S. government considered itself the errand boy of U.S. business, frequent misunderstandings often prevented agreement on the nature of "national interest." When the State Department tried to mediate a quarrel between Chile and Peru over the Tacna-Arica territory, an arms manufacturer complained that it was "interfering perniciously with legitimate business." While the government was internationalist, business remained isolationist; while presidents sought to make the country defense-conscious, the stock exchange consistently gave defense industries a lower rating than other firms and in recent years responded to peace rumors with bullish, to war with bearish behavior. As mentioned above, the *Wall Street Journal* and the right wing of the Republican Party were isolationist and antiinterventionist through two world wars, the Korean war, and even in Vietnam. They all thought it bad business to spend $30 billion a year to protect a piddling few million in trade and investments in Southeast Asia — never mind anticommunism and great-power aspirations. (As I make my final revisions, Henry Ford had to call off a profitable deal with the Soviet government; Secretary of State Laird vetoed it for strategic reasons — as if to prove my point.)

Neocolonialism

If business is no longer patriotic it may still display a "colonialist" stance vis-à-vis the underdeveloped countries. At international conferences like UNCTAD, charges were heard that the rich get richer and the poor, poorer; that the producers of raw materials enrich the makers of machinery; that the debtors feed the creditors. Yet the have-nots must ask for even more loans and complain that not enough funds come their way. U.S. capitalists prefer to invest in highly developed countries. Contrary to the Lenin-Hobson theory, capital is not under pressure to find investment opportunities. The opportunities are offered and the U.S. government vainly implores U.S. business to help industrialize countries suffering from under-development. Even though profit may be high, capital no longer takes risks; it demands, and gets, government guarantees; it expects the government to organize and finance preliminary surveys and research. Much of the international aid program is actually seed money — developing areas that may provide a hospitable environment for private capital. But as we have seen, U.S. capital prefers areas that already have developed markets. Only petroleum and ores, of necessity, have to be produced at the location where nature put them.

A word about the economics of these operations. The foreign companies, especially those in the oil and mining businesses, make enormous profits. But where are these profits realized? We must distinguish between two very different cases. The first is that of utilities, railways, and most of the manufacturing industries. Their profits are made off the natives and — unless reinvested, as is often required by law — are taken out of the country. An absolute loss; these nations would be better off if such companies were national-ized and profits were retained and used for development. Brazil now has a law making it obligatory for at least 50 percent of every company to be owned by Brazilian nationals — although, to make a profit from American know-how, they may have a management contract with an American firm. On the whole, this is a good arrangement that has also been adopted by other countries.

Quite different is the second case, which concerns the extractive industries — mines, oil, fruits, timber. These companies produce a commodity that cannot be consumed in the underdeveloped coun-tries. They must sell it, and they can sell it only to industrialized countries, above all to the United States. It is only here, in our country, that the profit can be realized. This is as true of bananas as it is of oil. The local powers in South America or Arabia may raise wage rates, ground rent, or royalty; they may write new laws or make new contracts; but neither the United Fruit Company nor ESSO will suffer. They will just raise prices and the American consumer will pay. Without monopoly powers in the consuming centers, however, the world market will set limits on the returns from other commodities, as coffee and cocoa producers have learned. Even though no United Fruit Company stands between them and the American consumer, their national and international cartels have been unable to stabilize prices. Incidentally, this also happened to the price of gold; its main producer, South Africa, has much in common with black Africa.

Developing countries with one-crop economies suffer from the vicissitudes of a world market they cannot control. The case of Cuba has shown how difficult it is to diversify and to find alternative markets. In many cases it is the structure of the market that leads to grievances against the big, wealthy customers: the terms of trade favor the industrial nations and discriminate against developing countries; the rich are always in a better bargaining position than the poor; the supply of industrial goods is easier to monopolize than farm products. Above all, the markets of the developed nations are not sufficiently open to late-coming competitors, and the highly industrialized countries are trading more with each other than with the underdeveloped world.

Since the developing countries are debtors, they should export more than they import, but the United States consistently achieves export surpluses in trading with underdeveloped countries. Americans buy Volkswagen cars and Sony radios, but pay low prices for their coffee. They buy less bauxite, magnesium, and chromium than they used to, since in many utensils metal is being replaced by plastic materials; and, unfortunately for the Manila government, Du Pont is producing fibers that will replace sisal. Another variation of this juncture: should the Arabs raise the price of their oil, it would pay to develop our own wells in Alaska. The world market is a game in which the producers of raw materials cannot win.

Brazil, Ghana, Colombia, and a few other countries have an agreement on coffee, but wholesale prices follow a declining trend. Industrial countries limit their production when prices fall; in backward countries farmers respond to the fall in prices not by cutting production but by increasing it, thus making the problem worse. As a result we have the phenomenon of the "scissors": industrial goods fetch ever-rising prices, while farm products and other goods that underdeveloped countries must export are constantly depressed. All underdeveloped countries lose in these exchanges; moreover, they are far more dependent on exports and imports than the United States. What is gravy for the United States is their meat and potatoes. They produce an excess of certain goods which they must exchange in order to satisfy their other needs, especially if they wish to industrialize. Now, unfortunately, our economy is so big that the 3 percent of GNP constituting our imports from other countries constitutes almost half of the world trade. When the United States sneezes, the underdeveloped countries catch a cold; when the United States catches a cold, they catch pneumonia. When our imports decline by an ever-so-small percentage point, their exports decline catastrophically. By the same token, a small concession on our part might provide significant relief for them.[37]

Pseudocolonialism—What's in a Name?

Many of the complaints that underdeveloped nations have voiced against U.S. trade practices are justified. At Caracas they requested freer access to U.S. markets and capital, renegotiation of licenses granted under duress, better terms of trade. Most of these requests, however, are no different from those discussed in trade negotiations between *any* two nations and do not imply an imperialist or colonialist relationship. The United States could allow tourists to bring wood carvings home from Haiti, or bird-lovers to buy seed in Ecuador. Denial of this demand would not prove "imperialism," nor would its granting remove the plagues of overpopulation and underdevelopment. But in bargaining about such (literal!) chicken-feed, the United States usually is in the stronger position, and its partners make up for their weakness by raising the hue and cry of "colonialism"; it may shame the United States into making concessions, but it will also create a mood of recrimination that converts business negotiations into a contest between haves and have-nots. I have called this tactic the pseudocolonialist bogeyman.

Pseudocolonialism has another dimension that, though not economically calculable and demonstrable, is nevertheless real. Citizens of an underdeveloped country are hypersensitive to the slightest lack of respect; they tend to feel humiliated by the mere hint that they may be petitioners or dependents. Whenever they have demands, they must feel righteous. Their poverty cannot be their fault; it must be the consequence of discrimination and unlawful exploitation. All their frustrations can, therefore, be blamed on Big Brother, and their demands will be presented as calls for liberation from an oppressive "System." This substitution of resentment for analysis can be termed psychoimperialism.

Actually, the U.S. government can do little to alleviate the underdeveloped countries' plight or to overcome their resentment; as long as they feel dependent on the decisions of their overweening partner, they will experience those decisions as encroachments on their sovereignty. If the United States buys their raw materials, it depletes their resources; if it does not buy them, it acts selfishly, perhaps in the interest of its oil companies. If the United States unconditionally supports the governments of underdeveloped countries, it helps to perpetuate an unjust system; if it demands reforms, it is meddling in other countries' affairs. The U.S. government has been blamed for helping the United Nations wage war in the Congo and for refusing to wage war in Biafra, Rhodesia, and Palestine. A United Nations study has shown that any serious effort at great power disarmament would most severely hurt the exports of the underdeveloped countries. No matter what great powers do, or leave undone, the Third World will be wronged in one way or another, and this is the definition of neocolonialism as a state of affairs.

The three optical illusions of pseudocolonialism, psychoimperialism, and neocolonialism prevent the people of underdeveloped countries from recognizing their true plight: they need to modernize their economy, and that often means considerable disruption of the time-honored web of social and cultural relations, of cherished customs and traditions. The foreigner often is the agent of that change,[38] a visible target for the hatred of the old ruling classes and for the anxieties of the unsettled proletarians. Even where the Westerner tries to be helpful, he seems to impose his ways, to tell others what's good for them, to threaten ancient cultures with extinction. He also threatens the old caste rule, staunchest obstacle to the most urgent and necessary reforms. At the Inter-American meeting in Caracas, the Latins desired "more action under the Alliance for Progress... [but] there was no talk of the social reforms that were its basic principles."[39] Instead, demagogic leaders of the underdeveloped nations brandish the banner of nationalism and anticolonialism; their solution to a number of insoluble problems is a nationalization that is often costly.

Economic nationalism cannot solve problems any better in the twentieth than it did in the nineteenth century. The problems of the underdeveloped countries are serious; they require fundamental restructuring of their domestic and foreign exchanges. To escape the thralldom of exploitation and competition, the raw-material-producing countries should accept international planning on a scale much greater than we have known hitherto.

Trade in the great international commodities must be brought under the control of international boards; mining operations, too, should be controlled by agencies modeled after the European Coal and Steel Community or Euratom. No private company has a right to exploit the natural resources of any country for its own benefit or for the benefit of a foreign country, just as no country has a right to reserve its natural resources for its own exclusive use.

These principles obviously are complementary, and their realization is not utopian. The United States government has provided a precious precedent in its draft proposal for the control of atomic energy through a worldwide agency (the so-called Baruch Plan, actually the work of Acheson, Lilienthal, and Oppenheimer). At present, the United Nations is discussing a similar proposal to ensure the resources of the seabed to all nations.

Aid Imperialism

Special arrangements must be designed to internationalize the supply of capital. It is generally agreed that the present developmental aid mechanisms are unsatisfactory. Low-interest loans must be provided for long-range projects. A world-development tax of 1 percent on national income could serve as the basic fund on which expansion of the world economy could be built with Keynesian techniques. Professor Paul Prebisch, the Argentinian economist and former chairman of UNCTAD, recommends, in addition, the creation of a "residual lender capable of providing capital without regard to returns."

When we compare these desiderata with the reality of "development aid," the contrast could not be greater. What is announced as development often is a promotion gimmick for U.S. exports, and what is pompously called aid is often export financing, a legitimate but certainly not philanthropic business. Loans have been tied to the purchase of certain goods; guarantees that were demanded have bordered on receivership.[40] Or "aid" serves as small change on the counter of political bargains: to buy votes at the United Nations, to support allied governments, etc. While it is unrealistic to condemn these practices, it is hypocritical to include the amounts spent in the statistics of "foreign aid." Also objectionable is the inclusion of loans that are purely commercial arrangements.

Only recently did the Latin Americans cause the Nixon administration to renounce the scandalous "additionality clause" (forcing them to buy more of the goods they had first received as grants) and to give them a wider choice of suppliers for goods bought with aid money.

Even genuine aid, however, has come under attack. "I fear the Greeks, even when they are bearing gifts," said Virgil, and many recipients of American aid have become critical of its results. Bilateral aid is often made conditional upon certain political services or on economic concessions that convert aid into shackles. The United States often speaks to recipient countries like a banker. Perhaps, too, what may appear to the donor as a reasonable guarantee for the grant's purpose is experienced by the recipient as an instrument of control or domination.

For all these reasons, U.S. aid has been denounced as a subtle form of colonialism; even grants have been criticized because they are in fact subsidies not for the needy but for our own industries.[41] This is certainly true of food shipments. But, after all, the money to supply them was collected in the United States, the needy received the goods (minus what their officials stole), and the beneficiary government usually was allowed to convert the counterpart funds into capital for development work. Yet most governments do not like aid programs designed and earmarked for specific purposes; they want the money free of conditions and strings, and here I beg to disagree with the advocates of national sovereignty: the purpose and use of international aid should be under rigorous control. Today much aid is given not for purposes of development but for pork-barrel projects. The World Bank complained in its report for 1962 that aid was often given for no economic reasons, or even against economic reason. Most seriously, when President Kennedy told the Latins, No reforms—no money, they sabotaged the Alianza para el Progreso.

The United States government should never have relaxed these "strings," and it should have insisted on another "string:" no aid to governments that buy heavy arms in the world market — or anywhere, for that matter. It is obvious that a government that can afford the luxury of arms does not need grants. If a government does not like such strings, which might embarrass its ruling classes, it is always free to refuse the "Greek gift." Incidentally, the alleged burden of political strings sits lightly on those who have repudiated all debts of such nature, as India has done often enough with impunity.

Proposals for Action

The plight of the underdeveloped nations does not stem from "imperialism" but from the concurrence of a health revolution (population explosion) with the pains of modernization. These nations must telescope the three industrial revolutions the West passed through into the lifetime of one generation. Colonialist practices often have started this process, but now they can only obstruct the path toward further progress and self-determination. Colonialist powers have earned extra profits from the services they have rendered and, as a matter of principle, should agree to pay restitution. However, the amounts involved may be too small and, even combined with realistic estimates of available aids and loans, will not be sufficient to provide the desirable amount of seed money. The main effort must come from the underdeveloped countries themselves, as it did in the older industrial countries. In most countries this effort will not come forth without fundamental changes in their social structure and without the psychological and political shock of a reformation or revolution.

The key reform of the international economy must be a higher price of labor in the underdeveloped countries and a subsequent increase in the price level of their products. In addition to paying these prices, the advanced countries could help by giving up rights acquired through unequal treaties with corrupt governments. Since much of the uneasiness in the Third World stems from the lopsidedness of our bilateral relations, we ought to handicap ourselves in negotiating with its representatives. To balance our advantage we should, in Gunnar Myrdal's words, "discriminate against ourselves,"[42] and agree to the following measures:

1. Common Market arrangements in Latin America and Africa, permitting these nations to protect their budding industries while not excluding them from our markets.

2. Conclusion of international raw-material and foodstuff agreements to stabilize prices and to allot production and import quotas (as in the case of sugar). Cash surpluses should be used to subsidize diversified farming.

3. Conversion of military budgets into development funds at least to the extent that cancelled defense orders' mean a loss of export for Third World countries.

4. Renegotiation of all mining and prospecting rights and royalties, with special regard to each nation's sovereignty over its natural resources. Establishment of international authorities for the world's fuel economy and for strategic materials.

5. Transfer, in underdeveloped countries, of industrial properties from foreign companies to state agencies or to international development boards.

This last measure in particular should help to overcome the image of neocolonialism. It would apply especially to establishments that

have caused resentment and whose economics are not well understood by the public. Such a proposal can no longer be considered
revolutionary. The pioneering precedent was set by Franklin D.
Roosevelt, more than thirty years ago. Up to the early 1930s the
State Department supported the oil companies in their dealings
with the Mexican government. But in 1938 President Cárdenas
expropriated U.S. oil properties valued then at a quarter of a billion
dollars. Roosevelt, much more concerned about the international
situation than about corporate rights, forced the oil companies to
settle for $40 million — one-sixth of the asking price.[43] The Ameri-
can taxpayers had to pick up part of the bill, and in future settlements the U.S. Treasury might indemnify the companies totally and
present the plants to the nations as a gift.

Using the latest figures, comparatively small sums are involved:
$4 billion in mining, smelting, and petroleum in Latin America; a
similar amount in all of Asia and Africa. In the manufacturing
industries, many firms may not lend themselves to nationalization,
nor have they aroused resentment. But it may be advisable to include
public utilities such as gas, electricity, telephone, and public transportation, which in most of Europe were nationalized long ago.
The entire expense would be equivalent to just a few years' foreign-
aid appropriations at the current level.

A Theory and a Strategy

This surgery, however, may reveal two ugly naked truths:

> ———the rivalry of the great powers and their ideological antagonism
> will not disappear; the cold war will go on in new forms;
> ———the gap between developed and developing nations will remain
> wide for at least one generation, and their relations will still be
> governed by the Gulliver complex.

Unfortunately, the problem of economic dependence that plagues
the underdeveloped areas is not directly connected with the problem
of political hegemony that plagues the United States. What con-

science-ridden Americans may do in one sphere hardly affects the other sphere; I therefore must give an ambiguous answer to my opening question.

Imperialist policies are not a necessary consequence of economic pressures, but they may have their own inevitable logic. Colonialist methods may not constitute the behavior pattern of U.S. relations with the Third World; but the Third World projects its own predicament into a pattern that the naked eye — or hate-tinted glasses — can hardly distinguish from colonial dependence.

Finally, the national revolutionaries of the Third World may be mistaken in identifying their enemy as neocolonialism, but they do provoke responses which they see as imperialist. As Canada's Prime Minister Trudeau said, it is uncomfortable to lie down with an elephant, be the beast ever so friendly.

It is necessary and possible, however, to separate the purely economic aspects of this relationship from the psychological and political irritations. It is not necessary, though it is possible, to confuse the negotiable issues of economic policy with the power issues of world politics. The first are accessible to reasoning; the latter, unfortunately, are charged with emotions and made manageable only through fear. But fear is also the agent that invites power to assert itself. It has often been remarked that in the cold war, as in earlier contests of alliances, each side interpreted the other's defensive moves as aggressive and therefore increased its own defensive preparations, which in turn escalated the other's fear. This game has been called "balance of power" or "deterrence," and it is obvious that the instruments of security that are useful in this game — military, political, and economic ones — should become values per se in the players' eyes. When that happens, when the means of security acquire a life of their own and become ends, we have imperialism: the desire to expand for the sake of expansion, the desire to have the strongest military forces, the strongest alliance, the greatest influence on other governments, the greatest economic penetration of other countries, and also an ideology claiming universal validity.[44]

It would be foolish to deny that money interests ride this engine. Even without money interests, however, the U.S. drive for hegemony in the Western world or its struggle with the Soviet Union would be no less vigorous. After all, Soviet imperialism has yoked to its wagon all those formerly independent nations without any prompting by such money interests. It is clear from the behavior of the two superpowers, as they are rightly called, that their game is one-upmanship, power lusting after power, with the agent becoming the master.

Some American liberals will disagree with this statement. They have been trained to believe that power is always derived from economic interests or directed toward economic goals. They are power-blind; they even manage to "explain" how a Hitler, a Stalin, a Nasser, a Genghis Khan may be driven "ultimately" by hope of economic gain. Even if that were to be granted, I would still argue that in the real world the "ultimate" never appears and "power" may have become autonomous (or in Marxian language: *verselbständigt*). The profundity that the profit motive explains all is utterly shallow and flies in the face of all the evidence about the motives of policy-makers.

Tribes, nations, races, states establish themselves as entities that define their identity in contrast or conflict with others. Moderating forces within and without may domesticate these drives, and perhaps the rivalry can be contained within certain channels; but what is contained here are the symptoms, not the disease. The disease itself is a constitutive element of our international system, which is a system of states; imperialist policies are nothing but exaggerated, perverted, unleashed functions of the legitimate security interests of national states. Imperialism is nationalism writ large, and it cannot disappear unless the national state itself withers away.

Colonialism as Lenin knew it was mostly liquidated after the Second World War; so-called neocolonialism is capable of being converted into measures to aid the development of backward countries; problems of pseudocolonialism may be difficult to solve but are a headache for the statesmen rather than a cause of real antagonisms. Imperialism, the self-justifying Will to Power, remains as the enemy of progress, justice, and peace. It is frightening to think how much deescalating and disarmament would be necessary to lower the tension even to the level that preceded the world wars, let alone the wars of the nineteenth century.[45]

The new means of destruction are not the only and not even the major reason why imperialist confrontations have become so much more dangerous in recent times; nor is the cold-war tension explained by the development of two worldwide empires whose interests clash at the fringes. It seems to me that empires can settle their differences as long as their leaders are aware of the overall interests that each must serve. But the means of competition, whether economic or political or military, may render themselves autonomous and create antagonisms that in turn degenerate into confrontations. Hobson, Schumpeter, and Arendt, starting from assumptions widely apart from each other, agree on this one point: that imperialist policies are parasitical, often atavistic outgrowths of particular forces that have superimposed themselves upon the body politic and exploit it rather than serve it. This is most evident in countries where the conduct of foreign policy is dominated by a military elite that considers the rest of the country merely strategic resources.[46]

Such a view, however, leaves one important question unanswered. Why would sound social forces within a country submit themselves to such pernicious leadership? I believe that we shall never understand imperialism fully until we know more about the importance of power in society. Tribes and nations are held together by certain mechanisms of a group relationship; every system of society is maintained and grows under the protection of a power apparatus that is specific and essential to its survival. At certain, rare stages of societal development such a special apparatus can be liquidated and replaced or supplanted by ritual and routine, usually at the expense of further development. At other stages the instruments of power may be liberated from supervision, initiate their own dynamism, accelerate evolution, or revolutionize the system. Then new elites, new classes come to the fore, armed with new techniques and uninhibited by the old codes of values or cultural traditions. Various power apparatuses — military, political, cultural, economic — are allowed to spread in all directions, to subdue the remnants of older social structures, to preach a new gospel, and to profess new ideas that justify the conquest as morally and historically right.

I am aware that I have taken up more space saying what imperialism is not than saying what it is. The reason is twofold: it is indeed hard to find a common root for the many phenomena that can be described as imperialist, and Lenin has misled an entire generation of antiimperialists by insisting that the root is always economic. Today we cannot be so sure, and it is perhaps better to describe different types of imperialism. In particular, it may be useful to distinguish the "youthful," dynamic style of an expansionism, based on the exuberance of new social forces, from the "late" imperialism described by Spengler or witnessed in the unsuccessful disengagement maneuverings of empires in liquidation.

9

Notes on
the Soviet Union

Fifty years after its emergence, the Soviet state has become one of the two superpowers. It is often said that as one grows older, and more prosperous, one learns to appreciate the value of things as they are; some may hope that in the same way the Soviet Union will turn into a conservative force — that in the future it will no longer endanger world peace but help to build it. This view, however, is based on the same assumption as its political opposite: the assumption that the cold war was caused solely by the Communists' plans for worldwide conquest.

The present book denies both the premise and the conclusions of this assumption. It stresses the historical fact that a great power — any great power — sometimes finds its advantage in conserving the status quo and sometimes in disrupting it. Communism is not the motor that directs the power of Soviet imperialism and its aim. The czars were also involved in power politics, disguising it now as a Christian and now as a Pan-Slav mission. The Bolsheviks inherited many of czarism's objectives and methods, added some of their own, and at any given time adjusted their global planning to the vicissitudes of the moment. So their strategy was now expansive and now defensive; their methods were now revolutionary and now diplomatic.

Introduction to *Weltmacht Russland* (Oldenburg: Gerhard Stalling Verlag, 1968).

In other words, the Soviet Union has come to behave as would any other state, assuming it were located on Soviet territory, blessed with its industrial capacity, and opposed to similar rivals.

There is also the matter of personal leadership. The statesman follows certain inclinations which combine his own personal preferences with the values that he has been taught by the party, the church, the school to which he belongs. Still other elements of his policies have been shaped by the history of his nation and by the political, social, and economic system he is engaged with. On this basis, he will either follow a policy of raison d'état and conduct a responsible politics, or else give way to the temptations of fame, power, or fanaticism, and so challenge the status quo.

The history of Russia, both before and after the October Revolution, offers ample documentation of how all these diverse variables have affected Russia's relations to its neighbors. Here is the question that will be asked: at any given moment, how much of Machiavelli, how much of Marx, and how much of Ivan — the traditional Russian peasant — can we discern in Russian foreign policy?

And here is a rough blueprint of the conclusions I reached.

1. The East-West contest is above all a struggle for global power — for creating a system of states which, after the convulsions of the Second World War and the national revolutions that followed in its wake, will have to take the place of previous power constellations.

2. In this struggle, each power follows its own raison d'état, which essentially depends on security conditions and on the particular state's natural position within the system of states.

3. In this struggle, ideologies are employed as weapons or camouflage; but they can rarely be identified as the sole motive for a political decision. Communism will by no means consistently promote expansionist tendencies.

4. On the contrary, the development of Russian foreign policy, from the czars to Lenin, Stalin, Khrushchev, and beyond, appears not as a series of differing conceptions but rather as the unfolding of what might be called a state personality. It will arise through diverse developmental stages where the state, in its struggle for a place in the sun, will make use of diverse means.

5. Soviet policy has used Communism just as cynically as Czar Alexander VI used Catholicism, or as Cardinal Richelieu used the Protestants; and Soviet policy has betrayed Communism no less than Napoleon betrayed the Revolution. For instance, whoever had counted on Communism and National Socialism being deadly enemies was brutally disillusioned in 1939.

6. Just as mistaken as those who identified ideology with reality were those who saw the so-called liberalization within Communist Russia as a harbinger of a more "liberal," less militant, less intransigent foreign policy. On the contrary: freed from the shackles of Marxist dogma, the Soviet Union in its foreign policy has been able to pursue its national goals more effectively than ever before. In addition, as it relies more and more on the ideology of national wars of liberation, the Soviet Union has revealed the essentially national character of the October Revolution.

7. Here is the paradoxical result: it is easier to coexist with Communist ideology than with the practical policy of the Soviet state. It is not necessary to bridge the chasm that separates the Communists' philosophy from that of the West; instead, the West can dispassionately recognize its existence. But when the West is in daily contact with the concerns of the Russian state, the resulting conflicts may one day lead us to the brink of another war.

8. Granted all that, there is hope for peace if we can gain a clearer insight. The confrontation, after all, is really based on conflicts of interest; that means it is accessible to raison d'état and even to intercession by other states. Only ideas know no compromise; interests know no principle and can be accommodated. There is no need to burden coexistence with philosophical debates; coexistence can grow, quite pragmatically, out of the daily routine of diplomatic strife. Coexistence is the constant effort to maintain peace, however unstable, however unsatisfactory a peace. Coexistence calls upon the diplomats to prevent the cold war from turning into the hot war.

9. Coexistence and cold war are merely two sides of one and the same relationship. To make sure this tension strikes no spark, we must ever more decisively strip it of ideology.

10

Who Are
the Palestinians?

Who are they, the Palestinians, and who has the right to speak for them?

Oppressed nationalities find it difficult to get a hearing because those who pretend to represent them are often political adventurers who merely exploit them — whether for other powers' imperialistic purposes or to vent on imaginary enemies their own hatred of the world. This is true of the Somalis, the Irish, the Bengalis, the Ibos; it is twice as true of the Palestinians because their country happens to lie at the crossroads of a world power struggle. Nowhere else do local enmities serve so many outside masters; nowhere else do foreign interests spread so much confusion about the very identity of the people whom they are pretending to save.

So, first of all let us agree: like most Irish, most Palestinians are not terrorists; but like many Ulstermen or Basques, many Palestinians will condone or even applaud acts of terrorism as long as they lack other means to express what they consider their just grievances, and as long as those grievances continue to be seen as just by others. Let us also agree that their plight is not of their own making; they have been objects of other people's policies for three thousand years.

Palestine, the land of the Philistines, a Semitic people that once was subjugated by Joshua and by David, has retained that name through the centuries as it was conquered by Hittites, Egyptians,

Dissent, Fall 1975.

9.   Beirut bombed by Israeli jets, June 11, 1982

(Photo: Wide World Photos)

Babylonians, Assyrians, Persians, Greeks, Romans, Arabs,[1] Christians from the West, Osmanli Turks, and the British. Until recently in modern times it was sparsely settled, mostly by Arab Bedouins, and considered part of Syria. A movement to liberate and unite the Arabs, then under Turkish domination, existed long before the First World War.

Then the British used Arab tribesmen to wrest Palestine, Mesopotamia (Iraq), and Syria from the Turks, promising them "sovereignty" and self-determination. After prolonged uprisings those parts of Syria that lay east of the Jordan River were given to Hashemite sheiks, who thereafter were called kings; the part west of the Jordan River was styled the British Mandate of Palestine and supposed to evolve toward self-government; northern Syria became a French mandate. The terms of the mandates were illegal even by the standards of the Covenant of the League of Nations, which was their covering law. Previously, a unilateral declaration by Foreign Minister Arthur Balfour had designated "Palestine" as a "Jewish homeland"; but at the same time Weizmann and Lord Harlech assured the Arabs that this should not interfere with Arab aspirations to sovereignty.

What these terms meant or how to reconcile them was never spelled out except in Balfour's memoirs, where he wondered how anybody could have been misled into thinking that they meant anything.[2] But on the evidence of contemporary customs and conditions, the Balfour Declaration was consistent with a Jewish immigration rate of 50,000 a year and a ratio of two to one between Moslems and Jews. In 1930, after serious Arab riots, immigration was severely restricted — just when Jews were desperate, not for a homeland but for a place of asylum. At the outbreak of World War II, the population consisted of 456,000 Jews and 1.1 million Moslems; at its end, the census counted 1.143 million Moslems, 583,000 Jews, and 145,000 Christians.

The Holocaust and the war left the Allies with a "disposal problem" in western Europe: nearly 100,000 East European Jews who had been made homeless by persecution and political changes were languishing in displaced-persons camps, fed by charitable contributions and government aid, mostly from the United States —

which, however, did not lift its own restrictions on immigrants from Eastern Europe. Responding to strong pressures from Zionist organizations — and minding the electoral situation at home — President Truman resolved the problem by agreeing to the foundation of a Jewish state in Palestine. Soviet diplomacy gladly gave its assent, viewing any diminution of the British Empire as so much gain for itself, and hoping to ingratiate itself with both Jews and Arabs.

At first the British wanted to build a base in Haifa because, ironically, they were about to fulfill another Arab demand: to evacuate the base in Alexandria. On the other hand, a White Paper of 1939 also promised independence to Palestine. Weary of Arab terrorism and immediately prompted by Jewish terrorism, the Labour Party government decided to abandon the thankless task of policing the peace between Jews and Arabs.[3] The deal was consummated by a United Nations Security Council resolution,[4] the only instrument of international law on which the state of Israel can base its existence.

It is therefore necessary to remember that the United Nations at that time created not one state but two on the west side of the Jordan: one Jewish and one Arab. The Jewish state so created was totally nonviable: it consisted of three noncontiguous parts encompassing most Jewish settlements and a like number of Arab settlements. Even Ben Gurion, however, accepted this rump territory because at that time he still assumed that Palestine would remain an economic unit where two peoples would be able to develop in symbiosis — a binational state in all but name.

A word about this assumed symbiosis. Not only Jews but Arabs too had come into Palestine, attracted by the higher wages and better working conditions under Jewish employers, or simply by the promise of prosperity that the Jewish immigration and its foreign backers brought to the country. The Jewish labor organization, Histadruth, had seen with alarm how fellow Jews were hiring Arab labor at low wages while Jewish immigrants were jobless. From the early 1920s on, therefore, the Histadruth had been waging a campaign "to fight for places to work."[5] Its strongly nationalistic appeal brought quick success to this campaign: by the 1930s Arabs worked for Jews mostly in menial positions that Jewish workers would not accept. Even so, a remarkable number of Arabs in Palestine prospered, learned mechanical skills, and went to college, so that former Palestinians now occupy enviable positions in all Arab countries as executives, opinion leaders, professional people, foremen, and skilled workers.

There is no doubt that the socioeconomic upset emanating from Jewish Palestine was one of the reasons for Arab sheiks, kings, and capitalists to fear the establishment of a Jewish state. Another was the threat of Jewish mass immigration and the growth of a new power center that was bound to subvert the status quo in the Middle East. At that time, only twenty years after the Balfour Declaration, Zionism was still considered a tool of British imperialism, and the Mufti of Jerusalem broadcast for Hitler from Berlin during the Second World War. To him, as to many Arabs and blacks today, Zionism was the imperialists' base in the Middle East.

A lot of silly arguments have been heard about this catchword, imperialism. Does it apply to Zionism? It is true that Orde Wingate trained the Haganah (Jewish underground defense organization); but another British officer, Glubb Pasha, led the army of Transjordan. And eighty years before these events, Lord Palmerston sponsored the unification of Italy; will anyone therefore charge that Garibaldi was a tool of British imperialism? The Jewish state was the goal of a *national* conquest; its conflict with Arab states or Arab interests is on the order of *national* rivalries, and this remains true even if Jews or Arabs or both are allied with imperial powers. At one time the British favored the Jews, but after 1930 they found Zionist presumptions increasingly embarrassing. Zionism exploited British power and then turned against it. The British, in turn, contrary to Lenin's theory of imperialism, did not mean to "exploit" Palestine economically but, as the mandate power, to prohibit the development of Jewish industries.

The United States has invested heavily in Arab oil developments. The charge that it uses Israel to keep the sheiks docile, however, is totally unfounded and, on the face of it, ridiculous. The policy of the oil companies and of the State Department has been consistently pro-Arab unless one defines as pro-Israel any policy not aiming at the destruction of the Jewish state. The responsibility for Israel's preservation, as for some other elements of the status quo the United States is committed to defend, has been a heavy burden. But it is in the nature of empires to be drawn into national border conflicts where their clients have interests, and very often they would rather not have to support them. Far from being used by the Russians or the Americans for their purposes, both Arabs and Jews have deliberately involved their big brothers in their own defense concerns.

Much has been made of the Histadruth's job policy. Obviously, in terms of Lenin's theory of imperialism, Jewish business has not been guilty of exploiting cheap Arab labor; rather, Jewish colonists have been guilty of making Arabs jobless and driving them from their lands. I have to explain here a subtlety of feudal law: *fellahin* can be sold along with the land on which they have been sitting, but the land cannot be sold without them; it cannot be pulled away from under their feet. When the Jewish agency, aware only of capitalist law, bought land from the callous *effendis,* it may honestly have thought that thereby it had acquired the right to expel the *fellahin,* which repeats the story of the "enclosures," well known to readers of Marx's *Capital.* As the Phoenicians had done at Carthage and the Athenians in Sicily, the Jews acquired land and Jewish colons "settled" it. This is the original meaning of "colonization."[6]

Notwithstanding Lenin, it may be called an imperialist policy on the part of the nation that hopes to prevail in such a fight for the land. Jewish settlers, who had naively begun to cultivate this ground — including *kibbutzniks* who did so in the name of socialism — wondered why the former owners or tenants of those grounds were firing at them or staging surprise attacks on their innocent children; from the vantage point of the expelled Palestinians, the settlers were usurpers, colonizers, imperialists in flesh and blood, not just the tools of mysterious powers across the sea.[7]

This is the background of the war of 1948, which resulted in Israel's conquest of a contiguous territory (within the boundaries of 1948-1967) and in the Hashemite annexation of territory west of the Jordan River, including part of Jerusalem and such Biblical cities as Bethlehem and Nablus. Perhaps even more important for our present purposes, it resulted in the flight of 600,000 Arabs from their native home.[8] In the light of the communal strife that had preceded the British pullout, that flight is totally understandable. A sensible person avoids being in anybody's line of fire, especially in this kind of civil war. The Jewish defense organizations had taken care to project an image of fierceness. Some, like Menachem Begin's Irgun Zwai Leumi and the Stern gang, were outright terrorists; their tactics appalled even Ben Gurion.[9] In June 1945 the Irgun blew up the King David Hotel, causing ninety-one deaths. British soldiers were shot by snipers; cars loaded with dynamite were driven into British army camps. Do these people have a right to complain about terrorism? Even the Palmach, the combat organization of the Haganah, blew up bridges and derailed trains. The crimes that had been committed in a few — fortunately very few — places had frightened the Arabs; when war came to their area, they followed the advice to stay clear of it. In so doing, they indicated that they were not taking part in the war operations. Clearly, in all wars of the past, displaced populations did expect to go back to their places of home, of work, of personal contacts. To keep them from returning, to forbid them a choice between staying abroad and accepting conquest, violates custom and international law — in fact it is a crime. Yet, for reasons of national policy, the Israeli government seized this opportunity to create a demographically homogeneous Jewish state.[10]

It was at this moment, and through this deed, that the issue of "the Palestinians" was created. So far, we have encountered Palestinians as the inhabitants of an area that might include all of the present state of Jordan, or only the population of the Mandate territory. Now the name has come to define almost exclusively the million Arabs who claimed that they had been expelled from their homeland and who were forced to live in primitive camps spread outside Israel in the Gaza strip, on the West Bank, in Lebanon, and in Syria. These camps were maintained by UNRRA, a United Nations affiliate, and financed mostly by American contributions.

Aside from the moral and humanitarian outrage they constitute, maintaining these camps was a political mistake of the first order. They became hotbeds of unrest, recruiting grounds for terrorist organizations, breeding places for corruption, blackmail, and crime. A few cents a day per head, amounting to many millions of dollars per year, meant an invitation to count many heads twice. The fraudulent claim that there are 2 million people in those camps is clearly exposed by the census figures of 1946. Even if every single Arab in all of Palestine had fled, there could still not be more than 1.2 million. Of course in the thirty years that have elapsed, the original 600,000 have been blessed with children and grandchildren; even some "dead souls" may have been procreative.

No one denies that many Arabs on the West Bank considered the miserable allowance in the camps preferable to their normal subsistence under Arab governments. On the other hand, genuine refugees from Palestine left the camps and found lucrative employment in other Arab states; many others died. All remain statistics in the camp population, and so are their children, although the children may live in other countries. By the most conservative statistics, therefore, more than half of the present camp inmates never lived in Israel. The Israelis who justify their claim to the land by the tribal memory of two thousand years obviously have no argument against people whose claim is based on tribal memories reaching back only thirty years. More than the expellees' actual misery, the bitterness of the sacrifice that was imposed on them intensifies the hatred that defines the Palestinians as a nation distinct from other Arabs.

Should the displaced Palestinians have been admitted by other Arab states? The Germans expelled from Eastern Europe after the Second World War have been among the Federal Republic's greatest assets. England has admitted West Indians and mestizos whose country had become someone's state. Why do not Syria, Egypt, Lebanon, or rich Kuwait, Algeria, Saudi Arabia help their Palestinian brothers — for whom they shed such abundant tears — get integrated into their countries? Although the oil sheiks have the means, they feel no obligation to do so.[11] Actually, they would rather use these unfortunate victims of national wars as pawn in their own game of power politics. They are not interested in healing this wound; they want it to fester — but in the body of Israel, and in the body of world peace.

How could this have been prevented? At some point between 1948 and 1968, the United States should have stopped subsidizing the refugee camps and Israel should have made an offer that might have, in one bold stroke, drastically reduced the number of "Palestinians" and disarmed their militancy. The offer should have been based on recognition of legitimate claims by those who could prove that they had lost their property, home, or job in the present territory of Israel. They should have been given the option of either a settlement in money or return under Israeli law. Since the conditions of life as a second-class citizen are never enviable, even when the nationalities are not emotionally hostile to each other, I believe that few Palestinians would have opted for return. Most would rather have taken the money, especially if at the same time U.S. subsidies had been ended. [12]

The Jewish authorities and public opinion have rejected such proposals on the twofold ground that Israel could not accommodate so many Arabs without disrupting her economy and without endangering the safety of her state. [13] The first part of this rejoinder sounds odd in view of their steady clamor for more immigrants from countries holding more Jews than there are Arab statistics in the camps. The second part is refuted by the results of the Six-Day War, which has added another million Arabs to the population of Israel — and many Israelis even speak of a "Greater Israel."

Most Israelis would probably want to keep the occupied areas if they could move the Arabs out, while Arab nationalism, strangely, demands the return of uninhabited desert first and liberation of the bemoaned brothers later.

In fact, Palestinians are not just the refugees in the camps of 1948. There are a million Arabs who live under military authorities in conquered territory. Despite the greater prosperity that annexation has brought to them, they are a source of unrest and an acute danger to peace. There can be no settlement, no truce, and no confidence between Arabs and Jews as long as their status is not determined equitably and as long as there is no international machinery to ascertain the will of the Palestinians themselves. Unless a political dialogue is initiated between Israel and responsible Arab leaders — a dialogue about concrete proposals that will satisfy legitimate claims — Yasir Arafat will step into the vacuum and pretend that he knows what the Palestinians want, and he will go on blackmailing his Arab friends and the international community. He also has rivals: should he not occupy the vacuum, some terrorist group or perhaps even the Communist Party will. The ball, therefore, is in Israel's court. It may not be easy, but unless Yitzhak Rabin finds a partner with whom to hold a dialogue, he may face another war.[14]

At the time of the Six-Day War, the Israeli government declared that it would hold the occupied territories only as pawns and evacuate them in return for a peace treaty. It has offered to pay compensation to those who have lost property in old Palestine — or rather, to allow the United States to make such payments; but it has not given refugees a choice of taking payment or returning. Prompted by Kissinger, Israel is now making diplomatic gestures — ever so reluctantly — that might have been helpful five years ago but that will not now divide its enemies. Meanwhile, the cancer of the Palestinians not only continues to fester but is being transplanted to the world arena, where it will eat away the possibilities of peaceful coexistence. A decision is urgently needed to attack the primary point of the evil. Neither recriminations about the past nor legal constructions of right and wrong are required. What is required is finding political answers to political problems.

The offer to receive or to compensate legitimate claimants might be made with greater confidence by the Israeli government if at the same time the Palestinians were to be offered a state of their own. It has been suggested that the West Bank and the Gaza strip — two noncontiguous territories — would constitute such a state. Unfortunately, that state would not be economically viable; hence it would be a pawn in the political game of the oil sheiks. Nor would such a proposal be politically acceptable without including the Arab part of Jerusalem. The Israelis are loath to give up any part of Jerusalem, and there is at this time no device of condominium or international control that would make the administration of the city possible without friction. It is clear that the real point of the quarrel is not viability but sovereignty. All the principals are too primitive in their tribal instincts or too immature as nations to be reasonable on questions where self-respect is at stake. Therefore, the solution for Jerusalem will have to be imposed by the great powers; it cannot be negotiated between the parties concerned. As long as they pretend to negotiate about it, they merely indicate that they do not mean to make peace.

By contrast, the return of the occupied territories must be negotiated by Israel itself with its neighbors, and the return of the refugees can be negotiated only privately between the Israeli government and those private parties who claim to have been residents of the area now under the government's jurisdiction. By its very nature, this cannot be a problem between Israel and Egypt or Syria, for neither of these countries claims sovereignty in Palestine. It could be negotiated between Israel and a state that can speak in the name of the Palestinians. These are a distinct people, different in background and culture from the Bedouins of Jordan, from the mercantile Lebanese, from the temperamental Syrians, from the millennia-old Egyptians. They must determine their own fate, both in Israel and in the West Bank area. They would probably prefer to sever their political ties with Jordan and might be interested in economic arrangements, to mutual advantage, with Israel. It stands to reason that they would rather not fight Boumédienne's wars and that the skimpy subsidies some of their guerrillas are getting from oil sheiks cannot substitute for a developmental plan and a technology to go with it. In the long run, a Palestinian state on the West Bank might easily fall into Israel's orbit, or become a client of Moscow, Peking, Washington, Teheran—who knows?

In the beginning, a Palestinian state would probably make obstreperous noises at international gatherings, and in some other ways it might not be the most desirable neighbor one could choose. Nonetheless, the unsatisfied demand for a Palestinian state is now a major source of posturing, gesturing, and confrontation. If Israel and Jews in the West could examine their interests rather than their emotional fears and historical memories, they might decide that approaching the Palestinians offers more chances for a lasting peace than speculating about Sadat's sincerity. Even supposing that he seeks a settlement with Israel—for whatever reasons—Sadat cannot deliver the Palestinians, and most likely no outside power can do that; they can be appeased only by a dramatic reversal in Israeli policy. (I have used the discredited term, appease, deliberately because no other applies; I am proposing a "solution" that will not last).

It is not necessary to believe that such an appeasement will bring an early cessation of terrorist attacks or a lowering of the level of invective in Arab rhetoric. But it may lay the foundation of a more constructive relationship between the Arabs and Jews on the local level and perhaps bring to old Palestine some kind of unity on the basis of economic interests and businesslike relations. In other words: it is necessary to strip this political problem of ideology. Although in this age everybody is "raising consciousness" or seeking to establish an identity, there is altogether too much of that in the Middle East. The Palestinians speak Arabic and worship in mosques; but they have come from many countries and have intermarried with many conquering nations. Their identity is of rather recent origin, through the misfortunes of war and yet another foreign conquest. Their appeasement ought to be less difficult than their arousal. They are looking for opportunities. I am even tempted to say that they can be bought; but they are being terrorized, and this may be the greatest obstacle to peace at this moment.

Arafat will speak for the Palestinians as long as they are not allowed to speak for themselves. His terrorism has so far not made him a hero to his people. He has imposed himself on the oil sheiks, but he is not widely admired and acclaimed. Arafat's threats, much like his predecessor Shukairi's, sound more like blackmail than fanaticism. He will have his little hours of triumph when Third World forces in international bodies need once again to show their "identity" by voting against the United States on an issue that is guaranteed to be without consequence. The Palestinians are neither better off nor worse when Arafat "represents" them in the ILO. No one has yet filled his belly by following the *Jihad,* though admittedly some heads might get filled with drunkenness.

Can Israel wager her security on the vague prospect that one day the Palestinians might not only awaken but also mature? There are no alternatives, and one must look for solutions that have some promise of lasting. One may hope to prevent an explosion though one may not be able to remove the dynamite. Above all one must divide, not unite, one's enemies.

Third World strategists have made the Palestinian issue into a cutting edge of their attack on Western positions in world politics. To blunt that edge, it is not necessary for the United States to take drastic measures, though it needs to radically rethink the issue. The friends of Israel — and, surprisingly, that includes many who have valiantly criticized "cold war attitudes" in U.S. policies — are tied to the confrontational patterns of the past decades; they think in terms of security rather than in political terms. They have missed valuable opportunities for peace in the past ten years. They gamble on the survival chances of a particular structure of the Israeli state, which is a dangerous gamble at best and is becoming more dangerous every day. The thought of having Arab citizens in their midst horrifies the Israelis; but while staring at that danger, they don't see the gathering of Arab armies outside the gate. They have too much confidence that the gate can be held shut for all time; this is an illusion for which others have paid dearly. In the long run, security lies only in the confidence of one's neighbors.

Aware that I have made some controversial statements, I want to make clear that the issue is neither moral nor judicial, but political. Those who wish to debate my proposal should refrain from reminding me who "started it" or who is "more to blame" or whose "rights" are better. Wherever I have touched upon such questions, my intention has merely been to show how Palestinians *see* them, and *that* is a political *fact,* not a moral judgment.

FOUR

Teachers of Marxism

11

Marx and the Jews

It is not because his life was too short that Moses could not enter the promised land, but because his was a human life.

Franz Kafka

Psychohistory vs. Marx

Histories of socialism usually begin with the Old Testament prophets, mighty preachers against usury and "those that buy the poor for silver," visionaries of a golden age, and messengers of perpetual peace. Their god was a god of Justice above all. Later, in the Diaspora, the Jews responded to persecution with a fervent messianic faith (which need not, of course, be socialist); but immediately upon emancipation, the buried message of social justice burst forth again in a crop of small and great prophets. Many Jews were followers of Saint-Simon, others helped to lay the foundations of social democracy: Moses Hess, Stephan Born, Ferdinand Lassalle, and, towering above them all, Karl Marx. In the generation of the Second International, Jews became so visible among the socialist leaders that Viktor Adler tried to restrain their zeal: Eduard Bernstein on the right wing and Rosa Luxemburg on the left, the brilliant Austro-Marxists and many of the Russians, both Marxist and Populist: Trotsky, Isaac Steinberg, Axelrod, Martov; in America, Mor-

Dissent, Fall 1979. All translations from the German, unless otherwise identified, are my own. —H.P.

ris Hillquit and the anarchist-feminist Emma Goldman. Among the martyrs of anarchism also were Gustav Landauer and Erich Mühsam.

However varied the ideas and careers of these men and women might have been, it is reasonable to assume that some elements of the prophetic and messianic tradition may have contributed to the formation of their intellectual profiles. Conversely, as revolutionary socialists, most of them had to shed other parts of the Jewish tradition (notable exceptions were Moses Hess and Isaac Steinberg). They had to reject their parents and liberate themselves from the confines of their social, national, as well as religious origins through a more or less vehement gesture of rebellion.

In an era of rapid modernization, members of an oppressed minority may have to make painful choices. Some may acquire a totally new identity: Johann August Wilhelm Neander (Mendel) became a great Protestant theologian, Friedrich Stahl became the theorist of German conservatism, Eduard Gans became the oracle of orthodox Hegelianism. Others, who also "bought the admission ticket" through baptism — Heinrich Heine and Ludwig Börne, both great German patriots and democrats, and Benjamin Disraeli, "the alien patriot" — never allowed anyone to forget that they were Jews. Conscious of both the paradise they had lost and the other one which they did not gain, such persons lived under tensions that could turn their genius toward total alienation and destructiveness (Otto Weininger, Edouard Drumont) or to the creation of a personal vision of paradise. To some Jewish rebels, however, a lucky combination of history and tradition provided the opportunity of converting the problem of personal or tribal salvation into a message for all mankind.

Such a turn from the particular to the universal requires an intellectual reorientation — or rather, a shake-up of all former premises, a tearing away from tribal, religious, and national moorings, the conception of a total revolution. The messianic-prophetic message has to be transposed from a context in which it no longer makes sense to one that transcends both the world of the minority and the greater surrounding world. A twofold tension then becomes the inspiration of a prophecy: to open the doors of the ghetto, which cannot accommodate the ideas of the new century, and to open the doors of bourgeois society, which is unable to contain all the new energies streaming into it. Where everyone can have utopian dreams at a certain age, the task of restructuring the world may become a lifetime obsession for some.

In many of these respects the life of Karl Marx was so typical that older biographers hardly felt the need to dwell on details. They were interested in the sources of Marx's ideas rather than his family relationships; in his interaction with his contemporaries rather than in his dreams about his ancestors.

Lately, the virus of psychoanalysis has invaded history departments, and posterity must now learn all about a subject's suckling and weaning, sex life and pathology. "To his valet no man is a hero," said Madame de Cornuel — to which Hegel replied: Precisely, because he *is* a valet! This valet's view of history sometimes yields interesting results on some level, but peephole information is not historical explanation.

The mischief is not as new as some of its practitioners think. Fifty years ago Otto Rühle — anarcho-Communist, friend of Karl Liebknecht and later President Lázaro Cárdenas' advisor on education — published a Marx biography based on the psychology of Alfred Adler, which explained that Marx's rebelliousness stemmed from feelings of Jewish inferiority, and his troubles in the First International from his carbuncles. In the past fifty years, however, psychohistory has progressed. With greater sophistication, we now know that the carbuncles were not the cause but the effect of Marx's failures, or, even more subtly, that carbuncles were his subterfuge to prevent himself from getting out of the routine to which he was irretrievably addicted, an addiction the infant is said to have acquired in order to stay dependent on his mother.

This is the theme of Arnold Künzli's erudite and voluminous *Karl Marx. Eine Psychographie.*[1] Künzli knows that little Karl objected to being weaned and begrudged his younger siblings their place at the mother's breast; Mrs. Marx was what one might call a smothering Jewish mother and never allowed Karl to grow up and develop mature relationships. Rejecting his parents, he developed a strong aversion to their Jewish background and behavior; Jewish self-hate in due time prevented him from coming to terms with his messianic heritage and forced him to look for another "chosen people." Thus, he invented the proletariat. Voilà Marxism exposed as the fantasy of the Jew who failed to grow up, and ony three small points remain to be explained:

> ——A million Jewish boys have overbearing and overcaring mothers, but one becomes Karl Marx, the other Portnoy. La petite différence!
> ——What do we know about Engels' Jewish mother? Or Lenin's, Liebknecht's, and Bebel's?
> ——Suppose Künzli is right; what caused millions of people to identify with the fantasy of this inefficient, immature Jew?

Watching a blimp, a psychoanalyst once pointed out to me that it was a penis symbol; I replied, Maybe, but doesn't it fly? Some Jews seem to take comfort in the revelation that the man who killed six million of them may have been a sex pervert; such talk merely distracts us from studying the phenomenon of fascism. Likewise, the considerable body of literature that has been written about Marx's *kvetches,* and especially about his "anti-Semitism," is largely irrelevant to an understanding of his thought; nor does it help us understand the sociological phenomenon of left-wing anti-Semitism. Toward comprehending and illuminating this important problem only Marx himself has made a contribution and, after him, George Lichtheim (in "Socialism and the Jews").[2]

The question of whether Marx was anti-Semitic centers mostly on his controversial essay "On the Jewish Question," which he published in 1843. It has been answered affirmatively, before Künzli, by Eugene Kamenka in "The Baptism of Karl Marx"[3] and by Edmund Silberner in *Sozialisten zur Judenfrage.*[4]

The recent biographers Fritz Raddatz[5] and David McLellan[6] come down on Künzli's exaggerations, and Jerrold Seigel in *Marx's Fate*[7] totally reverses Künzli. According to Seigel, Marx came into his own when in 1844 he eventually rejected the Christian-German philosophy and embraced "Jewish" materialism. The most recent review of the entire material, judicious and comprehensive but adding little really new, is Julius Carlebach's *Marx and the Radical Critique of Judaism.*[8]

My own approach will be historical. I shall try to show that the term anti-Semitic as we understand it today does not apply to the author of "On the Jewish Question" nor to his contemporary audience, which understood his meaning in the context of Hegelian philosophy and its language. I shall also contend that one is not entitled to draw psychological inferences from his essay unless one has a thorough grasp of its terms.

The Jews Marx Knew

When Franz Mehring wrote his classic biography of Marx sixty years ago, he was content to mention that the founder of scientific socialism was "descended from a long line of rabbis"; thereafter he did not think it necessary to refer again to the subject of Jewishness, except to express disapproval when Marx used epithets in bad taste against Lassalle. Times have changed, and with them our knowledge, our sensibilities, and our interests. In the latest biography Fritz Raddatz, the distinguished literary editor of *Die Zeit,* takes pains to trace the rabbis on both the father's and the mother's side back to famous Talmudic scholars of the sixteenth century in Lvov and Padua. (Going back thirteen generations, every Jewish family probably can come up with a famous Talmudic scholar.) More to the point, we learn that Mehring used an edition of the Marx-Engels correspondence that had been piously purged of dirty words and anti-Semitic expletives, and that he knowingly withheld from his comrades embarrassing information about the son Marx had fathered with his maidservant — information that had also been withheld from Mrs. Marx and the daughters, a touching reminder that the great challenger of middle-class morality and his immediate followers were still living this side of liberation.

That Marx and Engels were children of their time is, perhaps, nowhere as painfully apparent as in their attitude toward Jews, especially in their younger years. They saw them as "kikes" and used language that was common among their contemporaries. But Jews used that language too. As a black man may call another "nigger," Jews disseminate the lovingly self-depreciating jokes about scared, crafty, and *chutzpah*-prone coreligionists — jokes which the uninitiated consider a sign of Jewish self-hate but which the connoisseurs allow to melt on their tongues as fruits of refinement, and which they like to interpret as expressions of freedom or proof of maturity. We find these jokes in the works of two great apostates, Ludwig Börne and Heinrich Heine, next to passionate pleas for the civil rights of Jews and moving lamentations on the Jewish plight. Neither they nor Marx had turned their backs on Jewry, and Marx's daughter Eleanor proclaimed her Jewishness in public, although she knew nothing about Judaism.

At the same time these assimilated Jews were highly conscious of the chasm that separated them from the mass of their coethnics. They were an elite, not of their own tribe but of the German middle class. Marx's father Heinrich, himself a deist and liberal, had to convert in order to keep his government job, since some of the emancipation laws that the French Revolution had brought to the Rhineland were revoked after Napoleon's defeat. Characteristically, Heinrich Marx chose Protestantism in a Catholic province, and he remained on good terms with his brother, the chief rabbi of Trier. Several years later he found it necessary to have his children baptized, too, and only his Dutch wife held out a little longer.

Mrs. Marx may have had only a rudimentary education; her German was grammatically imperfect and her spelling atrocious; we do not know whether she kept some Jewish customs after baptism. Father Marx was as upright a patriot and liberal as one could find in Prussia; he was chairman of the local lawyer's guild, organizer of a "banquet" that dared to petition the absolutist government, and spokesman for the Jews. Two hundred other middle-class Jews lived in Trier with their families; but in the county there were ten times as many Jewish peddlers, cattle dealers, small-time usurers, and others whom the classmates of young Karl Marx had in mind when they spoke of "the Jews." They were the *visible* Jews, hated and despised by the gentiles. In Marx's time such Jews still had to step down from the sidewalk whenever a Christian gentle-man demanded it, and only one child per family was allowed to marry and live within the city.

I don't hold with *tout comprendre c'est tout pardonner;* still we all know the *embarras* of poor relations. One will never understand the attitude of Karl Marx to the "Jewish Question" unless one realizes that middle-class Jews had every incentive to emphasize what sepa-rated them from these lower-class Jews. By immersing themselves in German middle-class culture, classical literature, and patriotism, they hoped to fend off the specter of pogroms; by repudiating their poor relations they hoped to escape the opprobrium that was at-tached to the "dirty" Jews. Heinrich Graetz, the great Jewish histo-rian, wrote in his twelve-volume *Geschichte der Juden* passages like this:

> Twisting and turning, lawyers' tricks, wit, and prejudiced rejection of what transcends their horizon...are the characteristics of the Polish Jews. They don't know honesty and justice... they rejoice in cheating... The gentiles resented their superiority in Talmudic logic.[9]

(Graetz, incidentally, exchanged books with Marx.) Such expres-sions of liberal sentiments were typical among German Jews; they do not, in a man like Graetz, indicate Jewish self-hate or anti-Semitism, but parallel exactly the feelings a German gentile might express about Polish gentiles. It is the mimicry of a West-East differential in cultural development that already appears in eight-eenth-century documents: "I know, Sir, that the German Jews have nothing in common with the Portuguese Jews except a certain religious ritual, but that their mores betray no real similarity be-tween them," said the *Lettre à André Pinto* in 1758.[10] We shall again encounter this "Pinto the Jew," who crossed swords with Voltaire.

The middle-class German Jew tried hard to be seen as some-one very different from his distant cousin. For instance, among middle-class German Jews one never spoke of money; as German cant prescribed, one had a "calling" *(Beruf).* But the cartoonist's Jew, the Jew whom the anti-Semite knew, spoke candidly of profit, and the German Jew was ashamed for him. (To be precise, the middle class I have referred to here would probably be ranked as "upper middle" by American sociologists.) Neither Stendhal's Leuwen nor Balzac's Nucingen, both of whom were modeled after James Rothschild, have conspicuously Jewish features. Only poor Jews are dirty — and, of course, Marx thought Balzac a superb observer of the bourgeoisie.

Although obviously only a minority of Jews could be usurers, a man who was about to hock his watch might say "I am going to the Jew" as readily as, not so long ago, a New Yorker who took his dirty shirts to the laundry might say "I am going to the Chink." This was the world in which Marx grew up. It is well reflected in European literature, and its stereotypes were accepted even by Jews. A novel like Gustav Freytag's *Debit and Credit,* for instance, which today strikes us as anti-Semitic, could be found in many Jewish households, although the rapacious, unscrupulous Itzig—jargon, kaftan, and all—was presented there as the prototype of parasitical capitalism. Börne, Heine, and the young Marx had imbibed the ugly language in which "Itzig" (diminutive of Ignatius, a common name among East European Jews) stands for everybody who talks with his hands. Whenever Marx was angry at Lassalle's presumptuousness, he called him that—or worse—behind his back. In a letter to Engels (Marx/Engels Werke 30:259) he also called Lassalle "negroid" and added a low speculation about his mother.

The German Heirs of Philosophy

There is more of this in Marx's correspondence and notes. In the now-famous "Eleven Theses on Feuerbach" (1845) he criticizes the philosopher for contemplating theory only, "while practice can be grasped only in its dirty-Jewish form of appearance." The word Jewish is added here for emphasis; it is a gratuitous snicker for those who took this language for granted. As I shall explain later, however, it is not entirely unmotivated in terms of Marx's intellectual development. He was wrestling with the problem of the unity of

theory and practice; coming from the school of philosophical idealism, he was still looking for a way of endowing practice with some
kind of halo and was shocked to find it only in its "dirty," raw, and
unidealized form. His materialist turn would come soon.

Marx never published the "Theses," but even in his published
works he used anti-Semitic invective when it served a propagandistic
purpose. To discredit a loan that the hated czar tried to place at the
London Stock Exchange, he denounced the involvement of the
Jewish bankers who expected to profit from the transaction ("The
Standing of the European Houses" and "The Loanmongers of Europe";[11] a superb work of financial journalism). Incidentally, this is
the only place where Marx attacks the House of Rothschild.

Likewise, when he wished to denigrate a measure to increase the
circulation of money, proposed by the Prussian Minister of Finance,
Marx cited "a book On Circulation by the Jew Pinto, a famous
stockjobber of the eighteenth century," and thereafter always referred to the Minister as "Pinto Hansemann," as though the Jewish
nickname made him look foolish.[12]

Engels, too, was not above appealing to anti-Semitic prejudices
for purposes of propaganda, though in his case no Jewish mother
can be cited as the real object of his hatred. An example occurs in
his article on the Polish revolution, published in the same paper[13]
under Marx's editorship. Like all radicals, the Neue Rheinische Zeitung ardently supported the Polish cause, while the German National Assembly in Frankfurt opposed it, pointing to the great
number of Germans living in the provinces that Austria and Prussia
had annexed from Poland. Indignantly, Engels replied: "They
counted the Jews as Germans although this meanest of all races
could not have any relation of kinship with [the Assembly in]
Frankfurt, neither by its jargon nor by its descent, except perhaps
by its lust for profit." At the same time, he denounced the "Teutonic
money-grubbers," clearly intending to throw opprobrium on a
Prussian king who condescended to ally himself with Jews. The
article obviously was meant not to sow anti-Semitism but to exploit
an existing anti-Semitism and make a point.

Bad enough. But to judge such outbursts, one must compare
them with similar invectives against other races that had incurred

the wrath of these strict censors. One after the other the Russians, the Danes, the Prussians, the "Ur-Teutons," the "Balkanians," the Croatians, and the Slovenians stood in the path of the revolution and therefore were subjected to national or racial slurs. Other Slavic minorities in the Austrian monarchy were even worse off: though not guilty of counterrevolution, the Czechs and Slovaks were unable to bring about their own successful revolution; the Hegelian World Spirit condemned them to remain without history, *geschichtslos,* the worst insult a Prussian can fling at another nation:

> On the one hand the revolution: Germans, Magyars, Poles; on the other, the counterrevolution, i.e., all Slavs except the Poles; also the Rumanians, the Transylvanians. . . All history shows that only three nations are capable of living. The others have the mission [!] to be swallowed by the revolutionary storm and to perish.[14]

Later, when the Poles disappointed Engels, they too were thrown into the dustbin of history. The Jews missed the boat of history in 1849, when their leading cadres, along with the entire German middle class, abandoned the revolution.

Nevertheless, it is the Germans who were called by Hegel's World Spirit to take the lead in the next stage of history. With unconcealed pride Engels commented on Bismarck's victories in the Franco-German war of 1870, and Marx allowed that the superiority of the German arms would also help Marxian socialism to win out over Proudhon's brand. From their Olympian seat the two leaders judged Wilhelm Liebknecht's opposition to the founding of Bismarck's Reich "silly," for German unity had been one of their earliest political aims. To be fair: they often ridiculed and denounced the stupidity, meanness, and cowardice of the political establishment in Germany and condemned German nationalism and imperialism. But such strictures were political, never racial or ethnic; nor do the German bourgeoisie's historical betrayals ever doom the Germans as inexorably as other nations' betrayals doom them in the eyes of Marx and Engels.

As for Russia, by contrast, Marx's hatred of the czar and of the whole "Asiatic mode of production" seems to color his view of the

Russian people. When he writes a pamphlet against Bakunin, he begins, "The Russian, Bakunin," as though this characterization could forthwith dispose the readers against his opponent. Bakunin responded in kind by calling Marx a treacherous Jew. You really don't have to be Jewish, though, to display German haughtiness toward the Russians: when Bakunin tried to organize the Slavic resistance against German-Magyar domination in the Habsburg monarchy, Engels berated him in almost racist language, pointing to the gratitude the Slavs owed to the Germans who had civilized them, and to the impossibility of founding viable states with such slovenly nations. In the same article he applauded the efficient, culture-wielding, railway-building Yankees for having taken "rich California from the lazy Mexicans."[15]

Marx, too, had a poor view of the lesser breeds. While deploring the destruction of India's ancient culture, he saw it doomed anyway by frequent invasions and suggested that it would be better for the Hindus to be subjected by British than by barbarian conquerors: "The British have broken up the self-sufficient inertia of the villages, and railways will supply the new art of communication."[16]

In his private correspondence Marx was even harsher on backwardness. But while sharing the prejudices of all Victorians, he also gave warmhearted public support to all national movements: Indian, Italian, Czech, Polish, Irish, and especially those that were directed against German-Austrian overlords. No one can doubt the sincerity of Marx's internationalism, and we must often admire the soundness of his judgments on national revolutions.

In their political-philosophical beginnings both Marx and Engels had shared the Young-Hegelian hopes for the *Grossdeutsch,* the Greater German, revolution that was to bring "unity, justice, and freedom." As this hope grew more radical, they thought that the democratic revolution in Germany would transform itself into the social revolution, and that the underdeveloped German proletariat, being equipped with the heritage of German idealistic philosophy, would lead the socially and economically more highly developed West:

> In Germany no particular servitude can be broken without breaking all kinds of servitude. Radical Germany cannot be revolutionized without

revolutionizing everything from bottom to top. The emancipation of the German is the emancipation of Man. The head of this emancipation is philosophy, its heart is the proletariat. Philosophy cannot be realized without abolishing the proletariat; the proletariat cannot be abolished without realizing philosophy. [17]

This, of course, is pure Hegel, and its logic is carried along by the antithetical phraseology. As we shall have to remember presently, Marx enjoyed using this style, which he had learned from the master.

Schachern Detheologized

In this scheme of things the Jews had once occupied a place. Their historical function had been to introduce capitalism or, more precisely, a religion compatible with acquisitiveness, calculation, and money. (*"Où il y a de l'argent, il y a des juifs,"* said Montesquieu in *Persian Letters* LX.) Although only a few Jews had profited from the system, it had spread all over the civilized world; although the Jews did not rule, Marx said, their spirit did. "Mammon has become our God," Engels complained in the *Yearbook,* though of course he was not the first to say so. Precisely because it has reached its peak, Marx goes on, the tide must turn; by virtue of another Hegelian law Judah's fall is imminent:

> When society succeeds in transcending the empirical essence of Judaism — haggling *(Schachern)* and all its conditions — then the Jew becomes impossible precisely because his particular consciousness no longer has an object; the subjective basis of Judaism—practical need—is humanized, and the conflict between his individual, sensuous existence and his species existence is transcended. The social emancipation of the Jew is the emancipation of society from Judaism. [18]

These strange lines in the Hegelian manner form the conclusion of Marx's essay "On the Jewish Question," appearing in the same *Yearbook* from which I have quoted the idealistic exaltation of the German proletariat. Even stranger, they form a rather nongermane second part to a thirty-page essay whose bulk is a spirited defense of Jewish emancipation. Moreover, this same *Yearbook,* of which Marx was a coeditor, contains two further contributions with a strong pro-Jewish slant. One is a *chronique scandaleuse* about the Duchess of Baden and her Jewish lover, who was cruelly expelled by the peasants. The other is a skillful pastiche in which the commanding general's wife wishes to walk her dog in a public park "forbidden to dogs and Jews." After she has wrenched permission from her reluctant husband, the Jews come to claim that they ought to have the same rights as the dogs since they share their disabilities, too. The hilarious and sad incident, said to be true, is reported by Arnold Ruge, the coeditor of the *Yearbook* and a Young-Hegelian philosopher.

In a biographical context, the volume is of some interest because the three contributions by Marx reflect his rapid progress from Young-Hegelian idealism to Feuerbach's humanist materialism, and beyond toward historical materialism. Shortly afterward, Marx and Ruge were to part company; the essay "On the Jewish Question" was a reply to another former mentor, friend, and sponsor, Bruno Bauer. Bauer was a Young-Hegelian theologian who denied that Christ ever lived, and a radical democrat who did not believe in political action. He had accused Marx of lacking radicalism, because Bauer's own idea of revolution was that it must bring total liberation at once. Marx saw that this was possible only if one was content to "operate inside one's skull" in a manner that Hegel already had ridiculed. An example of Bauer's attitude: he had written two treatises on the Jewish question wherein he proved that a Christian state cannot emancipate the Jews without denying its own essence; hence, he concluded, Jewish emancipation would have to wait until everyone had become an atheist. Meanwhile, individual Jews had the option of emancipating themselves by converting to Christianity.

It is interesting to note that Marx was especially provoked by the impertinence of this latter proposition. He answered in great philosophical detail and, quoting the French and American Constitutions, showed that Bauer failed to distinguish civil from human rights. The former were meant to protect the latter. Civil emancipation did not mean equality in all spheres of human endeavor; it left each man free to err in matters of faith. By banishing religion from the public sphere,

> man was not freed from religion; he received religious freedom. He was not freed from property; he received freedom of property. He was not freed from the egoism of trading but received freedom to trade. The constitution of the political state and the dissolution of civil society into independent individuals is accomplished in the same act.[19]

Fine so far. But then Marx was tempted to deal with the relationships between the Jewish and the Christian religions, respectively, and human freedom. Bauer had argued that Christianity, being the "most highly developed" faith, was only one step away from total liberation. This led Marx to introduce, for the first time, what thereafter became "the economic interpretation of history," or *Ideologie-Kritik*. He had learned from Feuerbach that in erecting idols man worships only the image he has of himself. Now he proceeded to reduce this self-image of man to the social image: theology merely reflects economic conditions.

> Let us set aside the Sabbath Jew and consider the actual, secular, everyday Jew. Let us look for the secret of the Jewish religion in the actual Jew. What is the secular basis of Judaism? Practical need, self-interest. What is the worldly need of the Jew? Bargaining. What is his worldly god? Money. Very well: emancipation from bargaining [Marx always uses the Yiddish word, also used in German, *Schachern,* haggling] and money would be the self-emancipation of our era. [20]

At this stage of his development, Marx still saw money as the embodiment of all evil — the incarnate alienation of man from his creative powers. He saw Jews as the personified symbols of that power. In the passage just quoted, therefore, Judaism and Jewishness are metaphors, rhetorical devices to get at the substance, which is the money-grubbing gentile. Just as he tried to smear the czar, the Prussian king, and his finance minister by associating them with Jewry, so he now attacks the Christian businessman:

> Judaism has survived. . . because the practical Jewish spirit has perpetuated itself in Christian society, and here it even has attained its highest devel-

opment. [One has to hear the irony: Bauer had said that Christianity had attained the "highest development" in religion, which now stands revealed as a reflection of economic relations.] The Jew is only the special manifestation of bourgeois society's Judaism. Judaism has survived not in spite of but because of history. Out of its own entrails bourgeois society ceaselessly reproduces the Jew.[21]

The intention of the essay should now be clear, especially if we place it in the context of the *Yearbook* where it was published. Having pleaded in various ways for Jewish civil rights, Marx now turns to the Christians, asking, Who are *you* to deny us? Contrary to appearances, he is not attacking the Jews but is saying, That which everybody thinks is characteristic of Jews has been perfected by this Christian society: "The Jew has emancipated himself inasmuch as the spirit of money has become the practical spirit of the Christian nations. The Christians have become Jews."[22]

Except for the peculiar language and the elegant antithesis, these are not Hegelian subtleties. A hundred years earlier, Voltaire had said: "Christians are uncircumcised Jews," and Germans had always called their Christian usurers "white Jews." A French socialist wrote at about the time that Marx's *Yearbook* appeared, "I call by the despised name of Jew every dealer in money, every unproductive parasite who lives off other men's work."[23] Marx's contemporaries, therefore, needed no guidance to understand his meaning; for us, a little sense of humor is needed to place the essay in its "period" context. Marx was not writing on the Jewish question but on the question of money. He made that point with finality twenty years later, in *Capital:* "All commodities, however shoddy they may look, however malodorous they may be, in faith and truth are money, internally circumcised Jews."[24]

Said Saint Paul: " Not he is a Jew who is a Jew outwardly but he who is a Jew inwardly."

Marx Before Marxism

Although we can explain the essay "On the Jewish Question," we may still find it unsatisfactory. Jewish sensibilities have been hurt to the quick by Marx's bland identification of Judaism with money, and Jewish commentators have remarked that it was written without knowledge about things Jewish and without benefit of theological or sociological research. It was skewed because its intended target was hidden by the rhetoric of the manifest subject matter. It was simply trying to do too much at the same time:

———to answer an anti-Semitic argument made by Bruno Bauer;

———to plead for total emancipation, and for a secular, democratic state in general;

———to denigrate capitalists by branding them as "Jewish";

———to identify for primitive anti-Semites the enemy they should fight: "the Jew in themselves";

———to deny the Jews a particular and special existence as an estate, but to ensure their safety as citizens;

———to show that religious strife concealed economic strife;

———to introduce a new method revealing the social roots of ideological and theological conflicts;

———to say for the first time: in order to obtain political change, you must change the social system.

A heavy load, which the narrow approach of the essay could not carry! Marx did not yet possess the terminology to deal with the questions he was exploring (the most glaring defect: he still says money when he means capital). He covers his ignorance with brilliant formulations, but he is unsure and repetitious, groping for the right words, leaping from the economic base to ideological heights and back instead of studying the mediations; his idea of historical materialism is still too crude to be plausible.

The essay should be read as one that allows us a peek into Marx's workshop. Like many originally unpublished manuscripts that an unkind posterity later analyzes under the microscope, it is a warming-up exercise, decidedly pre-"Marxist" in both tone and idea. For its content it depends too much on ideas of the so-called German Socialists, whom Marx was soon to surpass and then condemn in the *Communist Manifesto* four years later. Those early socialists were indeed fighting the cult of the Golden Calf, and money was their enemy: "What God is for its *theoretical* life, money is for the inverted

world's *practical* life: the *alienated wealth* of men, their life-activity
that has been sold off...Money is the product of mutually estranged
men."[25] (Moses Hess's emphasis.)

10.   **Moses Hess**
(Photo: International Institute of Social History, Amsterdam)

The author, five years older than Marx and his close friend, was a mystic and messianist; later he became a precursor of Zionism, while still maintaining Marx's friendship. The article I cited was submitted to the *Yearbook;* it is therefore not surprising to read in the *Yearbook* (in "On the Jewish Question"):

> Money is the jealous God of Israel before whom may stand no other god. Money debases all the gods of man and turns them into commodities. It is the universal, self-constituted value of all things. It has robbed the whole world, both human and natural, of its specific values. It is the alienated essence of man's work and being; this alien essence dominates him; he worships it.[26]

These claims are made in an apodictic manner. Neither Hess nor Marx proves how monotheism connects with the leveling power of money. Modern sociology would demand a study of the mediating links, a baring of the psychological mechanism, a closer determination of the nature of the relationship — whether it is causal or a mere parallel. In his later practice of *Ideologie-Kritik* Marx would become more subtle.

From Usury to Capital

Anyway, the essay "On the Jewish Question," which has aroused so much controversy, does not reflect Marx's mature thought. A mere book review, it also is a mere transition piece. In the following section I shall show what place it occupies in the development of Marxism as against the primitive anticapitalism of Marx's predecessors. Let us begin with Marx's treatment of money:

> Whatever is found to be abstract in the Jewish religion: the contempt of theory, of art, of history, of man-as-an-end-in-himself, that is the actually conscious point of view of man-the-money-maker, his virtue. Even the relations between man and wife become an object of haggling: women are bought and sold.[27] ["Abstract," in Hegelian jargon, means one-sided.]

11. **The New York Stock Exchange on a quiet day, 1895**
(Photo: Jones, Brakeley & Rockwell, Inc.)

The last point is made frequently in early socialist literature; prostitution is used as symbol for the condition of the proletariat. Marx also quotes Thomas Münzer, the peasant leader of the Reformation, who declared it intolerable that creatures of God should be owned by others. Marx developed this angle in the "Economic-Philosophical Manuscript" of 1844:

> Money is the visible divinity; it is the conversion of all human and natural qualities into their opposites, the general confusion and perversion of things; it makes brothers out of incompatibles. It is the general whore, the procuress of mankind... it is the alienating and alienated, self-alienating potential of the human species.[28]

There he also quotes those lines from Shakespeare's *Timon of Athens* (act 4, scene 3), which still reverberate in a footnote of *Capital:*

Published for Bell's Edition of Shakespear. Feb.1.1776.

12.   Spranger Barry as Timon of Athens
(Photo: Billy Rose Theatre Collection. New York Public Library at Lincoln Center.
Astor, Lenox, and Tilden Foundations)

Gold, yellow, glittering, precious gold!. . .
Thus much of this will make black white; foul, fair;
Wrong, right; base, noble; old, young; coward, valiant. . . This is it
That makes the wappen'd widow wed again. . . Come, damned earth,
Thou common whore of mankind. . .

By this time, however, Marx had developed the full dialectics of exchange relations and was in possession of an adequate terminology for the analysis of capitalism. No longer did he need the synecdoche of "the Jew," citing the particular in place of the general. In his earliest studies of economics he had been baffled by the phenomenon of the division of labor. This seemed to him the very embodiment of all perversions, condemning man to a truncated existence. The specialization of the Jews, money trading, was at once the most outrageously dehumanizing and crippling activity and the most noxious for the community. The trader deprived himself of the pleasures of all-around activities, and he deprived the community of insight into the relations between its members. But by 1844, only one year after the publication of "On the Jewish Question," Marx was able to analyze this problem without resorting to the old visual aid — personalizing money in the Jew. In fact, without that distraction the problem became clearer to him and to his readers. From then on, he would no longer use the early socialists' language, the anti-usury, anti-Semitic ideology of primitive anticapitalism.

Other socialists, like Proudhon and Fourier, never outgrew the primitive stage and never reached Marx's analytical clarity. Their intellectual development remained arrested at a stage where they needed to see the abstract power of money embodied in the particular person of the Jew. Where they ought to have analyzed the functions of banking — good Christian firms like Neuflize. Hottinger, Périer, and Laffitte — they were content to shout, À bas les Rothschild! Bruno Bauer, too, had taken it for granted that "the Jews own all." In 1843 Marx had replied, Look at all those white Jews, the Christian bankers. By 1844 he was able to reply, Let us study the banking *system*.

In "On the Jewish Question" Marx took the first painful step away from primitive anticapitalist protest, but he still used the mystified language and imagery of that romantic rebellion. From then on we can watch him dissociate himself step by step: first explaining how imperfectly the symbol "the Jew" reflects the conditions that create the symbol; then analyzing those conditions and developing tools for a new social science; finally, in the *Communist Manifesto*, criticizing primitive socialism as a whole. In the 1848 revolution, Marx forgot altogether the Jewish reference frame of his earlier diction, and naively accused the bourgeoisie *in its entirety* of *verschachern,* selling the revolution down the river. "They value freedom only as the freedom to bargain *[schachern],*" the *Neue Rheinische Zeitung* declared on November 3, 1848. The language that had once been aimed at "usurers" now was leveled at the bourgeoisie *as a class.*

Anti-Semites Vs Marx

In the preceding sections we have encountered the romantic Marx, the warmhearted seeker after human nature and critic of inhuman conditions — a man different from the cool scientist and tyrannical dogmatist whom the public associates with "Marxism." That he was an angry man no one doubts; but then anyone living under the conditions of the Prussian police state and facing the intellectual crisis of the 1840s might have looked for a radical philosophy — witness the proliferation of radical and liberal magazines despite harassment by censorship and police. Whether he had a grudge against his father or suffered from a smothering mother seems irrelevant in face of the fact that thousands of others also mounted the barricades in 1848.

That Jews felt the "German misery" twice as hard is obvious; even socially successful, baptized Jews like Rahel Varnhagen complained about it. At the time Marx wrote "On the Jewish Question," he had just been through a harrowing experience. The pietistic-aristocratic relatives of his fiancée Jenny von Westphalen had objected to their marriage, and her family had cut his mother, then a widow. Marx knew that baptismal water does not wash birth defects away, and after the revolution he warned the Jewish bourgeoisie that "siding with the counterrevolution will not save you from being sent back into the ghetto." Yet when Jews were not with the oppressors but were the oppressed, he was on their side. A letter to Ruge, dated March 1843, reports that "the president of the Israelites here" (in Cologne, where Marx was editor of the liberal *Rheinische Zeitung)* "... has asked me to help with a parliamentary petition on

13.   Karl Marx as a student, from a group picture, 1836, lithographed by D. Levy (—Elkan)
(Photo: International Institute of Social History, Amsterdam)

behalf of the Jews; and I agreed. However obnoxious I find the Israelite beliefs, Bauer's view seems to me... too one-sided [*abstrakt*]."[29] Finally, when several Jewish writers answered Bauer, and Bauer rebutted them in his own paper, Marx came back to the charge and fully supported Bauer's Jewish critics, in 1845 (in two chapters of *The Holy Family*). An article describing the plight of the Jerusalem Jews is one of the few where this most unsentimental writer rises to chords of moving lament.[30]

In view of all these facts, the charge that Marx suffered from Jewish self-hate and tried to conceal his Jewish birth seems pure speculation, if not worse. It was voiced first by Eugen Dühring, an anti-Semite and Marx's rival for intellectual leadership in the German Social Democratic Party[31] — the same Dühring against whom Engels wrote the series of articles which then became the most popular introduction to "scientific socialism." In this book Engels mentions anti-Semitism only briefly as "a specifically East Prussian superstition inherited from the Middle Ages." Marx was also attacked as a Jew by one Eduard Müller-Tellering, who had been a contributor to the *Neue Rheinische Zeitung* and later in exile became an enemy, and by Wilhelm Marr, also a former associate, who was to become the foremost anti-Semitic agitator in the Bismarck era (in fact, he is credited with having invented the term anti-Semite in 1879). Ruge called Marx "a skunk and a slanderous Jew" and considered socialists "a gang of atrocious Jewish souls." More subtly, Proudhon seems to hint at Marx, writing: "Jews are counterfeiters in trade and in philosophy." Marx never answered these attacks but allowed Engels to deal with them; according to Bebel, who liked to quote the coinage, it was Engels who said: "Anti-Semitism is the socialism of imbeciles." (This phrase is not mentioned by Silberner, who cites a number of warmhearted pronouncements by Engels after his alleged "conversion" from his early anti-Semitism. Silberner believes that Marx and Engels were anti-Semites in their early career, while my point is that their views on Judaism were a function of their social philosophy.)

Had Marx tried to hide his Jewishness, he could not have succeeded. All who knew him and left memoirs have testified that he looked Jewish (Liebknecht, Ruge, Mevissen); his nickname was "the

Moor" because of his dark complexion, and he could have sat for Michelangelo as a model for one of his prophets. His quarrel with his mother (probably over finances) has fed the theory that he wished to deny his family; but he maintained the most cordial relations with his Dutch-Jewish uncles, and his wife and daughters shared these affections. Carlebach, the latest to review the entire material, says that no clinical evidence supports the theory that Marx acted out of Jewish self-hate. Carlebach also makes the astute remark that if there was hate, it was not necessarily "Jewish" self-hate.

Just the same, it seems legitimate to ask why Marx came down so hard on the Jews. The unpleasant fact is that he was no model character and especially nasty when he spoke of rivals. Hence the anti-Semitic expletives against Lassalle. But he also had a considerable stock of anti-German, anti-British, anti-Polish, anti-Russian invective. His letters burst with obscenities. In *The German Ideology* he compares philosophy with masturbation; in his economic notebooks most authors are shit-heads *(Scheisskerle)*, Malthus is ridiculed because of his many children, and only Adam Smith and David Ricardo (though a Jew) never seem to deserve any epithet.

All nationalities were objects of his slurs, and Jews cannot claim any privileged place in the order of Marx's wrath; they merely have more reason to resent such derangement of taste in one of their sons. As to their sensitivity to his approach in "On the Jewish Question," I hope to have shown that at least partly it is due to the difficulties that essay presents to anybody who is not steeped in the philosophies of Hegel and Feuerbach and in the language of early socialism. Shlomo Avineri has tried to correct this sort of misunderstanding in his essay "Marx and the Jewish Emancipation,"[32] in which he emphasizes Marx's distinction between civil society and political society, between human emancipation and political emancipation, between the brotherhood of men and their equality before the law, between bourgeois and citizen (both words are *Bürger* in German). But if Marx was concerned with man as a social being, why did he then confuse the social with the economic? He who knew Shakespeare so well might have quoted Shylock *(Merchant of Venice,* act 3, scene 1):

Hath not a Jew eyes? Hath not a Jew hands, organs, dimensions, senses, affections, passions? Fed with the same food, hurt with the same weapons, subject to the same diseases. . . . If you prick us, do we not bleed? If you tickle us, do we not laugh? . . . And if you wrong us, shall we not revenge?

The Unresolved Question

Again, I think the essay "On the Jewish Question" is unsatisfactory. It evades the real questions, and Fritz Raddatz says candidly that it does not make much sense. Jews will not be reduced to an economic paradigm. Nor is anti-Semitism simply a matter of economic classes. It existed long before capitalism. Jews were despised in ancient Rome because they would not eat with the gentiles nor sacrifice to the gods of the land or to the emperor. They did not participate in the rites that were needed to make the soil fertile and to weld the nation into blood brothers. They worshipped an invisible, alien, abstract god whom they carried everywhere — like money, indeed, but perhaps in a sense slightly different from the interpretation that Marx gave the association. In the Middle Ages the Jews were "dusty travelers" journeying from fair to fair, taking root nowhere, strangers everywhere. The service they performed might have been necessary, but it could be performed only by outsiders, unclean people — untouchables who were allowed to live on sufferance, as a privilege granted by the sovereign.

Then the roles were reversed. As in Hegel's famous chapter, the master became dependent upon the servant; the gods of the soil died; the king aggrandized the manipulators of money, whose religion was compatible with the abstract, invisible power that was encroaching upon traditional life. The representatives of the aristocracy and of the clergy expressed their resentment: Jews were the carriers of bureaucratic government, rationalism, commercialism. Impoverished handicraftsmen, too, became victims of this same liberalism that benefited the Jews: the revolution emancipated their persons from the shackles of privilege and their business from the shackles of the guild system. Next to the tree of liberty, therefore, grew "the poisoned root of socialist anti-Semitism."[33] Anti-Semites

14.   Otis Skinner as Shylock
(Photo: Billy Rose Theatre Collection. New York Public Library at Lincoln Center.
Astor, Lenox, and Tilden Foundations)

drew effective points from the resentments of the traditional classes, especially in Germany, where nostalgic resistance to the Enlightenment and liberalism was always confused with resistance to French domination:

> The Jewish religion appears to be totally a work of the intellect: a creation purposely injected into the organic world order to destroy everything natural, to subject it and to replace it by its own mode of operation. Just so capitalism, which places an artificial, calculated, and manufactured strangeling into the natural, creaturelike world. Rationalism is the word that unites Judaism and capitalism. [34]

Clearly, this goes back to Marx's indictment of "money"; but where Marx resolved the Jewish question into a question of capitalism, Sombart resolved the social question into a Jewish question. Then came the first world war, and the kaiser needed the help of every Jewish banker in Germany. Behold the great historian of capitalism who now finds no difficulty in ascribing all those Jewish traits of heartless, calculating mercantilism to the British![35] Not surprisingly, Sombart also adjusted himself to the Nazis and published a book on *German Socialism* in 1934. He declared that he was no anti-Semite but merely [!] wished to keep the Jews out of the German universities. If ever the crudest conception of the relationship between economic interests and ideology can be proven true, it applies to the German antirationalist philosophy, which is so closely connected with anti-Semitism.

But ideologies must be taken seriously, and Marx was too deeply involved in Hegelian and Feuerbachian rationalism to see the force of the romantic reaction. His analysis of the Jewish question shed light on only half of the problem: alienation in a money economy. "Abolish money and you will abolish the Jew," he had suggested; but "abolishing the Jew" does not mean abolishing anti-Semitism. Today "the Jew" no longer symbolizes money, yet the Jewish question is still with us – and precisely in those countries where not money but Marx is said to rule.

In the East as well as in the West, Jews are seen as representing the rule of rationality, alienation, abstraction, materialism, bureaucracy, and other invisible powers. Some who with good reason think they are disciples of the young Marx, write today: abolish the computers, and you will render the "Jew" impossible.

"Jewish" Marxism

Marxism is, or originally was, a protest against the "purposeful rationality" it called capitalism. Was it, then, an echo of the prophetic tradition, as some have asserted? Was Marx, perhaps, not an anti-Semite but, on the contrary, one who upheld the ethics of Judaism against the morals of the Jews? Alienation is not only a condition for the successful operation of capitalism, it is also the consciousness of being a stranger in that society. For Jews this has been both a theological and an existential problem, and it has been expressed symbolically in these lines from Heinrich Heine's poem "Prinzessin Sabbat":

> Hund mit hündischen Gedanken
> Kötert er die ganze Woche
> Durch des Lebens Kot und Kehricht,
> Gassenbuben zum Gespötte.
>
> Aber jeden Freitagabend
> In der Dämmrungstunde, plötzlich
> Weicht der Zauber, und der Hund
> Wird aufs neu ein menschlich Wesen.
>
> As a dog with doggish notions,
> All the livelong week he piddles
> Through life's slime and slops and sweepings,
> Mocked and jeered at by street-arabs.
>
> But on every Friday evening
> At the twilight hour, the magic
> Fades abruptly, and the dog
> Once more is a human being. [36]

Marx yearned to overcome the split between the Sabbath Jew and the workaday Jew, between workday and holiday. Whatever the emotional motive for this yearning may have been, the idea and the categorical instruments to deal with the problem had been received from Hegel and Feuerbach. The nineteen-year-old student explained this in a long letter to his father, and he acknowledges his intellectual debts in later writings. He, who was always scrupulously honest in quoting sources, never makes the connection between his own ideas and those of the Jewish prophets, or the church fathers (which might have been suggested by Hegel), or Saint Augustine. Moreover, he transformed these instruments to suit his own purposes. To him, alienation is not a general *Weltschmerz,* not the Kafkaesque consciousness of impotence in the face of unknown powers, but the specific separation of the worker from his work, from its product, from his fellow worker and, as worker, from his humanity. To confuse this with the sensibilities of a minority means to obliterate Marx's specific contribution to social psychology, nay to deny him credit for any original contribution.

Similarly, Marx's persistent expectation of the revolution has been interpreted as an echo of the messianic prophecies. Thus Mircea Eliade writes in *The Sacred and the Profane:*[37]

> Marx takes over and continues one of the great eschatological myths of the Asiatico-Mediterranean world: the redeeming role of the Just (the "chosen," ... in our day: the proletariat) whose sufferings are destined to change the ontological status of the world.... The classless society and the consequent disappearance of historical tensions find their closest precedent in the myth of the Golden Age.... [which Marx enriched by the Judeo-Christian ideology of a] final battle between good and evil.... He takes over the Judeo-Christian eschatological hope of an absolute end to history.

This is fantasy: in the *Communist Manifesto,* the victory of the proletariat is said to "end the *pre*-history of Mankind," and in *Capital* Marx compares the proletariat with the Chosen People only ironically: "As the Jews are... Jehovah's people, so the workers are the property of capital."

Finally, as Melvin Lasky points out in *Utopia and Revolution,*[38] "Marx was not interested in utopia but in revolution." Marx considered it his decisive contribution to the theory of revolution that he found it neither in a divine scheme of history, nor in the logic of a Hegelian World Spirit, nor in the ethical commands of reason, but in the socially active forces of people. As a young man he put it into verse:

> Kant und Fichte gern zum Äther schweifen,
> Suchten dort ein fernes Land.
> Doch ich such nur tüchtig zu begreifen,
> Was ich auf der Strasse fand.
>
> Kant and Fichte are fond of flying into the air,
> seeking there a distant land.
> I only try honestly to understand
> what I find in the streets.
>   (Lasky's translation, in *Utopia and Revolution*)

In the *Yearbook* he wrote: "We do not face the world with a new principle: 'Here is the truth, here kneel down.' We develop new principles for the world out of the principles of the world."[39] Elsewhere he denied that he had any message for the proletarians but meant "merely to make the workers aware of what they will find themselves led to do." In other words, Marxism is the opposite of a Sorelian myth, a Christian eschatology, or a Jewish prophecy. It is not apocalyptic but Promethean.

All previous revolutions, Marx says in another context, draped themselves in the garment of an ideal nation. The Puritans impersonated the Hebrews crossing the desert, the French bourgeoisie imitated the virtuous republicans of ancient Rome. The proletariat, by contrast, will have to build a bridge into unknown territory, develop principles of its own, create thoughts for which there is no model.[40]

The Marxian view of humanity and its future, therefore, is no closer to the Jewish prophets than to other visionaries like Joachim da Fiore, Thomas Münzer, some Russian Narodniki, or the British Levelers. There is no Marxian soteriology; the proletariat is no "Chosen People"; its historical mission is to abolish itself, neither to be elevated nor "saved": "The present generation is like the Jews whom Moses led through the wilderness. It has not only a world to conquer but must go under in order to make room for the men who are fit for a new world."[41]

This passage shows that Marx did not use Jewish symbolism in any way that would be different from the thousands of references in German magazine literature; since religious instruction was part of the school curriculum, writers and painters were able to draw freely on the rich imagery of the Biblical stories. The mere occurrence of such references, therefore, does not permit any inferences regarding the author's personal involvement. I do not find that the Jewish heritage is needed to understand Marx's intellectual development. His mature works transcend both the traditions he grew up with and his initial revulsion from them. What may need an explanation is the violence of that revulsion.

The Marginal Man

A useful concept in analyzing an aggressive reaction to cultural crises is "marginality," lack of identity between two cultures, failure to integrate, lack of "belongingness." Of marginal characters Jessie Bernard wrote that since they cannot be either Jews or gentiles, they must destroy everything they stand for.[42] Similarly, Salo W. Baron wrote: "They become a menace to the equilibrium of the general as well as the Jewish society around them."[43]

Marginality, however, occurs not only in the case of those who exist between two cultures coexisting simultaneously, but even more evidently when one culture is encroaching upon another or when a main culture disintegrates. Intellectuals are known to announce such disintegration; they are most sensitive to the shortcomings of the culture in which they grew up; they secede from it most vociferously; they articulate all contradictions and resentments. Therefore, what has been said of Jews may be even more true of intellectuals.

Hannah Arendt is probably right in remarking that first of all Marx was an intellectual: "The anti-Jewish denunciations by Marx and Börne cannot be understood except in the light of the conflict between rich Jews and Jewish intellectuals." In polemicizing against his father, Marx denounces middle-class society; in repudiating the Jewish religion he fights the state of alienation in which society forces the thinking human being to live. If he seems to flee from his family, he feels shame for all business-minded families. In different contexts, similar sentiments are found in Maximilian Harden, editor of *Die Zukunft* and a convert, in Walther Rathenau, and other Jewish intellectuals. They were "marginal" as Jews not only with respect to the main culture, but even more so with respect to the Jewish philistines. Thus, Marx said: "The existence of a suffering humanity that thinks and of a thinking humanity that is oppressed will be unpalatable to the philistines who are thoughtlessly enjoying themselves."[44]

The work of many Jewish writers demonstrates similar traits, either as an explicit topic or in more subliminal ways. Kurt Tucholsky created "Wendriner," a Jewish philistine whose inane comments on current events made both him and his enemies look foolish. But if Wendriner was an expression of Jewish self-hate, then Babbitt and Caspar Milquetoast must be called expressions of American self-hate and the term becomes meaningless. [45]

Marx hated Jewish Babbitts as much as he hated Babbitts in general, especially German ones. He criticized and denounced the Jewish bourgeoisie as part of the German and the English bourgeoisie. He was suspicious of Jews like Lassalle who wished to become part of the German establishment. He expressed his disgust with Jewish parvenus. Before him, Molière had proved that you don't have to be Jewish to behave like a nouveau-riche, and after him an American sociologist wrote a book on the ostentatiousness of the leisure class. But when Jewish jokes telescope that point in a brilliant punch line, other sociologists will write books on "Jewish self-hate." The truth is that the joke may do three things: it expresses *Schadenfreude* at the failure of misplaced ambition; it expresses sadness at the conditions that make the joke possible; and it disarms the anti-Semite by anticipating his scoffing comment. The joke is a protective weapon, a strategy to prevent others from laughing at Jews: "Wit is a good weapon, but more suitable for the weak than for the strong, more appropriate for the oppressed than for the overlords. . . . Hence its importance for the Jews."[46]

The great historian of mores Eduard Fuchs (incidentally, not a Jew), a friend of Rosa Luxemburg, felt that self-deprecation

> is that form of self-emancipation which relieves the Jew of the onerous pressure of social humiliation. . . . It disarms the enemy by saying in a witty way: Okay, Okay, you are right. There is no finer way of self-protection as long as one does not have a club or one's upbringing prevents one from using it. . . . The taste of this form of mimicry has developed into a special characteristic of the Jewish intellect.[47]

Apparently aware of all this, Saul Bellow says: "In America, certain forms of success required an element of parody, self-mockery, a satire on the-thing-itself."[48]

A self-deprecating joke may be a means of asserting superiority: he who reveals his weakness or his shame is the stronger in spirit. In reading Marx's denunciation of Jewish usury or pushiness, one gets the impression that he is doing just that. He is not preaching anti-Semitism but trying to defuse it. The same goes for Tucholsky, Börne, Heine, Kafka, Karl Kraus, and others. They all proved that the narrowness of the Jewish ghetto could be overcome only if *every* group left the narrowness of its ghetto and the larger city, too, was transcended. Liberation was to be complete.

Summary and Conclusion

The anti-Semitism that Marx knew in the middle of the last century was largely social; it was not yet an organized political force with a philosophy and program. These have existed only since the Dreyfus affair and have taken their toll in this century. Carlebach makes the distinction more sharply than it probably should be made, but on principle one can concede that it is anyone's damned right to dislike Jews or Italians or blacks or, for that matter, WASPs. What matters is whether private sentiments are converted into racist philosophies. In this political sense Marx and Engels cannot be called anti-Semitic, nor does their attitude to persons of the Jewish faith show any discriminatory pattern. They were both men of the Enlightenment — which anti-Semitism seeks to reject.

Both Marx and Engels used ethnic epithets against individuals. They shared certain national prejudices of their age, which may have colored their political judgment; their contempt for German institutions and German philistines, for instance, was overlaid by their hopes for the German future. It is possible, however, to explain and interpret these attitudes without resorting to psychoanalytical theories.

The same reservation should hold for Marx's attitude to his ancestors. One must assume that he was as conscious of the problem as other ex-Jews; but that does not mean to say that the problem wrought decisive quirks in his character or significantly influenced his thinking. In particular, his attitude to Judaism and Jews seems to be very much in tune with the notions that he found in his environment; these also developed and changed in response to changes in his social views, and in fact he contributed to the reshaping of the environment. I hope to have shown that his views on Jews and Judaism can and must be understood in their historical context, and that even those that we find unpleasant and deplorable did not in their original setting have the meaning we associate today with the notion of anti-Semitism. I have shown in particular that "On the Jewish Question" represents a transitional stage in Marx's thinking, and that his mature thought was totally free from any idols of the tribe, of the cave, and of the marketplace. It may even be that Marx was more critical of Jews than of other tribes because that is how most people show their concern for their family.

As a general rule, I would suggest to the psychohistorians a sort of Occam's Razor: that historical phenomena, and ideologies in particular, should be seen in terms of the situation out of which they have grown, and that psychological explanations should not be sought unless the analysis of general conditions yields no satisfactory explanation. In the case of Hitler there may be such an irrational residue; in the case of Marx's and Engels' attitude to race and religion, the evolution of their thoughts out of the Hegelian left is so logical, and the relatedness of that evolution to the political and social developments of their age is so direct and open, that the search for hidden psychological sources seems redundant or misleading. Marx's views on Judaism were a function of the development of his social thought.

A Short Note

Only after I read my article in galleys did I realize what it was about. Was it really necessary to rescue Marx from the charge of anti-Semitism? Should I not rather have written my essay from the inside out, praising Marx's emergence from the provincial German or sectarian Jewish world into the cosmopolitan world of the future?

Here is a man who overcame narrowness and nationalism. He is attacked by German nationalists for being an unpatriotic Jew and by Jewish nationalists for being an anti-Semitic renegade. Would not his best defense rather be to admit, Yes, I am all of those things, and proud of them. Obviously, to become a human being the German must stop being a German, and the Jew must stop being a Jew. In the *Communist Manifesto* Marx said that the workers have no fatherland, no nation, no religion. His philosophy was that of the great maskil, Moses Mendelssohn, who kept all the Mosaic laws but was disgusted with the Jewish language and customs. Similarly, those great defenders of Dreyfus, the brothers Théodore, Salomon, and Joseph Reinach — orientalist, archeologist, and statesman, respectively — excoriated Jewish traditionalism and deplored the backwardness and pettiness, even the "human inferiority," of Eastern Jews.

Likewise, Julien Benda, a Platonist of Jewish descent, characterized the narrow Hebrew as "enslaved by the passion for small lucre, patient, fearful, thrifty, hardworking, and a blind follower of customs that have lost their justification." I can see no reason why a Jew should not be able to denounce the shortcomings of his tribe, just as Signor Luigi Barzini has written about the Italians and Mr. Geoffrey Gorer about the Americans and Herr Kurt Tucholsky about the Germans.

12

The Ambiguous Legacy of
Eduard Bernstein

As much as political parties need a myth, they need heroes whom they can admire; although democratic socialism is a movement based on rationalism, it is no exception. A leader with a human face lends personal warmth to the idea; a founder's image bestows historical perspective upon routine practices. It is not surprising, therefore, that after the eclipse of the popular Willy Brandt and his replacement by the efficient Helmut Schmidt, the German Social Democratic Party should have scanned its history in search of an ancestor. Willy Brandt himself would have liked to revive the memory of August Bebel, the venerable cofounder who led the party from 1869 to his death in 1913. For all his sterling qualities, however, highly praised even by the cross-grained Marx, Bebel was not a thinker and perhaps too much of a boss; Marx, on the other hand, was out of the question. So some younger Social Democrats took matters into their own hands and recently staged a renascence of Eduard Bernstein (1850-1932), the critic of Marxism and father of "revisionism," well remembered by the pre-Hitler generation as "Old Ede Bernstein" and well suited, with his benevolent, bearded physiognomy, to play the role of ancestor.

A warning is necessary. Bernstein's revisionism of 1900 has almost nothing in common with today's search for a "socialism with a human face"; his opponents on the socialist left were dedicated, no

15.   **Eduard Bernstein, c.1912**
(Photo: International Institute of Social History, Amsterdam)

less than he, to democratic and humanist values. The party rarely had theoretical discussions about such values because it was too busy fighting for their realization and they were still unquestioned in the socialist camp. The early socialists took for granted that socialism proposed to expand the "realm of freedom" and to actualize those liberties that liberalism had failed to achieve. Only the enemies of socialism charged that public ownership would mean bureaucratic rule by bosses.

Although Gustave Le Bon (1895) and Robert Michels (1911) had attacked the spirit of mass movements, bossism, and the "iron law of oligarchy," Bernstein did not use their arguments, and while he criticized Marx and others, he never criticized the party. On the contrary, he was very much a man of the movement, and he hoped to formulate a theory that would fit the practice of its leaders. Occasionally he would warn the workers not to trust their May Day speakers, but he accepted machine rule when its decisions went his way. He declared decentralization a lovely idea, but in practical instances he came out for central organization and strong leadership.

In one respect, Bernstein's efforts aimed at exactly the opposite of what modern revisionists seek to achieve. They hope to underpin Marxism with philosophical, anthropological, and psychological "groundings" that would make it into an all-encompassing, universal— in the language of Lukács or Sartre: totalizing— *Weltanschauung*. Bernstein, on the contrary, tried to strip Marxism of all those transcendental claims that are not warranted by empirical findings, and he felt free to treat it as just another branch of social science, subject to periodical revisions.

It is mostly this undogmatic attitude that recommends Bernstein to modern socialists, but here again a caveat must be added: while the current labor movement needs an ideology, it was Bernstein's aim, seventy years ago, to keep ideology out of labor's activities. It is true, of course, that his residual Marxism was strong enough to make the socialist goal, and even more so the socialist attitude, matter; and he was far from wishing to convert the labor movement into a mere pressure group. But that was precisely the danger of his revisionism; it preached a sobriety that is perhaps overly dominant today. Where the present time needs new sources of inspiration, the socialists around the turn of the century were still feeding on the élan of a movement on the rise.

Bernstein's revisionism fit the period of the Second International, roughly from the 1880s to 1914, when the proletariat was growing —physically, morally, politically. Along with expanding capitalism, the trade unions were acquiring power while the parties were gain-ing votes in every election. Thus, Bernstein could take the position that no bloody revolution, perhaps no violence at all, was required to seize power: with the ballot the socialists would gain ascendancy step by step, and through legislation they would transform capitalism into a more humane system. To do that, however, they needed allies; above all the peasants and the intelligentsia. It was essential not to frighten them off by revolutionary gestures and fanatical programs; a party that wishes to rule must not bind its hands with ideological shackles. Socialist parties should be open to believers of all faiths; their programs should receive stimulation from all new developments in the arts and sciences; their tactics should be flexible. What mattered was not righteousness but a progress whose inevitability neither the orthodox nor the revisionists nor anyone else around 1900 ever doubted. The labor movement had been utopian as long as it was immature; now it could no longer afford to reject or deprecate immediate improvements on the ground that they seemed deceptive or puny in the light of the faraway ideal.

In this sense Bernstein spoke the words that made him famous: "*The ultimate goal* (Endziel) *is nothing to me; the Movement is everything*." In his main work, *Evolutionary Socialism,*[1] written in 1899, he qualified this to say that obviously the movement must have a direction, but that goals would develop concurrently with the movement's progress. Strangely, he shared this way of thinking with some on the far left, the French syndicalists and Rosa Luxemburg, who were certainly not his allies in any other respect. They, too, thought of revolution as an ongoing process, a movement rather than a unique event, and like Bernstein they felt that the power of the movement mattered more than the form of government under which it was progressing. At the end of this essay, the relevance of that idea will be examined, but first a review of Bernstein's life is in order.

"A Life for Socialism"

Eduard Bernstein was born in 1850, the son of a Jewish railway engineer in Berlin. His father sent him to high school — then unusual for workers — but he left at the age of fourteen with the certificate that enabled middle-class boys to cut their military service from three years to one. He was apprenticed to a banker, but his interest in socialism awakened early. At first he was attracted to Lassalle's ideas rather than to those of Marx, but having found Lassalle's disciples sectarian, he joined the Marxist-populist Social Democratic Workers' Party. This preference for movement over ideology foreshadowed his later views. In 1875 he took part in the Gotha Congress, where the two German workers' parties merged, forming the SPD (Social Democratic Party of Germany).

Persecuted under Bismarck's anti-socialist law, Bernstein fled to Zurich, where one Karl Hochberg, a rich, well-meaning philanthropist, sponsored a weekly paper, *Der Sozialdemokrat,* which was smuggled across the border. Since socialists in Germany found it difficult to communicate with one another, this exile paper soon was the most important link between them and became the party's official organ. Hochberg picked Bernstein to be its editor; did he sense even then that Bernstein was a moderate at heart?

Marx and Engels were suspicious of both men. But Bernstein acquitted himself with skill and, when he visited the masters in London, won their confidence. In 1888 the paper was transferred to London, and there Bernstein became so intimate with Engels that the old gentleman appointed him and Karl Kautsky — the high priest of orthodox Marxism — executors of his will. Bernstein justified this confidence by publishing a series of *Documents of Socialism* (among them part of *The German Ideology*).

In 1890 the SPD became legal once again, but Bernstein was still under indictment in Prussia and could not leave England until 1901. He used his long stay to study the seventeenth-century revolutions and write a remarkable book on the radical Puritans, which Max Weber recognized as a major contribution — in fact, as an anticipation of his own studies on the affinity between capitalism and Puritanism. In London, Bernstein met George Bernard Shaw and attended meetings of the Fabian Society. He watched the success of the "piecemeal revolution" they were advocating; he admired the civility of their discussions, so different from the blunt German manner; he was impressed by the gradual expansion of the public sphere in the supply of basic services and by the growth of democratic rights in industrial relations. In his book *Zur Geschichte und Theorie des Sozialismus* (1901),[2] he repeated the term piecemeal socialism but later on denied that the Fabians had been decisive in his intellectual development. He may have been right. Fabian socialism was not a popular movement but addressed itself to civil servants and other well-meaning members of the managing class. Bernstein, by contrast, was genuinely attached to the daily reality of trade union activities and the practice of class struggle rather than technocratic planning.

Although Bernstein had discussed Fabianism with Engels, its full significance may have become clear to him only later; also perhaps he did not wish to sadden his old friend and mentor. So he waited until Engels died in 1895. Less than a year later, he began to publish articles attacking Marxist philosophy and the theory of revolution. These articles were collected in *Evolutionary Socialism*.

Bernstein was hardly the first to point out discrepancies between Marx's predictions and the development of capitalism; nor were all his points well taken. He overestimated the significance of small business and paid too little attention to important changes in the structure of capitalism — the emergence of big business and monopolistic organizations, the collaboration of banking, industry, and government, the revival of the colonialist impetus — which were commented upon by writers in Kautsky's theoretical weekly, *Die Neue Zeit,* and elsewhere. On the other hand, he clearly saw that basic changes had occurred in the operating conditions of the labor movement and in the forms of its activity. He was not the only one to make these observations. Sidney and Beatrice Webb had just published *Industrial Democracy* (1897), the classic that Lenin translated and then quoted to show that by themselves the workers can develop only a "trade union consciousness."

Certainly Bernstein did not claim that he was offering a new theory. He merely presented his observations on the practice of politics and trade union action. To his surprise, however, the union leaders were not interested in being vindicated; they had no use for "revisionism" or any other "theory." The militants were annoyed with the "quarrels of intellectuals," which they feared might weaken the movement, and the party was in an uproar; sharp refutations were published in *Die Neue Zeit* and in various daily papers. Bernstein was censured at the party's congress and would have been expelled but for his personal friendship with many leaders. Nor did it help his reputation with the workers when he was invited by the University of Berlin to present his views to an academic audience. (He probably was the only German without a high school diploma ever to receive this honor. And twenty years later, when the files were opened, the suspicion seemed justified: the Prussian Minister of Justice had quashed Bernstein's indictment because it was hoped he would split the SPD.)

Bernstein gave his lecture an ambitiously Kantian title: "How Is Scientific Socialism Possible?" His answer, obviously, had to be that socialism is not a scientific necessity but a moral imperative. In the audience were such social-liberal professors as Lujo Brentano, Werner Sombart, and Gerhard von Schulze-Gävernitz, whom workers laughingly called "socialists of the lectern." But these paternalistic advocates of "social policies" were really fundamentally different from Bernstein. His aim was not to reform capitalism but to transform it; his social policies were not so much for workers as by the workers. What the professors considered a necessary, perhaps healthy adjustment of capitalism was for him merely the first mile on the long road toward a new social order. What they expected to be granted by the government, he foresaw as the movement's victories. Even in his two historical works on the Chartists and the Puritans, the emphasis had been on self-organization and action by the masses.

Why, then, was the party so shocked by Bernstein's views? Its everyday politics were no longer revolutionary. Kautsky himself had written that the SPD was a revolutionary party that did not make revolutions. It expected that somehow it would wake up one morning and find that the revolution had come — an event that was to happen in 1918. In the meantime, however, the party behaved as though infinite progress, step by successive step, was possible under the kaiser's regime. It was growing; already it was "the strongest of all parties" (as its hymn asserted); in 1903 it polled one-third of all votes; one day it would poll 51 percent.

16. Karl Liebknecht at a Mass Demonstration in Berlin, 1918
(Photo: International Institute of Social History, Amsterdam)

To make that success a certainty, the party needed the Marxist theory, which assured the membership that the outcome was preordained, that "ultimately" there would be a fundamental change, that all the suffering and fighting would be rewarded by a day of reckoning and consequent bliss. It was still dangerous to walk a picket line, and no man courts that danger for mere pennies. He must have a flag, an ultimate goal, an idea, a future, a community for which to risk his life. The great mass strikes in most countries were political strikes: not for economic gains but for civil rights, for the ballot.

Bernstein charged that the party's revolutionary rhetoric was no longer in line with its daily practice — which was precisely what the party did not wish to hear. He proposed to adjust the theory to the real conditions of class conflict — but would not the militants then have lost courage? He promised that a more realistic ideology would attract millions of middle-class voters — but did the proletarians to whom Marx had promised the future want that? Bernstein envisaged a movement of the whole people; but the party's life, its trade union halls, its May Day festivals, its social and cultural clubs were proletarian in speech, in manner, in dress, in habits, and in outlook.

The Dresden Congress of 1903 rejected "revisionism" by an overwhelming majority. Significantly, that majority included many who agreed with Bernstein on all practical matters but felt that the party could not abandon the ideology that had made it great. Bernstein's friend Ignaz Auer, who sympathized with this view, observed dryly: "My dear Ede, such things may be done, but one does not brag about them." Bernstein was isolated. Only a small band of intellectuals, parliamentarians, and trade union officials rallied around the revisionist magazine *Sozialistische Monatshefte,* which attracted progressive writers outside the party and dealt intelligently with modern poetry, drama, and fiction. Its reviews of contemporary literature and art compare favorably with those of *Die Neue Zeit,* which was hopelessly mired in the classical canons Marx had respected a generation ago. Bernstein was a regular contributor until the First World War revealed that the party had grown much more revisionist than he had intended. The *Sozialistische Monatshefte* in particular waxed ultrapatriotic; in the hour of national danger, it said, "Germany's poorest son is found to be her most faithful."

Bernstein, too, had originally agreed that in a "war against the bloody czar" no socialist could remain neutral (a judgment with which Marx and Engels would have heartily concurred). Soon, however, Bernstein learned that the German war aims were no less execrable than the czar's and he seceded both from the magazine and, more important, from the parliamentary SPD, which continued to vote for the kaiser's war appropriations. He was followed by a few "ethical socialists"; there were also radical war protesters on the left; they all met to form a new party, the Independent Social Democratic Party of Germany (USPD). Thus Bernstein was temporarily united with former antagonists: the orthodox Marxists, the old left—Kautsky, Hilferding, Ledebour, Haase—and radicals like Ernst Däumig and Liebknecht, who were later to prove influential in forming the Communist Party.

Although the USPD attracted only a minority of the old SPD, it embodied the best of the socialist traditions in Germany: it was revolutionary and pacifist; it had a solid base in the "councils" *(Räte)* that were springing up in the construction and defense industries; it became the driving force in the revolutionary events of 1918–19; it forced the Reichstag to sign the Treaty of Versailles.

Bernstein, however, never felt comfortable in this revolutionary ambiance. In November 1918 he tried to prevent "hasty" socializations that might disrupt production. Soon after the revolution he rejoined the SPD, yet he also maintained his membership in the USPD. When dual membership was declared inadmissible, he chose the SPD, although he did not abandon his effort to reconcile the parties until 1920. Then half the Independents merged with the Communists, while leaders of the old Marxist center (Kautsky, Hilferding) returned to the SPD in 1922. Two years later, on the occasion of Kautsky's seventieth birthday, Kautsky and Bernstein restored the friendship of their early days in London and proclaimed their total agreement. Forty years later, at a commemorative function, Carlo Schmid was able to state that "Bernstein triumphed throughout."

After he returned to the fold, Bernstein was given a seat in the Reichstag and became the party's expert on taxation. More important, as a former Independent he was useful to the party in arguing with the left; his pamphlets of the period are an apology for the SPD leaders' conduct during the 1918 revolution and a defense of the parliamentary Republic. His enemies, and in particular the Communists, now were the advocates of the council system. The Independents had favored a parliamentary republic in which the councils would have a legitimate place; now the labor movement was split into dogmatic advocates of parliamentary government on the one side and equally dogmatic devotees of the soviet system on the other.

The SPD still gave courses in Marxism to its youth groups, but by the middle 1920s it had exchanged class struggle for the defense of the Republic. At the Heidelberg Congress in 1925 it adapted its program to the new tendencies of "organized capitalism" and dealt with the new problems of industrial democracy and crisis management. In social legislation, the party still pursued policies along the lines of Bernstein's reform socialism. But the problems were of a new magnitude and nature that he had not foreseen: labor was deeply involved in administrative and economic decision-making; rather than transform capitalism, labor wished to "save" it.

In Prussia, which now was the most advanced German state, Social Democrats were planning and expanding public ownership. Bernstein, who had said that "a good piece of social legislation is worth more than a hundred nationalizations," had fallen behind the times. His powers were waning, and his later books are embarrassing. He died in 1932, at a time when history was shattering the liberal-labor ideologies and the pseudorepublican illusions of the SPD. If there was a better way to ward off the Nazi threat than support of Hindenburg, Bernstein did not know it. Peter Gay, Bernstein's biographer,[3] viewed "the dilemma of democratic socialism" as being caught "between the Charybdis of impotence vis-à-vis the enemy and the Scylla of treason vis-à-vis the cause." Our question must now be, Did this have to be the case? Does a democratic conviction exclude militancy and decisiveness?

Two Views of Revolution

Revisionism essentially is the view that progress toward social equality and power for the labor movement can be won without violent revolution; that the end cannot be achieved by a determined minority's actions but needs the support of the majority of the people; that revolution in the social sense — as opposed to "revolution by pitchforks" (Engels) — must be understood as a long-drawn-out process rather than a single act:

> Socialism will come, or rather is coming, not as a result of a great political showdown but as the result of a series of economic and political victories of the working-class movement in the various fields of its activities; not

as a consequence of increasing repression, of misery and humiliations but as a result of its increasing influence and of the improvements for which it has fought. The socialist society will emerge not from chaos but from an alliance of creative organizations in the field of economics and of creative innovations of militant democracy in the states and communities. In spite of reactionary counterblows, I see that class war assumes ever more civilized forms, and this is the best guarantee for the realization of socialism.[4]

This formulation was prepared by Bernstein for a speech he gave to socialist workers in 1898, reprinted in *Was ist Sozialismus?* in 1919. His conception was obviously modeled on the rise of the middle class, which had grown in the interstices of the feudal society and acquired power under absolutism. Revolution or no revolution, it had achieved a dominant position in all modern countries where it had developed its characteristic economic system and industry.

Marxists were convinced that the workers could not rise in the same fashion since they did not own the means of production and had not developed a characteristic economic system. The workers, rather, could come to power only by turning society upside down — not through prosperity but through a general cataclysm. The working class could not advance its principles within the old economy as its partner, rival, and successor; it had to be the midwife of "the new society that had been spawned in the womb of the old" — Marx was extremely fond of this metaphor, which he had inherited from Hegel.

Marx retained the spectacular and suggestive vision of an apocalyptic leap: the *social* revolution of the bourgeoisie had been accomplished before it acquired the symbols of political power, but it had to be completed by the *political* act that overthrew the "superstructure" of the feudal state. Strangely, he envisaged this same dialectic for the proletarian revolution, though with this difference: while in the bourgeois revolution the social–economic and cultural changes had *preceded* the seizure of political power, in the proletarian revolution the social-economic and cultural transformation was to *follow* the political seizure of power.

This scheme was no foreign element in Marxism. It was fitting for a weak proletariat and therefore was adopted wholesale by Lenin.

Even in an advanced country like Germany, however, the prophecy of a great cataclysmic revolution, a day of reckoning and renewal, helped to keep the militants' faith alive; even "pragmatic" socialist politicians felt that the party needed the fire-and-brimstone rhetoric of a revolutionary purgatory.

Bernstein considered all this an unfortunate heritage of the generation of 1848, when all radicals had looked back to the Jacobins and German radicals in particular were ensnared in "the trip wires of Hegelian dialectics" (the chapter so entitled is missing in the English version of *Evolutionary Socialism*). Had Marx not been trapped in the triadic schematism that requires the bloody qualitative leap, he might not have been blind to the chances of a more comfortable march into the future. Did not, by his own account in *Capital*, the workers win daily battles for the "political economy of the proletariat" — such as the ten-hour day and social security insurance — through trade union and legislative action, wielding ballots rather than bullets? Had not Engels, in the Preface to a new edition of Marx's *Class Struggles in France*, pointed out that modern city-planning, modern weapons, and modern police training had made the old tactics of insurrection obsolete?

Barricades might still serve as metaphors, and their memory might be celebrated in songs and on canvas. But in the most advanced countries — the Netherlands, England, the United States — Engels had thought it quite conceivable that a parliamentary majority might become the lever of the revolution. In Germany, the SPD had won 1.2 million votes and the next business slump would surely double this number; by the end of the century, Engels hoped to see socialism take power through democratic means.

Engels may not have been aware that, by embracing the ballot so enthusiastically, he was renouncing not only violence and dictatorship but also the entire either/or philosophy that pervades Marxist thought from the theory of value to the theory of the state. Marx's idea of revolution foresees a break in time, a sudden change of direction from the day before to the day after. Parliamentary tactics imply that pieces of socialist legislation can be introduced gradually and that the balance of power might shift from one class to another over a number of years. Just as the bourgeoisie had been able to use the state for its purposes even before the symbols of power had fallen into its hands, so the workers might acquire influence and power piecemeal while class struggle continued in the arenas of industry, parliament, culture, and law.

If the term "revolution" was to be used at all, it had to be redefined. It could no longer mean a military-political action that was to bring about a sudden change of regime. It would have to mean a protracted struggle, over many legislative periods, for the transformation of a private-enterprise economy into a mixed system where private and cooperative, municipal and state enterprises might compete but where all would undergo a process of democratization. So would all public functions. Class differences would gradually be reduced, and eventually disappear completely. Revolution, therefore, would be a continuous process, not a once-for-all-times surgical intervention. To return once again to Marx's favorite metaphor: socialism would not be brought into the world by Caesarean section.

Back to Lassalle and Proudhon

This development gave Ferdinand Lassalle, the meteoric initiator of German socialism, a posthumous victory over Marx. In his *Critique of the Gotha Program,* Marx had denied that the workers could "take over" the old state machinery. Lassalle, by contrast, had taught that once the workers had won the ballot, they would enlist the state's services in their fight against the liberal bourgeoisie. Lassalle did not mind allying himself with Bismarck for his purposes. In the united party, Marxist theory was still mouthed on solemn occasions, but in practical, everday dealings this staunch puritanism was an impediment rather than an aid; such rhetoric might justify class war but not direct it. Socialist congresses, therefore, were filled with curious debates about the relationship between socialist conscience and the need to win votes: should socialists agitate for farm loans when Marx had predicted the doom of the family farm? How was one to attract middle-class voters when the program condemned them to be ground down between the historical millstones of capital and labor? Was it permissible for the party paper in a small principality to mourn the demise of the local sovereign? Should Social Democrats at the end of a traditional Reichstag session, when the Speaker brought out the customary "Hurrah for the kaiser," rise politely but silently? or sullenly remain seated? walk out defiantly? Might the party paper serialize Zola's *Germinal* with its unflattering portraits of sturdy proletarians? Should socialists support the "petty-bourgeois" cause of Captain Dreyfus? In all these matters, practical measures of progress required acquiescence to the symbolism of the old regime, which offended the ethics and aesthetics of proletarian class consciousness. Yet a school of "pragmatists" among the labor leaders was quite prepared to sacrifice ideology for real increases in power.

Meanwhile, similar developments had spread "reformism" in other parties of the International. Filippo Turati formed the Italian Socialist Party and expelled the revolutionary syndicalists. In France the Parti Ouvrier, led by Jules Guesde and Paul Lafargue, wrote in its program: "The suffrage has been transformed from a means of deception, which it once was, into a means of emancipation" (the relative clause is there to appease the ghost of Marx). Certainly, in absolutist or semifeudal countries the state machinery had to be broken before any democratic development could be expected. It is also true that even in the West, socialist workers still thought of the revolution as "the day" — one of Kautsky's works was entitled *On the Day After the Revolution*. In their daily practice, however, the mass parties concentrated on electoral policies and social legislation; under the more liberal constitutions of the southern German states they occasionally provided the necessary votes to form a majority, and even orthodox Marxists were no longer suspicious of social reform. Rosa Luxemburg began her pamphlet *Social Reform or Revolution?* (1899), an eloquent polemic against Bernstein, by stating that these two terms ought not to be alternatives. Consequently, Social Democracy before the First World War was Marxist in name, but its actions were hardly guided by its program. When Bernstein proposed to purge Marxism of its Hegelian and Blanquist heritage, he meant nothing more than to bring the theory into harmony with the practice.

Revisions and Revisionism

Evolutionary Socialism is the work for which Bernstein is best known—unfortunately not an easy one, because Bernstein was not a systematic thinker. He was an able journalist who could handle facts and statistics well enough, but he was uncomfortable with ideas and often mistook "for instance" for an argument. His exposition also was warped by his ambivalent position on the fathers of the movement. Their orthodox discipline occupied the theoretical terrain, and instead of developing his own program, Bernstein had to present his views as deviations from established doctrine, sometimes exaggerating minor differences. Whatever Marx may have "really meant," the Marxism Bernstein knew was that of the late Engels and of Karl Kautsky; it was a Marxism that claimed to be "scientific" in the strict, deterministic sense of nineteenth-century materialism. Its function for the labor movement was to make its victory appear inevitable, as if it were a law of nature. Although Engels, too, had rejected the idea that anything "followed" from dialectics—as, for instance, in the *Anti-Dühring*—it was Bernstein who asked, Why then talk about dialectics at all? And Marx's famous law of value seemed to him sheer metaphysics: that the worker never gets the full product of his labor "is an empirical fact, demonstrable by experience, which needs no deductive proof. Whether the Marxist theory of value is correct or not is quite immaterial to the proof of surplus labor."[5]

Marx's propensity toward abstractions, however, had led him away from empirical reality. Predictions he had based on his alleged "laws" had failed to materialize. Bernstein noted in his diary: "Peasants don't sink, the middle class refuses to disappear, crises do not become ever more severe, nor do misery and slavery increase." Capitalism was not anywhere near the point of collapse, which Engels had set for the turn of the century. It was prospering. Instead of getting more polarized, class differences became more finely shaded. Instead of hurrying toward its doom, capitalism was developing tools of crisis management and organization: cartels, credit facilities, farm support, social policies. The middle class did not disappear; on the contrary, its expanding ranks gave strength to the economic structure and cushioned the business cycle.

Workers now had opportunities to rise or to find accommodations with the system, and socialists therefore found it more difficult to preach the total break that is revolution. A word often used, though not by Bernstein himself, stated the possibility of organic transformation *(Hineinwachsen)*, where it was not quite clear whether capitalism was imperceptibly "growing into" some sort of welfare state or the workers were acclimatizing themselves to capitalism. In either case, the conditions of class struggle had changed decisively since the *Communist Manifesto,* which still was the fundamental basis for the theoretical part of the program that the SPD had adopted at Erfurt in 1891. Bernstein himself had written the second, practical part of that program, with demands ranging from a universal, equal, and secret ballot to a progressive income tax and "free burial" — none of which was as explosive or "transcendent" as the famous "ten demands" at the end of the *Communist Manifesto.*

Bernstein's *Evolutionary Socialism* is really about this discrepancy. The first part summarizes the essential tenets of Marxism; the second shows that these no longer apply in the modern world; the third speaks of socialist actions in the real world, and especially of socialism's three main thrusts: trade unionism, cooperative enterprise, and parliamentary process. The last is presented with great eloquence:

> Democracy is in principle the suppression of class government, though it is not yet the actual suppression of classes... The right to vote in a democracy makes its members virtually partners in the community, and this virtual partnership must in the end lead to real partnership.[6]

After discussing the essential relationship between socialism and democracy, Bernstein comes to the question of patriotism. Contrary to Marx, he asserts that the workers do have a fatherland and, since they are "partners," they must defend it. "The complete breakup of nations is no beautiful dream," and the German nation carries out "its honorable share in the civilizing work of the world," especially in China, where the kaiser had just appropriated the base of Kiaochow:

In so far as the acquisition of the Kiaochow Bay is a means of securing [Germany's] right to... protest [against the partitioning of China], and it will be difficult to gainsay that it does contribute to it, there is no reason in my opinion for the social democracy to cry out against it on principle.[7]

"Protest" against colonialism is not the only purpose of acquisitions abroad. Five pages later we are told:

If it is not reprehensible to enjoy the produce of tropical plantations, it cannot be so to cultivate such plantations ourselves... It is neither necessary that the occupation of tropical lands by Europeans should injure the natives in their enjoyment of life, nor has it hitherto usually been the case... Moreover, only a conditional right of savages to the land occupied by them can be recognized.[8]

Even when better analyses of imperialism and colonialism became available — and they were soon an almost constant feature of *Die Neue Zeit* — Bernstein failed to see their significance. Just as his optimistic prognosis for capitalism was based on the survival of small business rather than on the really new features of monopoly and finance capitalism, so he missed altogether the meaning of the Boer War, of the Fashoda crisis, of Germany's frantic plunge into world politics, and of other signs indicating that the world was getting too small for national capitalism. In a book so totally devoted to the brightening horizons of labor under an increasingly benign and benignly increasing capitalism, one does not expect to find an apprehension of impending crisis. Far from being the seminal book that some pretend to see in it, *Evolutionary Socialism* is mostly a period piece, dated 1899.

With this important reservation: Bernstein must be given credit for closing the gap between social-democratic theory and social-democratic practice. He led the majority that had condemned him to repudiate Blanquist fantasies; he described the labor movement as it was. By doing so, he prevented disillusionment from turning into panic. The German labor movement was spared the experience of great defectors; it knew no Millerand, no Briand, no Viviani, no Laval, no Ramsay MacDonald, no Mussolini. We may attribute this to the existence of a revisionist theory, and also to the wisdom of

Bebel, who made room for the revisionists within the party, for those who could no longer follow Marx but remained Social Democrats.

This is no small feat when we consider what was being abandoned. To criticize Marxism did not mean simply to revise this or that judgment in the light of recent developments. Others did that —Rudolf Hilferding, Rosa Luxemburg, Heinrich Cunow, Lenin— with the intention of sharpening the scientific tools of class struggle. Karl Renner, the first president of the Austrian Republic, provided a far more cogent analysis of the new trends in capitalism, using Marx's methods of investigation and yet vindicating reform policies. What Bernstein abandoned was *the myth,* Marxism's claim that a comprehensive philosophy exists which guarantees (a) that capitalism is necessarily followed by socialism, (b) that socialism will be totally different from capitalism, and (c) that socialism will necessarily be better, will be "a higher stage of humanity." Bernstein did not feel that Marxism could make good any such claim or that it could be both scientific *and* tied to any particular class or party. For him there was no engaged science: "Just as there is no liberal chemistry, the notion of a socialist sociology makes no sense to me." *(Sozialistische Monatshefte,* 1901, p. 32.) By downgrading Marxism to a mere tool of social analysis, Bernstein not only deprived it of any attractiveness as a political philosophy, he also deprived the labor movement of its justifying ideology and socialism of its function as a Savior.

The Theory of Democracy

The price of abandoning the myth would be too high, unless something else could take its place. Did Bernstein suggest an alternative? Throughout his writings one senses an underlying idea — a fundamental devotion to democracy and its values:

> If at any time there was an economic demand of the socialist program that would have to be realized under conditions that would seriously endanger the development toward freedom, Social Democrats always

rejected it. The safeguarding of civil liberties has always enjoyed precedence over the fulfillment of economic postulates.

The development and safety of the individual *(Persönlichkeit)* is the aim
of all socialist measures, even those that may seem to be coercive. A
closer look will always show that any coercion that is required must
increase the total sum of freedom in the society. Coercion must give more
freedom to more people than it takes away.[9]

Bernstein liked to quote Lassalle's words, "We are all citizens"
(Bürger), and he complained about comrades who spoke of abolishing the *bürgerliche Gesellschaft* (the German language cannot distinguish between "civil society" and "bourgeois society"), instead of
the capitalist society.

Yet Bernstein had not worked out a theory of democracy. Like
other socialists of his generation he tended to confuse political and
economic democracy, participatory and representative democracy,
democracy as a way of life and democracy as a system of government, democracy as government by the people and democracy as
the assurance of due process, peaceful settlement of conflicts, law and
order. Combining the traditions of Rousseau and Lassalle, he had
an almost naive confidence in the goodness of the great majority
and in abstract democracy. He was convinced, like all social democrats, that socialism is unthinkable without democracy and that
democracy implies socialism.

Unfortunately, what had been postulated as a unity in lofty
thought became an ugly dichotomy when theory was translated
into reality. In 1917 the Bolshevik revolution suppressed democracy
in order to let "socialism" triumph. In 1918 the SPD bypassed
socialism in order to erect a democracy — of sorts; the militant
democratic movement became frozen into a static democratic order.
The man who had said that "the movement is everything" was now
concerned with writing a constitution which was no longer understood as an instrument of socialist politics but as an end in itself. Its
defense against critics from the left became Bernstein's major theme,
and he handled it as though democracy were synonymous with law
and order in a country where demonstrators were shot, divulgers of
what generals considered military secrets were jailed, press and
theaters were gagged by censors, democratically elected state gov-

ernments were deposed, the Republic's presidents ruled by emergency decree — all in the name of republican due process. It became clear that Bernstein's plea for "democracy" had really been a plea to compromise with the status quo rather than dispossess it. He defended the SPD leaders' conduct during the revolution of 1918-19 and therefore must share responsibility for the defeat of democratic aspirations. A *socialist* revolution was not on the agenda, to be sure; but the revolution of 1918 did not even fulfill the program of 1848, and the republican policies the SPD pursued in the fourteen years of the Weimar Republic were not even reformist. Indeed, one may cogently accuse the SPD of not being reformist enough.

Was revisionism to blame, or was the SPD's failure the result of personal failings and historical accidents? Conceivably, a social-democratic mass party, devoted to both democratic principles and reformist tactics, can simultaneously be dynamic, decisive, and militant. The Austrian Social Democrats provide a case in point: their defeat in the 1930s can clearly be attributed to external conditions. I shall therefore not make unfair use of hindsight in evaluating the historical significance of revisionism. In history, *post hoc* is not always *propter hoc,* and revisionism must be understood on the basis of the conditions prevailing around 1900.

In the preceding half-century, the working class had fallen heir to the democratic aspirations that the middle class had abandoned; these coincided with its own interests and with the necessities of class conflict. The trade unions were interested not only in better wage scales but in security and a dependable body of laws. As Lenin saw clearly, revolution was not in the immediate interest of the workers; only intellectuals indulging in utopias looked down upon the "legalism" of the trade union leaders. But to grow and to plan for the future, the labor movement had to strive not only for legal recognition and legal safeguards; it also had to insist on its own legality. It wrote contracts, it made political deals. Arguably, the leaders overvalued legality and respectability — just as Bebel always wore a frock coat in the Reichstag and exhorted the younger deputies to dress properly.

This is what the revisionists understood by democracy: if the establishment was to recognize the labor movement as a partner, the labor movement had to be responsible and law-abiding. And here we have the ultimate reason why Bernstein was so anxious to overcome the revolutionary phraseology and why he opposed the spontaneous stirrings of the working class during the revolution. Not the councils, the militias, the independent unions, not the unreliable local formations, but the well-established central organizations of labor were to determine the fate of the Republic. If any nationalization was proposed, let the Reichstag adopt a law — but beware of revolutionary intervention by the People's Commissars (the interim government that ruled until January 1919). In the hottest days of the revolution Bernstein gave his Delphic definition in *Was ist Sozialismus?* "Socialism is the sum of social demands and natural aspirations of those workers in modern capitalist society who have come to recognize their class situation and the task of their class."

Once again, the Movement is the message. The revolution had created an ideal framework for class struggle to proceed in a legal order: no more police at the bosses' command, no more weighted suffrage, no more aristocrats at the top of the local hierarchy. Now all depended on maintaining this democracy so that the labor movement would be able to act as the pressure group of the working class, without inhibitions. Its historic mission would thereby suffer some changes.

The historical significance of revisionism, hence, is to have reinstated the second half of the party's name, Social Democracy: "democratic" was not to qualify "socialism" but "socialism" was to qualify "democracy." The majority of the workers also understood the term in this sense, an insight that has been obstructed all too long by Leninist historiography and that even non-Communist historians have been reluctant to accept: the Social Democrats could not "betray" any revolutionary principles because for forty years they had failed to prepare the ground for the revolution; they were not caught in the dilemma of theory versus practice because the labor movement represented an interest rather than an idea.

Historians who assume that revolution should be on every proletarian's mind ask the wrong questions: Why revisionism? How did that aberration insert itself into an otherwise revolutionary social democracy? The answer usually names one of several "villains": the trade union bosses (Peter Gay), the party bosses (Robert Michels), the labor aristocrats (Lenin), electoral laws and parliamentary customs, the "mass society" (Marcuse), or simply the lack of proper Marxist training (Trotsky). My favorite villain, however, is inertia, and the question I find much more relevant and much easier to answer is, Why *not* revisionism?

It is Marxism that needs to be explained. People will not think about revolution unless they have been grievously provoked, and even in a revolution they would rather leave its execution to the proper organizations. The Social Democratic parties conducted pragmatic policies, tried to secure the most favorable institutional framework for those policies, and promised "socialism" only as a faraway ideal that might be approached asymptotically in the course of further history.

Ethical Socialism

It is true that militants need a faith, a symbol, or a myth. Democracy as a system of government, especially if it is defined legalistically, will usually not arouse the spirit, no matter how worthy it is of being defended with one's life. It is socialism that infuses the ardor of a transcendental goal into the political commitment. Since it was a grand theory, Marxism had been able to project such an ideal and to endow it with the aura of philosophical and historical necessity, fusing what ought to be with what will be. Since revisionism rejected the idea of committed science, or the confusion of scientific and moral judgments, it could not claim that its reading of the "facts" must lead to moral conclusions. Even if historical materialism were proven correct and capitalism were of necessity to be followed by socialism—for which Bernstein saw no proof—it still would not follow that socialism was the only *possible* alternative, nor that it was the most desirable outcome.

The determinist philosophy of Marx's immediate followers has been a source of embarrassment to many young Marxists, and Marx himself had observed (in the first "Thesis on Feuerbach") that idealism rather than materialism had developed the theory of action.

Revisionism, which aimed to create room for maneuver for the labor movement, had no use for a deterministic philosophy. Bernstein accepted the economic interpretation of history only with reservations: "Iron necessity [must be] modified in a way that increases the practice of social policy" *(Evolutionary Socialism)*. But that admission forced him to answer the questions he strove so hard to avoid: From where does one derive one's socialist faith? Where does socialist morality come from?

In his academic lecture "How Is Scientific Socialism Possible?" Bernstein came closest to an answer. The Kantian form of the question indicates where Bernstein believed the answer might lie: in the categorical imperative. This doctrine certainly implies a profound faith in the equality between men and also in the injunction to use no man as a means toward some end; it is democratic though not necessarily socialist. In the Kantian spirit, too, Bernstein suggested that social science may give socialists the tools to realize their goals; still it is unable to determine those goals. Where do they come from? The answer is ethical socialism, and many revisionists have indeed found the source of their socialist faith in ethical philosophy or religion. Important among them were Jean Jaurès and Kurt Eisner (a fellow Independent and martyr), and also the philosophers Hermann Cohen, Franz Staudinger, Karl Vorländer, and Paul Natorp. The latter were all members of the neo-Kantian school, and since they were the only professional philosophers writing on socialism, it has often been suggested that an affinity exists between revisionism and Kantianism.

Moreover, Bernstein permitted himself a pun at the end of his major work. Denouncing the hypocrisy of Marxist propaganda, he exclaimed: Away with this cant, let us go back to Kant; let us study "the preconditions [prolegomena] of socialism," as Kant had studied *Prolegomena of Any Future Metaphysics*. Bernstein knew this from reading Friedrich Albert Lange's popular *History of Materialism and Critique of Its Significance at the Present Time* (1866), a source he frankly acknowledged; but his other writings do not indicate that he had either read or understood Kant. As to the neo-Kantian socialists I have named, they were attempting to do precisely what was most repugnant to Bernstein: to deduce the necessity of socialism *a priori* from the categorical imperative, an endeavor at least as dangerous as Hegelian dialectics.

Nevertheless, there were neo-Kantians who were not revisionists, such as Max Adler, who made his political home on the extreme left of the Austrian Socialist Party, and there were ethical socialists who were not Kantians. I mention here only Tolstoy, Gustav Landauer, Oscar Wilde, Bertrand Russell, Ramsay MacDonald — some more radical than the Marxists, some less. The sources of socialist ethics are scattered over a wide spectrum, and though it is true that Marxists have dealt with Kant very unfairly, nothing permits us to assign a place in socialist history to him. Neither the thought of Bernstein nor that of Jean Jaurès or any other socialist stands in relation to Kant as Marxism stands in relation to Hegel; its mechanics are in no way derived from the earlier thinker.

Yet although he has not spelled it out himself, or implied it in a philosophical manner, I think that the query about the source of Bernstein's socialism can be answered. He was deeply committed to the movement: all his life he remained part of it and shared the experience of its members. His theories reflected the workers' understanding of the movement. He drew his ethical directives from the life of the party. His values were *solidarity, justice, equality, liberty, progress.* These are existential determinants of the working-class organization. They are not abstract philosophical notions; neither do they exist *a priori* nor are they derived. Rather, they are givens within that *Arbeiterwelt* in which Bernstein lived. They also constitute principles that guide and direct action. Bernstein's realism was not simply accommodating, but flexible. It has often been charged that revisionism leads to opportunism; the attitude of Bernstein and others — one thinks of Ramsay MacDonald in England and Kurt Eisner in Bavaria — during the First World War suggests otherwise. Bernstein always understood the movement to be a community of militants sharing humanitarian and laborite values. But unlike Sorel, he did not think that the movement was so much a value-in-itself that it could dispense with material successes and achievements.

Beyond Revisionism

In the days of the first Republic, and still more so since World War II, social democracy has lost much of its original moral impetus; it has become a representative of interests and a school of management. It owes more to Keynes and the Fabians than to Marx or Bernstein. The welfare state requires much more cooperation between the "social partners" than was thought possible by even the most "reformist" labor representatives of Bernstein's generation.

Social Democrats now must try to make capitalism recession-proof, inflation-proof, accident-proof, old-age-proof, etc. They must govern to make the system work, not to transform it — for transformations now are likely to come from other forces, including transnational corporations, nonsocialist governments, national revolutions, and international organizations. The programs that socialists now seek to develop or operate are also much more comprehensive than anything that was even thinkable at Bernstein's time: national planning for industry and agriculture, operation of nationalized industries, redistribution of income, public health and housing and other public services, price regulation, workers' participation in the management of corporations. All this more often requires cooperation than confrontation; any conflicts of interest or of conception must be negotiated and arbitrated rather than allowed to erupt in an open test of strength.

Reform policies in the first half of this century were essentially redistributive: one fought over the share of the product that was to fall to each class. The most advanced concept of that time was Hilferding's "political wage"; considerations of overall economic and social policy were still based on the assumption that the planning of production must be left to the enterprise, and that prices will be determined by the market. Today's reformers cannot leave such important decisions to the blind forces of the market. They are essentially regulators, and therefore different from the labor leaders who fought with individual businessmen. All this was seen much more clearly by Renner, who has been unfairly forgotten.

Earlier it was suggested that Bernstein's analysis of modern capitalism missed the significance of large-scale enterprise and monopolistic organizations; he was not up-to-date even then. Today his kind of reformism is as obsolete as Marx's model of revolution. Bernstein adequately described the opportunities of successful class action in the world before the First World War, but he would have had to learn a great deal in order to be at home in welfare-state economics and policies. These call for a larger horizon than is usually acquired in trade union schools. In his day, labor policies had to adapt themselves to the vicissitudes of capitalist development. Today the economy must and can be shaped to fit the vision of social planners.

It is therefore ironical that just now young German socialists are trying to revive Bernstein's memory as that of an ideologist. He, who was so averse to all ideologies, would have been very much surprised. He was anything but a prophet. Perhaps the explanation is psychological rather than political: what is needed is not so much an ideology as an attitude, a style "nonideological yet principled" (as Irving Howe has said), realistic yet not opportunistic, loyal to the party without surrendering to the bosses. Bernstein was a man with whom one can disagree while respecting his decency; his democratic modesty has created a tradition that is still alive in Western labor parties.

Another reason for Bernstein's revival after three quarters of a century is rather paradoxical. His early theories encouraged labor to seek reforms and to assume responsibilities even though the "system" was reactionary and the state in particular was antidemocratic. Today, the New Left has adopted the strategy of "marching through the institutions," disregarding their hateful, allegedly Fascist nature. Students who hope to become government-paid professors and researchers can only look with sympathy to the wise old man who taught the workers to forget the symbols of the police state and to make themselves at home in the enemy's house. They have interpreted Bernstein's ideas in a syndicalist sense that permits them to coexist with the establishment without acknowledging its legitimacy. The pragmatic, nonideological approach to politics also relieves the individual member of the "totalizing" tendency that inheres in every party.

Bernstein himself was fanatically anti–Communist, and he would be aghast at some young socialists' inability to distinguish between the East and West German states. But his positive attitude to patriotism and his "nonideological" approach may appeal to some of his new admirers as a legitimation for their own desire to keep the Eastern option open and minimize the difference between the two German states.

To conclude on a positive note: the implicit though unspoken commitment to an ethical foundation of socialism that can be ascribed to Bernstein may be cited to balance the all-too-visible drift toward technocracy in the Social Democratic Party. Although Bernstein cannot give guidance in this area, and although his thought was neither profound nor original, he shines as an example of an honest, courageous socialist, devoted first of all to the movement, and conscious of the fact that socialism is first of all a movement of people. He belonged to the generation of great humanitarian socialists, which also included Jean Jaurès, Rosa Luxemburg, Eugene Debs, and Norman Thomas.

13

Gramsci–
Stalinist Without Dogma

When Antonio Gramsci's letters from prison were first published,[1] ten years after his early death in 1937, Benedetto Croce, his
old teacher and adversary who survived him, hailed the martyred
leader of Italy's Communist Party (PCI) as "one of the great literati
of our country." Twenty years later, the provincial government —
not leftist but Christian-Democratic — of his native Sardinia called
a "Gramsci Congress," which brought together philosophers, historians, and critics from many countries. Today there is hardly a
major city in Italy without a Via Gramsci. In Rome, an Istituto
Gramsci piously guards Gramsci's papers pertaining to the turbu-
lent history of the PCI, as well as the 2,848 densely covered pages of
his *Quaderni* (notebooks), reflecting his wide reading in history and
the anxieties of the prisoner whose aspirations for a place in history
were, for a time, frustrated. The present English edition[2] is based
on the original Italian six-volume selection, which was edited by
Felice Platone and published in Torino by Einaudi, 1948-1951.

The *Prison Notebooks* bear witness that Gramsci was not afraid to
draw some conclusions at variance with the established school of
Marxism-Leninism; they were published at a time when, at the
other end of the philosophical spectrum, a pope was revising some
truths the Church had taken to be established. To be sure, John
XXIII did not repudiate the immaculate conception nor Gramsci

Dissent, Summer 1974.

17.   **Poster of Antonio Gramsci: Appeal (written by Georgi Dimitroff) to the international proletariat to rescue Gramsci from the fascist jail.**

(Photo: International Institute of Social History, Amsterdam)

the need for a party dictatorship. But the expectation of further "convergence" tempted commentators to greet Gramsci's numerous deviations from Stalinist rigidity as so many harbingers of a universal Spring of Heresy.

The Communist movement has taken advantage of this reputation and cultivates the myth that surrounds Gramsci. In the new English one-volume edition of the *Notebooks,* the Gramsci Institute makes a show of evenhandedness: the exhaustive Introduction gives due credit to Trotsky and Radek for their contributions to the Communist International; the importance of Amadeo Bordiga, the ultraleft founder of the PCI, and of Ignazio Silone is acknowledged critically but honestly; Gramsci's doubts about Marxist-Leninist dogma are not hidden but, where possible, pointed out.

Nevertheless, I must take issue with one major editorial decision. Gramsci had been under the influence of Benedetto Croce—the ex-Marxist, neo-Hegelian liberal philosopher—and the student's views on Machiavelli and other historical subjects still show an indebtedness to the teacher. In numerous passages one gets a glimpse of their differences; but a coherent sequence dealing with Croce — about two hundred pages in the original selection — has been totally omitted here. This is regrettable because Gramsci, like Lukács, often said that modern Marxists should relate to contemporary philosophers as Marx did to Hegel and Ricardo; i.e., develop their own ideas in the form of an immanent critique of their predecessors.

The Hoare-Smith selections deal with history, education, and philosophy, but their centerpiece is political power and organization. Much of the work is repetitious. Many ideas are tentative, contradictory, and inchoate. Few are original, although many may seem so to young researchers who have never seen them in a Marxist author's handwriting. Indeed they are very much in the tradition of Italian political thought, from Machiavelli to Mazzini and Gentile.

Gramsci's writing is neither elegant nor overly profound, neither enlighteningly precise nor gripping in human substance. These are indeed *Notebooks,* and just that — jottings of an intelligent reader who takes an interest in the philosophical discussions of his age and who has the leisure, in his forced isolation, to think about the condition of his country, his party, and the cause to which he has dedicated his life. None of this can be held against Gramsci; in prison one is apt to produce circular ideas rather than well–structured systems. But it should be noted that Antonio Gramsci was no Rosa Luxemburg and no Lenin, both of whom were able to work under similar conditions, nor a Machiavelli or a Dante, whom exile forced into greatness.

Within these limitations, Gramsci is important, and he can be compared with Georg Lukács and Karl Korsch. Their careers in the radical movement started similarly and then diverged in significant ways. All three came to Marxism after absorbing the vitalist and pragmatist philosophies prevailing at universities around the turn of the century. Their early sympathies lay with an activism that bears resemblance to the American IWW, and they were strongly influenced by such thinkers as Georges Sorel and Antonio Labriola, who injected a dose of "idealism" into Marxist theory and counted on the spontaneous creativity of the masses.

Indeed, much of Gramsci's fame stems from his deep involvement with the factory council movement in northern Italy–the *commissioni interne,* which in 1920 occupied the factories. He published a weekly, *Ordine Nuovo,* which made the slogan *democrazia operaia* (workers' democracy) popular and propagated the goal of *lo stato operaio* much along the lines of Marx's "free association of producers," or of Tito's shop councils. This was the truly heroic phase of his life; his writings in that period still have the earthy quality of populism.

In January 1921, when this great movement broke down, Gramsci helped found the Communist Party. Later that year he went to Moscow and stayed for eighteen months; he has never told anyone about his impressions, nor did he analyze, either favorably or unfavorably, the state of the Soviet Union. He returned to Italy to "bolshevize" the PCI, fought the "leftist deviation" of Bordiga as well as the "rightist deviation" of Tasca, who believed in trade union action and proletarian culture, and above all denounced the Social Democrats along with the liberals while leading the Communists out of the Aventinian alliance.[3] Gramsci thought that the PCI could operate legally under fascism, and he treated the socialists as the "major enemy." Like most Marxists then, he completely misjudged the character of the fascist state—a misconception which Mussolini proceeded to correct.

There is a tragic parallel between the ultraleft Marx, after the lost revolution of 1848–1849, and the attempt by some to bolshevize the European intellectuals after the lost revolutions of 1919–1921. Gramsci was least admirable in this period, when he was Secretary of the PCI. But, by then, he was a desperate man. Although he knew that the revolution had been lost, he tried to perpetuate its posture, embodied in the Communist Party, and he clung to the notion that a new kind of organization might preserve the revolutionary forces — as though it would be possible to take them out of cold storage intact, during a new period of revolutionary potentialities.

Meanwhile, the task was twofold: to shield those forces from reformist contamination, and to shield the one bastion the revolution had won, the Soviet Union. Hence, although he knew that Trotsky was right in fearing the bureaucratic degeneration of the Soviet state and the Bolshevik Party, Gramsci still fought ruthlessly for the Stalin-Bukharin line — or rather, for the "Russia First" line in the International and the PCI. In this period he was neither undogmatic nor accommodating; his political personality was a living lie. A Communist writer, therefore, could recently say that Mussolini actually did Gramsci a favor when he forced him to think in solitude.

Like Hegel's owl of Minerva, Gramsci's thought only spread its wings after dusk had fallen on the political landscape. In his ten years of prison life he gained insight into the workings of history. Yet, in Gramsci's review of his political experience it is amazing that he does not look for tactical mistakes or accidents of history. Rather, he subjects his entire conception of politics to a thorough revision. He does not follow the earlier revisionists who simply surrendered the revolutionary outlook. Instead he goes back, way back, into Italian history and tradition.

Gramsci asks these questions: Why didn't Italy produce the kind of revolution that shook Germany during the Reformation, or France in 1789, or Russia in 1917? Why didn't the rising medieval cities make the breakthrough toward modern capitalism? Why was the Renaissance the work of princes and not of the middle class? How could radicalism have been shunted aside in the Risorgimento?

Why did neither of the two Italian revolutions produce a Jacobin party? And what are the conditions for the rise of a revolutionary elite?

He never answered those questions. But in searching for answers he was led to ask other questions. What is the relationship between society and the dominant class, and between both and the leading elite? How can one class achieve "hegemony" over the others in a national revolution, and how does the revolutionary elite, which he also calls "the intellectuals of the proletariat," achieve "hegemony" over the revolutionary classes? While "absorbing" ideas from Pareto, Michels, and Mosca, Gramsci studied the revolutionizing effects of modern bureaucracies and other leadership cadres, which led him to these frightening thoughts: Perhaps a revolution can be achieved through the action of the elite without any need for the revolutionary class to participate? Did not the Prussian bureaucrats introduce the same reforms which the French Revolution had introduced? Is it possible that Fascism relates to the Russian Revolution just as the Prussian bureaucrats did to the Jacobins?

Gramsci calls such a revolution from above "passive" or "restoration/revolution." This notion also leads him to some astute observations on the Russian Thermidor: After the Kronstadt uprising of 1921, the period of revolution came to a close; the further development of the revolution no longer depended on the activities of the revolutionary class but on the performance of the bureaucrats, or *funzionari*.

It has often been observed that the counterrevolution fulfills the work of the revolution. And later Lichtheim quoted an unidentified "Comintern theorist" as describing "fascism as the bourgeois revolution in the age of bourgeois counterrevolution." Now Gramsci came to an uncanny, perverse understanding of what was happening in the Soviet Union: Trotsky's position had to be condemned not because he was wrong but because he was right! The "war of movement" (Gramsci's euphemism for the world revolution) had been replaced by the "war of position," which now

> demands immense sacrifices from the masses. An unprecedented hegemony [his word for dictatorship] is necessary. A more interventionist government must take the offensive against oppositionists... with controls everywhere reinforcing the hegemonial position of the dominant group.

Having accepted Stalin's definition of "socialism in one country," Gramsci understood the Russian Revolution as a national revolution; he expected the Italian revolution to be a continuation of national aspirations that had been at work ever since the time of the Risorgimento or even the Renaissance. He was deeply convinced, with Marx, that the Communists "do not try to realize any ideals" but must lead each nation toward the fulfillment of its destiny — molding that destiny in the process to be sure, but not changing it. Trying to change this objective development is the mistake of "voluntarism," while the opposite mistake, leaving that fate to be shaped by so-called objective conditions, is "economism." To find the right middle course between these two extremes, the party must have a better understanding of its role than Marx or even Lenin had bestowed on their heirs.

The mechanism of hegemony, therefore, is studied in a sequence of aphorisms, entitled "The Modern Prince," with a not too subtle allusion to Machiavelli and written in this vein as commentaries to paradigmatic events. Unfortunately, Gramsci does not get very far beyond Machiavelli; he is still suspended between *Fortuna* and *Virtù*; between the conditions ripening in civil society (Hegel's *bürgerliche Gesellschaft*) and the possibility of action by the leading party; between that party's need to possess moral authority — for which the code word is hegemony — and the necessity, alas, of using coercion.

Following Croce and other Italian philosophers, Gramsci calls these speculations a "philosophy of praxis," which he equates with Marxism. He was as averse to metaphysics as to sociology. Apparently he never read *Capital,* and his background in economics is weak. His Marxism was the kind of pragmatism, actionism, or vitalism that Mussolini and Gentile, too, were cultivating. Ideas were not either true or false, but either usable or unusable — or they could simply be flags: commenting on the factional fight in Moscow, Gramsci wrote that what mattered was not whose position was correct but who belonged to the faction holding a particular view. This was Stalin's opinion, too, and the insight is not only relevant but also rather confusing. For instance, Bordiga and Gramsci accused each other of lacking zeal in supporting "democratic centralism" when each really meant something very different. Gramsci quotes Vico's *"Verum ipsum factum"* (True is what I did myself) and a saying of Napoleon's that was also dear to Mussolini: "First one acts, then one thinks." A dangerous maxim, which in praxis opens the door to all kinds of opportunism. I mean to suggest, of course, not that Gramsci was a Fascist but that he was drawing on contemporary philosophies that were available to others, too.

What Gramsci feared most was a "passive" submission to the "given": better make a mistake than do nothing. "Positive" science and sociology condemned the proletariat to fight on its enemies' premises, which led to reformism. Gramsci therefore rejected theories that claimed objective validity, especially those based on material conditions. Did not the Social Democrats base their critique of bolshevism on the dogma that Russia was not ready for socialism? Was not Kautsky's complacent determinism to blame for the labor movement's collapse in 1914 and for the failure of the European revolutions after the First World War? No doctrine could be more pernicious to revolutionary politics than the belief in scientific predictions. Sociology was an ideology of the ruling class—politics an art!

Gramsci directed his most abrasive criticism against materialists and positivists, especially when they pretended to be Marxists. He ridiculed Plekhanov and Bukharin, who spent time and effort to prove that the universe was made of matter, that man was governed by inexorable, deterministic laws, and that Marxism was a science. His criticism of Bukharin's *Historical Materialism,* long the Comintern's catechism, is devastating though unfair.[4] His attack follows the line of Benedetto Croce, whose own teleological sophistry had been exploded a hundred years earlier by Kant. "How is history possible a priori?" Kant asked, and replied: "If the prophet contrives that which he predicts."

Had Gramsci lived longer, or had he been able to read German, he might have called his philosophy existentialism. Such statements as "Man makes himself," which Sartre later was to popularize, came easily to Gramsci from other sources, as they came to Lukács even before Marx's "early manuscripts" were available. He probably had learned from Croce and Lukács that Marxism should be considered not a system but a critique and a method — a method which, following Max Weber, could also be applied to the specific historical doctrines of Marx.

Such an extreme relativism can be justified only if some criterion is found to determine who shall be the agent of history (the historical subject, in Lukács' language). The proletariat as such is not that agent, since it is part of a civil society that lacks consciousness, and since its interests are not universal. Only the conscious strata of the proletariat can be the demiurge; or else the "intellectuals" who represent the proletariat and who—since their interests are "general" —constitute the political society. Gramsci calls this agent of history "the organic intelligentsia;" he distinguishes it sharply from the "traditional intellectuals," who can easily be identified with Mannheim's "free-floating intellectuals."

To explain Gramsci's aversion to "traditional intellectuals," it is necessary to note how he regards windbags like Settembrini, or his model Mazzini, who failed to understand what the people wanted in the Risorgimento; or perhaps it is necessary to go even farther back, to the Renaissance humanists who failed to see the national goal and continued to pursue the cosmopolitan ideals of medieval towns: the medieval town and its culture were "internationalist"; hence Renaissance humanists were "reactionary" — an interpretation which also stems from Croce. The party (i.e. the "modern prince") must reject the traditional, cosmopolitan humanist whose concern is with ideas; it must resolutely support the "organic intellectuals," who do not even have to be intellectuals: technocrats, bureaucrats, political leaders, and above all activists close to the national temper. Their hegemony helps the classes of the civil society to transcend their particular interests; it leads them into the political society through what is nothing more than Rousseau's "general will" or Lukács' "insight into the totality." Gramsci was not afraid to call his Jacobin party or political society "totalitarian." *Intellettualitá totalitaria* may refer both to the personnel and to the required attitude or conception of its function.

This, however, is not the whole story. Political society, or Jacobin democracy, is the highest form of consciousness the new class can reach both up to and during the revolution. Thereafter, however, civil society expands its functions at the expense of political society, and "the state withers away." Here Gramsci's submerged syndical- ism is allowed to surface for a furtive moment. In some passages he even seems to hope that the creative forces of civil society will continue to grow under fascism — perhaps also under Stalinism — and eventually submerge the rigid crust of political society. His actionist philosophy could tolerate murky definitions more easily than quietism. It is strange that Gramsci, who condemned positiv- ism and materialism precisely because they encouraged reformist illusions, should here teleologically indulge in a truly Hegelian synthesis: all paths lead to the fulfillment of History's ultimate command. It is never quite clear whether he looked toward a Jacobin state or expected dialectics to continue; his code word for socialism is not "free society" but "regulated society."

In an obscure passage, Gramsci refers to the Trotskyist opposition as "black parliamentarians" representing particular interests in a totalitarian state. Such moments, however, are rare in the English selections from the *Notebooks,* and totally absent in other published fragments. There Gramsci deals with subjects of fundamental inter- est to the "hegemonial" element: the leaders' education, the state's duty to punish criminals, rational production methods, bureauc- racy. He is concerned that technocrats could flout political control, and he recommends a rigid classical education for the political elite (no "progressive," let alone "permissive" educator, he distrusted the Dalton plan and educational "libertarians"). He was an admiring student of Taylorism and Fordism, and he never spoke of alienation; he railed against "libertinism" and agreed with Ford that "the new type of man demanded by the rationalization of production and work cannot be developed until the sexual instinct has been suitably regulated and until it too has been rationalized." While he condemns Trotsky's proposal to militarize labor, he adds: "The principle of coercion. . . in the ordering of production or work is correct; but the form it assumed was mistaken."

It must be clear by now why Gramsci had to support Stalin against the "cosmopolitan intelligentsia." *He had a better understand- ing of Stalin's historical role than Stalin himself.* He even understood Mussolini, and under the strange conditions in which he wrote he often confused the two: whether to conceal from his jailers his thoughts about fascism or to conceal his thoughts about Stalin, he was able to tell the truth about the one by citing the other. If this was perverse, the ultimate transvaluation of a personal and political tragedy appeared in the shape that these glimpses into the web of history finally took: condemned to inaction, the prisoner projected a philosophy of action which seemed to make history so transparent that the futility of action became manifest.

From Croce, Gramsci took the notion of the cathartic moment when theory and practice converge: the moment of revolution. This, however, leaves us baffled as to the relationship of theory and practice at all other times. His philosophy here gets avowedly idealistic: the hope for that moment is kept alive in the spirit while Stalin's and Mussolini's mills are grinding away. With less philosophical precision than Hegel — or Lukács, for that matter — Gramsci's dialectics nevertheless aimed at a similar reconciliation. The ultimate truth becomes the convergence of Stalin and Mussolini, Marx and Christ, revolution and religion. All differences are submerged in a total relativism and, paradoxically, the philosophy of practice has no handle to deal with reality. It is a philosophy born of defeat, more paralyzing than the positivism it proposed to overcome.

In this protean formlessness Gramsci's neo-Hegelian, post-Marxian, and preexistentialist philosophy became the suitable ideology for all — alienated ultraleft intellectuals who look for a councilist theory of action, left-wing Christian Democrats who look for an unorthodox Marxist with whom to hold a dialogue, and Communist opportunists who look for a certified martyr to legitimize their application for cabinet posts.

14

Orthodox Heretic,
Romantic Stalinist:
On the Ninetieth Birthday
of Georg Lukács

At the time of this essay, Georg Lukács would have been ninety years old. When he died, in 1971, he was eulogized for a number of conflicting reasons:

———To some, he was the guardian of orthodox Marxism and the only disciple who had ever dared to compose a complete "system," which included volumes that remained unfinished: a massive *Ontology*, an equally comprehensive *Aesthetics*, and the adumbration of an *Ethics*, which only his death prevented from growing to similar dimensions.

———Others remembered him as the iconoclast who, fifty years earlier, published a fiery book, *History and Class Consciousness*,[1] which had proclaimed precisely the opposite: that Marx had never *intended* a system, that the very idea of a system is repugnant to the spirit of dialectics, and that to be an orthodox Marxist one need not subscribe to any particular proposition in *Capital* so long as one follows the method of revolutionary dialectics.

———The Lukács, however, whom the obituarists praised most was a scholar who had made important contributions to the sociology of knowledge and especially of literature and who had written sensitively on the theory of aesthetics. His life's work, one critic felt, was "a

Dissent, Spring 1975.

18.   Georg Lukács

(Photo: Ullstein Bilderdienst, Berlin)

continuous... meditation on narrative, on its basic structures, its relationship to the reality it expresses, and its epistemological value."[2] Another had paid him the dubious compliment that "Lukács is actually a more 'bourgeois' and academic humanist" than "the Luxemburgs and Trotskys, far more imposing figures."[3] With Lukács, most commentators believed, Western intellectuals might hold a "dialogue" — provided there were any who could match his vast erudition or the breadth of his concerns.

The Quest

The question is not: Which was the real Lukács? But rather: How have these three views of the philosopher become relevant at different times? To answer such a question, a minimum of biographical data is necessary. György von Lukács, born in Budapest, was the son of an influential Jewish banker who had been knighted by the Habsburg emperor. The family must have been everything he hated. Sensitive and intelligent, he was alienated threefold from everything "real" by his race and religion, his language and nationality, his class and education. Liberalism was no answer to his problem of identity. At the turn of the century, the mainstream of Western culture had passed elsewhere. Lukács went to Berlin and Heidelberg as a dandy and aesthete. A brilliant adept of the exquisite circle of Max Weber and Emil Lask, he became attracted to the fashionable "vitalism" of Wilhelm Dilthey's school and communicated with disciples of the esoteric Stefan George as well.

These friends may have fortified his own neo-Platonic belief that "in the aesthetic sphere one might attain contact with ultimate reality through an act of intuition."[4] Their romantic protest may have been initially intended as a reaction against materialism, capitalism, and bureaucracy, but it also led to the irrationalistic and antirationalistic ideologies of nationalism and Nazism, which Lukács was to fight so bitterly in his later days. Some have wondered whether his later censorious and frequently unfair attacks on idealists, subjectivists, and positivists may not conceal guilty memories of those early associations.[5]

The intellectuals wanted to pit *Geist* (spirit) against gold. But when the First World War broke out, it was precisely the European *Geist* that broke down. Classical and neo-Romantic culture offered no shelter from the onrushing age of the barbarians; on the contrary, in that war they enlisted on both sides. In despair Lukács wrote a parable, *The Theory of the Novel*.[6] Under the guise of a somewhat pedantic analysis of various literary genres, the book proclaimed that modern man had forfeited his heritage: authentic cultures could produce myths and therefore leave epics as a residue; modern culture was able to produce only a poor substitute, the novel, and even that had by now sunk to the level of psychology and naturalistic description, reveling in the sensuous experience of matter instead of securing man in his universe. Wars were no longer fought by heroes, and the novel was no longer carried by characters that typified man's eternal nature.

This, of course, was not a matter of taste, or of losing some embellishment of life. It was the loss of something that had been central to *Geist*: "The novel is the epic of a world that has been abandoned by God." Along with the radical left, Lukács concluded that this wretched middle-class world was doomed. His eschatological mood drew him to the Russian Revolution: once again the Light was coming from the East and, as it happened, Lukács was preparing a *Habilitationsschrift* on Dostoevsky. He joined the Hungarian Communist Party and took part in its unhappy venture, the seizure of power in 1919.

The Spirit was pressing to be realized in the world, but did not know how to become Praxis. In his 1967 Preface to *History and Class Consciousness,* a veritable *apologia pro vita sua*, Lukács soberly states that then, in 1919, neither he nor his fellow revolutionaries had yet understood the workings and meaning of a social revolution. They were enthusiasts who went to war against the old world and would hardly ask the Hungarian peasants what they wanted. When he opened an Institute for Historical Materialism, Lukács announced that a new epoch in history had begun in which even the laws that Marx had discovered would be abolished.[7] But the revolution was beaten, and Lukács fled to Vienna.

In a similar situation Marx had decided that "the next revolution is as certain as the next depression." Such an easy answer was no longer possible for Lukács. His studies with Simmel and Weber had revealed the coming of an iron age where bureaucracy and purposeful rationality would rule human behavior, and where all thinking, even that which intended to oppose the system, would reflect that structure. Humans have to see themselves as functioning parts of the system; their lives have been not only robbed of mystery but "objectified."[8] From this viewpoint, thought itself is made a prisoner of the system; the workers, with their trade unions and their parties, do not overthrow it but, through their activities, help it to survive. A new variant of the discredited pauperization theory emerges: even if the workers are not getting materially poorer, they are getting poorer in spirit.

A story Lukács wrote in 1912 clearly shows the influence of Weber's and Simmel's ideas on alienation: "Work grew out of life, but has grown far away from it. It originated in man, but is inhuman, indeed antihuman." Both his anticapitalistic yearning and his search for a return from alienation were characteristic of Max Weber's circle in Heidelberg; what Marianne Weber called Lukács' "eschatological hopes" continued long into his Marxist period.

Lukács had at first sympathized with syndicalist ideas and with Rosa Luxemburg's "spontaneity" theory. These theories assumed that in daily combat the proletariat acquires more and more "class consciousness," culminating in the moment of revolution.[9] Now Lukács saw that this pattern of revolution was true only for the bourgeoisie, whose economic power and social position were increasing long before it achieved political recognition. The proletariat, by contrast, is being pushed farther and farther away from the revolution, right up to the moment when its utter despair must reverse the situation. No act that is not directly related to that point of reversal can be called revolutionary, and "class consciousness" cannot be defined in terms of an ever-growing awareness but only as that "moment."

We notice here both the heritage of Kierkegaard and Lukács' own independent discovery of Lenin's theory of the party.[10] All gradualist, meliorist tactics are called "passive"; all apocalyptic, millenarian hopes, whether of the anarchist type or Lukács' own previous ecstasies, are "abstract"; even Rosa Luxemburg, with her utopian hope of spontaneous creativity in class war, was a revolutionary "merely subjectively." Only the consciously directed effort of a disciplined party, guided by a correct theory, can crystallize the revolutionary energies during a period between revolutions. This is the famous "unity of theory and praxis." But in 1924, when Lukács wrote his brief monograph on Lenin, this theory of the avant-garde was still linked intimately with the hope of an early renewal of the revolutionary élan. He then quoted Lenin as saying: "Anybody who accepts the Bolshevik principle of party organization must believe that we live in a time of proletarian revolution."

Previously I had mentioned Kierkegaard, but the ideology should really be traced back to Saint Augustine: the City of God is the Church; between revolutions, the revolutionary idea can live only in the party. In the party there resides Hegel's World Spirit or the "identical subject-object" for which the romantic aesthete has been yearning and which he now finds embodied in an institution. The Party is not just an *instrument* of class war, necessary as that may be; it is above all the *incarnation of class consciousness itself*— "the tangible embodiment of proletarian class consciousness," he says in *Lenin,* after quoting the *Communist Manifesto.*

Lukács' involvement with Leninism can be followed in the sequence of essays he collected in *History and Class Consciousness,* notably "The Marxism of Rosa Luxemburg," "Towards a Methodology of the Problem of Organization," and "Legality and Illegality." The central piece is the famous essay "Reification and the Consciousness of the Proletariat," which maintained the old concern: that the Whole Man should be liberated from all estrangement — alienation *and* objectification. In this brilliant essay, Lukács showed how the philosophy of the bourgeoisie could not come to terms with the praxis of reification. As a result, the medium of liberation is no longer philosophy or aesthetic intuition, but the action of the party, the identical subject-object. *History and Class Consciousness* was *The Theory of the Novel* turned political. Indeed, the caesura in Lukács' development did not occur when he joined the Communist Party but much later, when he revoked the "Reification" essay.

The Frozen Flame

It is difficult to describe today the electrifying effect Lukács' book had on an intellectual vanguard back in 1923. Perhaps one might

compare it to the impact, more than a generation later, of Sartre or
Marcuse on a wider audience. While academic teachers had spoken
with resignation of the gap between humanity's yearnings and their
chances of fulfillment, of the split between ethics and knowledge,
or of the tragic conflict between essence and existence, Lukács proclaimed that theory and praxis form an indissoluble unity, that doing
and knowing are one, that action can lead to salvation, that it is in
the grasp of human reason to perceive the transition from "is" to
"ought."

To a generation that had come out numbed from the post-World
War I revolutions, this was an exciting promise. It was as though a
new Prometheus had stolen the fire from Hegel's *Phenomenology of
Mind* — written under similar circumstances — and transplanted it
into the twentieth century. In this fire, the dirty reality of class war
was purified and transformed into the gold of intellectual aspirations. Communism, Lukács said, was not simply a substitution, for
the law of the market, of a more intelligent or even more humane
system of distribution, but the liberation of the Whole Man from
alienation and loneliness. These ideas profoundly influenced the
thinking of the Frankfurt Institute and its friends — Erich Fromm,
Siegfried Kracauer, Walter Benjamin, Herbert Marcuse, Theodor
Adorno, Max Horkheimer, Jürgen Habermas — and through them,
a generation later, the New Left in Europe and even in the United
States.

No doubt Lukács was right when, in the Preface of 1967, he
claimed that

> the alienation of man is a crucial problem of the age in which we live. . . .
> Hence *History and Class Consciousness* had a profound impact in youthful
> intellectual circles; I know of a whole host of good Communists who
> were won over to the movement by this very fact. Without a doubt the
> fact that this Marxist and Hegelian question was taken up by a Commu-
> nist was one reason why the impact of the book went far beyond the
> limits of the party.

Moreover, the publication of Marx's early manuscripts in 1932
proved that Lukács had been right: they showed that for the founder
of Marxism the proletarian revolution had been more than the

liberation of the workers — it was the liberation of philosophy and of man himself. Rarely has a scholar's reconstruction of a lost text been so strikingly vindicated.[11]

But meanwhile Lukács had repudiated his own book. It is not true that he was forced to do so; Karl Korsch, who had simultaneously published similar views, never repudiated them. At that time, debates in the Communist movement were still lively; an adverse review in *Under the Banner of Marxism* did not yet make a martyr. Nor did the Comintern condemn a book because its content was unacceptable; books were condemned when they were written by the wrong authors, and it so happened that in the Hungarian refugee squabbles Lukács supported a faction that was out of favor in Moscow. When the Comintern leadership changed and his own faction was in sympathy with the new line, Lukács repeated his act of self-criticism; moreover, he criticized his romantic past in the guise of a study on Moses Hess,[12] the companion of Marx's Feuerbachian youth.

In the meantime he had changed over from the Communist ultraleft to the Communist right and had accepted Stalinism. It is not surprising, therefore, that the new Preface of 1967, reiterating the recantation once more, warns a new generation of romantic revolutionaries not to be tempted by the enthusiastic errors of the author's flaming youth: "I am afraid my book became famous for the wrong reasons."

The Preface lists, in particular, two "fundamental errors" in *History and Class Consciousness*: In 1923 Lukács had denied any "dialectics in nature," and he had failed to distinguish between "alienation" — the specific estrangement of the worker from his product — and "objectification," the general category of things as they appear to us. The latter is, according to Hegel, a necessary condition of progress and civilization. Much as enthusiastic intellectuals would like to abolish it, this source of their *Weltschmerz* is likely to stay with humanity. Only alienation, a specific mode of capitalistic production, will be overcome by the socialist revolution.

It is obvious that the two kinds of "errors" are related. Even in a socialist society man will be subject to general laws that govern his necessary dialogue with nature; moreover, in the Soviet Union all energies had to be bent to the increase of production. Iron laws were governing and are still governing the accumulation of socialist capital: this was the only excuse for a rate of exploitation that exceeded those in the Western capitalist countries. If that system was to be maintained, the revolutionary process had to be declared closed: once the Soviet system had been established, it had to be a self-contained unit in which no further dialectics was possible.

Here is the point at which Lukács turns to orthodoxy. His Leninist surrender to the party, which terminated his independence as a revolutionary thinker, paralleled his turn to right-wing realism in defense of the Soviet Union and all its institutions and policies. In fact, with revolution in the West far away, the twin existence of the party and of the Soviet Union was now substituted for the quest of the identical subject-object, or was passed off for its realization. Hence the necessity of a "system"; after all, every church has its theology.

Lukács had fallen into the trap that Marx had accused Hegel of having set for himself. He mistook for consummated that which, in *History and Class Consciousness,* he had announced as purpose: "As soon as mankind has understood and restructured its existence, truth acquires a wholly new aspect. When theory and practice are united, it becomes possible to change reality." The revolution Lenin had accomplished was unique, irreversible, and comparable to Kierkegaard's "leap." The practical command of ethics now was to side with the Soviet Union, and the point was not whether a little more or a little less freedom was enjoyed there by individual proletarians but that the metaphysical "proletariat" had made that leap into the realm of Freedom.

This led to a number of consequences. Class war was transferred to the international theater. Class consciousness meant supporting the Soviet Union; to be outside the Communist Party meant being deprived of class consciousness and even of "history." Lukács deplored "the fate that had befallen Karl Korsch," who thought he knew better than the party only to be expelled — and thereby deprived of history. Lukács, by contrast, bought his ticket of admission to further political activity, as the 1967 Preface candidly admits, by recanting.

Another consequence was that "a good Communist could not tolerate any criticism of the Soviet government" — and not just in the hour of greatest danger. When the Soviet Union was "facing

Hitler," such a pragmatic argument might still be understandable,[13] although it does not jibe with the judgment — made in the same essay — that the Hitler-Stalin Pact was a "technically correct decision." There was also the deeper, metaphysical argument of "historical necessity." Remembering the flimsy justification for the operation of the guillotine in 1793, Lukács had no illusion about the charges brought in the Moscow show trials of 1936 – 1937. But since Stalin was at the head of the Soviet state, he had *the historical duty to destroy the opposition*.[14] It is hard to tell what one should admire more: the candor, the naiveté, or the *esprit de système*.

According to Marx, cognition follows existence. Lukács' transformation called for a change in his understanding of the proletariat's role. Its consciousness had been usurped by the party; but it still was supposed to be the substratum of man's creative potentialities. The proletariat became divorced from its revolutionary function as a class that stands outside society and therefore is forced to subvert it while able to dispel its mystifications. In the same vein, labor became hypostatized into "work" as a metaphysical "foundation"[15] — a veritable ideology like so many others the young Lukács had denounced. Although Hegelian and Marxian dialectics excluded any ontology or epistemology separated from logic and history, Lukács did write an *Ontology* at the end of his life. It was at the same time that he recognized the "dialectics of nature." With a generous sprinkling of disparate Marx quotations he thus created a system, a veritable *summa* of Marxist philosophy, where what is superstructure — most ironically — is mistaken for the base.

A Teacher of Taste

The transfiguration of a Saint John into a Saint Augustine and from a Saint Augustine into a Saint Thomas Aquinas is imperceptible to its victim. Only a few words need to be changed. An appeal to the master's spirit can be transformed into canonical quotations. Yet, Lukács was simply too intelligent and too well trained in dialectics to be able to fool himself. With all his dialectical skill, he could not banish those "wrong reasons" that he had conjured up;

they came to pursue him like Peer Gynt's "imagined sins." Neither the party nor the Soviet government was that identical subject-object he craved to see, and Lukács' suppressed yearning found its natural outlet in a return to his first love — literature.

There is a line running from the German classics through Lukács' early work and right into the monumental *Aesthetics* of his old age: in the realm of "beautiful appearances" man experiences a liberating communion with truth.[16] Empathy is certainly no substitute for reason in Lukács' philosophy; but the master's works of literary criticism imply his conviction that the artist's imagination offers direct access to that truth and harmony which eludes him in the realm of politics. Twice at critical moments in his life, he tells us in his autobiography,[17] he forsook politics for literature: the first time after his efforts to reform the Hungarian Communist Party in exile had failed, the second time after the abortive Hungarian revolution of 1956. He also says, there and elsewhere, that he used literary criticism to smuggle intellectual contraband into Stalin's barbarian empire.

It is here that a humanist Lukács seems to emerge: neither a rigid doctrinaire nor a flaming rebel, but a sensitive man of letters who fought valiantly to preserve good taste in the midst of totalitarian horrors; who recognized the great value of the classical-bourgeois traditions and the permanence of their examples even for Marxists; who detested the colorless, schematic productions of "socialist realism." This was the Lukács who rejected agitprop art, and felt brutalized by the Five-Year Plan on the cultural front.

Since Lukács was convinced that good literature is essential for both a struggling proletariat and a socialist state, he appointed himself a teacher of taste in communism. Style carries a message, too, and it must be commensurate with content. The great writers of bourgeois realism from Walter Scott and Balzac to Tolstoy and Thomas Mann were his models; they knew how to construct a story, and they knew how to portray the human condition. Alas, contemporary Soviet writers did not know how to build full-blown characters, and contemporary bourgeois writers were concerned with all sorts of conceits rather than with substance. Their literature does not afford us the kind of insight that satisfies Lukács' craving for truth and harmony. In contrast, he preached the style of classical "realism" that alone, in his view, is revolutionary: it shows the world in its proper relationship to man; it deals with man on the human scale.[18]

Throughout his life Lukács differed from other socialist critics, such as Plekhanov, who grudgingly acknowledged the genius of a Dostoevsky and added a sigh of regret that such a great writer could not have been at least a bit more "progressive." Lukács is immune to such temptations; his judgments are incorruptible. In an article on Dostoevsky, he comes to grips with the problem boldly: literature supports the proletariat's struggle not by narrow partisanship or correct ideology but by teaching the reader how to face a reality beyond appearance, by presenting him with characters whose "type" makes the working of society transparent. Armed with such insight, the reader will then be able to rebel against pretense, distortion, and inauthenticity in bourgeois society ("das Verzerrende und Falsche in der bürgerlichen Gesellschaft"). Great art restores the genuine and harmonious relations between people because it restores harmony to man: "This dream [of the golden age] is the real, authentic core... of Dostoevsky's utopias, a state of the world in which people can know and love each other and in which civilization is no longer an obstacle to the development of man's soul."[19]

This sounds almost like the young Lukács, author of *Die Seele und die Formen,* where art was presented as a special form by which eternal truths could be known, and it corresponds with the intention of his late *Aesthetics,* where art appears as the way of realizing that elusive unity of fact and value, knowledge and practice, object and subject, all of which coincide in the act of creation. Thus at the end of his long life, after a diversion into politics that failed twice, Lukács seems to have returned to his original hope—whether neo-Kantian, Fichtean, or Hegelian is not important here —[20] that art offers a solution to the existential problem. The original title of his *Aesthetics* — *The Uniqueness of the Realm of Beauty* — reminds us of Friedrich Schiller and points to Marcuse. "In art, Thought materializes itself and Matter is not determined in any extraneous way but exists freely.... Nature and Freedom, the Senses and Reason find their right and gratification as one."[21]

In his *Aesthetics,* Lukács assumes a special "realm" where art permits cognition in its own peculiar manner. This was truly a paradoxical way for Lukács to end his philosophical career. Having devoted a lifetime to fighting philosophies of "passivity," he ended by accepting a practice that is entirely grounded in theoretical contemplation. Having meant to "realize philosophy" in the world, he now strove to save it from the world's harsh demands. How different things were fifty years earlier *when the word was pressing to realize itself in the flesh* and the deed was the answer to the question of philosophy! After the defeats of 1918–1923, the idea was crystallized and preserved in the party; now it lives on in art and literature — to be precise, in classical literature, in the exemplary, the model, the ideal. To the end of his life, beneath all the Marxist jargon, Lukács remained an idealist; as his beloved Novalis said: *Philosophy is transcendental homesickness.*

This insight permits us to measure the extent of Lukács' failure. The Faustian moment, which he tried to catch in *History and Class Consciousness,* passed him by;[22] the unity of theory and practice eluded him. It was a failure that happens only to those who have striven for the highest goal. But the respect owed to such an endeavor also forces us to consider the seriousness of the substitute goal. The literary criticism of his later years did matter to Lukács. On its success depended the realization of what the revolution had promised and had so far failed to deliver.

Literature as Political Weapon

This sounds almost trivial, but it is the essence of Lukács' thinking in his last years: his loyalty of fifty years to the Bolshevik conception of the revolution and to the Soviet Union would be vindicated if Soviet culture were to produce a Tolstoy rather than a Semyonov. It was with genuine joy, therefore, that he hailed the appearance of Solzhenitsyn as the "harbinger of a new socialist literature"[23] — although he had serious reservations about Solzhenitsyn's *narodnik* philosophy. Interestingly, he also had artistic reservations about

Solzhenitsyn far earlier than most critics: "What is not realized in literary terms does not exist."

Lukács' involvement in literature was not an evasive action. He considered his ideas on style a guarantee that socialism would survive the Stalinist distortion. As a student of Georg Simmel and Max Weber, he was aware of the universal trend toward technocracy. He saw the age of the savages coming, and he prepared a time capsule for the survivors: the message was humanist letters. Art "discovers the path of humanity"; artistic resolution is "imperturbable faith in the progress of mankind and nation."[24]

The same reasoning applied even more strongly to the Nazi regime. "At a time when German literary criticism led a servile or insignificant existence, Lukács' work stood pre-eminent."[25] What a moving sight: while the Nazi barbarians are booting down German art, a frail Hungarian Jew, an exile sitting in a Moscow library, tries to rescue Goethe, Schiller, Novalis, and Hölderlin for future generations of Germans![26] Or: that same Western Communist, not too sure that he will survive the purges, writes lovingly about the Russian character of Dostoevsky and Tolstoy, while Stalin's flunkeys are scribbling poems on the beauties of the tractor.[27]

It will simply not do to dismiss Lukács' literary criticism written in the Stalin period as "exercises in party regularity" or "crap."[28] On the contrary: these exercises are adroit maneuvers in a literary guerrilla war. The obvious flaws in the essays often betray the contrivance. In order to pass his beloved "classical realists" through the censorship office, for instance, Lukács has to touch them up with a little proletarian rouge; thus, the last act of *Faust II* is said to be a criticism of capitalism! Nonsense! Lukács knows better. But maybe such a view will help keep *Faust* in the libraries while Ilya Ehrenburg is raging against everything German. An innocuous poem of Goethe's is said to refer to the Peasant War; *King Lear* is a drama dealing with the dissolution of the feudal family. There is more of this "crap," and the better it achieved its purpose at the time of writing, the less can the unedited work be used as a guide to literature for the uninitiated reader.

I wish that were all. One could readily forgive Lukács an occasional boost for a mediocre writer who was a fellow traveler.[29] One might even understand why he forgot to mention the Dreyfus case in an article celebrating the centenary memorial for Zola — the year happened to be 1940, when Hitler was Stalin's ally.[30] But Lukács never was to disclose, later on, which passages in his voluminous writings had been "tickets of admission." I suppose he no longer knew when or where he had been sly; he had adopted the language of the dictatorship, his style had become dry and brittle, his thinking dogmatic and bureaucratic.[31]

Critic and Polyhistor

The price of deception grew exceedingly high. Lukács had to defend modern realism against the Nazis *and* the Stalinists, excluding on one side romantic idealism and irrationalism, on the other positivistic naturalism. This could be done only by applying a strict canon of aesthetics that excluded almost all experimentation and in particular the literary avant-garde, which Lukács himself, together with Ernst Bloch and others, had sponsored in the early 1920s. One would think that a Marxist critic should rejoice when a bourgeois writer like Kafka, willy-nilly, describes the disintegration of his world or his person; or that he would encourage a critical-satirical writer like Brecht when his allegorical plays take capitalist society apart. Far from it; Lukács deplores both of them as unconstructive and decadent. Their works may urge us to ask where we are going, but they do not show the transcendence that matters to Lukács.

In his critique of modern literature, Lukács tried to reconcile his growing conservatism with the revolutionary stance of his youth. But more was at stake for him: the coherence of a world in which the revolution was possible. Thus in the programmatic *Realism in Our Time* (1956) he charged that Proust "separates time from objective reality, transforming the inner world into a sinister flux." He objected to modern art for the same reason that caused Lenin to condemn modern philosophy. Just as his political decision had frozen all revolutionary dynamism into the order of the party, and just as his revolutionary dialectic was being frozen into a dialectical system, so he refused to agree that revolutionary literature could be experimental or avant-gardist. One knows that the symbolist writers, who had enthusiastically greeted the revolution in 1917, grew increasingly unhappy in Stalin's Russia. Lukács, who supported the idea of socialist realism — though not its stupid application by illiterate culture czars — felt that avant-garde expressionism and futurism sanctioned individualistic, irrational, petty-bourgeois sentiments that threatened the Five-Year Plan in Russia and helped create the cultural conditions in which fascism could thrive abroad. Thus he launched a literary offensive against Brecht, Bloch, and expressionism in general.[32]

The methodological error Lukács made in his sociology of literature is surprising. He assigns one style to a class at a particular period. Actually, creative artists react to their environment in highly differentiated ways. Although it is true that Marinetti and Benn were militarists, Barlach and Chagall religious, Nolde and Céline anti-Semitic, still the majority of the avant-garde artists, especially in countries where the bourgeoisie was nationalistic, sympathized with the left. Aragon, Éluard, Brecht, Gide, and Malraux were Communists at least in the 1930s. Only a sycophantic *esprit de système*, an Aristotelian anxiety about the "correct" rules, can label a style as petty-bourgeois without even a hint of analysis. Moreover, the sociological function of a style may change, or be ambivalent. Ernst Bloch suggested vainly that the criteria which help to understand Balzac and early-nineteenth-century literature might not apply to contemporary works. Lukács did not understand what Bloch called the "utopian potential" of modern art. One looks in vain for Mauriac, Martin du Gard, Melville, Dreiser, Malraux, Gide, Joyce, Proust, Musil, Broch, or Hesse in *The Historical Novel,* a book that praises many second-rate writers.

Lukács willfully shut himself off from modern literature. He simply had no ear for Brecht, Kafka, or Beckett, for poetry or music. Even after he had admitted Kafka's power of expression, he kept insisting: But it's wrong to have such fantasies. It was rumored, however, that Lukács, on emerging from Dracula's castle in deepest Transylvania — where he had been interned after the 1956 revolt — was overheard murmuring: "Maybe Kafka was a realist, after all." *Se non è vero è ben trovato.*

Lukács stated that modern art justifies uncontrolled demonism and gives recognition to the irrational. He came down severely on

his former friends, the German neo-Romantics. Intensely aware of
the allure of protofascist ideas,[33] he traced them back to their vitalist
sources. Incidentally, it can be shown that even in his Romantic
beginnings Lukács had never made concessions to irrationalism.[34]
Yet with equal zeal he opposed "positivism" — the very opposite of
irrationalism. In *The Destruction of Reason*,[35] he attacked the modern
sciences with ultra-Leninist fervor. He called Wittgenstein a
brother-in-arms of Heidegger; he charged that John Dewey considered changes in the social environment impossible; he accused Bertrand Russell and Herbert Marcuse, of all people, of spreading
imperialist and religious propaganda. He regarded atomic science
and biology as conspiracies to promote such vicious aberrations as
positivism and irrationalism.

One knows the allergy of neo-Marxists to positivism; it was
Lenin's bugbear, and it can even provoke a member of the Frankfurt
Institute to write a sentence that is comprehensible on first reading.
The reason is obvious: positivism destroys the metaphysical certainty that gives the master of the dialectical method inside knowledge of the World Spirit's next move. It sets up the specialized
sciences to rule on problem-solving procedures in the several fields
of human endeavor and thereby withdraws from a polyhistor such
as Hegel or Lukács the right to make pronouncements on matters
outside his own field — and, as Korsch once remarked, "reading
outside his field" is the real definition of an intellectual.

Perhaps the key to the riddle of Lukács can be found in the absurd
grouping of positivism and irrationalism. It is characteristic of
certain ideological partisans that they see all enemies as members of
the same camp — and dialectics is very helpful in establishing that.
In Lukács' case the *espirit de système* imposed its operating code
almost automatically: he was forced to prove that his rigid canon
applied to all fields and all issues; he was forced to take in more and
more territory and expand his pronouncements into areas where he
had no expertise. Moreover, not only would the system have to
explain the phenomena of the outside world; it would also have to
fit the conditions under which it had been conceived: *Lukács had to
build his own tower of orthodoxy within the ramparts of Stalin's fortress.*

The young Lukács had praised Marx for using his contemporaries' science and developing his own truth through immanent criticism of their findings. The older Lukács did not relate to his schol-

arly contemporaries as Marx had related to those of his time; he rejected them as vulgar epigones and as products of a continuous decline from the heights that had once been reached by Hegel, Ricardo, Balzac, and Darwin. What is not classical has no right to be. After noting that Marx was able to learn from Darwin and Morgan, Lukács says: "Obviously, nothing similar is happening today."[36]

The Historical Hero

It is a misconception that a Communist who cares for literature must be a "revisionist." Nothing could be farther from the truth. Lukács never made such a claim; on the contrary, he warned the Communists many times that "right deviations" and "revisionism" are — in typical Comintern language — the "main enemy." Even in those famous "Blum Theses" of 1928, which Lukács quoted as proof of his independence, he rejected the "democracy against fascism" slogan in favor of Stalin's watchword: "No pact with the pseudo-opposition [against Horthy];... fight against social democracy as a mainstay of fascism."[37] As late as in 1962, he called revisionism "the greatest danger."[38]

Was Lukács at least an anti-Stalinist? In that same article he pleaded that one should not forget Stalin's merits. He asserted that all through the late 1920s and the 1930s and up to 1948 – 49, Stalin had been right "tactically as well as theoretically against all opposi-tions" — but that then unfortunately "he mistook tactical necessities for theoretical truths and thereby degraded Marxism into an ideol-ogy." *Not Stalin's crimes were his sin but his philosophical myopia; not his system was at fault but an intellectual failing.*

It was not until Khrushchev gave the signal that Lukács joined the de-Stalinizers, and then he boasted: "I can truthfully say that I was objectively [!] an enemy of Stalin's methods even at the time when I still believed myself to be his follower."[39] Stalin had been a historical necessity in his time; now the time for critique had come. In the light of his own self-evaluations, Lukács was never a "revisionist."

He never stopped being a disciple of Hegel, who saw Napoleon as "the World Spirit on a white horse."

The public function of a thinker often differs from his private, narrow world. Lukács has passed for a revisionist not only because his early works have stimulated revisionist thinking but because repeatedly — however much against his wish and will — he clashed with the Soviet authorities. In Hungary, after a vain attempt to coexist with Mátyás Rákosi, Stalin's henchman, he helped found the Petöfi circle, joined Imre Nagy's insurgent government in 1956, albeit reluctantly, and left it before the end of its heroic stand. He was temporarily interned and suspended from the party for ten years. His late works have been savagely criticized in the East European press; his impressive collected works *(Gesamtausgabe)* in sixteen volumes had to appear in West Germany. After his death his disciples were suspended from the University of Budapest; they can neither teach nor do research — and yet Agnes Heller, his favorite, has repudiated his early masterpiece. [40]

Still, if Western scholars hoped for a "dialogue," Lukács made it clear that it would not be a two-way communication. In his opinion, Western theory was so decadent that he expected its partisans to capitulate; and he never accepted coexistence in the area of ideology. On the contrary, the essence of his teaching was that class war is also an intellectual *(geistig)* struggle. This part of his "idealistic" *History and Class Consciousness* he never retracted. He did not think that Marxism needed any complement from modern sociology, psychology, or anthropology.

Lukács fought a long, consistent, and often bitter fight against all humanist, existentialist, [41] and other "sentimental" or "revisionist" interpretations of Marx as well as against all attempts to link Marxism to Freudianism or any other science. [42] Naturally, he also rejected Maoism — as "subjectivist."

The Dialectical Paradox

For all that, the thought of the early Lukács remains a leaven throughout the satellite countries — and there its study may be as dangerous as the study of the young Marx. In the West Lukács' work has given rise to a considerable body of academic scholarship, and many of his followers may feel that to uncritically teach Lukács means to do revolutionary work. They are tragically mistaken. To freeze dialectical thought into a teachable canon is the opposite of revolutionary action. In this respect the disciples suffer from the same misconception as their master did when he taught the proletarian writers "realism." With them, as with the early Lukács, cultural criticism has replaced the permanent revolution, and it is a strange irony that "bourgeois" teachers of English or of sociology should now mine the treasures of Lukács' system for textbook excerpts and ideas.

There are, however, other diggers at work. As the young Lukács found his way to the forgotten draft manuscripts of the young Marx, so the work of the young Lukács, disowned by the older Lukács, is now taken up by a generation of young critics who will forever love the search more than its fruits.[43] This was the message of *History and Class Consciousness* back in 1923, and this message was the method.

Epilogue

Confessions of an Old-Timer:
Aphorisms on Socialism

Ideas change but their formulas remain. Two people a thousand years apart may be of the same mind despite their differences. To be sure, no bore is more boring than the disciple who quotes what I said twenty years ago. Yet I love him — not for the doctrine he continues to profess but because once in our lives we hated and loved the same things, sang the same hymns, and were clubbed by the same police. By the same token, I would have loved the man who said, twenty-five hundred years ago, "Good government is one of which the people know it exists; not quite as good is the one which they praise"; or the man who said, "The meek shall inherit the earth." I suppose I would have recognized their voices before I appreciated their ideas. So it is with other saintly fools or with my old fellow militants. Marching together made us into a movement. The idea was a flag, and some sacrificed themselves for the flag — I always thought they were dying for me, not for the flag. Solidarity was from each to all for one another — not from all to the flag.

Sometimes we were wrong — maybe more often than we knew or would care to admit; perhaps we are wrong even now. Yet, were we given a chance to live our lives over again, we probably would make the same mistakes, fight the same enemies, hold sacred the same illusions — or similar ones that also are based on the same assumption: that Man is good.

We were wrong most of the time when we tried to realize doctrines or when we followed a course of action that seemed to follow from the Scriptures. We were never wrong when we acted in solidarity with people who tried to shape their own destinies. How could we be wrong so long as we asserted our faith in Man? Even defeat could not disprove us; it only made our faith stronger. "Man is good." That is a proposition which is neither true nor untrue; it can be validated by the strong who believe in it militantly, or invalidated by the fainthearted.

※

Our real defeats were not the occasions when we were beaten; they came when we were told we had succeeded. Our ideas, let's face it, had a tremendous success; everybody stole them and "realized" them. The Nazis took May Day, the very name of socialism, and the pageantry of revolution. The Bolsheviks appropriated the doctrine of a planned economy. The Republicans have adopted the progressive income tax and the Democrats the welfare state. Nasser and King Saud nationalized large industries. Socialism has been hyphenated with nationalism, its mortal enemy, with anticlerical radicalism, and with clerical Christianity. It has been perverted into a totalitarian state philosophy and into the ideology of conservative labor parties. There is no cowardice that has not been justified by "socialist" consciences; no bold crime that has not been committed in the name of socialist efficiency.

They stole every part of the system, every single goal, and every doctrine; they claimed to have realized every socialist demand. Except one. They never stole the basic assumption that Man is good. Some will go so far as to admit that Man is perfectible, and they will proceed to educate him accordingly, by their own or even by our lights; but they will never let him educate himself. They will do everything for the people and eventually provide them with the most perfect socialist economy; but they will not allow these same people to act in their own behalf, make their own mistakes, and assert their own solidarity.

Socialism has become a doubtful word — not because it has been betrayed so often by its leaders, not because it has been diverted so often into strange channels, but because it has been institutionalized, taken over, and managed. Socialism is being *used!* Dare we protest? Dare we say that we never thought of Progress in terms of abstract

achievements: so much planning, so much welfare, so much nation-alization? Dare we return to the original meaning of socialism —
socii, the fellows — as that which people have in common?

※※

Many traits of "socialism" simply appeared when certain trends of modern industrialism were extrapolated. They call a socialist some-one who admits that free enterprise can no longer handle today's problems. Atomic energy must be kept under safety rules by the government; communications must be supervised by the state; great hydraulic works must be undertaken by national planning boards; weak industries such as farming must be subsidized. Worse: an efficient defense industry, a crash rocket program can be planned by despotism better than by free agents; the interests of nationalism point toward a "socialized" economy, with more integration, more interventionism, more welfare and planning, more compulsory ar-bitration. A moderately progressive kind of welfare economy has been "creeping" rather far and fast lately, and the more intelligent business executives know — or even admit — that it is here to stay. Outside congressional and Fourth-of-July oratory, classical free en-terprise is deader than a doornail, and socialists who continue to fight against its ghosts are museum pieces themselves.

It is about time for socialists to admit the facts: there is more "socialism" in the world today than capitalism or any other system. Although we don't like the kind of socialism that is being realized, we cannot simply repudiate or ignore it. Governments in most new countries are now in complete command of the national resources, either through ownership of the most important enterprises or by virtue of various control devices. Feudalistic and capitalistic forms of ownership are successfully checked by political means; the var-ious underdeveloped economies are being developed according to plans that may satisfy the desires of their elites and will certainly flatter their national ambitions. Even in the advanced countries, older capitalistic traditions yield to "mixed economies" that are largely regulated; production goals and distributive aims are formulated through political infighting and the influence of pluralistic pressure groups. Staunch defenders of free enterprise now acknowledge that elements of "socialist" economic thinking have become part of their system, while orthodox disciples of the "economic" view of history now admit that wage, price, and related disputes have become "political."

※※

Some socialists—the true ones, I think—do not agree that socialism is an extrapolation of present trends in the capitalist economy. The term socialism should have been saved from confusion with state capitalism or even state collectivist systems. Indeed, it should not be identified with any, not even the most perfect system; for originally socialism was a movement of protest against all systems. Its history in modern times begins with the Jacqueries and Martin Luther's indictment of the "Companies Monopolia"; it includes a sequence of anarchist, apocalyptic, and chiliastic rebellions against the domination and exploitation of man by man, against industrialism and the modern state, against commercialism and militarism. At times, these movements could merge in common hatred of an overriding symbol; capitalism provided the common denominator for all exploitation and domination. At all times, however, anticapitalism has had these two components: resistance to domination by an upper class, and resistance to an "inexorable law" which claims that exploitation of human "factors" is the necessary prerequisite of economic progress.

This democratic and humanistic root of socialism has flowered in conceptions like "industrial democracy" and "workers' control," in the "council" movements that recently sprang up in Poland and Hungary, in the American shop-steward law, and even in the German "codetermination" law. In a still more perverted form, it arises when workers repudiate socialist parties that (however ineffectively) try to defend their living standards, and follow the Communists who merely assert their freedom to protest. A minority of French Communists favors dictatorship and admires Bolshevik terror; most of them think they are defending democracy. In their propaganda speeches the Russians aptly refer to the "ruling circles" of the

West; this target, which evokes memories of the "Elders of Zion" and other world conspiracies of the upper class, most effectively rallies pseudodemocratic and pseudosocialist instincts of anticapitalist defense.

It was the merit of Marx to focus opposition on the specific "system" of capitalism and the "economic laws." He also attacked the social class that benefits from this system and is interested in its preservation. But for him this was only one aspect of a two-faced phenomenon. The more capitalism develops, the less some parasitic beneficiary — the private owner of capital — is the villain of the piece. This villain's gradual disappearance or submission under the abstract law of profitability merely confirms what should have been clear to readers of *Capital* from the beginning: that class situations are not properly described by the symbols "rich" and "poor" but by economic function, and that authority is derived not from property but from the right to use it. The managers of large corporations are not exploiting people; they merely translate the equation of rational efficiency into "personnel relations." Likewise, the managers of Soviet state trusts administer the law of growth of industrial enterprises. Socialism is a human reaction against both forms of command over man. Though not hostile to industrialism, socialism is not its fulfillment. Any society may use technological achievements without surrendering its own values. The Japanese militarists knew how to use industrialism; the Russian Bolsheviks abandoned themselves to its spirit. In the democracies the fight is still raging: will modern industry breed the perfect robot — or liberate man from drudgery and servitude? These alternatives require some reflection on the question of what socialism means today.

※※

We are learning better to know our enemy. Marx still wrote against capitalism; today all of society is under indictment. Marx still could say confidently that at the end of capitalist development nothing would be left to do except to "expropriate the few owners of already socialized factories"; today we are frightened at the sight of the "already socialized minds." After the owners of the communications networks had been expropriated, their function still would be "socialized" — maybe without minds.

Many socialists today are fighting the spread of what has been called mass culture. None of this has been new since Huxley's *Brave New World;* but today it is a problem for socialists. Huxley still believed that he was satirizing the trend of capitalism (he said specifically that the entire, weird arrangement of his world had been engineered for the sole purpose of ensuring maximum consumption of surplus production), and he still implied that socialism would break this fatal trend. In the meantime, the collectivist heaven has developed traits that are worse than the capitalist hell. Capitalism brought oppression from outside, but left the inner man largely intact — so much so that he was able to rebel. Collectivism captures a person totally; consent is being "engineered" or given "freely." People are "reasonable" because they no longer see alternative choices. Capitalism crippled people's sensibilities, to be sure; collectivism demands that these sensibilities wither away.

⁂

No doubt most socialists are horrified by the picture of "socialism" that has unfolded over the past forty years, and they will insist that this is not what they had fought for. Certainly they are right. But liberals and democrats could have protested, a hundred years ago, against the way liberal and democratic ideals were being realized. They had to take the responsibility because at least one thing could not be denied: liberalism was run largely by liberals. Socialism, on the contrary, is being run by everybody but socialists. Sometimes it can hardly be distinguished from its worst enemies — state capitalism, fascism, and nationalism.

We may vainly protest that the most important characteristics of socialism are missing in all these mixed, adulterated, and perverted conceptions; that a socialist system run by nonsocialists is simply unthinkable; and that socialism is an integrated whole from which no single feature can be omitted or integrated into another system. All this is beside the point — or rather, this is just the point: that the enemy has infiltrated the fortress and the socialists are not in com-

mand of their own house. It is simply impossible to ignore the
language of the common man and to insist that the name of socialism should be reserved for an esoteric notion of an esoteric sect; it is
even less possible if the missing element in all these pseudosocialist
systems is ill-defined. Socialists themselves have not agreed on its
nature, nor have they warned others of the impending confusion.
Moreover, the definition of pure or strict socialism, too, seems to
be hyphenated. The moment I say "democratic socialism" I admit
that there are other kinds, at least potentially, and that, to satisfy me,
I have to add to the definition of socialism a foreign ingredient taken
from another source. This attempt at evading the issue, therefore,
defeats the claim that socialism is an organic whole.

꩜

Can socialism be an organic whole? There really should be but one
such whole: Man. No institution, not the most perfect one, can or
should be an end. Whoever thinks that socialism or any other system
is the end of history stops thinking as a socialist.

I shall confide a sad truth to you. Those who want a perfect
socialism are not socialists. They substitute a system for the fullness
of humanity. They perfect institutions instead of making them fit
the needs of people. Beware lest they ultimately fit people to institutions. There can never be peace between man and man's works.
But it is true that there never was less peace between them than now.

꩜

Our society cripples people and inflicts on them the disease that
decimates "personality": A man is appreciated not for what he is
but for what he usefully contributes; he is cleft down the middle
into a public and a private being. The first is his material usefulness,
and it includes every one of the qualities that make him replaceable;
the other is hidden away, though it holds the unique qualities of his
humanity. Our society deprives itself, and him, of what is the
essential part of the personality.

In industrial-commercial relations, togetherness is neither freely granted out of the fullness of sympathy and generosity, nor is it ever allowed to bring out essential human impulses. It is a means to achieve productivity. Man himself is a means, not only for other men but for production goals. Wherever we see people together, their togetherness is either perverted or it turns away from society. Society, which does not need love, circumscribed it within a sphere of regulated and permissible behavior — just as the Church, unable to cope with man's totality, found a niche for pardonable sin. In this process society immunizes itself against feeling: it prevents the most human needs from affecting human relations. The totality of Man is never present in society; the best of him remains private.

***

Capitalism does not impede creativity; it misdirects it by capturing its specific virtue. On the whole, capitalism has promoted progress. But it has done something to the inventor. He no longer considers himself an artist or creates out of the fullness of his life in the community. The complaint that capitalism stifles creativity is ridiculous; we hear nothing but exaltations of so-called creativity. "Creative" of what? That is the question. The word makes no sense apart from any specific creation.

Productivity has been insulated; it has become an end in itself. This system also has permitted the advances of Soviet science. The price: science has been taken out of its political and philosophical context.

***

Lately, another flow of noble feelings has been isolated from its wellsprings of human generosity and perverted into useful techniques of management. Business today is all for social welfare, for planning, for greater equality, and, *horribile dictu,* for "solidarity," "togetherness," and "group thinking." After taking over most of the institutions and the material aims, the enemy is availing himself of a mock-version of the socialist spirit. To make the perversion complete, some socialist thinkers now have been moved to join the chorus of protest against "mass culture." When this clarion was first sounded, by Le Bon and Ortega y Gasset, it was the war cry of declared antisocialists; with the exception of Hendrik de Man, no socialist at the time protested against these aspects of the new socialism.

Such an analysis might be rejected on the following grounds: the present mass culture is characteristic of a capitalistic economy that still is being run by capitalists, and is working for their benefit; classes have not been abolished, and even where state capitalism prevails, its functionaries clearly constitute a new class of exploiters. If all this is true, socialists were even more mistaken than they seemed to be; they fought the wrong enemy on a false front. They laid all evils at the door of private capitalists or "bosses" instead of an institution that seems to be embracing considerably more territory than just private enterprise; we have called it modern industrialism, and its characteristics are a particular rationality and accounting mentality, a necessary division of labor, and a functional hierarchy.

Not private capital is the enemy but the capitalist calculability which defines man's worth by what he can contribute to the creation of value. Private capitalists are more or less needless costs in a modern industrial system and will be eliminated almost automatically, though slowly, should they prove to be too costly. Socialists still have to fight those who hold the levers of economic and political control, under whatever title; but on the ideological level these functionaries are better armed than the old capitalists. The capitalist had to justify himself in terms of his usefulness to the promotion of progress; often he could not show cause but was unmasked as a mere parasite. The functionary barely faces this difficulty. He clearly fulfills a function determined by calculations of an electronic brain; he can show that in terms of these calculations he is just as useful as anybody else; he merely executes the equations of the perfect plan. His wages are those of an administrator, and he has earned his share. Arcadij Gurland observed that the anticapitalist protest, from its very beginnings, was "political": under the conditions of a strict European class society, it was a protest against the owners of a monopoly. Opposition against the "manager," hence, can be aroused in the name of democracy only.

If socialism is the functionally most streamlined system of production and distribution, as provided by the most perfect electronic brains according to the economic equations, then the argument that the manager has earned his share is unanswerable. The little fat which the bureaucrats may skim off the national soup really does not matter if otherwise they give their citizens good service. Socialists then cannot quarrel with the accounting system either, because some accounting must be there to avoid unnecessary waste.

※

On technological grounds, a socialist expert of planning and accounting might not find too much to criticize in the budget of a pseudosocialist economy. Even so, a principled socialist opposition would be called into being whenever the definition of "national welfare" was at stake, i.e., if and only if the aims and goals of planning were subject to controversy. The government will always be able to show, figures in hand, that output and expenses should be increased, preferably in those places where greater customer satisfaction will eventually result in better production. Socialists may argue that they value leisure and easy production schedules more highly than national power and large production facilities, and that consumption allowances should be increased first for the aged and for retired people.

Here the human element in the argument disrupts the planners' calculations; the conflict between man and machine, or man and the organization, or man and the rationality of economic reckoning, has not changed, whether the executor of the abstract command of the figures is a private capitalist, a trust manager, or a bureaucrat. The socialist's function in this fight is still the same, whether the enemy be capitalism or socialism. The socialist represents humanity. To that extent, Marx's analysis of industrial labor is still correct: what he called "constant" costs still are the ones given by objective factors, and labor is the only "variable" cost. But he did not surmise that

19.   **Charlie Chaplin in <u>Modern Times</u>**
(Photo: The Museum of Modern Art, New York)

this criticism would still be valid under socialist conditions of production.

A graver drawback of recent advances toward socialism has been uncovered by Gunnar Myrdal. Planning, he says, is necessarily national planning first, and that means erecting protective barriers against the disruptive fluctuations that, periodically or constantly, are transmitted from the world markets to the national economies. Isolationism serves the interest of socialist planners; but it deprives the country's workers and consumers of all the checks on misplanning that normally control a national economy through the countervailing influence of foreign exchanges. Moreover, the closed economy leaves the government free to use foreign commerce for its particular political aims. For instance, the foreign transactions of the Soviet government are probably the single part of the world economy carried out with the least regard to cost; by that token, this operation might be called the "least capitalistic," but it is so conducted only for reasons of foreign policy. Any benefit to the people that might accrue from it is strictly accidental.

※※※

Socialism is not capitalism minus capitalists, nor the most advanced, streamlined system of industrial accountability; it cannot even be defined as a democratic system of such rational industrial relations properly institutionalized. On the contrary, socialists enter the picture precisely at the point where such a system breaks down and people refuse to obey the abstract law of efficiency. Socialists, at their best, always will represent the human protest against any system, and that is even more true when the system is more rational and more efficient and when the "human factor" is being managed more "scientifically." The human sense of dignity revolts against the dependence upon command powers, whether economic or political.

Our aim was to deprive people of the power to use other people as means to an end, however worthy the increase of productivity or the national welfare. This must remain the attitude of socialists under all systems. However, theoretical considerations and the evidence of recent history suggest that this conflict between man and things, or freedom and necessity, cannot be resolved. The aim then is to check the command powers through the countervailing powers of labor and other organizations.

The pluralistic system which this implies cannot be justified on the ground that it is more efficient than straight capitalism or straight despotism. It is not, and either of these systems will normally be more efficient. But it gives people a chance to wreck plans that were made without their consent, to assert their will, and to make their own mistakes. System-builders are so well-intentioned as to prevent people from making wrong decisions. They will do everything for the people except allow them to do anything for themselves. Even some enthusiasts of countervailing powers envisage those powers as a system, i.e., they assume that various powers sooner or later will become institutionalized and freeze into a well-organized system where, for example, wage conflicts will be superseded completely by a pyramid of negotiation and arbitration machinery which in the end will figure out what part of the national product each population group should get. Eventually this can be done by a special computer. Socialists may find a pluralistic arrangement more suitable for their purposes, but they must attempt to prevent its freezing into a system. They must be very flexible in promoting and checking the countervailing powers at the right times.

※※

Philosophy has not found a solution to the problem of conflict, nor does historical evidence suggest any avenue of escape. The famous "leap into the realm of Freedom" has not been defined as the *conquest* of Necessity but as the *insight* into its pattern or a choice between alternative aims. Reactionaries have seized upon this truth, in asking the silly (because incomplete) question, Freedom for what? Choice, the essence of freedom, is always a choice between possibilities; hence freedom is "for what" only to the extent that it is "from what." To conceal this dichotomy is a sleight-of-hand by which freedom is made to disappear. There is no genuine freedom when the choice is limited within a system. Freedom must always remain the liberty of refusing cooperation, of debating "necessity" and of disregarding "instrumental reason." Since necessity and instrumental reason will always be the specific patterns of the existing society, freedom can exist only if alternative frames of reference are offered by competing powers. Hence the system of countervailing powers should be as widely open as possible, the aim being not only to check the command powers of the ruling hierarchy but to establish the pattern of choices itself.

※

With regard to labor, socialists do not represent the human "factor" in the production equation; they represent the human element in society. That is to say, they break every equation. They are not interested in establishing a system with a better equation (though they often pretend they are doing so), but in saving man from being a factor in an equation. What matters to them is the point where the equation breaks down and man emerges, not where a new equation is formed and man is again integrated into a new system. Socialism, so understood as the action of socialists, is not a social and economic system; it is motion. Proudly expressing the essence of labor at its best, Bernstein said: "The ultimate goal is nothing to me, the Movement is everything." Marx's healthy contempt for wielders of "programs" is too well known to need quoting here, and even the great utopians used their programs only to realize their secret aim: to set people in motion. This is not to cite the Church Fathers as authorities but to answer the question of whether we can still call ourselves socialists in the same sense that they did. I think we can; socialism in this sense will be the slogan when in Poland, Yugoslavia, and elsewhere people present their demands for more self-determination and participation in deciding their own and their country's fate. Oppressed socialists under "socialism" are in the same position as Christians who uphold Christ against the churches.

Socialism first of all means movement; it is a freely organized movement. When the goal is reached, however, the movement may cease; "socialism" then dies for want of a cause. Nationalization, welfare, and planning — desirable as such — no longer symbolize man's aspiration to master his own destiny; they may well become the symbols of his inability to make responsible choices.

※

Socialism is not a thing to have; it cannot be abstractly defined. Suppose each worker owns his house and his car, and suppose the new techniques of economic control make it possible for capitalism to improve living standards, to give people economic security, and to narrow class differences: do we then still need socialism? I say yes, because it is a matter of attitudes. It is freedom, or the refusal to submit to commands. It is solidarity, or the refusal to forget people over the demands of technique.

✺

One cannot have socialism. One is a socialist.

Notes

2. THREE ECONOMIC MODELS

1. I do not wish to enter here into a learned discussion of marginal utility and the subjective theory of value. For a detailed analysis see Ben B. Seligman's truly encyclopedic and scholarly work, *Main Currents in Modern Economics* (New York: Free Press, 1962). For theoretical background, I have drawn heavily on this monumental publication, the most complete and the most modern of its kind to my knowledge. I am also indebted to Abba P. Lerner, *The Economics of Control* (New York: Macmillan, 1944), and Joseph A. Schumpeter, *Capitalism, Socialism, and Democracy* (New York: Harper, 1942).

2. In ancient Rome the capitalist way with fire brigades was revealed by Crassus, who would offer to buy a house on fire. If he got it, his slaves were standing ready to put the fire out; if not, they would leave the scene with their equipment. As Robert Heilbroner points out, the example also illustrates the divergence of private and social marginal products.

3. See Carl Landauer, *European Socialism* (Berkeley: University of California Press, 1959, vol. II), and Benjamin Evans Lippincott, ed., *On the Economic Theory of Socialism* (Minneapolis: University of Minnesota Press, 1938).

4. For that purpose even Adam Smith would grant a monopoly to a corporation!

5. It might be claimed that monopoly anticipates social benefits or development profits accruing from its investments. If we take this argument as seriously as it theoretically deserves, it leads us to recognize the advantages of state capitalism over private capitalism. Likewise, it might be claimed that without the land grants there might have been less railroad promotion and no opportunity for big-time speculators to expropriate the public's savings for the higher purpose of a national railroad policy. While this policy was not a deliberate scheme but resulted from the "cunning of history," in the case of our highway network a Depression was required to permit (and excuse) its planning on a national scale.

6. Ludwig von Mises, *Socialism,* revised edition translated by J. Kahane (New Haven: Yale University Press, 1959). Joseph Schumpeter, however, holds that monopoly is more efficient. See also Joan Robinson, *The Economics of Imperfect Competition* (London: Macmillan, 1933). Cf. my contribution, "Kapitalistische und Wohlfahrtsplanung in Amerika," in Robert Jungk and Hans J. Mundt, eds., *Wege ins neue Jahrtausend* (Munich: Desch, 1964), where I show that American planning is meant to restore, not to abolish, competition.

7. Malthus had no answer but war and pestilence when the problem was much less desperate; Ricardo and Marx assumed that periodic slumps forcibly restored the equilibrium. Today we have to use "countervailing" techniques permanently *and* maintain a defense economy. (See Section IV of this essay.)

8. The Rule of marginal utility says that output should be carried to the point where the cost of the last (marginal) unit matches the price it fetches, or where the

marginal social benefit matches the marginal social cost. Since the latter is also measured in prices, the two equations are identical. The assumption here is that social benefit and real social cost can be so measured; this I am going to deny.

9. In *Finanzkapital* (1910), Hilferding toyed with the idea of a "cartel général"; and in his last essay ("Socialističeski Vestnik," 1940) he rejected the term state capitalism, since "an economy without capitalists and without market cannot be called capitalistic." He coined the term bureaucratic economy for both the Nazi war economy and Soviet collectivism. The same idea, of course, underlies B. Riccio's "managerial society" — *La Bureaucratisation du monde*, by "Z" (Paris, 1939), to which James Burnham failed to acknowledge his indebtedness — and K. A. Wittfogel's "oriental despotism." Important as the nature of the ruling elite may be, we are here concerned with abstract models of pure economic mechanisms; "capitalism" exists wherever capital must earn its keep. It is interesting to note that by now the Soviet Union is forced to abandon the "uneconomic" (i.e., noncapitalistic) methods of price-fixing and accounting. Khrushchev admonished the managers to earn an honest profit, and Kosygin allows a wide discussion of Evgin Liberman's neosocialist theories. There is, of course, a semantic and political advantage in setting "statist economy" aside as a special category; but my interest here is theoretical.

10. As state capitalism tends to encourage totalitarian government (see later in Section III), it tends to create artificial shortages, too.

11. *Ekonomia Polityczenna* (Warsaw, 1959); in English, *Political Economy*, translated by A. H. Walker (New York: Macmillan, 1963–1971) and *Essays on Economic Planning* (Calcutta, 1960). Quoted by Landauer, *European Socialism*. Jaurès was of the same opinion: "Collectivism can be regarded almost as a special case of capitalism" (*ibid.*, p. 1606).

12. For this reason I speak of only three basic types of economy. State capitalism and monopoly capitalism are derivative forms. Under conditions of scarcity, state socialism, too, will be hard to differentiate from state capitalism, with special incentives for the managers destroying the chances for one of Lange's "three advantages" — equality. Strangely, or maybe not so surprisingly, Lange fails to claim a fourth advantage that ought to go with socialism of any kind — public accountability.

13. It is now official doctrine of the U.S. State Department that foreign governments may "nationalize" American investments, provided they pay compensation (for which the U.S. Treasury usually will compensate them). What matters is not that the United States is being robbed but that the principle of property is maintained — even at the expense of the U.S taxpayer.

14. In its degenerated forms, it may also be a "limited liability" economy that merely preserves the welfare of politically powerful groups (or elites). It socializes losses and plans the conservation of guild privileges. This problem of the welfare state is well illustrated by the debate in which each year various pressure groups are pitted against each other. On a higher level, we have witnessed the debate between Dr. Leon Keyserling and Professor John Kenneth Galbraith; the latter advocates expansion of the public sector, the former would rather raise the income level of the underprivileged. Dr. Keyserling has argued his own priority preferences per-

suasively, though on purely pragmatic grounds, and theoretically no general rule can be established for all countries at all stages of development.

15. In the Soviet Union these public consumer services now amount to 15 percent of wage income, and are supposed to rise to 50 percent. This is substantially what Galbraith and Robert Theobald are suggesting: the constant enlargement of public services.

16. Anton Menger notes as one of three basic rights "that each member of society may claim that the goods and services necessary to the maintenance of his existence shall be assigned to him, in keeping with the measure of existing means, before the less urgent needs of others are satisfied." *Das Recht auf den vollen Arbeitsertrag* (Stuttgart, 1891); in English: *The Right to the Whole Produce of Labour* (London, 1899). The other two rights are Louis Blanc's "right to work" and Ferdinand Lassalle's right to a just (not the full!) share of the product of one's labor. These "rights" fall short of abolishing inequality and exploitation, but their realization is a condition for a classless society.

17. England has done better with the so-called public corporations, which Eldon Johnson has called "a cross between a governmental adjective and a capitalist noun."

18. The Socialist International proclaimed in its Frankfurt Manifesto of 1951 that planning does not presuppose public ownership of all means of production. But when the Manifesto continues "it is compatible with private enterprise in important fields," I would add "under controlled conditions."

19. Peter F. Drucker, *The New Society* (New York: Harper, 1950), p. 76.

20. Daniel M. Friedenberg, "Real Estate Confidential," *Dissent* (1961), 8:260.

21. We are constantly drawing on such assets as air and water, and only occasionally are we reminded that they may have "value" — whenever the water level sinks and someone can sell us some water that he owns. Value is property! And property — *c'est le vol!*

22. In at least two respects, though, a socialist economy is more economical than any preceding society. One is its concern for human beings, the other conservation. As air and water pollution become ever-growing problems and we no longer can take nature's immensity for granted, an economy which saves nothing but that which can be owned becomes a threat to the survival of the human race. Once it used to be said that capitalists would charge a price for the air we breathe if only they could make it scarce. Now, precisely because they are making it scarce, socialism becomes a practical necessity.

23. I have dealt with the philosophical and ethical aspects of socialism in "The Right To Be Lazy."

24. This allusion to multiple centers of decision-making and competitive — or even antagonistic — organs of shop democracy must suffice here. My essay deals with only one aspect of the socialist economy, its theory of value. It will take another essay to describe its second, no less essential aspect, the democratic organization of work.

4. THE IDEA OF PROGRESS IN MARXISM

1. "Manifesto of the Communist Party," in Karl Marx and Frederick Engels, *Selected Works* (Moscow: Foreign Languages Publishing House, 1962), 1:33–65.

The first expression of such a purely historicist view is found in a contribution by Engels to Robert Owen's magazine, *The New Moral World and Gazette of the Rational Society*, November 4, 1843, entitled "Progress and Social Reform on the Continent," reprinted in German translation in *Marx/Engels Werke (MEW)* (Berlin: Dietz, 1957), 1:480 ff. My contention is that Marx and Engels abandoned this historicist view when they turned to the "naturalist method," which is usually called materialism.

2. Karl Marx, *Capital*, translated by Samuel Moore, Edward Aveling, and Ernest Untermann (Chicago: Charles H. Kerr, 1907–9), 1:13; 3:517.

3. "No social order ever perishes before all the productive forces for which there is room in it have developed; and new, higher relations of production never appear before the material conditions of their existence have matured in the womb of the old society itself. Therefore mankind always sets itself only such tasks as it can solve; since, looking at the matter more closely, it will always be found that the task itself arises only when the material conditions for its solution already exist or are at least in the process of formation. In broad outlines Asiatic, ancient, feudal, and modern bourgeois modes of production can be designated as progressive epochs in the economic formation of society. The bourgeois relations of production are the last antagonistic form of the social process of production...." Karl Marx, Preface to *A Contribution to the Critique of Political Economy*, in Marx and Engels, *Selected Works*, 1:363–64.

4. In the preface to the second edition of *Capital*, Marx approvingly quotes a Russian reviewer: "Of still greater moment to [Marx] is the law of... their transition from one form into another, from one series of connections into a different one... [Marx] proves... both the necessity of the present order of things, and the necessity of another order into which the first must inevitably pass over... (1:22–23).

5. In his book on Feuerbach, Engels explains historical dialectics in this simple way: "There is no final, perfect state.... Each stage is necessary, and therefore justified for the time and conditions to which it owes its origin. But in the face of new, higher conditions which gradually develop in its own womb, it loses its validity and justification. It must give way to a higher stage which will also in its turn decay and perish." Frederick Engels, "Ludwig Feuerbach and the End of Classical German Philosophy," in Marx and Engels, *Selected Works*, 2:362. He specifically denies here the "illusion" of a predetermined goal of history.

6. G. W. F. Hegel, *Reason in History*, translated by Robert S. Hartman (New York: Bobbs-Merrill, 1953), p. 25. Lenin saw the approach to truth — the most paradigmatic progress — in this asymptotic image; see his *Materialism and Empiriocriticism*.

7. Similarly, the young Marx in his letter to Ruge: "The reform of consciousness exists *merely* in the fact that one makes the world aware of its consciousness, that one awakens the world out of its own dream.... Our slogan therefore, must be: Reform of consciousness, not through dogmas, but through analysis of the mystical consciousness that is unclear about itself.... It will be evident, then, that the world has long dreamed of something of which it only has to become conscious in order

to possess it in actuality." *Writings of the Young Marx on Philosophy and Society,* translated and edited by Loyd D. Easton and Kurt H. Guddat (Garden City, N.Y.: Doubleday Anchor Books, 1967), p. 214; emphasis by Marx.

8. See Sir Karl Popper, *The Open Society and Its Enemies,* 5th ed. (Princeton: Princeton University Press, 1966) and Eduard Bernstein, *Evolutionary Socialism,* translated by Edith C. Harvey (New York: Schocken Books, 1961).

9. From Karl Marx, "The Poverty of Philosophy," in Easton and Guddat, eds., *Writings of the Young Marx,* pp. 489–90; emphasis by Marx.

10. Frederick Engels, "Speech at the Graveside of Karl Marx," in Marx and Engels, *Selected Works,* 2:167.

11. Karl Marx und Friedrich Engels, *Ausgewählte Briefe* (Berlin: Dietz, 1953), pp. 150 and 155. On January 16, 1861, to Ferdinand Lassalle: "Darwin's book is very remarkable; it suits me as a foundation, in natural science, of historical class war. . . . Despite all its defects, here for the first time teleology has received its death blow as far as natural science is concerned, and the latter has been made rational empirically." And on June 18, 1862, to Engels: "He is dealing with the animal kingdom as though it were the bourgeois society." By contrast, compare Stalin's pompous view: "Evolution is not a circular movement, not the simple repetition of the old, but a progressive movement, as a movement in ascending line, a transition from an old qualitative state toward a new qualitative state, as development from the simple to the complex, from the lower to the higher." J. V. Stalin, "On Dialectics and Historical Materialism," in *Fragen des Leninismus* (Berlin: Dietz, 1950, p. 650).

12. Easton and Guddat, eds., *Writings of the Young Marx,* p. 486.

13. Karl Marx, *Die Frühschriften,* edited by Siegfried Landshut (Stuttgart: Kröner, 1953), p. 517.

14. Lukács himself revoked his 1923 *History and Class Consciousness,* translated by Rodney Livingstone (Cambridge: MIT Press, 1971); see his interesting Preface to the 1967 edition. Korsch was expelled from the Party; see his 1923 *Marxism and Philosophy,* translated by Fred Halliday (London: NLB, 1970), his *Karl Marx* (London: Chapman and Hall, 1938), and (written in 1929 against Kautsky) *Die materialistische Geschichtsauffassung* (Frankfurt: Europäische Verlagsanstalt, 1971).

15. Another tenet of this "return to Marx" is the charge that Engels introduced "vulgar Marxism" and wasted his old age trying to reconcile natural science with his own poor understanding of dialectics. To which Engels might reply that some of the most original contributions to Marxism are contained in his own early writings. For example, the title of Marx's first economic work and the subtitle of his major work are anticipated in Engels' essay of 1844, *Outlines of a Critique of Political Economy.* His *Anti-Dühring,* which indeed is shallow in parts, was written in collaboration with Marx; had Marx wished to correct any misunderstandings, this last overall survey of their common views would have been the occasion to do it. But he was not interested — or perhaps he was no longer capable of building a coherent philosophy out of the fragmented hints of his youthful works. This task was left to the epigones. It is reported that the painter Max Liebermann once said:

"God bless the art historians! When we are dead, they ascribe our ill-conceived canvases to our students." Marx benefited from the reverse procedure: no philosopher since Socrates has had his esoteric masterwork thought up entirely by his admirers.

16. See the 1844 manuscript "Private Property and Communism" (Easton and Guddat, eds., *Writings of the Young Marx*, pp. 301–14), where Marx seems to proclaim the "complete emancipation of all human senses and aptitudes" and the "complete and conscious restoration of man to himself. . . ." But Marx adds significantly: ". . . as a *social*, that is, human being" (*ibid.*, p. 304). Shlomo Avineri has recently pointed out, refuting some "trendy implications" of the amazing pages on sexual liberation in the same manuscript, that "it is not the content of sexual relations that interests Marx but. . . their structure" as a paradigm of relations between people in society *(Dissent*, Summer 1973, pp. 323–31). Incidentally, this was a device frequently used by the "True Socialists." The example of prostitution especially finds itself in essays by Otto Lüning, Karl Grün, and Hess. Like Hegel, they all saw the restoration of "true man on a higher level," which of course was "social." Some of this reasoning is common to later Marxists. Even Rosa Luxemburg tried to prove the probability of communism by pointing to the primitive community of savage tribes.

17. Karl Marx and Frederick Engels, "Address of the Central Committee to the Communist League," in Marx and Engels, *Selected Works*, 1:108.

18. In the "Critique of the Gotha Program" Marx rails against "ideological nonsense about right and other trash so common among the democrats and French Socialists" (Marx and Engels, *Selected Works*, 2:25). There he also protested against lumping bourgeoisie and petty bourgeoisie together as "one reactionary mass" (*ibid.*, 2:26). The former have a historically progressive function; the latter are by nature reactionary, unless they *join* the revolutionary proletariat.

19. See Shlomo Avineri, ed., *Karl Marx on Colonialism and Modernization* (Garden City, N.Y.: Doubleday Anchor Books, 1969), especially the essays on India.

20. Karl Marx und Friedrich Engels, *Historisch-kritische Gesamtausgabe*, Abt. 1, Bd. 6 (Frankfurt: Marx-Engels-Archiv, 1932), p. 521; my translation.

21. Marx and Engels, *Selected Works*, 1:64–65.

22. Frederick Engels, "Outlines of a Critique of Political Economy," in Karl Marx, *Economic and Philosophic Manuscripts of 1844*, translated by Martin Milligan (New York: International Publishers, 1964), p. 199.

23. *Ibid.*

24. Karl Marx, "The Future Results of British Rule in India," in Marx and Engels, *Selected Works*, 1:358.

25. *Communist Manifesto;* preface to *A Contribution to the Critique of Political Economy;* the last chapter but one of *Capital*, vol. 1; likewise Engels in *Anti-Dühring.* The preface to *Capital* says: "And even when a society has got upon the right track for the discovery of the natural laws of its movement. . . it can neither clear by large leaps, nor remove by legal enactments, the obstacles offered by the successive

phases of its normal development. But it can shorten and lessen the birth-pangs" (pp. 14–15).

26. Marx, *Capital,* 1:836–37.

27. See chapters 12 and 13 of *Anti-Dühring.*

28. Easton and Guddat, eds., *Writings of the Young Marx,* p. 214.

29. There occur very often in Marx's writings expressions such as "conditions under which there will be no more classes" or "social revolution will cease to be political revolution." In such passages he indicates his confidence that the future will be qualitatively different from the present, not just later than the present. In fact, the change he envisages is so deep that it is to be distinguished from all earlier changes. It will "end the prehistory of mankind" *(Communist Manifesto)* and even change man's relationship with his environment—which sounds a little like Fourier promising that under socialism the earth would have more moons (did he mean sputniks?). I owe to Shlomo Avineri the insight that the famous passage "To do one thing today and another tomorrow, to hunt in the morning, fish in the afternoon, rear cattle in the evening, criticize after dinner, just as I have in mind, without ever becoming hunter, fisherman, shepherd, or critic" is actually a response to Fourier, who used a similar example. Quote is from Karl Marx, *The German Ideology* (New York: International Publishers, 1970), p. 53. Of course it must be read literally: Fourier expressly says that the person attends *committees* dealing with these matters; Marx simply uses the metaphor to indicate that communism must overcome specialization and the division of labor. He goes on to say: "This fixation on social activity, this consolidation of what we ourselves produce into an objective power above us, growing out of control... is one of the chief factors in historical development up to now." In the "Critique of the Gotha Program" he makes the point that under socialism the division between manual and intellectual labor would be overcome.

30. Karl A. Wittfogel, *Oriental Despotism* (New Haven: Yale University Press, 1957); Daniel Bell, *The Coming of Post-Industrial Society* (New York: Basic Books, 1973); Shlomo Avineri, *The Social and Political Thought of Karl Marx* (London: Cambridge University Press, 1968). In his famous letter to Vera Sassulich, Marx also asserted that a direct transition from the Russian *mir* to socialism was thinkable. The two long drafts of this letter (printed in Marx und Engels, *Ausgewählte Briefe,* pp. 408 ff.) show that he hesitated to commit himself scientifically to such a view. In this section I have drawn on the unpublished lectures of Karl Korsch.

31. Marx, *Capital,* 1:834.

32. "Bureaucracy possesses the state's essence, the spiritual essence of society, as its *private property"* (Easton and Guddat, eds., *Writings of the Young Marx,* p. 186). Emphasis by Marx.

33. For other views on Marx and the intellectuals, see G. D. H. Cole, *The Meaning of Marxism* (Ann Arbor: University of Michigan Press, 1964) and Lewis S. Feuer, *Marx and the Intellectuals* (Garden City, N.Y.: Doubleday Anchor Books, 1969).

34. Avineri, *Social and Political Thought of Karl Marx,* p. 49. See also Avineri's "From Hoax to Dogma — A Footnote on Marx and Darwin," *Encounter* (March

1967), pp. 30–32, and "Marx and the Intellectuals," *Journal of the History of Ideas* (April–June 1967), 28:269–78.

35. "Private Property and Communism," in Easton and Guddat, eds., *Writings of the Young Marx*, p. 302.

36. Stephen Eric Bronner, "Art and Utopia: The Marcusean Perspective" in *Politics and Society* (Winter 1973), 3:1.

5. COMMUNISM AND CLASS

1. ADGB: *Allgemeiner Deutscher Gewerkschaftsbund*, the umbrella organization comprising the free trade unions; socialist-minded, but in general more moderate than the Social Democratic Party. Also called Free Trade Unions.

SPD: *Sozialdemokratische Partei Deutschlands.*

KPD: *Kommunistische Partei Deutschlands;* its last head: Ernst Thälmann.

USPD: *Unabhängige Sozialdemokratische Partei Deutschlands;* founded in 1917 by revolutionary, antiwar, antiauthoritarian Social-Democrats; for a few years a mass party, politically located between SPD and KPD.

KAPD: *Kommunistische Arbeiterpartei Deutschlands;* to the left of the KPD.

2. *Thälmanns Antwort auf 21 Fragen von SPD-Arbeitern,* 1932, pp. 5 and 11.

3. Michael Altenberg in *Marxistische Tribüne,* 2:363.

4. Dimitri Manuilsky, *Die Kommunistische Partei und die Krise des Kapitalismus* (Hoym, 1931).

5. Arthur Rosenberg, *Geschichte des Bolschewismus* (Hamburg: Rowohlt, 1932).

6. Georg Friedrich Hegel, *Grundlinien der Philosophie des Rechts* (1821), paragraphs 311 and addendum to 258. Translated with notes by T. M. Knox, *Hegel's Philosophy of Right* (Oxford: Clarendon Press, 1942), pp. 202, 279.

7. V.I. Lenin, *Ausgewählte Werke* (Wien: Verlag für Literatur und Politik, 1925), pp. 45 and 48.

8. Translation from Howard Selsam and Harry Murtel, eds., *Reader in Marxist Philosophy* (New York: International Publishers, 1963), pp. 286–87, 310.

9. Cf. his *Two Tactics of Social-Democracy in the Democratic Revolution.* Translation from V.I. Lenin, *Selected Works in One Volume* (New York: International Publishers, 1974), p. 105.

10. *Sammelband,* p. 419. (Lenin's emphasis.)

11. Thälmann, *Volksrevolution über Deutschland,* p. 59. — EDITOR'S NOTE: On councils, see "Was Weimar Necessary?" in Henry Pachter, *Weimar Etudes* (New York: Columbia University Press, 1982).

12. Kurt Sauerland, *Der dialektische Materialismus* (NDV, 1932), pp. 286, 297, 298. Typical of this sophomoric work, which reels from platitudes to absurdities, is its assertion that the theory of the Third International "had been concretized by Stalin and Lenin long before the war."

13. *Ibid.,* p. 285.

14. Karl von Clausewitz, *Vom Kriege* (1832); quoted from *On War,* translated by O.J. Matthijs Jolles (New York: Modern Library, 1943), p. 587.

6. FASCIST PROPAGANDA AND THE CONQUEST OF POWER

1. The term is used here to cover both National Socialists and Fascists.
2. Quoted in Ladislas Farago, ed., *The Axis Grand Strategy — Blueprints for the Total War* (New York: Farrar & Rinehart, 1942), p. 485, from Eugen Hadamovsky, *Propaganda und nationale Macht* (Oldenburg: Stalling, 1934).
3. Hitler, *Mein Kampf* (Munich: Franz Eher, 1942), pp. 531–32, 548–49.
4. *Ibid.,* pp. 535–36.
5. Hermann Rauschning, *Gespräche mit Hitler* (New York: Europa-Verlag, 1940), pp. 198–99. English title: *Hitler Speaks* (London: Thornton Butterworth, 1939).
6. *Mein Kampf,* pp. 371–72.
7. EDITOR'S NOTE: See "Aggression as Cultural Rebellion" and "Irrationalism and the Paralysis of Reason" in Henry Pachter, *Weimar Etudes* (New York: Columbia University Press, 1982).
8. Heinrich Heine, *Lutetia I* in *Heinrich Heines sämtliche Werke* (Stuttgart: Cotta), 11:219.
9. Synthesizing the political outlook of an ideal-type agitator, Leo Lowenthal and Norbert Gutermann, in *Prophets of Deceit* (New York: Harper, 1949), pp. 141–42, write: "Oppression and injustice, as war and famine, are eternal. . . . Idealists who claim otherwise are fooling themselves. . . . I offer you no promise of peace or security. . . . If you follow me, you will ally yourself with force, with might and power — the weapons that ultimately decide."
10. Ernst Kris and Hans Speier, *German Radio Propaganda* (New York: Oxford University Press, 1944), p. 73.
11. Quoted in Heinrich Hoffmann and Josef Berchtold, *Hitler über Deutschland* (Munich: Franz Eher (the Nazi publisher), 1932), pp. 7, 17.
12. *Rheinische Zeitung,* March 1943. This article was broadcast.
13. *Journal of Clinical Psychopathology* (1943), 4:445 ff.
14. Rauschning, *Gespräche,* p. 104.
15. Filippo Marinetti, *Il Poema Africano* (Milan: A. Mondadori, 1937), pp. 27–28.
16. See Werner Betz, "The National-Socialist Vocabulary," in M. Baumont, J.H.E. Fried, and E. Vermeil, eds., *The Third Reich* (New York: Praeger, 1955), pp. 784–96.
17. More examples in Heinz Paechter, *Nazi-Deutsch — A Glossary of Contemporary German Usage* (New York: Frederick Ungar, 1944), and Victor Klemperer, *LTI — Die unbewältigte Sprache,* new edition (Darmstadt: Melzer, 1966).
18. Mussolini, *The Doctrine of Fascism* (Florence: Vallecchi, 1935), p. 37 and first sentence.
19. *Mein Kampf,* p. 514.
20. Rauschning, *Gespräche,* p. 177.
21. *Mein Kampf,* pp. 512–13.
22. *Ibid.,* p. 650.
23. *Ibid.,* p. 187.

24. *Ibid.,* p. 654.

25. Although the Nazis frequently borrowed vocabulary and imagery from religious institutions of all times, I cannot agree with those who speak of a "Nazi religion." The psychological mechanism which the Nazis manipulated to build faith in the leader is different from the one that satisfies a metaphysical craving. Not that Goebbels didn't try — but Hitlerism as such died with Hitler and could be revived only by another Hitler, while religions thrive on dead founders.

26. Rauschning, *Gespräche,* p. 198.

27. *Mein Kampf,* p. 197.

28. *Ibid.,* p. 198.

29. *Ibid.,* p. 200.

30. *Ibid.,* pp. 252–53.

31. *Ibid.,* p. 203.

32. Rauschning, *Gespräche,* pp. 222–23.

33. Thriller writers like Arthur Koestler answer the question "Why do accused traitors confess?" instead of asking "Why are such confessions believed?" American would-be fascists have successfully used the Yalta Conference as a symbol of "worldwide conspiracy" against the traditions of their country and are forever hunting "traitors" whom they would hold responsible for a painful reality they refuse to recognize. However, our discussion suggests that, despite some terroristic traits, this propaganda will never achieve the wantonly destructive glamor of fascist propaganda. On the other hand, anti-American propaganda in Europe and Asia lately has assumed some weird features of the polarized sham universe. Comparison of continental reactions to British wealth, in the nineteenth century, with continental resentment of American power today reveals the fascistoid components which paralyze significant action.

34. Circular of the Ministry of Foreign Affairs, 83–26 19/1 Ang. II, dated Berlin, 31 January 1939, on the subject of "The Jewish Question as a Factor in German Foreign Policy in the Year 1938," Nuremberg Document 3358-PS; reproduced in German in *Trial of the Major War Criminals before the International Military Tribunal,* Nuremberg, 1948, 32:234–45; reproduced in English translation in Office of U.S. Chief of Counsel, *Nazi Conspiracy and Aggression* (Washington, D.C.: GPO, 1946), 6:87–95.

35. Amplifications on other aspects of the totalitarian sham reality will be found in Franz L. Neumann, *Behemoth — The Structure and Practice of National-Socialism* (New York: Oxford University Press, 1942); Ernst Kris and Hans Speier, *German Radio Propaganda* (New York: Oxford University Press, 1944); Theodor W. Adorno et. al., *The Authoritarian Personality* (New York: Harper, 1950); Hannah Arendt, *Origins of Totalitarianism* (New York: Harcourt, 1951); Harold D. Lasswell and Abraham Kaplan, *Power and Society: A Framework for Political Inquiry* (New York: Norton, 1948); Daniel Lerner et al., *Propaganda in War and Crisis* (New York: Stewart, 1951).

8. THE PROBLEM OF IMPERIALISM

1. V.I. Lenin, *Imperialism, The Highest Stage of Capitalism* (original title: *Imperialism, the Latest Stage of Capitalism*), 1917.

2. Ronald Segal, *The Race War* (London: Jonathan Cape, 1966).

3. For argument's sake, I am exaggerating the difference between the two types. Obviously, the real situation is more complex and the points made are confused: radicals denounce individual culprits, while moderates in Congress also attack institutions.

4. Gabriel Kolko, *The Roots of American Foreign Policy — An Analysis of Power and Purpose* (Boston: Beacon Press, 1969), pp. 51, 53, 55. Since no breakdown by countries is provided, the reader remains unaware that the bulk of strategic goods comes from such countries as Canada, Russia, Australia, England, and Chile, which are economically independent. Moreover, were raw-material prices to rise, it would become profitable for U.S. corporations to produce them here or to develop substitutes. Nor does Kolko account for the fact that countries without empire, such as Germany and Sweden, can prosper. Their "confident access to raw materials" is ensured by that archcapitalistic device — buying them. Most countries are more import-dependent than the United States.

5. Karl Kautsky, "Ältere und neuere Kolonialpolitik," in *Die Neue Zeit,* 1898, pp. 809 ff.

6. John Strachey, *The End of Empire* (New York: Random House, 1959; Praeger, 1964).

7. Rosa Luxemburg, *The Accumulation of Capital* (Berlin: Singer, 1913). Rosa Luxemburg is part of a long line of nonclassical economists, beginning with Malthus, Sismondi, and Rodbertus, and including Hobson (see below), who denied that capitalism can expand its scope, as it must, unless it finds resources outside its circuit of exchange. Lord Keynes, a disciple of Hobson, found a way out of the dilemma. For a detailed criticism of Luxemburg's theory, see Paul Sweezy and Leo Huberman, *The Theory of Capitalist Development* (New York: Oxford University Press, 1942; Monthly Review Press, 1960).

8. In contrast to the theories relating imperialism to big business, William Appleman Williams argues in *The Roots of the Modern American Empire: A Study of the Growth and Shaping of Social Consciousness in a Marketplace Society* (New York: Random House, 1969) that the American farmer in the nineteenth century was desperate to find outlets for his surplus and therefore tried to extend his market philosophy to other nations. See my article, "A Pre-Leninist Theory on American Imperialism," reviewing this book, in *Dissent,* July–August 1970.

9. William Appleman Williams, *The Tragedy of American Diplomacy* (Cleveland: World, 1959).

10. "The Myth of the China Market, 1890–1914," in *American Historical Review* (February 1968), pp. 742–58. "If government support of consular service is a measure of how seriously Washington took the...interests in China,...[it] approximated apathy."

11. John A. Hobson, *Imperialism* (London: Allen & Unwin, 1902; Ann Arbor: University of Michigan Press, 1965). See also Hobson, *The Evolution of Modern Capitalism* (London: Scott, 1894).

12. Hobson, *Imperialism,* 1948 ed., pp. 77–78. Hobson was even more outspoken in *Modern Capitalism.* The bland assertiveness in these two lonely references to U.S. imperialism contrasts with Hobson's well-balanced, circumspect analysis

of the multiple sources of imperialism in countries he knows first-hand. The famous chapter in *Imperialism* on "the economic taproot of imperialism" is one of fourteen chapters dealing with the sociology and psychology of the parasitic classes. As a liberal, Hobson placed the emphasis on the parasitic character of imperialism; from this Lenin concluded that capitalism itself had grown parasitical.

13. Rudolf Hilferding, *Das Finanzkapital* (Berlin, 1910) and Lenin, *Imperialism*. Both works are exciting examples of Marxism's ability to present a coherent picture of all observable phenomena. The single motor of imperialism is Marx's "law of the falling rate of profits": as capital finds no more profitable employment in high-wage areas, it is driven into a mad scramble for overseas investment.

14. Paul Baran and Paul Sweezy, *Monopoly Capital* (New York: Monthly Review Press, 1966); Harry Magdoff, *The Age of Imperialism* (New York: Monthly Review Press, 1969); Ernest Mandel, *Traité d'Économie Marxiste* (Paris: Julliard, 1962); also Kolko, *The Roots of American Foreign Policy*. For a critical review of this conception, see Michael Harrington, *Toward a Democratic Left: A Radical Program for a New Majority* (New York: Macmillan, 1968), and Strachey, *The End of Empire*.

15. Needless to say, the "social Darwinists" tried to turn all these characteristics into assets, making imperialism praiseworthy. See Archibald P. Thornton, *Doctrines of Imperialism* (New York: Wiley, 1965).

16. Joseph Schumpeter, *Imperialism and Social Classes* (Tübingen, 1919); translated by Heinz Norden, edited by Paul Sweezy (New York: Kelley, 1951).

17. A.J.P. Taylor, *The Struggle for Mastery in Europe 1848–1918* (London: Oxford University Press, 1954). It is remarkable that the great historian manages to tell his story without mentioning weapons technology or arms manufacturers, and defense budgets only when they become objects of rivalry. A better source is William L. Langer, *The Diplomacy of Imperialism 1890–1902,* 2 vols., (New York: Knopf, 1935). See similar arguments in Raymond Aron, *The Century of Total War* (Garden City, N.Y.: Doubleday, 1954; now a Beacon paperback).

18. Hannah Arendt, *Imperialism* (originally chapter 2 in *Origins of Totalitarianism*) (New York: Harcourt, Brace, 1951); now available as Harcourt, Brace & World paperback. Imperialism here is seen as the alliance of capital with the mob.

19. One can verify this in Thomas Mann's World War I book, *Betrachtungen eines Unpolitischen* (Berlin: S. Fischer, 1918), "Reflections of a Nonpolitical Man," which merely reflects the ravings of famous German professors; their war was the defense of *Geist* against the mercantile *(Krämer-)* mentality of the British "shop-keepers" who greedily grabbed all the world markets for themselves. The kaiser's ideologists saw the German Siegfried, young, pure and innocent in spirit, of noble race and chivalrous bearing, forever fighting the dragon of mammon. Following this Wagnerian mythology, the Nazis conjured up the foggy ideologies of "blood and soil" and exalted the rebellion of primeval tribal instincts against the rationalist spirit of Western plutocracy. Similar observations are true of D.H. Lawrence, along with a host of others.

20. Max Weber has shown that the desperate attempt to preserve the big Prussian estates made it impossible for eastern Germany to become the industrial center whose emergence might have changed the course of history for all of eastern Europe.

21. Fritz Fischer, *Griff nach der Weltmacht* (Düsseldorf: Droste, 1961).

22. Also from Canada and from some Latin-American countries that have reached a certain stage of industrialization and now feel that they could do better under national management.

23. In contrast to Claude Julien, *L'Empire Américain* (Paris: Grasset, 1968), Jean-Jacques Servan-Schreiber, *The American Challenge* (New York: Atheneum, 1969), is neither shrill nor anti-American. The more seriously must we take his charge.

24. Thucydides, *The Peloponnesian War,* chapter 1.

25. The principle of the Open Door was first enunciated by Jefferson in a memorandum of December 16, 1793, "On the Privileges and Restrictions of the Commerce of the United States in Foreign Countries": "Should any nation, contrary to our wishes,... [continue] its system of prohibitions, duties and regulations, it behooves us to protect our citizens, their commerce and navigation, by counter-prohibitions.... Free commerce and navigation are not to be given in exchange for restrictions and vexations."

26. "Our navigation involves still higher considerations. As a branch of industry, it is valuable, but as a resource of defence, essential." From the same Jefferson memorandum, quoted in Ruhl J. Bartlett, *The Record of American Diplomacy* (New York: Knopf, 1960), p. 74.

27. In their classic study *Dollar Diplomacy* (1925; Monthly Review Press paperback, 1966), Scott Nearing and Joseph Freeman have shown how capital used the opportunities offered by U.S. diplomacy. But they have failed to show — if that was their intention — that capital interests guided U.S. diplomacy. By skilfully manipulating their quotations they have conveyed the impression that Knox and Taft were contemplating something more sinister than what their own use of the term dollar diplomacy implied. For the original conception see Willard Straight, *The Politics of Chinese Finance* (published address, May 2, 1913, East Asia Society, Boston), and Herbert D. Croly's biography of Straight, who was Consul General in Mukden and later J.P. Morgan's agent: *Willard Straight* (New York: Macmillan, 1924).

28. "We must have the Floridas and Cuba," quoted by Thomas Bailey, *A Diplomatic History of the American People* (New York: Appleton, 1958), p. 165. Also, possession of the island "would fill up the measure of our political well-being" — quoted by Julius W. Pratt, *History of United States Foreign Policy* (Englewood Cliffs, N.J.: Prentice-Hall, 1955), p. 293.

29. *Ibid.,* p. 420.

30. It is ironical that the French Communists at that time declared they "had not joined the government to liquidate the French empire."

31. See Morris L. West, *The Ambassador* (New York: Morrow, 1965), a novelistic account based on pertinent information.

32. See Theodore Draper, *Castro's Revolution: Myths and Realities* (New York: Praeger, 1962). It is well known that Batista's officers deserted him when Eisenhower stopped supplying him with arms. The Latin American desk at the State Department, the *New York Times,* and influential New York bankers had openly supported the insurgents since 1958.

33. As a principle of international law and as a maxim of diplomacy, one should recognize all governments — right or left — exercising sovereignty in a given territory. Recognition means neither moral approval nor attestation of legitimacy. Withholding it makes sense only if one expects the government to be overthrown shortly. Nonrecognition is very popular as a form of public pouting.

34. Velasco bought full-page ads in several U.S. papers to assert that in Peru the press is free and foreign capital safe. Incidentally, the largest bank in Peru is Italian, the biggest cotton textile plant Japanese, the railways are British. But the U.S. presence is resented because U.S. policies bear a greater threat to Peruvian sovereignty. It is true that the big Cerro de Pasco mines and the International Petroleum Company are American; but next door in Bolivia, the mines are owned by the Argentinian Señores Aramayo, Patiño, and Hochschild, and the United States is still considered the imperialist. Obviously, the people have not read Lenin but know where power lies. Indeed,

> in the well-developed countries the bourgeois dictatorship is the result of the economic power of the bourgeoisie. In under-developed countries . . . the leader stands for moral power, in whose shelter the thin and poverty-stricken bourgeoisie of the young nation decides to get rich. . . . In spite of his frequently honest conduct and his sincere declarations, the leader as seen objectively is the fierce defender of these interests. . . The leader, who has behind him a lifetime of devoted patriotism, constitutes a screen between the people and the rapacious bourgeoisie. Frantz Fanon, *The Wretched of the Earth* (New York: Grove Press, 1963), p. 134 ff.

35. A German Jewish industrialist, author of technocratic books, 1922 Foreign Minister of the Weimar Republic. EDITOR'S NOTE: See the essay on Rathenau in Pachter's *Weimer Etudes* (New York: Columbia University Press, 1982).

36. This is one of those arguments that cannot be won. When U.S. policies seem to favor Israel, it is said that the oil companies want to use it as a spur in the flank of their Arab retainers; when U.S. policy veers away from Israel, the oil companies are said to fear for their property in Arab lands. In New Left lore, oil and Zionism usually appear as twin evils, though actually oil has always been hostile to the Jewish state. The "long arm of Zionism" was unveiled by *L'Opinion de Rabat* (organ of Istiqlal, Morocco's United Independence Party) when it said that the Paris student riots of May 1968 had been instigated by the CIA in complicity with the Zionists to punish de Gaulle for his pro-Arab, anti-American stand the year before. (Quoted by *Le Monde,* May 30, 1969.)

37. I must warn against a common fallacy. One compares "their" lot and "ours"; one deplores that, whatever we do, we come out on top. But one cannot conclude that they are poor *because* "we" are rich, or that they are poor because they are *exploited* by us. Their wage level was low before "we" came in; it is much higher among employees of U.S. firms than among their compatriots, and it would be much lower if those firms were to disappear.

38. Albert O. Hirschman, *How to Divest in Latin America, and Why* (Princeton: Princeton University Press, 1969). See also John Hans Adler, ed., *Capital Movements and Economic Development* (New York: St. Martin's Press, 1967).

39. *New York Times,* February 9, 1970. See also Frantz Fanon: to the national bourgeoisie, "nationalization quite simply means the transfer into native hands of those unfair advantages which are a legacy of the colonial period." (*The Wretched of the Earth,* p. 124). By contrast, Soviet economists distinguish between big, bad imperialist capitalists and the nice national bourgeoisie, which is "opposed to the [U.S.] interests." See R. Avakov and G. Mirsky, "Class Structure in Underdeveloped Countries," in Archibald P. Thornton, *The Third World in Soviet Perspective* (Princeton: Princeton University Press, 1964), p.278.

40. These criticisms should not be interpreted, however, as denying the usefulness of development aid. Nor is aid through international agencies always better than bilateral aid, and it certainly is not cheaper. Even Magdoff (*The Age of Imperialism*) admits that without U.S. prodding, Pakistan could not have improved its productive capacity.

41. It is well known how reluctant Congress is to award grants to nonvoters. Presidents, therefore, have used the most bizarre arguments to prove that foreign aid is good for American business. Kolko and Magdoff, in turn, have not failed to exhibit these quotations as so many proofs that the United States gives foreign aid in order to aid American business.

42. See two works by Gunnar Myrdal: *An International Economy* (New York: Harper, 1956), and *Economic Theory and Under-Developed Regions* (London: Duckworth, 1957).

43. Robert Engler, *The Politics of Oil* (New York: Macmillan, 1961). The precedent for Franklin D. Roosevelt's good-neighbor policy had been set by Woodrow Wilson, who stubbornly stood by Mexico's President Carranza in his fight against the Standard Oil Company.

44. I would give less weight to ideology and the defense of capitalism, for as early as 1916 Woodrow Wilson began to worry that a world war might result in Europe's subjugation by the czar. The United States has emerged from the two world wars as the only power capable of containing the Russian advance. Smaller Western nations and their friends in the United States have criticized the way in which this was done; they would have preferred a multicentrist to a polarized structure of international relations. But it is erroneous to think that only the polarized structure is imperialist.

45. See Raymond Aron, "The Leninist Myth of Imperialism," in *The Century of Total War,* pp. 56–73.

46. Juan Bosch, *Pentagonism — A Substitute for Imperialism,* translated by Helen R. Lane (New York: Grove Press, 1968). It is understandable that the martyred Dominicans should single out the Pentagon as the main enemy of small nations in this hemisphere. On a world scale, the Nassers and Giaps share at this moment the responsibility for the escalation of tension, and the Soviet general staff has more influence on foreign policy than is good for the world's peace.

As we go to press, a review article by Robert Heilbroner draws my attention to Seymour Melman's new book, *Pentagon Capitalism: The Political Economy of War* (New York: McGraw Hill, 1970). I gather that Melman's view is similar to the one presented here: that the power drive, in this case the military establishment's drive, takes precedence over the profitability calculus.

10. WHO ARE THE PALESTINIANS?

1. Arabs today identify themselves only by speech. Originally the term means conquerors coming from the Peninsula.

2. In 1922, Colonial Secretary Winston Churchill rejected the interpretation that Arab laws and customs had to be subordinated to Jewish interests, and Arab representatives rejected every constitution the British or the League of Nations tried to impose on the country. The Arab Congress in 1928 demanded a "fully democratic" government—whatever that meant in terms of Arab constitutions.

3. Foreign Secretary Ernest Bevin was no "anti-Semite"; he simply dropped a hot potato that cost England 50 million pounds a year. He was not the only Englishman, however, to wonder why the Jews were turning against England— of all nations — which had fought Hitler. Gratitude is not a political word, but bitterness is.

4. The United Nations then had fifty-seven members; obviously the resolution would not pass today. Except for states recognized in the Westphalian Peace Treaty (1648) and at the Vienna Congress (1815), no other state has received such sanction. States usually are a product of violence.

5. This was the term used abroad; the Hebrew term sounds less offensive.

6. A reader points out that the number affected was comparatively small and that terrorism developed mostly in the cities. Unfortunately, the symbolic and political value of the object does not depend on its size or price.

7. "The revolt is largely manned by the peasantry, that is to say by the people whose life and livelihood are on the soil but who have no say whatever in its disposal; and their anger and violence are as much directed against the Arab landowners and brokers who have facilitated the sales as against the policy of the mandatory Power under whose aegis the transactions have taken place. The fact that some of those landowners have served on national Arab bodies makes them only more odious to the insurgent peasantry and has rendered it less amenable to

the influence of the political leaders as a whole." George Antonius, *The Arab Awakening; The Story of the Arab National Movement* (New York: Lippincott, 1939), pp. 406–7. The Jewish leaders — except for the Communists, Martin Buber, and some chalutzim — never thought of allying themselves with these victims of colonization. See Bernard Avishai in *Dissent,* Spring 1975.

8. Some say the number was 800,000 — more than had been living in the Jewish half of Palestine.

9. Obviously, what applies to Arabs must apply to Jews. Most Jews may not have approved of terrorism — though my father, usually one of the most law-abiding citizens, did; but Arabs are even less able than Jews to distinguish between factions in the other camp. The crime must be condemned; an entire people must not be condemned for it. But I am not arguing here about the morality of terror; my aim is to establish the fact that the Arab population *felt* threatened.

10. Unfortunately, socialists like *Dissent* contributors Avishai and N. Gordon Levin have defended this theft on the ground that "socialist values" can be realized better in a securely Jewish environment. Would they agree with the Soviet government that "Soviet values" can be realized better in an environment that does not include Solzhenitsyn, Pasternak, or Trotsky?

11. Israel claims that she accepted a million Oriental Jews, mostly expelled from Arab countries. The rationale of the Jewish "homeland," however, conflicts with the suggestion that these should be balanced against the Arab expellees. They would be entitled to Israeli citizenship even without being harassed in Bagdad. Besides, a forcible population exchange is repugnant from any internationalist perspective.

12. Gordon Levin rejects the notion that readmission could "serve [any] real human interests besides a satisfaction of Arab honor." But that is a question of deep concern, and it is in Israel's power to restore that sense of honor.

13. It seems that Zionism has abandoned its earliest propaganda, which claimed that a Jewish state would make its Arab citizens happy and contented.

14. Arab notables in the occupied areas are subject to intimidation; some Israelis therefore think that Arafat is the only *available* partner. It is certain that no parley is now conceivable without him, a calamity that conforms to the pattern of the Israeli's poor grasp of diplomatic realities: they have always been forced to choose between two evils after they had rejected an alternative that would have been, after all, second best.

11. MARX AND THE JEWS

1. Arnold Künzli, *Karl Marx. Eine Psychographie* (Vienna: Europa Verlag, 1966).

2. George Lichtheim, "Socialism and the Jews," first published in *Dissent* (Summer 1968), now in his *Collected Essays* (New York: Viking, 1973).

3. *The Hibbert Journal* (1958), 56:340–51.

4. Edmund Silberner, *Sozialisten zur Judenfrage* (Berlin: Colloquium Verlag, 1962); see an English version of the part relating to Marx in *Historia Judaica* 11 (April 1949).

5. Fritz Raddatz, *Karl Marx: Eine politische Biographie* (Hamburg: Hoffmann & Campe, 1975).

6. David McLellan, *Karl Marx — His Life and Thought* (New York: Harper, 1973).

7. Jerrold Seigel, *Marx's Fate — The Shape of a Life* (Princeton: Princeton University Press, 1978), p. 145.

8. Julius Carlebach, *Marx and the Radical Critique of Judaism* (London: Routledge and Kegan Paul, 1978).

9. Heinrich Graetz, *Geschichte der Juden*, 12 volumes (1853–1875; English: 1889–1895).

10. Ephraim Justifié, *Lettre à André Pinto, Juif Portugais*, 1758.

11. *New York Daily Tribune*, November 9 and 22, 1855.

12. *Neue Rheinische Zeitung*, April 1849, *passim*.

13. *Ibid.*, April 29, 1849.

14. Quoted by Roman Rodolsky in *Archiv für Sozialgeschichte* (Hanover: Verlag für Literatur und Zeitgeschehen, 1964), 4:187.

15. *Neue Rheinische Zeitung*, February 15 and 16, 1849.

16. *New York Daily Tribune*, August 8, 1853.

17. "Toward a Critique of Hegel's Philosophy of Right," *Deutsch-Französische Jahrbücher*, 1843 (hereafter referred to as *Yearbook;* my translation). For the context, see *Writings of the Young Marx*, Loyd Easton and Kurt Guddat, eds. (New York: Anchor Books, 1967), p. 264. Hereafter this edition is referred to as Easton and Guddat, eds., and cited only for identification of context.

18. Easton and Guddat, eds., p. 248.

19. *Ibid.*, p. 240.

20. *Ibid.*, p. 243.

21. *Ibid.*, p. 245. The German term *bürgerliche Gesellschaft* is used ambiguously, meaning both civil society and bourgeois society.

22. *Ibid.*, p. 244.

23. Alphonse Toussenel, *Les Juifs, rois de l'époque. Histoire de la féodalité financière* (Paris, 1847).

24. Marx, *Capital*, vol. I, German edition, p. 162.

25. Seigel, *Marx's Fate*, p. 125.

26. Easton and Guddat, eds., pp. 245–46.

27. *Ibid.*, p. 246.

28. *"Nationalökonomie und Philosophie"* in Karl Marx, *Die Frühschriften*, Siegfried Landshut, ed. (Stuttgart: Kröner, 1953), p. 299.

29. McLellan, *Karl Marx*, p. 86.

30. See also Helmut Hirsch, *Marx und Moses — Karl Marx zur "Judenfrage" und zu Juden*, vol. 2 of the series *Judentum und Umwelt* (Frankfurt: Peter D. Lang, 1980),

which has collected a long list of passages where Marx shows compassion for and solidarity with Jews. It is full of Marxological gems, since the author has made it his business to read every book Marx ever quoted from; he knows as much about what Marx left out as others know about what he said.

31. Eugen Dühring, *Kritische Geschichte der Nationalökonomie und des Socialismus* (Leipzig: Naumann, 1900), p. 512.

32. *Journal for the History of Ideas* (July–Sept. 1964), 25:445–50.

33. Lichtheim, *Collected Essays*, p. 415.

34. Werner Sombart, *Die Juden und das Wirtschaftsleben (The Jews and Modern Capitalism)* (Leipzig: Duncker, 1911), p. 242.

35. Werner Sombart, *Händler und Helden—Patriotische Besinnungen* (Shopkeepers vs. Heroes—Patriotic Musings) (Munich: Duncker, 1915).

36. Hal Draper, *The Complete Poems of Heinrich Heine — A Modern English Version* (Boston: Suhrkamp/Insel, 1982), p. 651.

37. Mircea Eliade, *The Sacred and the Profane— The Nature of Religion,* translated by Willard R. Trask (New York: Harcourt, Brace, 1959), pp. 206–7.

38. Melvin Lasky, *Utopia and Revolution* (Chicago: University of Chicago Press, 1976).

39. Easton and Guddat, eds., p. 214.

40. Karl Marx, *The Eighteenth Brumaire of Louis Bonaparte.*

41. Karl Marx, *Class Struggles in France,* Clemens Palme Dutt, ed. (New York: International Publishers, 1934), p. 114.

42. Jessie Bernard, "Biculturality: A Study in Social Schizophrenia," in Isacque Graeber and Steuart H. Britt, eds., *Jews in a Gentile World* (New York: Macmillan, 1942).

43. Salo W. Baron, "Modern Capitalism and the Jewish Fate," in *Menorah* (1942), 30 (2): 116–38.

44. Easton and Guddat, eds., p. 210 ff.

45. See Everett Stonequist, *The Marginal Man* (New York: Scribner, 1937), and Kurt Lewin, *Resolving Social Conflicts* (New York: Harper, 1948).

46. Fritz Engel, quoted by Eduard Fuchs, in *Die Juden in der Karikatur* (Munich: Langen, 1921), p. 304.

47. Fuchs, *Die Juden,* pp. 304–5.

48. Saul Bellow, *Mr. Sammler's Planet* (New York: Viking, 1969), p. 70.

12. THE AMBIGUOUS LEGACY OF EDUARD BERNSTEIN

1. Eduard Bernstein, *Evolutionary Socialism,* translated by Edith C. Harvey (New York: Schocken Books, 1961); German title: *Die Voraussetzungen des Sozialismus und die Aufgaben der Sozialdemokratie.* Unfortunately the English version is unreliable and often incomprehensible to readers not familiar with the German text. Who, for instance, would guess that Bismarck's "socialistic law" (p. 145)

refers to his ban on socialist agitation, the *Sozialistengesetz?* Moreover, important chapters have been left out.

2. Eduard Bernstein, *Zur Geschichte und Theorie des Sozialismus* (Berlin, 1901).

3. Peter Gay, *The Dilemma of Democratic Socialism—Eduard Bernstein's Challenge to Marx* (New York: Collier Books, 1962).

4. Bernstein, *Was ist Sozialismus?* (Berlin: Arbeitsgemeinschaft für staatsbürgerliche und wissenschaftliche Bildung, 1919).

5. Bernstein, *Evolutionary Socialism*, p. 35.

6. *Ibid.*, pp. 143, 144.

7. *Ibid.*, p. 173.

8. *Ibid.*, p. 178.

9. *Ibid.*, p. 150. (my translation). Political theorists may note that Bernstein's formulation provides a bridge from Bentham to Rawls.

13. GRAMSCI—STALINIST WITHOUT DOGMA

1. Antonio Gramsci, *Lettere dal carcere* (Torino: Einaudi, 1947).

2. Quintin Hoare and Geoffrey Nowell Smith, eds., *Selections from the Prison Notebooks of Antonio Gramsci,* abridged from the original Italian six-volume edition (New York: International Publishers, 1972). Other works: Antonio Gramsci, *The Modern Prince and Other Writings,* translated and with an Introduction by Louis Marx (New York: International Publishers, 1967). Antonio Gramsci, *Letters from Prison,* translated by Lynne Lawner (New York: Harper, 1973).

3. The Roman people, in the fifth century B.C., staged an exodus to Mount Aventinus (Mons Sacer) to obtain rights from the Senate—the first political strike recorded in history. When the center and left parties were boycotting Mussolini's parliament, they remembered this and met on Mount Aventinus. Only the Communist Party returned to the Capitoline hill.

4. Gramsci's unfairness shows in infractions of elementary logic. One of many examples: Bukharin is taken to task for adopting the natural sciences' definition of prediction as the test of truth. How can I predict, asks Gramsci, when any prediction changes the premises? This is nonsense. My prediction refers to the conditions extant before any new element is added. If my prediction changes these conditions, then I must also predict how my prediction will affect the outcome. Gramsci's logic is never very tight; his philosophy is journalistic.

14. ORTHODOX HERETIC, ROMANTIC STALINIST: ON THE NINETIETH BIRTHDAY OF GEORG LUKÁCS

1. Georg Lukács, *History and Class Consciousness* (1923), translated by Rodney Livingstone, with Lukács' new preface to the 1967 edition (Cambridge: MIT Press Paperback, 1972).

2. Fredric Jameson, "The Case for Georg Lukács," in *Marxism and Form* (Princeton: Princeton University Press, 1972), p. 163.

3. Alfred Kazin, in the Introduction to Lukács' *Studies in European Realism* (New York: Grosset & Dunlap, 1964), p. v.

4. George Lichtheim, *Georg Lukács* (New York: Viking, 1970). My hunch is that for Lukács, as for other Jewish intellectuals of his generation, Cabbalistic reminiscences took the shape of ultramodern philosophies.

5. Morris Watnick, "Relativism and Class Consciousness," in *Revisionism: Essays on the History of Marxist Ideas,* Leopold Labedz, ed. (New York: Praeger, 1962), pp. 142–165. See especially Lukács, *Die Zerstörung der Vernunft* (East Berlin: Aufbau, 1954; Neuwied: Luchterhand, 1974), 3 vols.

6. Lukács, *The Theory of the Novel,* with his 1962 Preface, translated by Anna Bostock (Cambridge: MIT Press, 1971).

7. Lukács, *History and Class Consciousness.* A similar claim was made when he returned to Hungary in 1947.

8. Although Lukács has often been hailed as the founder of the "sociology of knowledge," it is important to acknowledge his neo-Kantian sources. Emil Lask referred to Marx and Simmel as having studied reification *(Verdinglichung)* — the hypostatizing of abstract concepts (such as Natural Law) as though they had a real, independent existence apart from the social-cultural realities they symbolized. Heinrich Rickert also condemned the illusion that "true history" could be written without "a definite idea of cultural values."

On Lukács and Mannheim see Martin Jay, "The Frankfurt School's Critique of Karl Mannheim and the Sociology of Knowledge," in *Telos* (Summer 1974), 20:72 – 89. On reification see Heinrich Rickert, "Geschichtsphilosophie," and Emil Lask, "Rechtsphilosophie," both in Wilhelm Windelband, ed., *Die Philosophie im Beginn des zwanzigsten Jahrhunderts, Festschrift für Kuno Fischer* (Heidelberg: Carl Winter, 1905), 2; 51–135 and 1–50.

9. The point is elaborated by both Watnick, *Revisionism,* and Andrew Arato, "Lukács' Theory of Reification," in *Telos* (Spring 1972), 11:25-66.

10. Although Lukács mentions the earlier debate in *Die Neue Zeit,* he does not seem to have known *What Is to Be Done?*; it had not yet been translated into German.

11. It does not detract from Lukács' achievement if I note that he used Marx's "Introduction" of the now famous *Grundrisse,* which Kautsky had published as the Introduction to the *Critique of Political Economy* in 1902, and the *German Ideology,* which Bernstein had published in his *Dokumente des Sozialismus.* (After all, it is not quite true that these two "reformists" were insensitive to the cultural and Hegelian side of Marx.)

12. English translation, "Moses Hess and the Problems of Idealist Dialectic" (1926), in *Telos* (Winter 1971); 10:3–34; also in Lukács, *Tactics and Ethics,* translated by Michael McColgan, edited by Rodney Livingstone (New York: Harper & Row, 1972). With Lukács' *Der junge Hegel: Über die Beziehungen von Dialektik und*

Ökonomie (Zurich and Vienna: Europa Verlag, 1948), this is Marxist intellectual history at its best.

13. Advanced in a letter to *Nuovi Argomenti* (1962), nos. 57 and 58 (in *Marxismus und Stalinismus — Politische Aufsätze — Ausgewählte Schriften IV* (Hamburg: Rowohlt, 1970), pp. 172–91.

14. Lukács, *Marxismus und Stalinismus*.

15. See my essay, "The Right To Be Lazy."

16. "Man becomes truly himself when he creates his own world in the reflection of the world in him and makes it his own." G.W.F. Hegel, *Ästhetik* (Stuttgart: Frommann, 1927), 1:477. Because of limited space, I omit citations of the relevant passages from Friedrich Schiller.

17. "My Road to Marx" in Lukács, *Marxismus und Stalinismus*.

18. Lukács, *Realism in Our Time*, translated by John and Necke Mander (New York: Harper Torchbooks, 1964).

19. Lukács, *Der russische Realismus in der Weltliteratur* (Neuwied: Luchterhand, 1964), p. 176.

20. Lukács, "Subjekt-Objekt-Beziehungen in der Ästhetik," in *Logos* (1917), pp. 1–19; see also his *Die Seele und die Formen* (Berlin: Fleischel, 1911); English: *Soul and Form*, translated by Anna Bostock (Cambridge: MIT, 1974), and *Ästhetik: Teil I, Die Eigenart des Ästhetischen*, 2 vols. (Neuwied: Luchterhand, 1963).

21. Hegel, *Ästhetik*, 1:95.

22. In his *Goethe and His Age*, translated by Robert Anchor (New York: Grosset & Dunlap, 1968), p. 217, Lukács concludes that "Goethe could not see in the world he knew any objective social force which would have been able to combat Mephistopheles successfully"; previously he had identified Mephistopheles as representing capitalism.

23. Lukács, *Solzhenitsyn*, translated by William David Graf (Cambridge: MIT Press, 1971). He blames Solzhenitsyn for uncritically accepting the opinions of his protagonist Ivan Denisovich, whom Lukács compares to the inarticulate peasant Platon Karatayev in *War and Peace*. The translator says "plebeian" (p. 81 ff.) and fails to point out that in the Soviet context *narodnik* is a grave accusation. It is ironical that in earlier essays Lukács himself has asked for "folkishness" (*Volkstümlichkeit*) in literature.

24. "Balzac" (1940), in *European Realism*.

25. George Steiner, in the Preface to Lukács' *Realism in Our Time*, p. 13.

26. Lukács, *Goethe and His Age*.

27. Lukács, *Der russische Realismus*. The Preface of 1946 fulminates against "counterrevolutionary calumniators" who pretend that "the new Russia has rejected classical Russian literature" (p. 9).

28. Lichtheim, *Georg Lukács*.

29. E.g., Lion Feuchtwanger, a German novelist then much in vogue; he asserted that the "confessions" in the Moscow Trials rang true.

30. For connoisseurs: Lukács mentioned Voltaire's defense of Calas — to salve his conscience. Incomprehensibly, this essay was printed unchanged in postwar East German editions (Berlin: Aufbau, 1951), while Dreyfus does appear in a new edition, printed in 1963 in West Germany.

31. He even made elementary mistakes unbecoming the great scholar he was. I will cite only a few examples; I hope they will not be interpreted as nit-picking, for I mean to ask why a man like Lukács had to forget what he knew. "Balzac: The Peasants," a famous chapter in *European Realism*, begins as follows: "In this novel, the most important *[bedeutendste]* of his maturity, Balzac wanted to write the tragedy of the doomed landed aristocracy." Nonsense: the "doomed landlord" is a Napoleonic general whose father was an upholsterer and who is constantly referred to as a *roturier* (bourgeois), whereas his prosperous neighbors belong to the aristocracy, and the peasants, as we should expect from Balzac's imagination, support these traditional nobles against the upstart intruder. Yet to fit an admiring passage in Marx's letters, they have to be representatives of "capitalism."

In that same work Lukács remarks that Don Quixote is "a story of lost illusions... The nascent bourgeois world destroys the still lingering feudal illusions." Miguel Unamuno confuted *this* illusion in 1914, and it can generally be said that whenever Lukács does not invent an idea he is usually forty years behind in scholarship. In Ibsen's *Rosmersholm*, Rebecca has allowed her rival to go mad "in slow, imperceptible steps," and the tragedy reaches its climax when Rebecca realizes she is a murderer; Lukács decrees that this is no drama since no precipitous action is shown. He totally fails to see that the drama is in the revelation (as in, say, *Oedipus*). This time it is the schematism not of Marx but of Aristotle that stands in the way of Lukács' perception.

He also fails to see that Hebbel's *Judith* is a psychological drama whose theme is familiar to the post-World-War-II audience from Sartre's *Dirty Hands* or *Hiroshima Mon Amour:* Judith goes out to seduce Holofernes, the enemy general, and to kill him in order to save her people; but she is attracted by his ferocity and kills him in a rage of offended womanhood. Lukács thinks the playwright should have allowed her to kill in cold blood so as to keep the tragedy "pure" and without "accident." The last psychologist Lukács had read was Pavlov, and the Comintern vocabulary lacked the term "ambivalence." The two examples are from Lukács, *The Historical Novel*, translated by Hannah and Stanley Mitchell, Preface by Irving Howe (Boston: Beacon, 1962). They must suffice here to show that from the late 1930s on Lukács was writing below the level of his intellectual eminence and that these works cannot serve as a guide either to literary appreciation or to Marxist analysis, or to the significance of Lukács' work.

32. "Grösse und Verfall des Expressionismus," in Fritz Raddatz, *Marxismus und Literatur* (Hamburg: Rowohlt, 1969), vol. 2. On the "expressionism debate," see Stephen Eric Bronner's excellent article in Bronner and Kellner, eds., *Passion and Rebellion: The Expressionist Heritage* (South Hadley, Mass.: Bergin, 1982). Ernst

Bloch, in *Erbschaft dieser Zeit* (Frankfurt: Suhrkamp, 1962), replied sharply to Lukács' "socialist-realistic" denunciation. See also Brecht's answers in his *Gesammelte Werke* (Frankfurt: Suhrkamp, 1967), vols. 18 and 19.

33. Watnick, *Revisionism*.

34. Lukács, *Die Seele und die Formen*.

35. Lukács, *Die Zerstörung der Vernunft*—his weakest work.

36. Lukács, *Marxismus und Stalinismus*, p. 229.

37. Lukács, *Tactics and Ethics*, p. 251.

38. *Nuovi Argomenti*.

39. Lukács, *Marxismus und Stalinismus*, pp. 239–40.

40. In *New Hungarian Quarterly* 24 (Winter 1966), a magazine published in Budapest, she speaks of his "valid work since 1930," thus by inference excluding *History and Class Consciousness*.

41. Lukács' direct answer to Sartre (1948) in "Existentialism or Marxism?" (in George Novack, ed., *Existentialism Versus Marxism*, New York: Dell, 1966, pp. 134–53) is surprisingly unphilosophical and weak. That could not be otherwise: only the standpoint of *History and Class Consciousness* could have provided a satisfactory foundation for a critique.

42. Lukács, *Marxismus und Stalinismus*.

43. Here I certainly would include Lukács' pre-Marxist writings.

Index

Adorno, Theodor W., 84, 301, 342*n*35
Alianza para el Progreso, 191, 193
Alienation, 6-9, 67, 79-84 *passim*, 235-37, 246-48, 250 f., 299, 300-2
Allende, Salvador Gossens, 50
Anarchists, xix, 147, 152-54, *155-57*, 320
Anti-Semitism, xii, 117, 124, 128, *140-44*, 222-27, 231, 234, 239, *240-46*, 252 f., 346*n*36; *see also* Jews
Arendt, Hannah, xviii, 172, 198, 251, 342*n*35, 344*n*18
Aron, Raymond, 344*n*17, 348*n*45
Aventinian coalition, 111, 287, 352*n*3
Avineri, Shlomo, 79, 243, 338*n*16, 19, 339*n*29, 30, 34

Baran, Paul, 170, 182 f.
Bauer, Bruno, 231-34, 239, 242
Bell, Daniel, 57, 79, 339*n*30
Bernstein, Eduard, xv f., 70, 219, *256-83*, 330, 351*n*1-352*n*9, 353*n*11; Works: *Evolutionary Socialism*, 259, 271, *272-75*, 279, 337*n*8, 351*n*1, 352*n*9; How Is Scientific Socialism Possible? (lecture), 262, 279; *Was ist Sozialismus?* 267, 277, 352*n*4; *Zur Geschichte und Theorie des Sozialismus*, 261
Bloch, Ernst, 309 f., 355*n*32
Borkenau, Franz, xxi
Bosch, Juan, 348*n*46
Brecht, Bertolt, xxi, 309 f., 355*n*32
Bronner, Stephen E., 84, 340*n*36, 355*n*32
Bureaucracy, xxix, 26, 43, *55-58*, 59, 81 f., 289, 334*n*9, 339*n*32

"Calling," 5, 7, 225; *see also* Work
Capital, xxv, 16 f., 17, 20, 23-25, 30-33, 42, 65, 168, 176-78, 185, 187, 189, 191 f., 234, 302 f., 321, 344*n*13, 345*n*27, 347*n*38

Capitalism, xxv-xxviii, 6-8, 11 f., *16-28*, 32, 60, 65, 71, 75 f., 78-82 *passim*, 120, 165-87 *passim*, 239, 246 f., *261-81 passim*, 302, 319-22, 324 f., 333*n*1, 2, 6, 334*n*9, 343*n*7, 11, 12, 351*n*43
Cartel général, 17, 334*n*9
CIA, 179, 180, 181, 182, 346*n*36
Codetermination, 45, 60 f., 320
Coexistence, Cold War, xx f., xxii f., 164, 172, 181, 195-98, 200, *202*, 214, 347*n*44
Collectivism, 36, 320, 322, 334*n*9, 11
Colonialism, Neocolonialism, 71-73, 162, 165-68, 171, 173-75, 186 f., 189 f., 193, 196, 197, 261, 273, 343*n*5, 347*n*39; *see also* Marx on Colonialism
Comintern, 70, 72, 84 f., 100 f., 102, 104, 109, 286, 288, 302
Communist Party, xii f., xvi f., xix, xxvii, 19, 84, *89-109*, 152 f., 265, 284-88, 290, 292, 298-300, 303 f., 305, 337*n*14, 340*n*1-12, 345*n*30; *see also* Lenin's Concept of Party
Comte, Auguste, xxvii, 68, 78
Conservation, 15, 40-42, 45, 335*n*22
Control vs. Ownership, xiii, xxvi, 18, 31, 184, 321, 335*n*18
Corporate State, Corporativism, 17, 54, 120
Councils, *see* Soviets
Countervailing forces, 27 f., 328 f., 333*n*7
Croce, Benedetto, 284-94 *passim*

Democracy, xiii, xix-xxi, xxx, 34, 38, 44-48, 58-63, *106-9*, 175 f., 272-82 *passim*, 333*n*1, 335*n*24
"Destiny," xix, 116, 122, 126-28
Determinism, xiii, xxvii, 65-70, 78 f., 169 f., 259, 263, 274, 278 f., 291, 336*n*4, 5

Dictatorship, xxi, 26, 44, 46 f., 50, 53–55, 61, 63, 68, 81, 95 f., 104, 106–8, 179–83, 286, 289–93
Disarmament, xxiii, 12
Division of labor, 7, 13 f., 239, 325, 339*n*29
"Dollar Diplomacy," 177 f., 345*n*27
Drucker, Peter F., 32

Efficiency, xxi, xxv, xxix, 5–8, 12–15, 22, 25, 33 f., 42, 328
Eliade, Mircea, 248
Engels, Friedrich, 37 f., 66–82 *passim*, 223–54 *passim*, 260–71 *passim*, 335*n*1, 337*n*15; on USA, 229. Works: *Anti-Dühring*, 76, 242, 271, 337*n*15, 338*n*25; *Feuerbach*, 336*n*5; *Outlines of a Critique of Political Economy*, 74, 337*n*15, 338*n*22, 23
Evolution vs. Revolution, 73, 156 f., 259–73, 276–78, 279
Expropriation, *see* Nationalization

Fanon, Frantz, 346*n*34, 347*n*39
Fascism, xiv f., xvii–xix, 92, 97, 100–2, 105, 107 f., *110-46*, 149 f., 287 f., 289, 293, 297, 341–42, 344*n*19
Fischer, Fritz, 172
Foreign Aid, 21, 187, 191–95, 347*n*40–43
Fourier, Charles, 14, 239, 339*n*29
"Freedom of the Seas," *see* "Open Door Policy"
Free Trade, Protectionism, 72, 166 f., 172, 181, 194, 327, 345*n*25

Galbraith, John Kenneth, 334*n*14, 335*n*15
Gay, Peter, 278
Goebbels, Joseph, 110 f., 124, 131, 132, 141 f., 342*n*25
Goodman, Paul, 61
Göring, Hermann, 117, 121
Gramsci, Antonio, xii f., *284-94*, 352*n*1, 2, 4

Harrington, Michael, 344*n*14
Hayek, Friedrich von, 18, 27, 47 f.
Hayes, Carlton, 171
Hegel, G. W. F., xxvii, 46, *66-68*, 71–84 *passim*, 93, 108, 169, 221–54 *passim*, 267,

290, 293, 301–4 *passim*, 306 (quote), 338*n*16, 354*n*16; *see also* "World Spirit"
Heilbronner, Robert, 53, 333*n*2, 348*n*46
Heine, Heinrich, 120, 220, 224, 226, 247, 252
Heller, Agnes, 313, 356*n*40
Hess, Moses, 71, 219, 220, *235 f.*, 302, 338*n*16, 353*n*12
Hilferding, Rudolf, xvi, xxiii, 169, 265, 274, 281, 334*n*9, 344*n*13
Hirsch, Helmut, 350*n*30
Hitler, Adolf, 59, 110 f., 112–17, 121 f., 123–30 *passim*, 134–39 *passim*, 142 f., 145; *Mein Kampf* 112, 113, 117, 120, 129–39 *passim*
Hobson, John A., 21 f., 168–70, 172, 178, 198, 343*n*7, 11, 12
Horkheimer, Max, 84, 301
Howe, Irving, xxiv, 282

Imperialism, xxiii, *161-99*, 200, *207*, 273, 343, 344, 347*n*40, 44, 348*n*45, 46; *see also* Lenin's Concept of Imperialism
Independent Social Democratic Party of Germany (USPD), 103, 264 f., 340*n*1
Individualism, xxx, 37–39, 64, 275
Intellectuals, xviii f., 82, 94, 114, 117 f., 130, 134, 250 f., 259, 276, 288, 289, 292, 293, 298, 301 f., 311, 339*n*33, 34
International Agencies, 43, 185, 191, 194
Irrationalism, xii, xviii, 118 f., 129–32, 135, 141, 171, 244 f., 297, 310 f., 341*n*7, 344*n*19

Jay, Martin, 353*n*8
Jefferson, Thomas, 177, 345*n*25, 26, 28
Jews, xxiv, *205-15*, *219-55*, 346*n*36, 348*n*2-7, 349*n*9-14, 349*n*2, 350, 351*n*42, 43, 46, 47, 353*n*4; *see also* Anti-Semitism
Jünger, Ernst, 9, 123, 124, 126, 127

Kafka, Franz, 219, 248, 252, 309 f.
Kautsky, Karl, xv, xxvii, xxix, 32, 50 f., 70, 73, 84, 165–68, 260–271 *passim*, 291, 353*n*11
Keynes, John Maynard, 28, 192, 281, 343*n*7
Keyserling, Leon, 334*n*14
Kirchheimer, Otto, xx f.
Knox, Philander, 177, 345*n*27

Kolko, Gabriel, 165 (quote), 343*n*4, 344*n*14, 347*n*41
Korsch, Karl, xii f., xxix, 70, 287, 302, 303, 311, 337*n*14, 339*n*30
Kris, Ernst, 123 (quote), 124, 341*n*10, 13, 342*n*35

Labor, *see* Work
Labor Service, 11 f., 15, 40
Lafargue, Paul, *9*, 270
Lange, Oskar, 19, 25, 26, 334*n*11, 12
Langer, William L., 344*n*17
Language 125, 127, 130, 341*n*16, 17
Lasky, Melvin, 248 f.
Lassalle, Ferdinand, *9*, 219, 226, 251, 260, 269, 275, 335*n*16
Le Bon, Gustave, 114 f., 116, 258, 325
Lenin, Vladimir I., xvii, 21 f., 48 f., 53, 73, 267, 274, 303, 311. Concept of Imperialism, xxiii, 162, 164–70, 173, 178, 184, 197, 199, 207 f., 343*n*12, 344*n*13, 348*n*45; Concept of Party, xvi, xxvii, 93–96, 98 f., 101, 106, 261, 276, 278, 299 f., 303. Works: *Left-Wing Communism*, 103; *Materialism and Empiriocriticism*, 336*n*6; *What Is To Be Done?* 94, 353*n*10
Lerner, Abba, 22, 32, 333*n*1, 8
Libertarians, *see* Anarchists
Lichtheim, George, 222, 244, (quote), 289, 349*n*2, 351*n*33, 353*n*4, 354*n*28
Liebknecht, Karl, 263, 265
"Little Man," xviii, 116 f., 118, 122
Löwenthal, Richard, xiv, xxi
Lukács, Georg, xii f., 70, 258, 286, 287, 291 f., *295-314*, 337*n*14, 353–56. Works: *Aesthetics*, 295, 305, 306 f., 354*n*20; *Ethics*, 295; *European Realism*, 308, 355*n*31; *Existentialism or Marxism?* 356*n*41; *Gesamtausgabe*, 313; *Goethe and His Age*, 354*n*22; *The Historical Novel*, 310, 355*n*31; *History and Class Consciousness*, 295, 298, *300-3*, 307, 313, 314, 356*n*40, 41; *Der junge Hegel*, 353*n*12; *Lenin*, 300; *Marxismus und Stalinismus*, 304, 305, 312 (quotes), 354*n*13; *Moses Hess*, 302, 353*n*12; *Ontology*, 295, 304; *Realism in Our Time*, 306, 309; *Der russische Realismus*, 306, 354*n*27; *Die Seele und die Formen* (*Soul*

and *Form*), 306, 354*n*20; *Solzhenitsyn*, 307 f., 354*n*23; *Tactics and Ethics*, 312 (quote), 353*n*12; *Theory of the Novel*, 298, 300; *Die Zerstörung der Vernunft* (*Destruction of Reason*), 311, 356*n*35
Luxemburg, Rosa, xxiii, xxix, 46 f., 70, 73, 219, 259, 274, 299, 338*n*16. Works: *The Accumulation of Capital*, xxiii, 166, 343*n*7; *Social Reform or Revolution?* 270

Magdoff, Harry, 170, 347*n*40, 41
Mann, Thomas, 118, 305, 344*n*19
Mannheim, Karl, 292, 353*n*8
Marcuse, Herbert, 71, 83, 84, 182 f., 278, 301, 306, 311
"Marginality," 250–52, 351*n*42, 43, 45
Marinetti, Filippo, 124, 126 (quote), 310
Market Society, 17, 19 f., 43
Marshall Plan, 181, 183
Marx, Marxism, xii f., xxvii f., *9* f., 12, 22, 40, 47, *65-85*, *219-54*, *256-81* passim, 284–88, 290, 291 f., 295, 298, 301, 303, 304, 330, 333*n*7, 335*n*1–340*n*35, 344*n*13, 350*n*4–30, 351*n*39–44, 353*n*8, 11; on American Civil War, 75; on Colonialism, 71, 73, 75, 166, 167, 229, 338*n*19; letters, 69, 77, 226, 240 f., 248, 336*n*7, 337*n*11, 339*n*30. Articles: 73, 227, 229, 242, 338*n*24. Pre-1848 works: 67–82 *passim*, 94 f., 226, 230–251 *passim*, 260, 301 f., 314, 338*n*16, 339*n*29, 340*n*35, 350*n*17, 28, 353*n*11. Later works: *Capital*, 53, 55, 65, 69, 70, 76, 80, 81 f., 208, 233, 237, 248, 268, 321, 336*n*4, 338*n*25; *Civil War in France*, 81; *Class Struggles in France*, 250 (quote), 268; *Communist Manifesto*, 37, 38, 65, 71–79 *passim*, 166, 234, 239, 248, 254, 272, 339*n*29; *Contribution to the Critique of Political Economy*, 336*n*3, 338*n*25, 353*n*11; *Critique of the Gotha Program*, 269, 338*n*18, 339*n*29; *The Eighteenth Brumaire*, 81, 249
"Mass Culture," 322, 325
"Means and Ends," xvii, xxv, 101, 123, 152 f., 178 f., 196, 198
Meidner Plan, 60
Melman, Seymour, 348*n*46
Michels, Robert, xxix, 258, 278, 289

Mills, C. Wright, 56
Mises, Ludwig von, 18, 20, 21, 27, 32, 34, 333*n*6
Money 30, 230, 232-39, 244, 246
Monopoly, 17, 20-23, 168 f., 170, 333*n*4-6, 334*n*12, 344*n*14
"Movement is Everything, The," xv f., 151, *259 f.*, 275, 277, 283, 330
Multinationals, 183-85, 281
Mussolini, 59, 111, 114 f., 120, 124 f., 129 f., 131, 138-140, 145, 290 f., 293 f.
Myrdal, Gunnar, 194, 327, 347*n*42

"National Dividend," 30, 31, 39, 41, 63, 335*n*16
Nationalism, xxiii f., 54, 119, 124 f., 138 f., 170 f., 182, 191, *197*, 211, 264, 272 f., 282, 297, 319
Nationalization, Socialization, Expropriation, xxvi, 24 f., 28, 30 f., 36 f., 39, 51, 76, 82, 183, 186, 187, 191, 195, 265, 266, 277, 321 f., 334*n*13, 335*n*18, 347*n*39, 43
National Socialism, *see* Fascism
Neumann, Franz, xviii, xx, 342*n*35
"New Class," 55-57, 81, 184, 292, 334*n*9
Nihilism, 9, 116-19, 123-27; *see also* Terror

"Open Door Policy," 167, 176 f., 178, 273, 345*n*25

Pinto, André, 225, 227
Planning, 13, 25, 28 f., *30-34*, 36 f., 39-61, 63, 191-92, 194-95, 281 f., 326-28, 333*n*5, 335*n*5
Popper, Karl, 337*n*8
Popular Front, xiv, xvii, xix, 148, 149, 155, 312
Positivism, xxvii, 68, 291, 293, 294, 297, *311*
Progress, xxvii, xxviii, 12, 65-85, 318 f., 324 f., 335*n*1, 336*n*3-5, 338*n*18, 25, 339*n*29; *see also* "World Spirit"
Proletariat, *see* Working Class
Protectionism, *see* Free Trade
Proudhon, Pierre-Joseph, 67, 69, 228, 239, 242, 335*n*21 (quote)

Raddatz, Fritz, 223, 244, 355*n*32
Raison d'état, xxii f., 201, 202

Rathenau, Walther, 111, 185, 251, 346*n*35
Rauschning, Hermann, 129, 142 f., 341*n*5
Reform, Reformism, xv, xxviii, 49, 52, 73, 94, 96, 103 f., 259, 260-82 *passim*, 291
Renner, Karl, 274, 281
Revolution, xiv f., xvi f., xxxviii f., 48-53, 57, 63 f., 80, 82 f., 93 f., 95-98, 103-6, 108 f., 154-57, 229 f., 231, 248 f., 259-81 *passim*, 291, 294, 298-303, 314, 339*n*29
Robinson, Joan, 333*n*6
Rosenberg, Arthur, xvi, xxi, 92 f., 104, 340*n*5
Ruge, Arnold, 77, 231, 240, 242
Russia (pre-1917), 54, 95, 167, 200 f., 228 f., 264, 339*n*30, 347*n*44

Sartre, Jean-Paul, 258, 291, 301, 355*n*31, 356*n*41
Schumpeter, Joseph, 31 f., 170 f., 198, 333*n*1, 6
"Self-Activity," xv, xxviii, 45 f., 47, 62, 68, 80, 249, 262, 287, 328 f.
Seligman, Ben B., 333*n*1
Servan-Schreiber, Jean-Jacques, 345*n*23
Shop stewards, *see* Soviets
Simmel, Georg, 298 f., 308, 353*n*8
Smith, Adam, 18, 74 f., 243, 333*n*4
Social Democratic Party of Germany (SPD), xv f., 70, 73, 89-92, 102-5, 108 f., 111, *256-83*
Socialism, xiii, xx, xxv-xxx, *11-15*, 17, 22, 23, 26 f., *29-35*, *36-48*, 50, 79, 80 f., *256-83*, 293, 301 f., *317-31*, 333*n*1, 3, 6, 334*n*12, 335*n*22-24, 339*n*30, 349*n*2
"Socialism in One Country," xiii, xvii, 97, 105, 106, 290
"Socialist Realism," 305, 308-10, 355*n*32
Socialization, *see* Nationalization
Sombart, Werner, 246, 262, 351*n*34, 35
Sorel, Georges, 67 f., 249, 280, 287
Souchy, Augustine, 157
Soviets, councils, *Räte*, 19 f., 34, 49, 53, 60 f., 96, 97 f., 106-7, 265, 287, 320, 340*n*11
Spanish Civil War, xiv, xix f., 49, 60, *147-57*
Spitz, David, 45
Stalin, Stalinism, xiii, xvii, xxi, 59, 73, 98 f., 181, 286, 288, 290, 293 f., 302, 305, 311, 312 f., 337*n*11

State Capitalism, State Socialism, 11, 17, 20-23, *23-26*, 32 f., 35, 58, 60, 320, 325, 333*n*5, 334*n*9, 10, 12
State "withering away," 81, 82, 107, 197, 293
Steinberg, Isaac, 219, 220
Sternberg, Fritz, xxi
Streicher, Julius, 134, 142
Syndicalism, 17, 19 f., 60 f.

Taylor, A. J. P., 344*n*17
Terror, Terrorism, xviii f., xxiv, 110 f., 117-19, 133, 203, 206, 209 f., 214, 304, 312, 348*n*6, 349*n*9
Thälmann, Ernst, xiii, 89 f., 97, 340*n*1
Third World, xxiv f., 42, 53 f., 63, 81, 101, 157, 179 f., 182 f., 186-96, 203-15, 319, 346*n*34, 347*n*37, 39, 40, 42, 348*n*46, 348*n*1-349*n*14
Trade Union Activity, 8, 11 f., 60, 61, 94, 104 f., 168, 258-82 *passim*, 287, 340*n*1
Trotsky, Leon, xvi, 51, 53, 83, 104, 219, 278, 286, 288, 289, 293
Tucholsky, Kurt, 251, 252, 255

United Front, xvi f., 89-92, *100-5*, 108 f.
United Nations, xxiii, 173 f., 186, 190, 191, 192, 206, 209, 214, 348*n*4

U.S.A., xxii, 161, 162-65, 166-69, 174-91, 192-97, 205 f., 207 f., 210, 212, 334*n*13, 336*n*6, 342*n*33, 343*n*4, 8, 9, 10, 12, 344*n*14, 345*n*23-28, 346*n*32, 34, 36, 347*n*37, 40, 41, 43, 44, 348*n*46
U.S.S.R., xvii, xix-xxiii, 24, 39, 42 f., 49, 51 f., 57, 83 f., 91, *102-7*, 109, 147, 149 f., 161, 162, 167, 174, 180 f., 196 f., *200-2*, 206, 212, 288, 289 f., 302-4, 307 f., 310, 320 f., 334*n*9, 335*n*15, 347*n*39, 44, 348*n*46

Weber, Max, xxviii, 260, 292, 297, 298 f., 308, 345*n*20
Welfare State, xxv f., 16, 22 f., 23 f., *28-29*, 55, 63 f., 272, 281 f., 319, 333*n*6, 334*n*14
Williams, William A., 167, 343*n*8, 9
Wittfogel, Karl August, xii, 57, 79, 334*n*9, 339*n*30
Work, labor, job, xxix f., *3-14*, 17, 23, 36, 40, 41 f., 293, 299, 304, 321, 326 f., 330
Working Class, xiii, xiv, xv f., xxvii-xxx, 6-12, 27, 51-53, 68, 71, 74 f., 77, 78, 80, 82, *89-109*, 111, 154, 184, 229 f., 237, 248, 258-80, 287, 291 f., 299, 303 f., 320, 353*n*9
"World Spirit," xxvii, 67, 68, 78, 80, 83, 93, 96, 228, 249, 300, 311, 313

Youth Movement, xi f., 118